ONE LONG TUNE

THE LIFE AND MUSIC OF LENNY BREAU

RON FORBES-ROBERTS

FOREWORD BY GENE LEES

University of North Texas Press
Denton, Texas

Permissions:
University of North Texas Press
1155 Union Circle, #311336
Denton, TX 76203-5017

The paper used in this book meets the minimum requirements of the American
National Standard for Permanence of Paper for Printed Library Materials,
z39.48.1984. Binding materials have been chosen for durability.

Library of Congress Cataloging-in-Publication Data:

Forbes-Roberts, Ron, 1953–
  One long tune : the life and music of Lenny Breau / Ron Forbes-Roberts ;
foreword by Gene Lees.
    p. cm.
Includes discography (p.), bibliographical references (p.), and index.
ISBN-13: 978-1-57441-210-9 (cloth : alk. paper)
ISBN-10: 1-57441-210-8 (cloth : alk. paper)
ISBN-13: 978-1-57441-230-7 (pbk. : alk. paper)
ISBN-10: 1-57441-230-7 (pbk. : alk. paper)
  1. Breau, Lenny. 2. Jazz musicians—United States—Biography. 3. Guitarists—
United States—Bibliography. I. Title.
ML419.B742F67 2006
787.87'165092—dc22

2006000134

For Betty Cody-Binette and Bob Erlendson:
Two remarkable musicians and great spirits who gave the best of themselves to the subject of this book

"I just improvise and keep it going and see what happens. Sort of like adapting to your environment and playing however that environment makes you feel. Just one big, long tune."

—Lenny Breau, quoted in Joan Sadler,
"Shed No Tears for Lenny"

Contents

Foreword

Back in the 1960s in New York when I was writing a lot of fiction and practicing a lot of guitar, I invented in a short story a guitarist whom I conceived of as using harmony in the manner of Bill Evans. In fact, before it was published (in some now-forgotten magazine), I showed the story to Bill. The problem with this conception was that what Bill did on piano was virtually impossible on the guitar for two (and more) reasons, one of which is that many voicings that are easy on piano are not easy on guitar; the other is that certain of these voicings require seemingly impossible stretches of the left hand and an enormous strength in the fingers.

So even in writing the story, I didn't think it could be done.

And along came Lenny Breau and did it.

Every great guitarist I have been privileged to know—and the list includes Oscar Castro-Neves, Mundell Lowe, Gene Bertoncini, Ed Bickert, Reg Schwager, the late Emily Remler, and more—has considered Lenny a *wunderkind* at minimum, even some kind of musical miracle. The universality of Lenny's interests on the instrument led him to the most total technique on guitar I have ever heard, and my own interests on guitar extend from country-and-western guitarists like Hank Garland and Thumbs Carllile through the great classical guitarists to flamenco players. And Lenny combined it all. When you look over the guitar literature of the past, Sor, Tarrega, the transcriptions of Segovia and more, when you look back down through the instrument's history to the time before it had six strings, you are compelled to think that more than just maybe, Lenny Breau was the most accomplished guitarist in history. I think so, anyway.

Consider only Lenny's use of harmonics. If you are not familiar with the term, a harmonic is an overtone of a note. If you pluck a note and touch the string in a certain way, it kills the "fundamental" and leaves the overtone an octave above it ringing with an odd, ethereal, bell-like sound. There are natural harmonics and false harmonics on the guitar, and Lenny had totally mastered them. Other guitarists will at times play short passages in harmonics, but it is difficult to mix the two kinds of sound. Not for Lenny. He could throw in harmonics seemingly anywhere he felt like, and always to exquisite effect.

Lenny could play with a plectrum, or pick. But he became so absorbed with the classical guitar (and his ability to memorize anything he heard is legendary) that he used the full four-finger technique. And sometimes he would use a mixed technique, fingers and thumb pick at the same time. One of the great musicians of our time is Don Thompson, who plays just about every instrument there is, and all superbly. Don used to play bass with Lenny, a duo gig at a Toronto club where I heard them a number of times. Please take my word that Don has a pair of the most incredible ears I've ever encountered. Don told me, "Because I was standing behind him, I couldn't see his hands, and I couldn't figure out how he was doing some of those things."

I suppose Lenny's work has to be called jazz, but it is beyond that (or any other) category of music. It is a thing unto itself.

When I was first shown the manuscript to this book, I realized that its author, Ron Forbes-Roberts, had to be Canadian, because he has so much knowledge of the country and its musical worlds, and that he must also be a guitarist, because his information was so wide-ranging and accurate. Both turned out to be true. As it happens, I'm Canadian, and Lenny considered himself Canadian, although he was actually born in Maine. You'll see the reasons for this as you make you way through this most excellent biography.

When I first read it, I had a second copy sent to my friend Mundell Lowe. And Mundell thought, as I do, that it's a book every guitar student should read. Indeed, the ideal for any guitarist would to be to gather up a fair collection of Lenny's recordings, sit down with them and this book, and just let it all blow your mind.

There has never been anyone like Lenny Breau, and never will be again, and I am grateful to Ron Forbes-Roberts for what he has done for Lenny, for the instrument, for music itself, and for all of us.

—Gene Lees

Acknowledgments

This book could not have been written without the input of every one of the two-hundred-plus interviewees who kindly shared with me their anecdotes and observations of my subject. I'd like to thank the following people for their specific contributions to this book: the Breau, Cody-Binette and Breau-St. Germain families for their generosity, hospitality, and candidness, and Gene Lees for his enthusiastic support and advice and the insightful foreword that he kindly contributed to this book. I'm grateful to Dan Casavant who pointed the way and persuaded me that I could tell this story, Craig Dobbins for sharing his archival knowledge of Chet Atkins's recordings and guitar style, Kent Hillman for his insights into Lenny's playing and his encouragement and support, Paul G. Kohler of Art of Life Records for sharing his resources with me and for making so much of Lenny's great music available, my patient and hardworking editor Karen DeVinney for giving this book a chance, and Ed Benson of *Just Jazz Guitar Magazine* and Daryl Angier of *Coda* for getting the word out. My thanks also to my parents and sister—Dick, Dorothy, and Jacquie Forbes-Roberts—for their encouragement and help, Catherine Luke for her endless patience, support, and sincere interest in this book, Lucinda Johnston whose wise words kept me from scrapping this project at a crucial moment, and to her son, my boy Raven who at the age of four framed the question I would ponder for the next six years: "Just who is this Lenny Breau"?

I am also grateful for assistance far beyond the call of duty from staff members of the University of Manitoba Archives and Special Collections, CBC Archives in Toronto and Winnipeg, the Manitoba Provincial Archives, the archival department of Vanderbilt University, and the Los Angeles Police Department.

Lenny Breau at The Establishment, Winnipeg, 1964.
Courtesy of Archives and Special Collections—
University of Manitoba

Introduction

Apart from a bell-bedecked washboard that he strummed in his parents' country band, Lenny Breau's first instrument was a child-sized, secondhand accordion that his father bought for him at a flea market. Lenny, then five years old, was delighted with the gift, even after discovering that one of its keys produced no sound when pressed. Undeterred by this defect, Lenny set about learning a French jig on his new instrument, relying on his ear to locate its melody on the accordion's flawed keyboard.

Lenny liked to practice the tune in his parents' bedroom where he could watch himself in the large mirror of his mother's vanity. In the next room, his mother sat listening to her son repeat the tune again and again, always anticipating the instant when—within a few notes of completing the melody—Lenny would press the broken key. He would then stop, mutter a child's innocuous curse *sotto voce*, and, after a gentle reprimand from his mother, start the tune over again. It was as though the boy believed that his dogged persistence would eventually overcome the obstacle of the broken key, and he would be able to complete and perfect the melody that he heard in his mind.

Lenny's interest in his accordion waned a year or two later and was replaced with a passion for guitar, but the determination with which he'd approached his first instrument never faded. For the rest of his life, Lenny stubbornly challenged the commonly accepted strictures of the guitar in order to give full voice to the sounds roiling in his vast musical imagination. By his early twenties, he had evolved an unorthodox and complex approach to the guitar fretboard and created a battery of techniques that are now synonymous with his name. But his genius had less to do with mechanical legerdemain than the profoundly eloquent expression that his technique was designed to serve. Lenny's greatest gift was his ability to channel raw emotion through a highly refined musical sensibility to make music that was at once challenging and accessible—a paradox that was at the core of his art.

Chet Atkins became aware of Lenny and his music in 1967, and invited him to Nashville to make what would be the first of two records for RCA. In a CBC documentary chronicling this session, Atkins virtually designated Lenny as the new golden boy of the guitar—a crown that Atkins had worn twenty years earlier.[1] In one segment of the film, after offering up a string of hosannas to the abilities of his young protégé, Atkins commented, "I think his potential is unlimited."[2]

It's not clear whether Atkins was referring to Lenny's artistic or commercial potential when he made this comment, but if he meant the latter, he was sadly off the mark. Lenny Breau's professional ambitions simply did not match his relentless drive to master his instrument. As Steve Grover, a drummer who played often with Lenny in the seventies, puts it, "If Lenny could have made a living just sitting around on the couch in someone's living room, playing for people after a good home cooked meal for fifty bucks, he would never have wanted to do anything else." (Unless otherwise indicated, all interviews were conducted by the author. See Appendix "List of Interviews.") While Lenny did not reject commercial success out of hand, he feared that its demands would interfere with his zealous devotion to his art. This paralyzing ambivalence, a substance abuse problem, depression, poor management, and a music industry and record-buying public that were indifferent to jazz all contributed to the faltering of his career right out of the gate. Within a year of recording a second album for RCA, Lenny began a vertiginous slide into professional oblivion. For the rest of his life, he led a chaotic, darkly quixotic existence, playing sporadically in small, out-of-the-way clubs and recording albums of uneven quality, mainly for ad hoc labels. At the time of his murder in 1984, his only regular work was a one-night-a-week gig at a Los Angeles jazz club. He had lived on the far margins of the jazz world for so long that many jazz fans were surprised to hear about his passing simply because they'd assumed he had died many years earlier.

Yet despite the downward trajectory of his professional life after the early 1970s, Lenny Breau's evolution as a musician remained in ascendance, and his playing and ideas continued to astonish his fans. One of these was jazz guitarist Sid Jacobs, currently an instructor at the Guitar Institute of Technology and author of *The Music of Bill Evans for Guitar*. "It was amazing how beautifully he played," Jacobs says of a gig he attended a month before Lenny's death. "He was incredible. Any bit of flashy guitar playing was completely gone. You heard no individual personality, just music that was totally pure without one note out of place. If I sound like I'm overstating it, it's because words fail me, but it really was like his playing had gone to a higher level than I could have imagined."

Through addiction, penury, a perniciously abusive marriage, aimless wandering, and a string of personal tragedies, Lenny Breau somehow managed to pursue his artistic vision with the same faith and passion that had fueled his efforts as a persistent child straining to triumph over his malfunctioning instrument in front of his mother's mirror. The magnitude of that faith and passion, and the sublime beauty of the music that was its consequence were the inspiration for this biography on Lenny Breau.

1.

On the Trail of the Lonesome Pine
ca.1916—October 1948

"Whoever'd think that a little Frenchmen could play like that?"
—Denny Breau on his brother Lenny

"Oh, Come out and listen while I sing and play for you/I am the Lone Pine Mountaineer."
—Hal Lone Pine[1]

The towns of Auburn and Lewiston face one another across the Androscoggin River thirty-five miles due north of Portland, Maine. Most of the squat, red brick mills in both towns are deserted now, but for more than a century after the Civil War a ceaseless stream of textiles, building supplies, footwear, and other commodities flowed from their dusty, cacophonous depths. The mills were manned mainly by French Canadian immigrants and their progeny who were drawn to the region by the relatively high wages to be earned there in the latter part of the nineteenth century. By the time Lenny Breau's maternal grandparents, Aldina and Alphonse Cote, arrived in Auburn with their family from Sherbrooke, Quebec, in April of 1922, the region had become an entrenched enclave of Franco-American culture where 65 percent of its 40,000 residents spoke French as their first language, and still held tightly to the cultural traditions earlier generations had brought with them from the townships of Quebec.

One of the most highly valued of these traditions was the practice and appreciation of music, and the Cotes were well equipped to make a significant contribution to the region's culture in this regard. Alphonse Cote, a journeyman carpenter, built fiddles in his spare time, and Aldina sang traditional French folk songs, church music, and light classics in a beautiful soprano voice. All of their eleven children possessed musical gifts, but the one whose talents would become known to the broadest audience was their sixth child, Rita Francis. Born in Sherbrooke, Quebec, on August 17, 1921, Rita grew up singing her mother's stock of songs as well as pop tunes of the time. Then, in the early 1930s, she and thousands of young people of her generation were captivated by a new sound that swept out of the southern states on radio and records by Jimmie Rodgers, the Carter family, and other early country singers. "It just hit so fast in Maine," she says. "The French people really went for the country music. Everybody was trying to learn guitar and sing in those days."

Rita began emulating female country singer and yodeler Patsy Montana, and at the age of fifteen was singing professionally with Curly and the Country Boys at local dances and on WCOU radio in Lewiston. Rita, who was just beginning to speak English, was known to her audiences as "The Little French Girl," a stage name that her husband, Harold Breau, would replace a few years later with the countrified sobriquet—Betty Cody—by which she would be commonly known for most of her life.

Born on June 5, 1916, on his parents' farm near the village of Pea Cove, Maine, Harold John Breau was the eldest of six children born to Arthur Breau—a Canadian immigrant—and wife Flora Belle (nee Holmes), a native of Oxford, Maine. Fourteen years later, the family moved to Old Town, a small community ten miles north of Bangor where Harold began singing traditional English and Scottish ballads with his high school glee club. It was here that Harold heard his first Jimmie Rodgers record, an experience that affected him so profoundly that he decided on the spot to pursue a career as a country singer. After winning several talent contests, he landed a noontime spot on WLBZ radio in Bangor as "The Radio Cowboy," and t formed a trio called the Lone Pine Mountaineers. When the .... folded a few months later, Harold dubbed himself "The Lone Pine Mountaineer"[2] and continued performing as a solo act. By the age of seventeen, he was a popular entertainer in northern Maine and appeared regularly on theatre stages and radio stations throughout the region.

In November of 1939, Pine—as he was commonly known to friends—came to Lewiston to play a series of shows, and hired a local band called The Sons of the Westerners as his back-up group. When Pine asked the band's leader and guitarist, twenty-year-old Ray Couture, to recommend a back-up singer for the group, Couture suggested his friend, Rita Cote. "He was broadcasting from Bangor as The Lone Pine Mountaineer," Betty recalls, "but I'd never turned on WABI so he was all new to me. I'd never even heard of him, but he hired me." In keeping with the western image he wanted his group to project, Pine dubbed his new singer Betty Lou Cody.

Initially, the group performed as The Lone Pine Mountaineer with The Sons of the Westerners and Betty Lou Cody[3] and was later augmented by Betty's sisters, Lucille, Flo, and Maggie, who performed as "The Three Little Sisters." They also took on an ex-Vaudevillian comedian/clown named Billy Hall who called himself Bozo the Tramp. Later, Pine invited Gene Hooper, a young guitarist/singer from Machias, Maine, to join the show. This marked the beginning of a working and personal relationship between the men that would endure until Pine's death in 1977.

The group's working day began with a noon-hour appearance on WCOU, after which the band might drive for several hours for a performance in a theatre or community hall in some far-flung New England village. Their four-hour show was split into two hours of music and comedy routines followed by a dance of the same length. With their striking good looks, winning personalities, and the flashy western attire that Pine had specially made by a tailor in Philadelphia, the gregarious, outgoing king of Maine's country music scene and his demure, charismatic, and golden-throated queen easily won over their audiences the moment they stepped on stage. Not surprisingly, it wasn't long before they won each other's hearts as well. On June 29, 1940, after a six-month courtship, Pine and eighteen-year-old

Betty Cody married. There was no honeymoon; immediately after the wedding the band set off on a tour of the southeastern United States. "Our manager had bought a big tent and we lived in that and traveled down south through a lot of the larger cities," Betty says. "We were traveling by car and staying in tents, one night after another. We'd hired a cook who cooked all our meals on the ground and we were eating outside. It was a rough, gypsy's life, all new to me."

The grueling trip came to an abrupt end in December of 1940 when Betty discovered that she was pregnant. The troupe folded their tents, bade goodbye to the Southland for the time being, and returned to Auburn where on August 5, 1941, Betty gave birth to Leonard Harold Breau. Named after Betty's younger brother, with Pine providing his middle name, Lenny was born in his grandparents' home at 52 Fourth Street in Auburn surrounded by a coterie of adoring relatives and musicians from his parents' immediate and extended family. All were delighted with the infant despite the physical anomaly that naturally caught the eye of the attending amateur and professional musicians. "The little fingers on both his hands were twisted like his grandmother's," says Betty's sister, Flo. "I remember Betty looking at him and saying, 'Gosh he's got fingers just like his grandma Breau; he'll never be able to play guitar like that.'" Lenny's pinkie fingers were curved and twisted slightly and would never entirely straighten out. This was a congenital feature inherited from his father's side of the family, which Lenny in turn would pass on to his own son. In other regards, Lenny was a petite but robust, healthy baby. "He had beautiful skin and dark eyes as big as quarters: a little black-headed beauty," says Gene Hooper. Lenny would grow to resemble closely his diminutive, dark-eyed mother although by his teenage years his body language and vocal cadence were very much his father's.

Shortly after Lenny's birth, Pine and Betty returned to the road and were often gone for weeks at a time. Lenny was left with family members in Auburn or Bangor or with a nanny named Mrs. St. Pierre whose young son was also named Leonard. To distinguish between the boys, she called her new charge Sonny, a name by which many of Lenny's family and relatives still refer to him. (The spelling of the diminutive form of his name fluctuated. While he signed his name "Lenny," up until the late 1960s, he was often referred to as "Lennie" in promotional material and in many articles written about him.) Lenny was two years old when his parents bought an old farm on Turner Road about ten miles outside of Auburn and it was here, a year later, that his parents caught their first glimpse of their son's musical talent. The couple was practicing in the barn when Lenny, attracted by the music, wandered in. "We'd started rehearsing 'Cattle Call,' the Eddy Arnold song," recalls Betty. "Lenny was listening and then, by gosh, we hear him harmonizing, doing the perfect third part. He was right on the dot on each note. We said 'do that again' and he did. He just made it up because neither of us were singing that part."

Lenny was soon performing with his parents, singing high harmony above his mother's vocal line in a perfectly intonated voice. He had inherited his mother's perfect pitch, and would become incensed when his father—whose own sense of pitch was often tenuous—would occasionally lose the melody line and be pulled towards Lenny's harmony. His son would stop in exasperation and complain loudly, "Daddy, stop singing my part!" Betty made her son a cowboy outfit complete with a small hat and toy gun in a holster and Lenny wore this outfit for his first promo shot, which became a best seller at the group's shows. In the photo, Lenny is holding a guitar that dwarves him despite its diminutive size. The phrase "Keep Smiling" is written on the photo to the left of his image and "Lone Pine Junior" is signed in his father's hand on the right. This appellation would adorn his promo pictures until the year of his first marriage.

Lenny's first live performances were on his parents' noontime radio show on WCOU and later on WLBZ in Bangor. With his parents flanking him, he would stand on a stool heightened with two telephone books, allowing him to sing into the microphone his repertoire of tunes, which included "Popeye the Sailor Man" and "Coat of Navy Blue." His earnest, reedy voice was a hit with listeners and attracted so much fan mail that before long he was taking the stage with his parents at their local shows. Besides singing a few solo numbers and harmonizing with his mother and father, Lenny worked with Bozo the Tramp. The two quickly developed a strong affinity and rapport that delighted their audiences, says Betty.

With Lenny it all came natural; he would do anything on stage. He would do a soft-shoe shuffle with Bozo and kibitz with him. One day Bozo was teasing Lenny a little and Lenny didn't like it. He didn't know it was just in fun. He said, "Ah, I don't like you anyway, Bozo. You're just a dirty old tramp." Bozo looked hurt and pretended he was crying and said, "I never thought you'd say that to me." Lenny got upset and said, "Oh Bozo, I didn't mean it. You're a clean tramp!" Everybody laughed so hard. He was about four and it was already just coming out of him.

Lenny used a toy guitar as a stage prop, but his first real instrument was a washboard with an array of attached bells and whistles for which Pine made a case emblazoned with the legend "Lone Pine Junior." Lenny did solo spots on his washboard and accompanied the band on a few songs. "His rhythms were not fancy," says his aunt Flo, "but always in time and in just the right place."

Lenny was five when his father gave him a child-sized accordion and he was soon picking out simple melodies on its recalcitrant keyboard. "I had a vanity with a full-length mirror and Lenny would practice in front of it," Betty says. "He'd look at himself in the mirror and make believe he was putting on a show. He had a key that stuck and when he'd hit that note he'd say, [stage whisper] 'Jessusssss!' I'd say, 'Lennnnyyy!' Then he'd start it all over again. He was already quite a character!"

By the late forties, Pine and Betty had worked Maine and surrounding states so thoroughly that they'd burnt out their territory, and audiences had dwindled drastically. When station CKCW in Moncton, New Brunswick, offered the band their own radio show, the Breaus decided this was an opportune time to move on to a new locale. On October 2, 1948, an item in the *Lewiston Evening Journal* announced the sale of the Breaus' Turner Road farm and declared "Harold Breau, the Lone Pine Mountaineer of Stage and Radio . . . [and] singer of Western ditties is leaving soon on a Canadian tour."[4] A month later the Breau family—one member larger since the birth of their second-born son, Dickie—along with Ray Couture, and Gene Hooper and his soon-to-be bride, Flo Cote, settled in Moncton, New Brunswick, where they broadcast daily as "Lone Pine and his CKCW Jamboree Gang." Because of their busy touring schedule, the

Breaus deposited their sons with Ida and Alphie Babineau on a farm outside of Shediak, a town about twenty miles east of Moncton. The Babineaus had met the Breaus on an earlier trip to the Maritimes and after becoming fast friends with the couple, offered to look after their sons. Dickie Breau was three years old at the time and recalls his five years on the Babineaus' farm with great fondness. "The Babineaus were very nice," he says. "Ida was a doting kind of person who was always waiting on you hand and foot. They were more like parents to us than anyone who took care of us. The most normal childhood I had was on the farm. In fact, I've often said to my wife and friends, 'those were the best years of our lives.'"

Lenny was less enthusiastic about the new situation than his younger, more adaptable brother. While he got on well with the Babineaus, Lenny lived for his parents' bi-monthly visits, which generally coincided with their shows in the area. Lenny often performed at these shows where his candor and zeal elicited much appreciative laughter from audience members, Gene Hooper says.

> One night we played a hall outside of Moncton and the pipes had dripped and it was kind of dirty. You could tell it hadn't been cleaned for a long, long while and in those days they didn't have no running water. The toilets had two or three holes. As we got into the hall we could smell the toilets and we started cleaning the place up, dusting and sweeping. Pine says, "You know, this is the dirtiest hall I think we ever played." When it came time to introduce Sonny, who was eight or nine, he says, "Howdy, folks," and took his little cowboy hat off the way Pine had shown him. Pine said, "Well, Junior, do you have anything to say?" He says, "Yes, I sure do. You know folks, this is the dirtiest hall we ever played in! And those toilets! Boy, do they ever stink. Somebody should clean this dump up!" Christ, we could have gone through the stage but it was the biggest hand of the evening.

In performance, Lenny rarely suffered from the stutter he had developed at the age of six or seven. Lenny would later claim that his stutter was the result of alternating constantly between French and English schools as a child. Betty, however, says that while Lenny was fluently bilingual as a child, he never attended an exclusively

French-speaking school and did not change schools frequently, in any case. Whatever its origin, his stutter would stay with him all his life, usually manifesting itself when Lenny was nervous, angry, or under pressure.

In 1949, Pine and Betty's move to Sunnyside, Prince Edward Island, about ninety miles and a ferry ride away from Shediak, coincided with an upswing in their careers. The following year, they traveled to Montreal to record Ray Couture's composition, "Prince Edward Island is Heaven to Me" backed with "When it's Apple Blossom Time in Annapolis Valley" for RCA Canada. The company released the 78 on their budget subsidiary Bluebird label, and within the month the record was a significant radio hit in the Maritimes, making the Breaus superstars in Atlantic Canada. On Valentine's Day 1950, they took to the air as "The Noisiest Gang on Radio," on station CFBC in St. John, New Brunswick. The popularity of the show led to a thrice weekly, nationally broadcast spot on CBC radio. Later that year, Pine and Betty toured the Maritimes with country legend Lefty Frizzell and then relocated to Truro, Nova Scotia. From here, Pine commuted regularly to Bangor to host a show on WLAM radio that was nationally syndicated on the ABC network. By this time, RCA had released "Prince Edward Island" in the US where it enjoyed heavy radio play in New England. On the strength of this, the Breaus (accompanied by Ray Couture) returned to live in Bangor in mid-1951, leaving Dickie and Lenny on the Babineaus' farm. Lenny did not take this well, says Gene Hooper, who remained in New Brunswick. "He missed his folks very bad. It was hard on poor Sonny, very, very hard." Fortunately, by this time, Lenny had discovered a pastime that would help to make his parents' absence almost bearable.

Throughout his life, Lenny was always pleased to tell interviewers at exactly what age he began playing guitar and from whom he'd received his first instruction. Unfortunately, his accounts varied almost from interview to interview. In 1968, he told CBC's Lee Major that he began playing at the age of six,[5] but months later in another CBC radio interview, he explained that he had picked the instrument up "by the age of eight."[6] Betty Cody confirms the latter, but her son's interest in the instrument had actually begun some time before he became serious about playing it, says Ray Couture. "He would ask me a question every now and then, like 'what are you playing there?' and I'd say 'Well, this is the key of A,'" says Couture. "But I don't ever recall him playing guitar at that time. He'd come to my room and listen to me. One day in Bangor, I said, 'Lenny, I want you to hear a real guitar player.' I played him a [seminal French jazz guitarist] Django Reinhardt record. And he listened for awhile, and I said, 'Well what do you think?' He thought for a minute and said, 'That guy sure plays funny.'"

Couture would eventually teach Lenny a great deal about the guitar, but his earliest teacher was the Babineaus' fourteen-year-old son, Norman. The basic chords and strumming patterns that Babineau showed Lenny were augmented by experience gained first-hand at local barn dances and country hoedowns, as he told interviewer James Marck in 1983. "Some of the first music I learned how to play was the kind of jigs and reels that they would play at these things," Lenny recalled. "From the age of six to twelve, that's all I listened to. I'd watch the guitar players' hands and then we'd all look at each other and somebody'd nod and that's how we knew to change to the other chord."[7] Lenny was soon picking out melodies on his guitar, pieces like Arthur Smith's "Guitar Boogie," a simple instrumental built on a bass pattern used in the Boogie-Woogie piano style. His parents were unaware of their son's evolving guitar skills until they visited their children after a two-month road tour towards the end of 1949. Betty says that shortly after their arrival at the farm, Lenny insisted that they listen to him play a song he had learned on Norman Babineau's guitar. "[Norman] had bought a record of Hank Snow playing some reels," she says. "Lenny had learned one just from listening. There was Lenny playing the tune, his little hands going so fast all over the fretboard—first the high strings, then he started on the bass notes, and he would never miss a note. It was just in him and he wanted so much to play music. But we never pushed him. We just let him go."

Lenny needed no encouragement. When Pine discovered his son's burgeoning facility on the guitar, he bought him a small-bodied, Gibson acoustic guitar—model unknown—that Lenny played constantly with a discipline and intensity that belied his age. Lenny loved to play, and took great pride in his rapid progress on the instrument, but apparently there were other motives fueling his desire to master the guitar. Many years later, Lenny would tell friends and journalists that as a child he believed that if he excelled on his instrument, he would earn a permanent position in his parents' band.[8] For Lenny, the pleasures of family life were inextricably bound up with his parents' vocation and the circumstances in which they practiced it. To be on stage with his parents, to bask in their approval and hear the praise that followed his performances constituted the apex of his relationship with his family. There was little else, says Dickie Breau: "It wasn't your typical family life. We never really did much together as a family. I don't remember picnics or cookouts or going to an amusement park together. Our parents were always on the road. Sonny grew to know my parents better than I did, but until he started playing with them, it would have been a similar thing: he really wouldn't have had much time with them."

Like Norman Babineau and other guitarists in the area, Lenny used a flat pick to play the fiddle tunes, country songs, and instrumental riffs that made up his expanding repertoire. However, in late 1952 or early 1953, while twirling the dial on the Babineaus' radio, Lenny came across a guitarist who was playing "Fig Leaf Rag"[9] in a style that simultaneously baffled and mesmerized him. "I had the radio on one day and I heard a guitar player playing who sounded like two guys playing at the same time," Lenny later told interviewer Lee Major, "and I didn't believe that he was playing his rhythm and his melody at the same time because I had never heard of anybody doing that. And it stuck in my head, and I went out and bought a record and listened to it and I thought it was a trick recording at first."[10]

The guitarist whom Lenny heard on the Babineaus' radio that day was Chet Atkins. He was using a technique that would become so closely identified with him that it is often referred to as Atkins-style picking, but is also commonly called thumbstyle, fingerpicking, or fingerstyle. Broadly speaking, the technique has its roots in the European classical guitar tradition, but the specific fingerstyle approach that astonished Lenny originated in the American South during the late nineteenth-early twentieth century with African-American musicians. These guitarists used their right-hand thumbs to play a rhythmic pulse on the bass strings of the guitar while one or more fingers plucked an often syncopated melody on the treble strings. This allowed the player to play two notes simultaneously on non-adjacent strings and opened up possibilities not available to the pick-style guitarist. The style was adopted and given a different spin by various white players including guitarist Mose Rager (1911–1986) who taught it to several fellow Kentuckian guitarists. One of these was Merle Travis (1917–1983), who in the early 1940s began a long and successful career as a popular recording and performing artist. Travis applied the style to traditional tunes and originals often flavored with a ragtime or country jazz feel. Many of these pieces became popular radio hits during the forties, and they caught the ear of Chet Atkins, then a budding young guitarist and fiddler who was born in Luttrell, Tennessee, in 1923. Just as Lenny would do many years later, Atkins practiced constantly to master "Travis Picking," as the technique was then known, eventually refining it by using three fingers and the thumb of his right hand rather than just thumb and index finger as Travis had done. Atkins began his career working with country acts like The Carter Family and singer/yodeler Roselie Allen but he also applied his fingerstyle technique to classical pieces, Broadway show tunes and jazz numbers. His eclectic, sophisticated style often seemed as out of place in his countrified surroundings as his natty houndstooth jackets and tailored slacks did amongst his faux cowboy attired co-musicians on the Grand Ole Opry where he often worked. In time, this same eclecticism would characterize Lenny's playing and he would develop the Atkins style to a degree that its originator had never imagined. Initially, however, Lenny had little success imitating the sounds he heard on Atkins's records and, with no one in Shediak to teach him the style, its rudiments would remain a mystery to him for another year.

While their son was grappling with the onerous task of learning the Atkins style by ear, the Breaus' star continued to rise. In July 1952, RCA president Steve Sholes invited Pine and Betty to Camden, New Jersey, to record several sides for the company. It was Sholes who gave Pine his most enduring stage name. Pine had long since shortened "The Lone Pine Mountaineer" to "Lone Pine" and RCA signed the group as Lone Pine and The Mountaineers. But Sholes decided that the handle had an anachronistic ring and added Hal, a diminutive of Harold, to Lone Pine to create a handle under which Pine would record and perform for the rest of his life.

At their first meeting, Sholes knew Betty only as the group's back-up singer but after hearing her sing and yodel on the Ray Couture composition "Tom-Tom Yodel," he was so impressed that he signed her to her own contract (and removed "Lou" from her stage name). This would mark the beginning of a dramatic ascent in Betty's career but would also fuel Pine's professional jealousy towards his wife, an issue that was already creating tensions in the couple's marriage. These tensions were compounded by Pine's sudden and inexplicable shift from a militant teetotaler to a recklessly heavy drinker. "When we married, that guy was straight as an arrow," says Betty. "But then he started going the other way and it was all different. He was a person who never should have had a drink. He was an alcoholic, but he didn't know it." These problems would eventually destroy their marriage but during the next few years, they preserved for their audiences the illusion of the devoted, starry-eyed country sweethearts from small town Maine.

Shortly after the RCA sessions, country singer Doc Williams invited the Breaus to join "The World's Original Jamboree" where Williams had performed for many years with his wife Chickie and their band, The Border Riders. Based in Wheeling, West Virginia, and broadcast over radio WWVA, the Jamboree debuted in 1933 and by the early fifties was one of the most popular country radio shows in North America. Seven days a week its performers, who included Little Jimmy Dickens, Hank Snow, and Hawkshaw Hawkins, could be heard from Mexico to northern Canada via its 50,000-watt signal, one of the most powerful in North America.

In August of 1953, Pine, Betty, and their third son Denny (Dennis) relocated to Wheeling, where Lenny and Dickie—driven to Wheeling by Gene and Flo Hooper—joined them three months later. While Betty and her sons shared a large house owned by WWVA stars Wilma Lee and Stony Cooper, Pine chose to live elsewhere, Betty says. "When we hit Wheeling, things weren't that great between us. He wanted to break away from me, but Wheeling wouldn't hire us unless I went."

Lenny may have been puzzled by this arrangement, but he was elated to be reunited with his parents, whatever the circumstances. He was also pleased with the musical resources that were available to him in Wheeling, and began picking the brains of every guitarist with whom he came into contact including Ray Couture, who had arrived in Wheeling a few months ahead of the Breaus.

When we moved to Wheeling, Lenny was always with me because his mom and dad were always too busy doing this and that. But he loved the guitar and all he wanted to do was play and learn as much as he could. One day he said, "Hey Pan [Couture's nickname], show me that tune you play with Dad on stage." I said, "I don't think you're ready for that. You just know a couple of chords. That's written in the key of E and in a couple of positions and even past the twelfth fret." The tune was something I'd written called "Messing Up the Frets." He said "Well, play it for me." So I played it for him twice and showed him the fingering on it real fast and the picking on it: up and down real fast on the last two strings. He tried it a couple of times and said, "Well, I'm gonna practice on it." Right after that we left on tour for about three weeks. I'll never forget when we came back, he had this guitar around his neck and he called me in his bedroom and said "Hey Pan, come here. Listen, you know that tune you play with my Dad? Well listen to it and see if I'm playing it right." Well, he played it and he played it better than I did and added triplets to it. I couldn't believe it. I told Betty, "You'd better send that kid to school 'cause that boy's talented."

Through his interest in Django Reinhardt, Couture had come a long way as a guitarist since hiring on with Pine in 1939. Much of his guitar work on Pine and Betty's RCA sides is marked by fast single note runs that, while not harmonically sophisticated, have a definite jazz flavor in their phrasing and rhythms. Lenny naturally absorbed this feel as he diligently practiced Couture's riffs on the Fender Telecaster that he'd acquired soon after arriving in Wheeling. (Lenny exchanged the Telecaster for a Fender Stratocaster sometime in late 1954.) By the age of thirteen, Lenny had mastered Couture's style, says Gene Hooper. "Lenny'd be playing behind you and you'd swear it was Ray Couture. I remember Hawkshaw Hawkins [with whom Lenny occasionally played] just couldn't get over it." Accordingly, publicity pictures taken of Lenny in Wheeling were now captioned "The Guitar Wizard!"

Couture was a flat-picker, but he was able to provide Lenny with the basics of the Atkins style, having learned them firsthand from their originator while recording with Betty at an RCA session the year before. Steve Sholes had enlisted Chet Atkins, a session musician for RCA at the time, to play behind Betty on the song "But-terfly Heart." Couture played rhythm guitar on the tune and observed enough of Atkins's technique at the session, and another following, to grasp the fundamentals of the style. "I saw Chet use a thumbpick," he says, "so I got one and learned a few tunes and taught them to Lenny." With these new skills Lenny was able to learn an Atkins medley called "I've Been Working on the Guitar" based on the traditional tune, "I've Been Working on the Rail Road." Couture says that beyond these basics, he had little fingerstyle technique to show Lenny, but was able to introduce him to people who did. The most important of these was Bill Tustin, a young semi-professional guitarist who occasionally played with Jamboree star Bob Galleon. "I used to follow him around like a little dog," Lenny told inter-viewer Walter Carter, "[I'd say] '. . . Hey man, show me this, show me that.' I'd watch him like a hawk."[11] Even with Couture and Tustin's help, learning Atkins's style was hard going as Lenny explained in an interview many years later. "It took an awful long time just to get a smooth sound and keep my thumb going, you know, keep the rhythm while I played the melody. . . . It seemed like I would do that nine hours a day. I would drive my mom crazy because I was always playing in the house. She would say 'why don't you go play in the cellar?' So I'd go down in the cellar, play until midnight, then get up in the morning and go to school."[12]

In school, Lenny was an average student who was unswervingly obedient and polite to his teachers. Although friendly, outgoing, and possessing a quick sense of humor, he had no real friends among his schoolmates, preoccupied as he was with learning the craft of his eld-ers. "You couldn't ask for a better kid, very soft spoken and very pleasant to be around," says his aunt Flo. "Not at all shy or nervous. But Lenny was grown up even as a kid. He grew up too fast. He never had kids to play with. See, no matter where he was, he was always with grownups."

There were exceptions, however. Norman "Buddy" Spicher would go on to become one of the most recorded and respected fiddlers in country music. But when he came to Wheeling from Dubois, Penn-sylvania, at the age of sixteen in 1954, he lacked the skills necessary to pass his audition with Hal Lone Pine. He remained in Wheeling where he met Lenny not long after his failed audition. "Lenny was the talk of the town," says Spicher. "Everybody was saying 'You've gotta watch this little guy play the guitar.' I met Lenny in the same dressing room area in the Virginia Theatre where I auditioned for Hal. There was a bunch of us who were just gathered around listening." Afterwards, Spicher struck up a conversation with Lenny who, upon learning that Spicher was a fiddler, offered him some advice. "He said, 'You should get some Stuff Smith albums,'" recalls Spicher. "Stuff Smith was the first great jazz violinist. Lenny was hip to everybody but I didn't know Smith. Later I went to Lenny's house and he got out a Stuff Smith album and played it for me and said 'You hear that? That's a flat five [a musical interval common in blues and post-1945 jazz].' That was one of Stuff's signature licks. He liked the flat five. I bought all of Stuff Smith's albums as a result of Lenny introducing him to me and I became a Stuff Smith clone. To this day, people will say that I sound like Stuff and I take it as a compliment."

According to Spicher, Lenny was already incorporating some elementary jazz riffs—probably lifted from Couture's Django Reinhardt records—into his playing, much to Pine's chagrin. "The only time I ever seen Pine aggravated was when he and the band would be singing a song and Lenny would throw in a flat five or something," says Spicher. "He'd get a dirty look from his dad. Lenny was havin' fun and experimenting, and he was doing it for us because he knew we were off to the side listening." By this time, Lenny was also working occasionally with other performers on the Jamboree, says Gene Hooper. "Lenny was backing up Jamboree acts when he was only twelve. Soon everyone around Wheeling in country music knew him and it seemed like every day he improved. He'd play the same run for an hour until he'd get it right. His hands were so small, I used to wonder how he did it."

In December of 1953, Betty's recording of "I Found Out More Than You'll Ever Know" reached the top ten on the Billboard Country Chart and eventually sold over 80,000 copies. A string of hits followed over the next eighteen months and Betty's career soared. In late April of 1954, she and Pine did a fourteen-city tour with "The RCA Victor Country and Western Caravan," a traveling show that included Hank Snow, Minnie Pearl, and Chet Atkins. (Lenny stayed in Wheeling but years later Atkins recalled that during the tour Pine and Betty often spoke to him of their son's guitar prowess.) Colonel

Tom Parker, later Elvis Presley's manager, promoted the show and was greatly taken with Betty. "Colonel Parker invited me to be his protégé," Betty says. "He said 'Betty, if you would be interested in coming with me to Nashville, we could do the big time for you. You're star material. The thing is you'd have to leave your children for at least six months and be all music.'" Betty refused this and another of Parker's offers. "He wanted to take Lenny on the road to play behind [early rock/pop singer] Tommy Sands who he was managing, but I said 'no way.' He was only thirteen and too young to leave his family like that."

But as the offers rolled in, Betty began losing interest in pursuing the career that was widening the rift between her and her far less successful husband. In late 1954 when Steve Sholes asked Betty to come to New York without Pine for another recording session, she turned him down. Shortly afterwards, the Breaus left Wheeling permanently to take a job on a small radio station in Schenectady, New York, one of the very few offers Betty received that included her husband.

In Schenectady, Lenny continued to spend all of his time concentrating on the Atkins style although, as he explained to John Knowles in 1982, it was a tougher go now that he no longer had Tustin or Couture, who remained in Wheeling, to help him along.

> I was on my own. Then I started taking Chet's records and slowing them down. I would listen and hunt around on the guitar. I would try to find open strings and find out what key Chet was in. That was very important. At first I didn't know that "Black Mountain Rag" was in an open tuning; I was just trying to play it in G and it wasn't very easy. I said to myself, "He's playing up here [on the higher frets] and that bass note is staying the same, man, he can't be holding that G with his thumb!" I finally realized what was going on. Boy, that was a breakthrough! I was so happy![13]

In June of 1955, Betty gave birth to her youngest son, Robert (Bobby) Breau. Complications with the birth necessitated surgery, and afterwards the Breaus returned to Auburn where Betty could be in the care of her family. The Breaus had not recorded or performed on a major radio network for over a year at this point, but to the citizens of Auburn/Lewiston, they were still genuine celebrities and this status was naturally extended to Lenny. Larry Donovan was a friend of Lenny's and recalls his first day at Walton High in Auburn. "He caused so much commotion that the principal had to announce a message over the PA system asking all students to please let Lenny be. He was so handsome, famous and talented, and polite to everyone, teachers and students. It took at least a week before the girls stopped following him down the corridors and staring at him through classroom windows. Through it all, Lenny was respectful and polite."[14]

Lenny had indeed become a remarkably handsome young man with a broad, open smile enhanced by even, pearly white teeth. His thick jet-black hair was perfectly coiffed but for a few stray "kiss curls" dangling down his forehead in the manner of the early rock and roll teen idols. He had inherited his father's love of fancy clothes and favored white suits, often worn with dark shirts and white ties, either fashionably narrow and straight, or country-style string bow ties. "He wouldn't go nowhere 'less he had a suit on and a necktie," recalls Gene Hooper. "He was a sharp dresser even in Wheeling; always nice and clean cut."

Lenny did not feel like a specimen under glass at Walton High for long. He was a reasonably good student, but showed little interest in his studies and soon began skipping classes. He spent his days listening to music, often at the home of a newfound older friend named Maurice Hebert who had known Lenny's parents for several years. Hebert had an enormous jazz record collection that ranged from Armstrong and Ellington to Charlie Parker and Miles Davis. "On Seventh Street [in Auburn] back in those days," says Hebert, "it was, 'well, if you want to hear what's new in jazz, Hebert's got it.' So Lenny approached me and soon he started coming over. He wasn't playing jazz at that time and never talked about any particular jazz guitarists that he liked. We'd just talk about jazz and he'd ask me about people. He felt right at home. He knew where the house key was, and during the day he'd sneak in and listen to Miles Davis and Charlie Parker and all the jazz stuff I had. It was OK with me."

The school soon reported Lenny's absences to his mother who scolded her son and ordered him to attend his classes. He toed the line for a time, but soon his seat in class was again vacant more often than not. The school notified Betty once again and she checked his whereabouts with friends. "His mother gave me a call one day and said 'I don't know where Lenny is. He's not going to school half the time,'" says Hebert. "I said 'Well . . .' That's when I told her about Lenny [coming to his house] and that didn't go too, too good with her. So after that when he'd sneak into the house while I was at work, I'd say 'Lenny, you go to school. What's the matter with you?' He'd say, 'ye-ye-yeah, Mr. Hebert.'"

Lenny simply moved the base of his listening operations to a Lewiston music store and continued to miss school. Finally, Betty and the school's principal agreed that Lenny was never going to put aside his musical obsession for academic study and gave Lenny permission to leave school to pursue music full-time. Lenny joined his father's band six months shy of his fifteenth birthday, only slightly younger than his parents had been when they had become professional musicians.

Pine was working regularly on Bangor's WABI TV and WMTW TV in Poland Springs, a few miles outside of Auburn. This station broadcast a popular noontime country show called *Rhythm Ranch*, which was hosted by various Maine country performers including Pine, future country music star Dick Curless and country singer Ernie Lindell. Lindell's guitarist was a Newport, Rhode Island, native named Paso Golios, better known as Sleepy Willis, who emulated country/jazz guitar speedster Jimmy Bryant. Before long, Willis was playing with Pine in his new band, The Kountry Karavan, often holding down the bass chair while Lenny played guitar. "Lenny came to town and drove everybody crazy with his guitar playing," Willis says. "He was a super guitar player even back then, playing in the Atkins and Travis style. He got so good at it, Atkins could have died and Sonny could have taken his place and nobody would have known the difference."

Lenny backed his father on the old country standards and hokum tunes that were the backbone of Pine's act. He also did a few solo spots, playing an Atkins or Travis instrumental or singing a number like Jimmie Rodger's "Any Old Time." Pine often introduced his son with "He's the best in his field. In fact, that's where his mother and I found him: in a field," or would refer to Lenny's voice as being "somewhere between the six o'clock whistle and a pig's squeal." Lenny took it all amicably, just happy to be working on stage with his father.

A southerner named Curtis Johnson joined the group around this time. Johnson originally played steel guitar with The Kountry Karavan, but when Pine discovered that he did an uncanny imitation of Elvis Presley, he insisted that Johnson do a rock and roll set with Lenny backing him on guitar. Says Willis, "Curtis was a real good lookin' kid, tall with sideburns like Presley and Presley-type clothes and sounded just like Presley. Between him and Sonny, they were an absolute smash: Pine's bread and butter."

Lenny was developing a stage presence that, while less dynamic than his father's, radiated more confidence than Willis remembers him having off stage. "Lenny was pretty outgoing on stage then but normally he was sort of quiet, not really an outgoing type at all. He stuttered a lot so maybe that was the reason that he was kind of quiet." Willis cites one performance in which Lenny was even more outgoing on stage than usual. At a dance in Harrison, Maine, Willis and several of the musicians were surreptitiously drinking vodka/cola cocktails from Coke bottles. A musician left his bottle within Lenny's reach and Lenny began to sip from it, oblivious to its alcoholic content. "The next thing I know," Willis recalls, "he's playing louder than hell. The more he's playing, the louder he's getting and I said, 'Man, your volume is a little—you know.' He goes, 'Ohhh yeahhh?' He was just happy as hell and I said to him, 'What the hell's going on?' I looked at [fellow band member] Roy Aldridge and said, 'Didn't you have a Coke bottle over there?' and he says, 'Yeah, but there's only half left out of a full one.' So here he was sloshed on Roy's coke! He made it through the show and we just took him home. He was fine in the morning."

This incident foreshadowed things to come, but despite the rock and roll act he did with Johnson, Lenny was no fifties-era "rebel without a cause." He was eminently respectful and obedient to his elders, especially his father who was quick to show his son approval and affection, particularly after a good performance. "Pine was always hugging Lenny and telling him how great he was and how proud of him he was," says Betty. His father's praise was important to him and Lenny asked for little else. However, Betty recalls one atypical incident where Lenny summoned the nerve to question his father. "Sonny always got paid the last and if there was no money, he didn't get paid at all even though he was the biggest asset in the band," she says. "I said, 'You don't have to do that no more; just quit.' So Lenny said, 'Dad, I deserve a little more money.' Hal told him that he was all done with him. Lenny was fifteen and Hal fired him. Two or three days later, the musicians told Pine, 'If you don't rehire Lenny we're quitting.' So Hal rehired him but never did pay more money."

In the spring of 1956, Pine booked a session at a newly opened recording studio called Event Records. Located a few miles west of Portland in the village of Westbrook, the studio was owned and operated by Al Hawkes, a musician, country music scholar, and electronics wizard who had built the facility in a former blacksmith's shop on his property. He had just put out Event's first record, which featured country singer Charlie Bailey, when Pine contacted him about arranging a session at Event to provide him with records to sell at the Karavan's shows. Hawkes knew Pine's music and reputation well but had not met him until Pine arrived at the studio with his group for the first session. Hawkes recalls that he was as impressed with Pine's take-charge manner as he was by his son's acquiescence. "Hal was a strong individual and always in control," says Hawkes. "He had a military stance, like 'I am in charge, I am the master sergeant. Pay attention.' I didn't disrespect him for that although I didn't think him a very warm person, and he could be egotistical. But people often needed to be like that to survive in show business and he was a survivor of that era. [Lenny] looked like he was twelve years old: very young looking but very dapper, debonair and very well mannered. He was very respectful of people including his father. [Pine] would say to Lenny, 'I don't like it that way, do it another way,' and Lenny would just automatically do it without question. I never heard Lenny tell his father to do anything."

Lenny made his first professional recordings at Event Records on May 26, 1956.[15] He and The Kountry Karavan recorded "Prince Edward Island" (which Pine would record at least six times over the next two decades) and an old hokum tune by Frank Crummit called "Down by the Railroad Tracks." On the former, Lenny is lost in the mix but on "Railroad Tracks" he can be heard playing high speed slurs in the style of Chet Atkins behind his father's vocals. Later that day, the group's fiddler, Harold Carter, recorded "Hot Mockin' Bird" and "The German Waltz," which Lenny kicks off with some natural harmonics and, at one point, adds a counter melody to

Carter's playing. Dick Curless, who played with the Karavan on many of their shows, did the final session of the day and recorded "Foggy, Foggy Dew" with Lenny on rhythm guitar.

For reasons now forgotten, Betty Cody did not come to this first session but did sing with the Karavan when they returned to Hawkes's studio on July 7. Lenny backed his mother on Patsy Montana's "I Want to Be a Cowboy's Sweetheart" and "Treasure Island." Neither side was issued nor were two tracks that Gene Hooper cut that day with Lenny backing him. Once again Hawkes was astonished by Lenny's playing and invited him back to the studio for further recordings. Over the next eighteen months, Lenny played numerous sessions at Event Records with several musicians including Dick Curless and Curtis Johnson. Most of these sessions were country oriented but Lenny and Johnson would score Event's biggest hit with a rock and roll tune called "Baby, Baby." Hawkes had composed the song and worked out a simple rockabilly guitar riff for the tune's intro. The facile lick was far below Lenny's technical level, Hawkes says, but getting him to play it the same way on subsequent takes was not easy.

> Lenny was an experimenter even then. He would take a break and just make it up because everything was head arrangements—there was nothing written down. But maybe the guy's voice wasn't just right or someone was off beat or something. We'd have to do it again and we'd say "Lenny, do it just like you just did," and he'd say "Uh, what did I do? Can you play it back to me?" We'd play it back and he'd say "Oh, that's what I did." Then when we'd do it again and he'd do 90 percent of what he did but he'd add something to it. And then in many cases he'd embellish it even further. That was always his attitude: "I can do it better." He was constantly improvising. It was like his mind wouldn't let him duplicate it. He was always hearing something else.

In general, Lenny disliked rock and roll, and his difficulty with the intro to "Baby, Baby" probably had as much to do with his disdain for the song's genre than his desire to improvise. Still, the guitar work on many early rock records interested Lenny because much of it was influenced (and in a few cases played) by Chet Atkins who backed Elvis on some early RCA sides. Atkins's influence is absent on "Baby, Baby," but on Johnson's rendition of a rockabilly number called "I Don't Care if the Sun Don't Shine" recorded around the same time, Lenny uses Atkins's patented alternating bass, double stops, arpeggios, and slurs throughout the tune.

Lenny's most significant recordings at Event Records were done mainly as a lark during casual visits to the studio to listen to Hawkes's 20,000-unit record library or between sessions when Hawkes kept the tape rolling while the musicians jammed. Almost forty years later, these tapes were discovered by Dan Casavant, then a researcher for Guitarchives Records, and released by the label on the album, *Boy Wonder*. The CD's twenty-seven cuts provide an excellent overview of Lenny's playing at that time. The material falls into three stylistic formats: acoustic and electric solo guitar instrumentals, duets with Sleepy Willis, and group jams with Willis and other Event musicians. Lenny used Hawkes's small-bodied 1934 Gibson L-001 on most of the solo material, but also did a few of the pieces on the new orange Gretsch model 6120—designed and played by Chet Atkins—that had replaced his Fender Stratocaster sometime in 1956. This solo material consists of almost note-for-note versions of Travis and Atkins numbers and arrangements like "Chinatown, My Chinatown" and "Cannonball Rag," all of which Lenny played with a precision and flair rivaling the men that originally recorded them. Hawkes recorded the duo guitar session (titled "Sonny And Sleepy—Country Hot Guitar Club" on the log sheets) on August 12, 1957. The seven tracks from this session range from the uptempo swing blues of "Speedy Jazz" to standards like "Out of Nowhere" and "September Song." There is little of what might be labeled as real jazz improvisation on these cuts although both guitarists— Willis in particular—play with a strong swing feel and drop in some convincing jazz/blues riffs here and there. The group material, which Hawkes recorded at various sessions during 1956 and 1957, is mainly in the country/swing vein. "Mystery Swing" (incorrectly listed on *Boy Wonder* as "Muskrat Ramble") is clearly a stab at the Gypsy jazz of Django Reinhardt although neither guitarist really does the style justice. The tune "Blues Doubled" is an anomaly— the consequence of a lesson in studio recording techniques that

Hawkes used to show Lenny how Les Paul achieved his super-humanly fast licks.

> He didn't know anything about the multiple overdubbing process. I told Lenny that Mary Ford [Paul's vocalist and second guitarist] was doing overdubs and four-part harmony and Les Paul is doing four and five part guitars. Dick Greeley [studio engineer and co-founder of Event Records] was there and he said "What Les Paul does if he wants it fast, he runs the tape slower, [records] at that speed and then runs it up to fifteen inches [of tape per second] to double it, you know." Lenny said, "You gotta be kiddin' me! How do they do that?" Dick said "Go out to the studio with your guitar and I'll show you what to do." And he made "Blues Doubled." You should have seen his eyes when he came back in the studio. He said "Dick, we gotta do this some time. We gotta sit down and just do this." But we never did.

In 1957, Gene Hooper, Lenny, and his friend Shep Spinney attended a Merle Travis performance at The Lone Star Ranch, a popular outdoor country venue in Reed's Ferry, New Hampshire. Before the show, Hooper says, Lenny managed to get backstage to meet Travis and persuaded him to allow him to try his guitar. Travis reluctantly gave in, and was so astounded by what he heard that later during his performance he called Lenny up on stage and had him play a few numbers, including a duet version of Travis's "Cannonball Rag" with Shep Spinney. After the applause, Hooper says, Travis removed his hat and placed it on Lenny's head saying, "Well, folks, tonight there's a better guitarist in the house than me." Travis wasn't merely being kind; as Lenny's playing on *Boy Wonder* demonstrates, he had mastered the style down to its smallest nuance and developed a touch every bit as adept as Atkins and Travis.

As Hawkes got to know Lenny better through his frequent visits to Event Records, he became intrigued with the paradoxical mixture of naiveté and sophistication that Lenny's personality comprised. "He was really very innocent in general but in some ways very mature; at fifteen years old, he was more like a twenty-five-year-old guy," Hawkes says. "Once he told my wife Barbara that he'd slept over night with a girl in Vermont. He said something like 'I'm not gonna go with any more young girls.' My wife said, 'What do you mean?' 'Ah', he says, 'It's too hard work. They don't know anything.' Being in that business, he had to grow up fast. He had all this input from older musicians. Even though he was young, he had such a great ability that they couldn't ignore him. He was one of them."

Yet, while sophisticated beyond his years, Lenny could still demonstrate a charming, childlike guilelessness as he did on an important gig in New York City in late September of 1957. Dick Curless had won a spot on CBS's *Arthur Godfrey Talent Show* by auditioning with a rockabilly type rendition of Merle Travis's song "Nine Pound Hammer." When the show's programmers scheduled him for his appearance, Curless asked Lenny to accompany him. Lenny was game, but there was a problem: network regulations barred performers under the age of sixteen from appearing on the show. Lenny was a month short of his sixteenth birthday, but on the flight to New York, Curless counseled him to "just look 'em in the eye, smile big and say, 'sixteen'" if he were asked for his age.[16] Lenny nervously agreed but artifice did not come naturally to him. "They used a bass player from the show and the trio got a good thing going," says Al Hawkes. "When they finished, the producer said, 'That's just great—terrific!' Then she turned to Lenny and said, 'You sure play well for somebody your age. Just how old are you?' Well, Lenny looked at her and blurted out, 'f-f-f-f-fifteen, ma'am!' The studio went dead quiet and Lenny, realizing what he'd done, stuttered out, 's-s-s-s-sixteen, ma'am!' The producer turned to her assistant and said 'Get that kid out of here! He's off the show.' So he had to sit there and watch." Asked about the incident years later, Curless said, "Sonny didn't want to lie and I always loved him for it."[17]

Lenny had just finished recording "Nine Pound Hammer" at Event Records with Willis and Curless when he learned that once again he and his family would be moving on to new territory. Country entertainers Ray and Anne Little—longtime friends of the Breaus—had been hosting a daily half-hour show on CKY radio in Winnipeg, Manitoba. When they decided to leave the show, they recommended Pine and Betty as their replacements. The Breaus knew nothing about Winnipeg or its surrounding environs, but recalling their popularity and good fortune in the Canadian Maritimes, they decided to take this new job in "the provinces."

In early December of 1957, the Breau family piled into their Cadillac and began the five-day journey to their new home. Dickie Breau says that Lenny seemed to have no misgivings about the move. "I don't remember anybody having a problem with going to Winnipeg. Lenny was never concerned about going anywhere. He was out of high school and didn't have anything to hold him at that point." Geographical location had never had much importance to Lenny for whom the realm circumscribed by his guitar and family was the only world of real consequence. Winnipeg would, however, come to have special significance for Lenny. In the hard-edged, prairie city, isolated and remote from North America's major jazz centers, Lenny would serve a rigorous musical apprenticeship and develop into one of the greatest guitarists in the history of jazz. In the process, he would also become a hometown hero, although his relationship with the city would be tested in years to come.

Song of the Prairie
December 1957—April 1960

"Back in those days Lenny was a musician on the road with his family. Music, family, and the road; that's all he knew."
—Ray St. Germain

Winnipeg, a gritty prairie city with long, frigid winters and oppressively humid summers, is located in the exact east/west center of Canada, sixty miles north of the Manitoba/North Dakota border. In 1957, it was a sprawling railroad town with a large meatpacking industry and a rich cultural scene that included a world-class ballet company, an excellent symphony, a disproportionate number of music stores, and myriad nightspots with live music of all kinds.

Even before the Breaus had left Maine, CKY Radio had heavily publicized their arrival in the city with constant on-air plugs and out-dated posters heralding "RCA Stars Hal Lone Pine, Betty Cody and

their son, Lone Pine, Jr., The Fourteen-Year-Old Guitar Wizard."
The family had barely moved into their three-bedroom bungalow at
679 Sinclair in Winnipeg's North End before Lenny and his parents
were playing dates that CKY radio had arranged to promote their
upcoming daily show. After one of these dates, the Breaus visited a
downtown Winnipeg nightspot called the Rainbow Dance Gardens
where seventeen-year-old Ray St. Germain, a popular Winnipeg
singer/entertainer, was performing with his band. St. Germain had
started out in country music, but by the time the Breaus arrived in
Winnipeg, he was also playing rock and roll, and had a particular
affinity for Elvis Presley's music. He recalls that he was playing an
Everly Brothers song when the Breaus, resplendent in their sequined
Western wear, walked into the club. "They'd just come from a gig,
and they were dressed like stars," says St. Germain. "I'll never forget
Lenny. He had a white suit on, white shoes, white bucks. He was carrying his guitar, a Gretsch, in a white leather case. He had wavy
black hair and was small in stature, a cross between Sal Mineo and
Tony Curtis. The girls in the audience gasped. They didn't know
who he was, but knew he must be a star." St. Germain recalls that
the Breaus watched the band play a few numbers before Pine
requested an Elvis Presley song.

We did the tune and a couple more, and I was invited over to the
table. We talked for a while and he said they needed a rock and roll
singer for the show and would I be interested. They asked how old
I was and said I'd be a perfect age for a companion for Lenny. So I
accepted even though I was still in school and still living at home. I
asked Lenny if he wanted to sit in with the band that night because
he had his guitar; didn't want to leave it in the car. Hal said, "Sure,
it'll give him a chance to learn some of your stuff." Lenny got up
and I sang a couple of tunes, but the people were screaming for
Lenny. I mean, he was a radio star. It's important to realize back in
'57, radio was king and these were radio stars. They came from the
States on top of it. Anybody who came from the States to Canada
must be better than anyone else. Anyway, we ended playing all
Lenny's songs that night because they just wanted more and more
of Lenny so we just ended doing the background for him.

Ray and Lenny hit it off immediately and when Ray asked if he would be interested in playing a New Year's Eve gig with his band, Lenny—after getting the OK from his parents—eagerly took him up on the offer. A few days later, Lenny dropped by Ray's house to rehearse and was introduced to the St. Germain family. The family was impressed with Ray's new friend, particularly Valerie, Ray's sixteen-year-old sister. "I thought he was very handsome," she recalls. "He reminded me of Elvis. His eyes hypnotized you, looked right through you. They had secrets in them. His teeth, his mouth, his hair, his nails, everything about him was perfect. And he seemed so much in control with a lot of charisma and very mannerly."

The pair met again a week later when Valerie went with the band to their New Year's Eve gig in a nearby town. "We were in the car; he was in the front seat and I was in the back," Valerie says. "He kept lighting cigarettes and holding the match up, looking at me and smiling and going 'oh wow.' At the dance, I sat on the stage and he kept looking at me while he was playing, turning his head and then turning away. But there was another girl who was really interested in Lenny, and she ended up in the car with us for the ride back. We came back to town and I was dropped off. I thought, 'oh well, I'll probably never see him again.'" Valerie needn't have worried; she had just had her first date with her future husband and father of her two children.

The CKY Caravan did their first fifteen-minute show on CKY at 4:00 on Monday, January 6, 1958. Initially, the band was made up of the Breaus, Ray St. Germain, and bassist Jimmy Daughtry, who had worked with Pine in Maine before coming to Winnipeg with Ray and Anne Little. A few months later, Pine hired fiddler Jack Paget who subsequently became the group's steel guitarist when the Caravan acquired seventeen-year-old fiddler Stan Winnistock. Soon the Caravan was performing in the myriad small towns and villages within the range of CKY's powerful 50,000-watt signal, often leaving Winnipeg minutes after signing off to rush to a gig in North Dakota or northeastern Saskatchewan. When possible, they would return home after the show, sometimes at one or two o'clock in the morning, says Dickie Breau, who shared a room with Lenny. "I remember Lenny coming home after those shows. He'd give me all the change that he'd made selling his pictures at the show that night and then he'd start practicing his guitar and would play for several more hours. He'd wake me up and I'd think, 'Oh, he's going to play again.' He would and it would go on sometimes until five or six a.m."

Sometimes the family would be on the road for days at a time, playing in a series of remote towns while CKY broadcast their taped shows in the Caravan's radio slot. Ray St. Germain says that these road trips took them deep into the prairie hinterlands, driving long miles on often unpaved roads in Pine's 1954 Cadillac.

Lenny would spend his time practicing in the back of the car. He was always practicing, very dedicated to his craft. He had a little cigar box that he had extended with a little neck on it and rubber bands stretched as tight as he could get them. He'd just practice on the rubber bands. He'd also started squeezing balls for strength. In a lot of these towns, they still had hitching posts for the horses and spittoons in the hotel lobbies. We stayed in small rooms with the bathroom down the hall. No lamps, just overhead light bulbs. They all had fire escapes for sneaking up local ladies. [Laughs] When we had any spare time before a show or something, we played pool. Lenny was a heck of a pool player. He was good— dedicated to becoming the best like everything else he did. We'd hit town and we'd set up at a local movie theatre or community hall. We had a light show with us: two little black lights. Our outfits were painted with invisible paint that turned color when the lights were off. Lenny's Gretsch was orange, but he had that invisible paint so whenever [the black lights] went on, you just saw this glow. And of course, all this white fringe with white hat, teeth and clothing. The PA consisted of two ten-inch speakers and a record player in the middle that had the amp. You'd fold it up to about eighteen inches square. We had an old microphone, a really big thing. The only electric instrument was Lenny's with his amp; the rest were acoustic.

On days that the Caravan did not travel, Lenny would leave after their broadcast to meet Valerie, who worked on Main Street a few blocks from the CKY building, and the two teenagers would go to a nearby restaurant to eat and talk. "We just connected very quickly," Valerie says. "The first time I was with Lenny, he said 'you know, I'm going to study all the great guitar players in the world and their styles, and then I'll develop my own style. I'll be about thirty-five when that happens and I'll be one of the greatest guitar players in the world. I'm going to have a son and I'm going to name him Chet.' Just like that! He was very clear and positive. He knew where he was going and what he had to do to get there. He showed me there was something else out there besides going to work from nine to five. He opened up a whole new world to me. We started going around with each other pretty steady and he gave me a ring, a black onyx, four leaf clover set in white gold with a diamond in the middle."

A few months later on Lenny's seventeenth birthday, Valerie's brother gave Lenny a very different sort of gift. "He was always talking about jazz and Barney Kessel, about what a great player he was," says St. Germain. "He said he had heard him back when he was in Maine, and had always wanted to try to play that music but his dad didn't like it, and he was never around any players who knew how to do it. So knowing that his birthday was coming up, I bought him a Barney Kessel album and he was so thrilled to get it.[1] The next day I picked him up to go play some pool and he said, 'listen!' And he played the whole album note-for-note. He'd sat up from the time I'd left him and he'd learned it. He was that quick. By then, I was so close to him that, well, I was amazed, but in a way it didn't surprise me."

While Lenny could easily parrot Kessel's solos, the theory underlying them was a mystery to him. But in the fall of 1958, a chance meeting with a well-connected local musician would serve to bring Lenny into contact with musicians who could reveal to him the secrets of jazz improvisation and theory. One afternoon, Lenny was playing guitar for some friends in the back of Rosenbaum's Music Store—a popular hangout for the city's musicians—when the late trumpet player and CBC producer/writer Paul Grosney overheard him. Grosney, who was just putting together a new CBC television show, was impressed. "What I heard just blew me away," says Grosney. "I said to him, 'OK, you're starting a television show with me in two days.'" Lenny agreed but as Grosney talked further with him, he discovered that Lenny did not have a union card, which was required for work at CBC. Undeterred, Grosney took Lenny to the Winnipeg union office, lent him the money for his card and two days later

Lenny played "Sweet Georgia Brown" on Grosney's show, the first of countless CBC dates that Lenny would play over the next decade.

The most immediate benefit of this experience was that Lenny's union membership made it possible for him to work in the pick-up bands that the union put together and booked to play casuals around the city. These groups were manned largely by older, more experienced musicians who had much musical knowledge to pass on to Lenny. Reg Kelln, who would become a close friend and drummer with the original Lenny Breau Trio, was one of the first of these players whom Lenny would meet. Four years older than Lenny, Kelln had been playing professionally since 1954. By the time he met Lenny four years later, Kelln was an accomplished jazz drummer perfecting his craft mainly at after-hours jams in the homes of like-minded musicians. Most of his paying gigs at this time were non-jazz dates but this didn't stop him from slipping in jazz riffs at straight ahead functions as he was doing at the Rainbow Dance Gardens the night he first met Lenny.

It was a dance job: polkas, waltzes, regular wedding type dance music with accordion, fiddle, guitar, bass, maybe a saxophone. At half time, we went down the elevator to have a smoke outside. He said "I've never played with drums before. While we were playing that polka, you were playing, 'ding diddle ding diddle ding.'" It was a jazz riff, cymbal ride, I told him. He said, "is that ever neat. Cymbal ride, huh? And then you guys would be playing that polka and they'd play and then you'd be playing and—." I said, "Well, we were trading fours in a polka." He goes, "Oh, so you'd play four and then they'd play four?" I said, "Yeah, that's it." After that job, we went to a jam where we were playing jazz. He didn't know the tunes so he sat out, just sitting there listening. After a while he said, "Well, can I get some albums to learn some of these tunes?" We said, "Oh yeah," and gave him three LPs: one big band swing with well-known tunes, one a quartet with jazz tunes, and a flamenco album. He says, "OK, I'll take them home and I'll learn these." So about four or five days later he phones me up and says, "OK, I'm ready." I said, "Wait a second, we gave you three albums." He says, "Yeah, I got it all down." I thought, no, that can't be. But when we go to the next session, there he is, ready to play; plays every tune perfectly. I remember thinking, "there's something weird about this guy." Afterwards he said, "Well, next time you guys get together to rehearse, let me know." We all looked at each other and just said, "OK."

Lenny began to drop by Kelln's apartment regularly to listen to jazz records and pick the drummer's brain. On one of his visits, he met Gary Gross, a friend of Kelln's, who was learning to play bebop on accordion. "Lenny had such an inquiring mind musically and he was always in the mode of wanting to move forward," recalls Gross, later a well-known jazz pianist and TV writer. "This was pre-jazz guitar for him, as far as I know. Reg had a portable record player and I put on a Tal Farlow record [with] the tune 'Lover.' Lenny sat right next to the player and his whole demeanor changed when that track started to play. He went into a kind of semi-trance, just flipped out. He kept saying, 'I can't believe it. Hey man, put that back, put that back!' He didn't want to hear the second track; he had to get that first one in his mind to understand it. He flipped out over the feeling and the improvisational greatness of it all. I believe to this day that hearing 'Lover' was certainly an epiphany for him."

This may or may not have been the first time Lenny heard Farlow, but there's no doubt that Farlow's brilliant bop lines and unique harmonic concepts would have a profound influence on Lenny, as he admitted to Farlow himself almost twenty-five years later during a cameo in the Lorenzo DeStefano documentary *Talmage Farlow*.

I only started listening to jazz when I was fifteen and naturally I wanted to listen to guitar players so I listened to you and I have to confess that most of the records I had were yours . . . I was about sixteen or seventeen. I didn't hear you play chords that often but when you did, some of the chord changes you used, some of the voicings, they just completely threw me off because I didn't know what you were doing. I didn't understand it . . . I just never heard anybody play those chords . . . those were great chords, man. Just the voicings alone—it took me a few years. I finally got onto them after I got into piano . . . all of a sudden I said, "oh yeah, that's what that was."[2]

Lenny did acquire some rudimentary piano skills a few years later, but in the main he used his ear to learn Farlow's music and relied on the same method he'd used to pick up Atkins's pieces. Slowing down Farlow's records to 16½ rpms from 33 on a variable speed turntable, Lenny (or a friend enlisted for the purpose) would repeatedly move the needle back to the beginning of the phrase he was trying to learn until Lenny found it on the guitar. Using this method, Lenny was able to pick up Kessel's and Farlow's riffs as well as their chord melody arrangements of standards. In January of 1959, he played one of these arrangements on a CBC radio show called *The Trans Canada Talent Caravan*, a weekly contest program that featured five local performers who were judged in front of a live studio audience. Before Lenny's spot, the show's host, George Murray, interviewed him briefly. Polite and cheery (and sounding remarkably like his father), Lenny tells Murray, "I like jazz the best, but I like western too, you know, but actually I like jazz the best." Asked to name his favorite guitarist, Lenny replies without hesitation, "Mr. Johnny Smith is my favorite guitar player."[3]

Smith's style had little to do with what followed, however. Backed by rudimentary bass and drums accompaniment, Lenny played a virtual note-for-note copy of Barney Kessel's version of "Mean to Me" from *The Poll Winners* album, throwing in a rehearsed, bebop-based single note solo. He gives the tune's B section a rubato treatment, playing the melody in the bass against arpeggiated chords on the treble strings, a technique used often by Chet Atkins. After rattling off one of Atkins's patented slurred riffs, he returns to the A section in tempo, once again playing Kessel's arrangement of the tune. Lenny easily won the contest and Murray presented him with a check for a hundred dollars while the audience cheered wildly.

This performance illustrates well just where Lenny was with his jazz playing in early 1959. His phrasing and facility were excellent and he played with a precision and tone that already surpassed Kessel at his best. However, while Lenny was picking up odds and ends of the jazz lexicon from records and friends like Kelln, his formal musical knowledge at this point was still so restricted he could do little more than reproduce the music he was pulling off his icons' records and pool their ideas into a rehearsed pastiche that replaced authentic improvisation. What Lenny needed at this point was a mentor who could teach him the nuts and bolts of jazz theory and improvisation, just as Bob Tustin and Ray Couture had helped him with the Atkins style. Although Lenny didn't know it, a few weeks before appearing on *Talent Caravan*, he had met such a mentor, a man who would help him to unlock the riddles of jazz and, in the process, become his close, lifelong friend.

Bob Erlendson was born in 1931 in rural Manitoba, but grew up in Winnipeg where he studied classical piano as a child. He became interested in jazz in his early teens after hearing Nat King Cole, and then immersed himself in the bebop of Gillespie and Parker. He began playing professionally with legendary Canadian bandleader Johnny Bering in his early twenties, and in the years following, modeled his playing on a number of players including Lennie Tristano, Dave Brubeck, and Horace Silver. Erlendson left Winnipeg in 1954 and for the next five years gigged throughout Canada and the eastern United States, often in the company of the late tenor sax player Don "DT" Thompson, an important figure in the Canadian jazz and pop scene. Erlendson returned to Winnipeg in the fall of 1958 to take a steady gig at the Town and Country Inn, but was fired a week later when the room's manager decided that jazz did not draw customers. Strapped for money, Erlendson kept himself afloat for the next few months playing casual union gigs. In late December, Paul Grosney asked Erlendson to play vibes at a union-sponsored gig at Stony Mountain penitentiary with a band for which Lenny had also been hired. Erlendson recalls being intrigued with the well-dressed young guitarist who was doing his best to follow the swing tunes that Grosney called. "I knew he was something special because he obviously didn't know the tunes, but could fake his way through them," Erlendson recalls. "Lenny wasn't simply convincing, he was f—marvelous, and when the gig was done, I made sure that I got his phone number."

At this time, Erlendson and a sax player/singer named Frank Lewis were putting together a vocal group modeled on The Four Freshmen with local bassist Bob Jackson and a female singer named Dinie Gillis. The group—Four Guys and a Doll—lacked one male voice and Erlendson, eager to work with Lenny, called him to ask if he would be interested in joining the quintet. Lenny was game, even though his guitar playing would be secondary to his singing. He met with Erlendson prior to his first rehearsal with the group and the pianist soon realized that Lenny's abilities far exceeded his practical musical knowledge. "It was startling how little he knew," says Erlendson. "He wasn't even absolutely sure of the names of the strings of his guitar so I started to feed him theory. That was Lenny's first sight-reading experience, reading the arrangements that Frank and I wrote. He was such a fast study. I would teach him [the parts] note by note with me singing his part and him memorizing it. His voice was fine, just beautiful. He had perfect pitch so he could sing in tune and was just fine as that third voice. He also liked the material because it was a whole other ballgame."

While Lenny's friendship with Erlendson was getting under way, his parents' relationship came grinding to a halt. Pine decided that the family could no longer afford a nanny to look after the children, and ordered Betty to stay home with their sons when the band was traveling. Betty was stunned, but complied with her husband's wishes. Soon after, she discovered that Pine's edict was motivated by his affair with nineteen-year-old Jeannie Ward, one half of a singing sisters act Pine had hired just before firing Betty. Still reeling from this discovery, she learned from the Breaus' landlord that Pine had not paid rent on their house for several months. "Pine wouldn't support us," says Betty. "And then I got sick. My doctor said that I should leave Winnipeg and go home to Lewiston. I didn't have no money so I called my parents and they sent us plane fare." Betty asked Lenny to return to Maine with her and his brothers, but he had become engaged to Valerie in November of 1958 and the couple planned to wed the following year. "He just didn't want to leave," she says. "He was young and in love. He said 'Gee, mom. I've got my job here with my father and I'm engaged so . . .'" Betty respected Lenny's wishes but his naiveté and lack of life skills made her uneasy about leaving her son behind. "I had made Lone Pine promise to take care of Lenny when they were on the road," says Betty, "but he didn't and was always introducing him to older women and that sort of thing."

Shortly after Betty left Winnipeg, Pine learned that his contract with CKY would not be renewed when it ended on July 1, 1959.

Fortunately, his old friends, Ray and Anne Little, happened to be leaving their job on CHAB radio in Moose Jaw, Saskatchewan, and once again recommended Pine as their replacement. The station agreed to sign Pine but had slightly different plans for him and the Caravan. CHAB had just opened a television studio and wanted Pine to host his own daily half-hour live show. Pine signed on with the station and, with no warning, Lenny and the rest of the band were informed that they would be relocating to Moose Jaw in time to do their first show as the CHAB Caravan on July 7, 1959.

Lenny was not pleased with this news. Besides putting six hundred miles between him and his fiancée, the move curtailed his position in Four Guys and a Doll. "He left before we did any gigs," Erlendson says, "He wasn't really happy about it; it was just duty, that's all. He certainly had loyalty to his dad who was doing what he could do to follow immediately the success he'd had on CKY. But, no, he wasn't happy about it."

The framework of Lenny's life changed little in Moose Jaw. When the Caravan's daily show was done, they would troop off to play local dance halls or theaters or hit the road to play rural community halls indistinguishable from those that Lenny and his father had worked countless times over the past four years.

This routine was broken when Lenny returned to Winnipeg to marry Valerie on her eighteenth birthday—November 14, 1959. The groom, who had reached his full height of 5 feet, 6 inches and weighed about 135 pounds, recited his vows to his young bride while wearing a blue pinstripe suit that he had bought for the occasion in the boy's department of the Hudson Bay Company department store. Only members of Valerie's immediate family were present at the small ceremony. Lenny's father did not deign to attend, and Betty, recovering in Maine, was unable to travel. Like his parents, Lenny had no honeymoon. He returned to Moose Jaw alone and was on the road playing when Valerie arrived a few days later to set up housekeeping in the small apartment the couple would share.

When the couple returned to Winnipeg for the Christmas holidays, Lenny discovered that during his absence two jazz-loving Winnipeg businessmen had opened an after-hours jazz club called the Rando Manor in a renovated restaurant on the northeastern outskirts of the city. The men hired Bob Erlendson to play piano in the club from midnight to 5:00 a.m., and the venue had quickly become Winnipeg's hottest after-hours jazz club. During his Christmas visit to Winnipeg, Lenny visited the Rando Manor and, playing his recently purchased Gibson ES-125 guitar, jammed with Erlendson, Gary Gross, and a bass player named Dave Shaw. An audience member taped this impromptu performance and the recording provides an interesting sample of Lenny's jazz playing in late 1959. He was playing single lines with a flat pick at this point, still emulating Kessel and Farlow and recycling their riffs. However, his improvisational abilities were beginning to evolve, guided by his innate musical sensibility rather than any academic understanding of theory and harmony. He was now creating lines out of short melodic fragments rather than simply running through worked out riffs although he often fell back on fast slurred licks when stumped for ideas. He was most at ease with simpler, blues-based tunes like "Billie's Bounce" and "All Blues," from Miles Davis' groundbreaking album *Kind of Blue*, which had been released a few months earlier. His articulation, phrasing, and sense of swing on the recording are consistently superb, and on "I'll Remember April," he purposefully drags the beat so much that at one point he is playing with a perfect 3 over 2 feel, a rhythmic figure that would later become a signature of his style.

Lenny attended a few more jams at the Rando Manor before returning to Moose Jaw where the music he played on stage was confined to country. But his desire to play jazz remained strong, bubbling to the surface at—as his father saw it— inappropriate times. Ray St. Germain says that one night when the Caravan was playing the Don Gibson hit "Oh Lonesome Me," Lenny mischievously threw in a bebop-styled solo during his instrumental break. Pine smiled gamely, but after the show, St. Germain says, he reprimanded Lenny and then slapped him. Paget and Winnistock dispute this, insisting that Pine would not have hit his son under any circumstances. Valerie Breau, however, says she once witnessed Pine hit Lenny for talking back to Betty, and Gene Hooper claims that his own personal experience with Pine's hair-trigger temper leads him to believe that the backstage incident is entirely credible. Whether or not the slap was a literal one, there were powerful tensions between father and son that encompassed more than musical issues. Lenny was still upset over his parents' separation, and Valerie Breau-St. Germain says that he had not forgiven his father for jettisoning his mother. Pine added insult to injury by paying newcomer Jeannie Ward, an inexperienced, run-of-the-mill singer, the same cut as his son, long the undisputed star of the show. Lenny, uncharacteristically, complained to his father, but backed down when Pine stonewalled him. "Pine was very controlling over Lenny," says St. Germain. "He would have hated to lose him. Lenny went through his teenage years with his dad as his boss—not a normal life."

These squabbles suddenly came to an end in late March of 1960 when, without warning, Pine announced that he was dissolving the group. He offered no explanation for his decision but since the advent of rock and roll, the audience for his kind of country music— heavy on mawkish chaff like "Fuzzy Wuzzy Teddy Bear" and long outdated comedy skits—had dwindled significantly. It's likely that he simply recognized the financial benefits of working in a smaller unit, and for the next several years he traveled, performed, and occasionally recorded alone or with Jeannie Ward, who would become the mother of Pine's daughter. Lenny was ambivalent about the break-up of the band. While he was now free to concentrate on jazz, the dissolution of the group meant a sudden cutting of ties with his father and the end of the band that had been the hub of Lenny's universe since infancy. As a small, lonely boy, Lenny had worked hard to hone the skills that would allow him entry into his parents' group and, by default, their world. Once accepted into this magical realm, in the guise of the fictional character known as Lone Pine, Jr., Lenny had been called on to do little more than remain an entertaining, charming child who was granted many of an adult's liberties with few of the accompanying responsibilities or expectations. While he learned many essential musical and stage skills in the process, no one ever imparted to him any pragmatic understanding of the world beyond the bandstand. Now an eighteen-year-old husband with a pregnant wife and all the attendant pressures of adulthood, he was ill prepared to leave the comfort and safety of his unorthodox and protracted childhood, and never would entirely. In ways that would forever be alternately appealing and disconcerting to those close to him, Lenny Breau's adult character would always resemble that of the engaging, needy, and guitar-obsessed boy wonder known as Lone Pine, Jr. As

Ray Couture puts it, "You just couldn't help but love Lenny, but if you loved him, he expected you to look after him because he couldn't look after himself."

Lenny and Valerie returned to Winnipeg in late March 1960 and moved in temporarily with Valerie's parents. In the weeks that followed, Lenny struggled to understand what might be expected of him during and after the birth of his first child. "The night Val went into labor," says Valerie's younger sister, Judy, "Lenny was really scared and he said to Dad, 'what do I do if the baby starts coming?' I remember his eyes were so big. And Dad said, 'oh don't worry, Len. Just start pulling if the baby starts coming.' And Lenny said, 'No, you don't mean that, do you?' He just didn't know anything about it." The couple's first child was born on April 14, 1960, and given the name that Lenny had chosen for her. Petite, dark-eyed, and fine-featured, Melody would favor her father physically and possess, Valerie says, his artistic sensibilities. Lenny adored his daughter from the moment of her birth, but initially suffered the sort of insecurity one might expect from an only child who fears his privileged position in the family hierarchy will be usurped by the arrival of a sibling. "When Melody was born, he sat by my bedside, taking my hand and looking into my face," Valerie says. "He said, 'Will you love Melody more than you love me?'"

After Melody's birth, Lenny began to look in earnest for work around the city. He and Ray St. Germain formed a duo called the Mississippi Gamblers, playing folk, country, and pop tunes on occasional radio spots and doing out of town and local gigs. One of these was at Winnipeg's North Main Drive-In where they entertained during intermission after hauling their equipment up onto the roof of the theatre's concession stand. Lenny also played lead guitar in St. Germain's rock group, The Satins, which had a regional hit on Chateau Records with the Presley sound-alike number, "She's a Square."

While these gigs provided Lenny with badly needed income, the three-chord songs that he and his brother-in-law played were essentially a stale reprise of the material he'd performed in his father's shows since his early teens. Jazz was now his passion and he wanted to spend all his time unlocking its mysteries and playing with musicians who shared his musical inclinations. The possibility of fulfilling this desire must have seemed hopelessly remote to Lenny as he and his brother-in-law played the latest Everly Brothers hit to a lot-full of blank car windshields while the projectionist set up *Revenge of the Teen-age Werewolf* for the drive-in's restless patrons. Unbeknownst to him, however, a few miles away in downtown Winnipeg, a local entrepreneur/musician had just opened a new club that might well have been fashioned from the very fabric of his jazz dreams.

3.

Lullaby of Birdland
April 1960—May 1962

"Some of my greatest fun was playing at the Stage Door back in the old days. I learned so much playing there; it was like going to school."

—Lenny Breau[1]

"The activity at the Stage Door was fabulous, like Birdland in New York City or the closest thing to Birdland that Winnipeg will ever have: a big, fabulous learning scene for all of us."

—Ron Halldorson

Known to his friends as "Shap," the high-rolling, loquacious Jack Shapira was a pianist who had led a number of dance bands in Winnipeg during the 1940s and '50s, and later had a career in television and radio production at the CBC. Shapira was not a jazz musician, but loved the music and wanted to start a club that would feature it exclusively. "There were all these local musicians and entertainers from out of town who had nowhere to go once all the clubs closed down at 1:00 a.m.—not even any all-night restaurants," he says. "So I said, 'why don't we have a jazz club?' And that was it. I started it just as a place for us to go." After buying out and shutting down the struggling Rando Manor to eliminate competition, Shapira opened the Stage Door in April 1960.

The cramped, dimly lit club occupied the bottom floor of an office building in Winnipeg's downtown core. Entering the club through a small foyer, one reached the restaurant area by climbing a few stairs to a raised section where chairs and tables with red and white checkered tableclothes were set up. Along one wall was an eight-inch-high stage that was just big enough to accommodate the battered house upright piano and a half dozen tightly packed musicians with drums set up on the floor beside the riser. The kitchen beyond the stage was overseen by a Chinese cook who specialized in Italian food. Officially the unlicensed club's specialty was strawberry shortcake, but those who knew the password could surreptitiously order a cup of coffee liberally spiked with rye. Shapira decided that everything from the spaghetti to a cup of regular coffee would be $1.50.

Shapira had just fired the club's first house band when a local guitarist named Monty Levine dropped by the Stage Door one evening with Lenny in tow. Shapira knew of Lenny through local buzz, but was not prepared for what he heard as Lenny, dressed in the mauve country-cut suit jacket, string tie, and cowboy boots he wore when performing in the Mississippi Gamblers, sat down and took out his guitar. "He looked like a country hick," says Shapira. "But when he played I couldn't believe it. I hired him right away."

Shapira then contacted Bob Erlendson who had just finished a six-week gig playing bass with a local band. "Jack said, 'I'm going to get Lenny Breau to come in tomorrow night. Why don't you come too?'" recalls Erlendson. "Lenny hadn't gotten ahold of me [since returning to Winnipeg] for whatever reason. So I went down and we played two consecutive nights—Tuesday and Wednesday. Shapira dug it and said 'alright I'll hire both of you.' So all of a sudden we're working together six nights a week from 10:00 p.m. until 4:00 a.m. and later if there were people there or a lot of jamming going on."

Shapira paid the musicians $35 each per week and kicked in meals, a side benefit of which, Shapira says, Lenny took full advantage by eating at the club four times a day on occasion. Despite the meager wages, Lenny was thrilled to be working with Erlendson, who over the next year and a half would provide Lenny with a comprehensive musical education that would serve as the foundation of his jazz playing for the rest of his life. "Bob got me into understanding what I was trying to do," Lenny later told John Knowles. "Before that if I played a Dm9 chord, I didn't know what it was called . . . At first I didn't want to be bothered with all of that. I just wanted to learn by ear without knowing all the details. But after a while, what he told me really became important."[2]

During this process, the two men would become close, lifelong friends bound by their love of jazz and a deep mutual respect and affection. "I considered Lenny to be my very best friend," Erlendson says. "He was jolly to be around. When we were talking music, it was intense, but he was fun-loving and always cracking jokes. Sometimes we would be playing and we would just start laughing because it was fun; not only fun but very, very creative."

The duo's first task was to learn enough repertoire to keep their audience interested through three or four nightly sets. This had to be done quickly and was, particularly for Lenny, an uphill push, as Erlendson recounts.

> We worked our asses off. Not only did we do six nights a week for the first six months but we were rehearsing two or three times a week and [I was] spending a lot of time teaching Lenny all the things that were necessary to get him caught up. He couldn't read charts, chord symbols—none of that. He was learning mainly by ear, as I would bring new stuff in. By the end of that year and a half, we'd learned and played over a thousand tunes. We'd each made a book listing those titles. We were doing it by ear and I would write them down. I figured that was one way I could help Lenny—to write out these things because I was doing more research than Lenny was, as far as [finding new] tunes are concerned. He did do some. He was slowly but surely accumulating records: Miles, Coltrane, the Art Blakey bands, things like that. There would also be some cuts on records that he would really like so he would learn them by playing along with them and bring that information to a discussion. During our afternoon sessions he would say, "OK, here's what I've learned." And I would say, "I like that chord, I like that one but I don't like this one." I spent a lot of the time working out by myself a consistent pattern for fingering chords on the piano

and showing Lenny how to integrate this into his own playing. This was a big part of what Lenny wanted to know: chord changes and voicings. He didn't understand anything about scales or soloing over changes; he was improvising totally by ear by that point. But he asked these vital questions: "What are you supposed to do with this chord? How do you voice it?" And I'd say, "Well, here are the four positions of that chord. I can show you on piano and you can transpose it to guitar."

To accelerate this educational process, Erlendson, a quick study on any instrument, learned some basic guitar technique with Lenny's help in order to show him scale positions, note names, and recurring patterns on the fretboard.

Even though he was doing some remarkably interesting jazz improvisation things right from the minute I met him, a lot of it was just running the E string and paying no attention to the B and G strings except to play one or two notes on them. What I was trying to get him to understand was [that] even though he was way up on the high E at the twelfth fret, he should be able to go all the way down right to the low E string and see the connection between the scale positions clearly, to practice and master this rather than saying something like "Oh, I'll try this one day and see what it's like." I tried to get him to where it became intimate knowledge. This also included chords and triads. Many times, it started off the same way. He'd say, "What did you just do?" I'd say, "I played these three notes." He'd say "Well, play them one at a time." This was at a relatively primitive stage. I'd say, "Well, I'm playing this and this. Find it on the guitar." He'd see a string that it worked on, put his fingers on it and say, "Oh, I can play that. What do you call it?"

In the summer of 1960, Erlendson purchased an electric bass: a cello-shaped Hofner model that would later become commonly known as a "Beatle bass" when Paul McCartney made it his axe of choice. While Erlendson would occasionally play the bass on gigs, he'd bought the instrument with Lenny in mind. As Erlendson explained to his friend at their next practice session, having to provide the harmonic underpinning for the duo's music on bass would help Lenny gain a thorough knowledge of how chord progressions worked. Lenny was not thrilled with Erlendson's plan, but agreed to play at least half of the duo's sets as a bassist and soon saw the wisdom in Erlendson's suggestion, as he explained to John Knowles. "[It] was one of the best things I ever did because I learned the forms of tunes that way. I had to learn the chord sequences or structures of tunes. It also made my left hand strong. . . . In those first gigs, they would call out a tune and I'd say, 'Man, I don't know that tune!' And Bob would say 'Well, you will. One-two-three-and—. Talk about scuffling. That's when I first learned chord progressions by numbers."[3]

As Lenny began to understand the chord numbering system, and how chords are linked to create progressions, he developed his own musical vocabulary to express certain recurring chord sequences, labeling them with names that often reflected his country and western background, says Erlendson:

He had to learn the musical language in order to ask the question. He'd fumble around just to get it out and slowly but surely his vocabulary got there. He invented nicknames [for musical terms]. Like a chord sequence that goes "1-3-6-2-5-1" has been used in a zillion tunes, and variations of it happen all over the place. So he just said, "Let's call that a 'Down the Line' so when we learn a new tune, we can say it's a Down the Line with a flat 3rd instead of a 6th." When you're looking at specific tunes, you start seeing chord patterns that cover the whole of each new composition. So I'd say, "We've got to really understand that within one scale, [an example of] a chord pattern that would really make sense would go 1-4-3 minor, 6 (either a minor or with a dominant 7th), minor 2nd to the 5 chord—the dominant 7th—and back to the 1. So [the progression is] '1-4-3-6-2-5-1, which Lenny nicknamed 'Down the Line.'" So I could say, "I've found a song and it's a 'Down the Line' in this way but has variations like a [chord built on the scale's] flat 3rd instead of a 6th." I would say "Down the Line, flat 3" and he'd know what I meant. And we'd play the tune as if we'd played it before and it was the very first time we'd ever played the song. Or I could say, "It's got a 'Down the Line' progression but look at what we do at bar six, that's different." Lenny was intrigued with the idea that you can take the written chord out and substitute it with something else. There were times on the bandstand when something would occur to me and just on the spot I would notice a better chord than the one we had talked about, try to yell it at him just before I played it. And if he missed it, he would just laugh. But his memory was good so when we got to the next chorus he was ready for me. He would hear the alteration right away. It got to the point in a year and a half where I would hardly even yell because I was sure that if I played it and even if he was a semi-tone out, he'd slide into it with a gliss and make it sound like he meant to do that.

In September of 1960, the Stage Door house band became a trio when Bob Erlendson persuaded Shapira to hire Reg Kelln, by then Winnipeg's premier jazz drummer. Soon there was a constant parade of the city's best musicians across the club's small stage as they turned out to sit in with the trio after their regular gigs around town had ended. One of these musicians was jazz singer and future CBC broadcaster, Mary Nelson. A musician friend had asked Nelson to drop around to the Stage Door to sing a few numbers one night and while Nelson doesn't recall the tunes she sang, her first impression of Lenny is still vivid. "Even at the age of nineteen, he was brilliant—brilliant!" she says. "Lenny didn't try to make you in awe of him; you just were in awe of him. I guess it would be like being in the presence of someone like Chopin when he was young. That's what I felt at that moment."

Nelson sang regularly with Lenny and Bob during the next two years on various jobs around Winnipeg, but it was their work together at the Stage Door that she recalls most clearly.

We'd meet down at the club and I'd sing with Lenny doing all those Julie London/Barney Kessel tunes from that album.[4] That album was something we had in common because Barney Kessel was one of Lenny's favorite guitar players. Lenny had more of an attraction to that impressionistic, ballad stuff rather than the burning stuff. Lenny was a romantic. Not to say he couldn't play as fast and as outside as anybody else, but left to our own devices we would do nothing but ballads: "Lush Life," and "Round Midnight," and "Invitation." Lenny would sit on the stool playing the guitar and it would come time for his chorus, and we would be watching him breathlessly because two bars would go by and three bars would go by and then the fourth bar would come in and he would play maybe three notes. But Lenny said more with silences than most musicians could say with a bazillion notes because every note he played was perfect.

His less-is-more musical approach, says Nelson, paralleled a subdued but charismatic demeanor that expressed much in few words. "His stuttering was constant and not just when he was upset or pressured, so he mostly spoke through his instrument," Nelson says. "He was just so shy but he was magical. You couldn't see the man without feeling drawn to him. There was an innocence and a joy about him. And as soon as you heard a note from his guitar, and saw those long nails on one hand, and the short nails on the other—how could you not sing, how could you not play, how could you not be just so happy in the presence of somebody so innocent, so wonderful, and so talented?"

One night, the Shelly Manne Trio—Manne on drums, pianist Russ Freeman, and Ray Brown on bass—dropped by the Stage Door after playing a show at the Winnipeg Auditorium. The three men sat at the back of the club watching the house band until the set break when Shapira asked them if they'd like to do a few tunes, Nelson recalls.

> They said, "Sure, we'd love to do a set." So the band is trooping off the stage and Lenny's the last and as he's walking off Shelly puts his hand on him and says, "No, not you, man. You stay right here where you are." And Lenny did. There he was, sitting up there on his stool just being Lenny, so totally unassuming. He was very stage shy but he played his ass off. After the set was over, the guys got off the stage and went over and sat down. Lenny comes floating across the stand to where the cash is and I looked at him and grinned and he was just in seventh heaven. He said "whoa, sh-sh-sh-it,"—the only cuss he used—"whew! Playing with Shelly and the boys!" Ah, it was wonderful. "Shelly and the boys!" Just wonderful!

The laid-back atmosphere and camaraderie among the audience and musicians at the Stage Door created an atmosphere conducive to musical chance taking and spontaneity, which on some nights led the musicians into the realm of free form playing, Erlendson says. "We would just play off the cuff to see where it took us. No set tune. I would say, 'I don't know what I'm gonna do. I'm just going to close my eyes and punch the piano. See what it means to you.' And I would just go 'thunk' and let my hands fall anywhere on the key-board. And he would just start to play. And I would say, 'That makes me think of this' and—'thunk'—I would respond to what he did. To me, that was important. I was thinking back to the early Lennie Tris-tano [innovative post-bebop pianist] things that he did in 1947–48 [and] were really just part of honest, spontaneous playing."

Despite these experiments, Lenny was never interested in aban-doning melody as the guiding precept in his improvisations and, says Erlendson, always showed a natural inclination to play beautifully realized melodic lines.

> Lenny was a very melodic thinker, honestly melodic partly because of the country thing. If you play country, especially if you're the lead man or singer, you'd better learn the melodies of the songs. If you're hearing a bunch of melodies—good, bad or indifferent—eventually the good ones will lock into your brain and you'll say "that's good!" That's where he was coming from. And because I really approved of that, especially at the beginning of the Stage Door, what I was trying to do was feed him real cushions of sound that were providing [him with] something that would dictate a lovely melody. Let his mind respond with a good melody. So we were making these off-the-wall [harmonic/melodic] choices. At first it was me leading, but after we did it for a few weeks, I said "don't forget, it doesn't have to be just me dictating where it might go. If something occurs to you, just play it and it's up to me to respond to it." After awhile he got really, really good at it. Watching that hap-pen along with everything else Lenny was doing night after night, I was in awe a lot. But it was a kind of funny thing because there was a take-it-for-granted part of it too. The more I got to know him, the more I got confident in what he could play, I just said, "Oh, there's another thing that Lenny's doing. First time I've seen him do that!"

That fall, Lenny made his second appearance on CBC television when Jack Shapira hired him to play with the band on his weekly talk/variety show, *Sit Back with Jack*. Shapira recalls the admixture

of naiveté and blazing musical intelligence Lenny demonstrated on
this early session:

> I wanted Frank Lewis [the show's bandleader and arranger] to do a
> swing arrangement of "You Are my Sunshine," and he wrote the
> arrangement with a sixty-four-bar solo for Lenny. Now, Lenny had
> a fantastic ear and could play anything you wanted in any key. He
> knew how to count bars but he couldn't read music. So in the first
> part of the arrangement, he ran across the word "tacit," which
> means you don't play. So he yelled at me, "Hey, Shap. What does T-
> A-C-I-T mean?" And a guy yelled back, "It means take it, man.
> Take a solo." Lenny didn't appreciate it. Anyway, we gave him a
> solo 'though we knew he couldn't read it. I said to Frank, "When
> you cue Lenny, just nod your head and he'll know when to come
> in." And Lenny took an unbelievable sixty-four-bar solo on "You
> Are My Sunshine." Everybody from the stagehands to the producer
> was amazed. You couldn't listen to him without saying, "I don't
> believe this guy." That's how great he was, and him just an inno-
> cent little kid with a pretty little wife.

Lenny's "pretty little wife" was coming to understand the trials
and tribulations of being married to a musician, yet was still patient
and accepting of her husband's constant practicing and late night
club dates. After leaving the St. Germain's home in June 1960, the
Breaus had moved into a two-story house on Lipton Street in Winnipeg's West End. Lenny may have been keen to keep up with all that
was current in contemporary jazz, but when it came to his marriage,
he preferred a traditional arrangement, Valerie says. "[At the beginning of our marriage] Lenny said, 'I'll take care of the music and
making money and you take care of the kids.' So my job was clean-
ing, cooking, laundry, and taking care of our family and finances. I
always managed the money." While Lenny's parents and his various
caretakers had never expected him to contribute to household
chores, he was not above occasionally pitching in to help Valerie
with domestic work although with some reservations. "He'd take out
the garbage," Valerie says. "But he wore gloves to do that and to hang
out the diapers because he always looked after his hands. He liked the
house clean, perfect, like he was, always spending a lot of time on his

hair and clothes." Even prior to their marriage, Valerie says, she had happily cared for Lenny's clothes, taking great care to observe her husband's fastidious standards. "He'd come in from the road and I'd hand wash and press all his shirts just the way he liked them; no starch. He loved the way I did it. All his clothes were hung up perfectly in the closet with his shoes all shined and lined up underneath."

Lenny would occasionally babysit Melody on afternoons when Valerie worked as a model at the local Eatons department store, doing his best to balance his daughter's needs with the advancement of his guitar skills, as his friend, country singer and guitarist, Eddie Laham relates.

> He used to phone me up and say, "I need your help." He lived just a few streets away so I'd go over. Barney Kessel and Tal Farlow were his idols then and he'd want me to help him with picking stuff up from their records. He'd play a record and I'd pick up the needle and put it over to where he wanted it. Meantime, I'm taking care of Melody and flipping the record over for him at the same time, moving the needle over so he could pick up certain things on the guitar. I'd say, "Here's your little girl; she needs changing." He'd say, "Can you do it?" He wasn't much of a family man—not devoted. He cared, but it was not a hands-on kind of thing. He loved his children but he didn't have that fatherly feeling about him. Lenny was self-centered in his music, which you're supposed to be if you love something that much. And he really loved it. I have a picture of Lenny when he was [nineteen] and he's sitting in my house with a pair of gloves on—in July! I said, "What's the gloves for" and he says, "I don't want to hurt my fingernails!" All he thought about was his hands and his music.

Besides his nightly gig at the Stage Door, Lenny was playing occasionally at other clubs around the city with various musicians including the late vibraphonist/pianist Jimmy King. Nicknamed "King Jim," he was a highly respected patriarchal figure in the Winnipeg music scene, and particularly generous and encouraging to young musicians. King also wrote a weekly music column for *The Winnipeg Tribune*, and in 1960 gave Lenny his due in one of his articles:

Few experiences in jazz are as swingingly intense as a Lennie Breau performance. In addition to a bursting passion in all his playing, there is a constant sense of exploration. With clean precise technique he will take flights into the unexpected at a speed that will make his harmonic texture so dense it becomes almost a sheet of sound. His utilization of time and space along with convincing melodic structures are two elements pervasively present in his playing.[5]

By the late fall of 1960, Lenny was working intermittently with King in the Selkirk Room of the swank Royal Alexandra Hotel where King's group played background and dance music. Between sets, King would often feature Lenny on solo guitar, fingerpicking a jazz ballad or an Atkins tune for the hushed audience. The King band played until 11:00 p.m. and after the gig, Lenny would loosen his tie and take a nine-block cab ride to the Stage Door where he'd join whatever musicians had happened by to play that night. King would sometimes accompany Lenny to the Stage Door after the Selkirk Room gig and jam with the band. When the club finally closed around daybreak, he and Lenny would drop by a nearby restaurant to drink coffee and talk music or, if the morning were fine, sit outside as the sun came up and snap their fingers to the rhythmic patterns they heard in the songs of awakening birds. "We must have looked pretty strange to anyone who saw us," King said many years later. "Two grown men sitting on a doorstep and snapping our fingers."[6]

King expected great things of Lenny and was concerned that his lack of sight-reading ability would hinder his opportunities. Lenny had made a few half-hearted attempts over the years to improve his reading skills but had never persevered at these studies. Valerie recalls Lenny telling her, "Honey, all those notes just look like little dots all over the place. I just have to hear it once and I know how to play it and the other guys are bent over their guitars still trying to read the notes." King managed to persuade Lenny to study reading with Ray Moga, a bassist/guitarist who worked often in King's group. One afternoon, Lenny dropped by Moga's house and submitted to a ten-minute lesson before giving up and telling Moga that his time was better spent playing. He then turned the tables on the older musician and taught him Barney Kessel's version of "Mean To Me." "I learned more that afternoon than I had in years," says Moga.

"Here he was coming to me to learn to read and I was getting a wealth of knowledge from him. He showed me some chords, some real nice changes, and I said 'where'd you get those chords?' He said 'Oh, Mickey Baker [a popular jazz guitar method book]' and he gave me the book. It opened my eyes to a lot of things so I had a lot to thank Lenny for." Moga and Lenny talked guitar through the afternoon, and when Moga's wife arrived home, she asked him to stay for dinner. Lenny was pleased to accept the invitation but did not let the meal interrupt his guitar playing. "We played until it was time for dinner," Moga laughs. "He got up and brought his guitar to the table with us. Here he is having dinner with us and the guitar is sitting on his lap. He'd take a few mouthfuls and play a few riffs. I was just amazed by it all. Lenny told me that sometimes he went to the bathroom with his guitar. Lenny lived it, he really lived it."

The Stage Door was now one of Winnipeg's most popular clubs and jazz fans and musicians packed it nightly. On a typical night, a group of younger players (often including sixteen-year-old Bernie Senensky, later one of Canada's finest jazz pianists) would take the stage around 9:00 p.m. to play a set or two. The house trio—Erlendson, Lenny, and Kelln—would then take over and play for a few hours before other musicians joined them on stage for jams that lasted into the early morning hours. Bassist Dave Young, who would play often with Lenny over the next two decades, was one of the club's regulars. Many nights, before joining the band for a set, Young would sit in the audience and watch Lenny play bass. "I really admired his bass playing," Young says. "I didn't hear him that much; obviously he didn't play when I was around, but he really knew the bass—the concept of bass. It wasn't a guitar player playing bass. It was a guitarist who knew bass the way bass should be played." Bob Erlendson concurs:

By 1961, I swear Lenny was the greatest bass player in the world. I don't care about acoustic or electric. This was partly a result of getting all of this theoretical stuff organized. He'd play these things on guitar on one tune and then be playing bass on the very next tune so he'd start to see the big picture by playing the bottom end and getting intimate with what notes you choose, how do you make the bass line less boring than dum-dum-dum-dum [sings a major third on beat three] and learning how to run lines. It was guitar thinking in a sense but soon it became the norm for bass. He was using a thumb pick and got to be just dynamite at it. He could change the tone of the bass by doing semi-muff tricks. If he wanted a more percussive part, he just used the edge of his hand to muff that string so the note would die sooner [a technique Lenny picked up from the playing of Atkins and Travis who often damped the bass strings of the guitar with the palms of their right hands]. And it's a guitar now, not a bass. He really got to understand that on the first beat of the bar you want the I [root] of the chord and if that means that you sometimes let it ring for two beats, let it ring. He was playing lovely solos on the four stringer [bass]. But he would also play you exactly what you wanted for bottom. It was just unbelievably graceful watching him do it. I'd tell people that Lenny was the best bass player in the world and they'd say "you're out of your head." But someone who agreed with me was Red Whooten who was in town with Benny Goodman's Sextet. Whooten jammed with us at the Stage Door and when he left he said, "I'm going back to Hollywood and I'm going to buy an electric bass. I've been sneering at it but if you can play an electric bass like Lenny Breau, maybe it's a good instrument."

One night, Lenny brought a friend of his to the club to introduce to Erlendson and the rest of the Stage Door habitués. Ron Halldorson was two years Lenny's junior and had been something of a boy wonder himself, having played steel guitar professionally at dances and on radio for about four years when he and Lenny met in 1958. Halldorson was a regular and devoted listener to the Breaus' daily CKY broadcast and would hurry home from school every afternoon to listen to Lenny play on his parents' show. One evening he was shocked to receive a phone call from Lenny who had apparently heard him playing on a radio show. "This stuttering voice on the other end of the phone said, 'Hi, this is Lenny Breau. I re-re-really like your playing,'" Halldorson recalls. "The hair on the back of my neck stood up. I couldn't believe it because here was my idol. Even before I met him, I knew he was extraordinary and that proved to be true. A few days later we got together and played at my house." The teenagers quickly discovered that they shared a love of jazz and this became a focal point for the jams that took place in Halldorson's kitchen. "Lenny was playing a lot of jazz and subsequently I was too," says Halldorson, who was also learning to play six-string guitar. "So when we were getting together, we were playing mainly jazz and jamming mostly on jazz or western swing. We'd play jazz tunes like "Four" or play on swing tunes like "Sweet Georgia Brown." Or sometimes we'd just play country—"Maiden's Prayer" or something—but jazz more than anything else because it was hard for both of us to find people who could play that kind of music."

Halldorson had brought along his steel guitar on his first visit to the Stage Door, but Lenny had other long-term musical plans for his friend. Eager to play more guitar on stage, Lenny needed someone to take over bass chores in the Stage Door house band and had decided that Halldorson was the ideal candidate for the position. "Lenny roped me into the job," Halldorson admits. "Before that I'd picked up the bass a few times and maybe played it a bit in country bands, but I had no interest in being a bass player. The only reason I did it was to spend more time playing with Lenny. I realized how much I could learn playing with Bob and those guys and I decided that was worth doing. The opportunity to play with Lenny and Bob would have been appealing if it had been on bagpipes." Fortunately, this wasn't necessary; Erlendson lent Halldorson his Hofner bass, which Halldorson would use on Lenny's first two albums and still owns. Lenny's choice for the bass chair was auspicious. Over the next decade, Halldorson would develop a bass style that was a sensitive complement to Lenny's guitar work and would be an integral part of Lenny's musical explorations in performance and on record.

While Lenny was devoting most of his time to playing jazz, he was also investigating other stylistic horizons. Lenny learned his first classical piece—"Spanish Romance"—at the age of thirteen from Ray Couture who had picked it up from a guitar-playing bartender in Wheeling. A relatively simple piece from the soundtrack of the 1952 French film *Forbidden Games*, it consists of a repetitive right-hand arpeggio on the treble strings with a simple melody confined to the high E string. In the late fifties, under the influence of Chet Atkins, Lenny began to further pad his repertoire with classical pieces. "I noticed how Chet was into classical," he said in 1978, " so I started stretching myself out and listening to classical."[7] Lenny beefed up his repertoire with Chopin's "Minute Waltz," "Waltz in A flat" by

Brahms, and Lecuona's "Malaguena" (all of which Atkins had recorded during the fifties), playing them on his Gibson ES-125 and a Martin D-28 that his father had given him. However, learning precise classical guitar technique and repertoire to the exclusion of other music was not Lenny's goal. "I could never be a classical guitarist myself," he told an interviewer, "but I appreciate them for their knowledge of the instrument. I'm just incorporating some of what they know into my jazz playing."[8]

Apart from hearing Atkins's versions of classical standards and a few Segovia records, Lenny's exposure to classical music had been slight. His friend, George Reznik, a Winnipeg jazz pianist with an extensive classical background, tried to rectify this. One night at the Stage Door, Reznik explained to Lenny that a jazz turnaround he'd used in a tune had its source in a J. S. Bach piece. Lenny was fascinated and the next day he dropped by the pianist's house where Reznik played him a record of the Bach G minor Keyboard Suite. Lenny borrowed the record and when he returned it the following afternoon, he claimed to have learned the entire suite. Reznik was naturally skeptical but when Lenny took out his guitar and played the whole work, astonishment replaced disbelief. "He does it and then says, 'Yeah, what do you think? I memorized the whole thing.'" Reznik says. "He'd memorized the whole thing overnight, this piece that took me years to learn by reading and memorizing it all. He'd just adapted it for guitar and played the figure with the two-part invention and the whole thing. It's impossible that anybody could just take it home and get it in his ear and unscramble it, then transfer it to his hands and play it. But he did it. And that's when I knew I was talking to a genius."

While Lenny's interest in classical music would never rival his love of jazz, flamenco was another matter. Lenny was so powerfully drawn to the passionate music of the Spanish gypsies that it very nearly supplanted his jazz ambitions. "One day," recalls Ray Moga, "Lenny came over to my house with a classical guitar under one arm and a record by [renowned flamenco guitarist] Sabicas under the other. He played the Sabicas record and said, 'that's what I want to play like. But better.'"

It's difficult to know precisely when and where Lenny first heard flamenco. Reg Kelln recalls giving Lenny a flamenco album not long after first meeting him in 1958 and this may well have been Lenny's first taste of the music. Whatever the origin of his interest in flamenco, he "went through a flamenco period for three years" and "listened to Sabicas, Montoya [and] people like that," as he told Walter Carter in 1978.[9]

Lenny approached flamenco with the same zeal that characterized his passion for jazz and was faced with some of the same challenges that the former had presented. But where he had Bob Erlendson to guide him through the intricacies of jazz, there was no one from whom to learn the mysteries of flamenco. Initially at least, Lenny fell back on the same method he had used to learn the lines of Kessel and Farlow, as he explained to Lee Major in 1968: "I never met Sabicas, but I think he's the greatest of all. He's got the greatest hands in the world. I listen[ed] to his records and he plays really fast so I had to put the records on 16 [rpm] speed in order to learn the runs . . ."[10] This method only went so far, however. Besides the style's demanding technique, fledgling *flamencoistas* must also learn the various song forms of flamenco: bulerias, soleas, taranta, etc, which are defined in large part by their cycle of rhythms and beat patterns. Improvisation is allowed only in specific areas of the form and must not depart from the structure of the piece. Grasping by ear the rules governing the strict rhythmic phrasing and various forms of flamenco song is a Herculean task, but somehow Lenny unlocked the science as well as the techniques of flamenco, Ron Halldorson says. "Lenny knew all about the rhythmic stuff in flamenco, could talk about it and play it perfectly." In lieu of firsthand instruction, Lenny learned the complexities of flamenco as he had every other musical style for which he had developed a passion: through close listening, tireless analysis, and disciplined, constant practice.

Lenny's study of flamenco provided him with an array of new guitar techniques that he eventually assimilated into all aspects of his playing. Slurring, for example, became an integral part of his jazz work. This technique involves plucking a note with the right hand and then using the left hand to produce one or more notes with fingers pulling off or striking down on the string. Because the player does not have to pluck every note with the right hand, lines of notes can be played with dazzling speed, a technique that became a signature of Lenny's style. In one interview, Lenny explained the origin of a technique he often used that involved playing a rapid flurry of notes while muting the strings with the heel of his right hand on the guitar bridge. "It came from playing those Sabicas pull-offs and the Montoya stuff and muffling it," Lenny said. "It's hard to tell which notes are picked and which aren't because the idea is to get the pull-offs as loud as the [picked] notes . . . to create the illusion of balance. I worked on this technique quite a bit on a steel-string Martin."[11]

Lenny's right-hand technique was also shaped significantly by his flamenco studies, particularly his use of the *apoyando* or rest stroke in which a right-hand finger strikes a string and continues across it until it rests against the string below. This movement in tandem with alternating right-hand fingers striking the strings (i.e. index-middle-index-middle, etc.) produces great right hand velocity and power. Lenny found a way to practice this technique even during the rare moments when he did not have a guitar in his hand, says Gary Gross. "I recall Lenny practicing rotary finger plucks on matchbook covers so he'd get that taka-taka-taka-taka going faster and faster. Ring-middle-index/ring-middle-index/ over and over to get his strokes even." This exercise became almost a constant, nervous tic for Lenny when his guitar was not close at hand.

In years to come, Lenny would become widely known for blending flamenco with jazz in original compositions like "Spanjazz" and "Taranta," a concept that may well have been sparked by the 1960 Miles Davis recording, *Sketches of Spain*. This jazz milestone featured Davis's trumpet work over a Gil Evans arrangement of Spanish composer Joaquin Rodrigo's Concierto De Aranjuez—a concerto for guitar that drew heavily from the music of the Andalusian region of Spain where flamenco was born. Mary Nelson recalls afternoons at Reg Kelln's apartment when Lenny would listen to the album repeatedly, enthralled with what he heard. "I can remember quite vividly when *Sketches* came out; he just loved it," Nelson says. "We'd spend the whole afternoon listening to that album over and over with Lenny picking out that classical/jazz Spanish thing that that music was."

Almost to the end of his life, Lenny would play flamenco and apply its techniques to his jazz work. But in 1961, his fascination with the music of the *flamencoistas* was suddenly overshadowed by his passion for the work of a musician whose influence on Lenny would be far greater than Sabicas or Montoya. As Gary Gross puts it, "the axle upon which everything turned—including Lenny's jazz, flamenco and later the Indian bag—the axle upon which all that spun and wove its web was Bill Evans." Evans's music would not only galvanize Lenny into developing many of his most innovative guitar techniques, he would also assimilate into his own music the poetic, bittersweet, and lyrical qualities that characterize Evans's playing. Lenny later said that he fell so deeply under the sway of Bill Evans upon hearing "Nardis" from his 1961 album *Explorations*, that he went "a few years after that without even listening to guitar."[12] Bob Erlendson had first brought Evans to Lenny's attention in December 1959 when he played him Miles Davis's groundbreaking album *Kind of Blue*, with Evans on piano. "I bought that album soon after it came out [in March 1959] and played it till the grooves turned white," says Erlendson. "He became my main man, and Lenny got into him through me." Bob and Lenny had immediately learned one of the album's best-known cuts, "All Blues," and jammed on it at the recorded Rando Manor session. Lenny's playing on the tune was more than competent, but it's clear that he had no grasp of the modal concept that was the backbone of "All Blues" and the rest of the material on *Kind of Blue*. This changed during the latter half of 1960 when, with the help of Bob Erlendson, he began to study modal theory and incorporate it into his playing. Erlendson was already familiar with the modal system, having studied composer George Russell's seminal work on modal theory *The Lydian Chromatic Concept* in which the Lydian mode replaces the major scale—aka the Ionian mode—as the essential scale. This treatise had an enormous impact on Miles Davis and John Coltrane, and inspired much of their work on *Kind of Blue*. Bob was therefore able to teach Lenny modal theory and its use of quartal harmony—chords constructed from fourths—that was the harmonic foundation of much contemporary jazz from the late 1950s onwards.

> Quartal harmony was influenced by what Miles and McCoy Tyner with Coltrane were doing around that time, but it still comes back to Bill Evans's whole approach to playing. We started working on building chords, understanding how the fourths work and how you can voice them on the guitar. We did a whole bunch of work on that during the Stage Door period. It was useful on piano as well

but I was trying to figure it out from guitar through what he was teaching me as a guitar player so that I could have stuff ready to lay on his head: all the practical work on it, how to build it up, how to construct the chords, how to move them all over the guitar was stuff that I was working on to help him do it. Understanding fourths is relatively easy on the guitar. You just bar. [Barring three bass strings at any fret on the guitar creates a suspended 4th chord.] But it seemed to be really essential for us to get to understand really well how to move it around, to shift it to major or minor just by moving one finger.

It wasn't long before the pair began writing modally based tunes to use as exercises for their quartal explorations, Erlendson says. "One was called 'Lydiin' with no G on the end. A private joke because it was in the key of G! I think Lenny just made its melody up [and] we fooled around with it at all kinds of tempos from ballads to pretty fast. There was an eight-bar melody that would be played at the beginning but the rest of it was used just to blow on the Lydian mode. We worked really hard on all that stuff and by 1961, he was hip to all the modes."

Lenny was also intrigued by the two-note chords (dyads) Evans played with his left hand while soloing with his right. These dyads had little or no rhythmic function, but were used to provide a sparse harmonic basis for Evans's right-hand lines. Lenny began looking for a way to incorporate this technique into the unique guitar style that he was slowly piecing together. "I had been trying to figure out how to get a style of guitar that would be my own," he told Walter Carter in the late '70s. "I was playing jazz with a straight pick, and I said there must be another way I can use my fingers," cause I like playing with my fingers and I already knew how. So I got the idea from listening to piano, wondering if it's possible to play the melody and to play the chords like [Evans did]. If it's possible to go one-two-three-four . . . with the thumb and play melody with the fingers . . . it must be possible to just play the chords [rather than single bass notes as Atkins had done]. I started working on it. It came very slowly."[13]

One of the first steps in placing Evans's keyboard style on the fretboard required paring his chords down to a manageable size. Through his studies with Erlendson, Lenny knew that a chord could be reduced to two notes and still retain its essential quality. For example, a G7th chord, which contains the notes G-B-D-F (Root-3rd-5th-minor 7th), can be sketched in with a dyad comprising B and F, or 3rd and 7th: an interval of an augmented fourth or tritone. When the notes of the C scale (or G mixolydian mode) from which this chord is built are played over this dyad, the chord is in effect completed with the various chord tones it lacks: root, 5th, 9th, 11th, and 13th. Lenny found that it was possible to play these dyads on adjacent bass strings of the guitar, and began using them to comp (play accompaniment) behind Bob Erlendson's solos. "The whole thing started off with me saying 'we've got to be able to play some blues,'" Erlendson says. "So if you're playing blues on your own, you can comp for yourself if you just play the 3rd and the 7th. So he learned how to play the 3rd and 7th of the blues chords [dominant 7ths] as a left hand comp. So I was just playing left hand bass while he was playing those little comp tricks. He got better and better at it so that he was using two or three of his [right hand] fingers to play the solo and the other two fingers were comping fingers. Soon he got it so that it sounded perfectly natural." In time, his mastery of this technique would develop to the point where he could support his own complex single note lines with dyads (or guide tones as they are sometimes called) played with such independent rhythmic finesse that one was left with the impression of two guitars playing different parts simultaneously. This technique—along with chordal harmonics—would become the most recognizable trademark of Lenny's style.

Evans's use of dyads and smaller chords in the left hand were not the only aspect of the pianist's harmonic concept that inspired Lenny. Especially on ballads, Evans used lush chord voicings that were derived from or heavily influenced by the harmonic ideas found in late nineteenth/early twentieth century classical music, particularly those of the so-called Impressionist composers, Claude Debussy and Maurice Ravel. Prior to encountering Evans's music, Lenny had relied mainly on standard jazz chords and voicings as well as the Freddie Green comping style—three note chords played on the bass strings—favored by swing rhythm guitarists, and Johnny Smith's unique, closely voiced chords. Lenny would continue to use all these chordal concepts throughout his life, but the harmonic ideas for which he became celebrated, particularly in his ballad playing, resulted from work begun in 1961 when he became determined to capture Evans's voicings on guitar.

This task presented Lenny with a whole set of logistical problems. Many of Evans's voicings are not difficult to play on the keyboard but problematic or impossible to reproduce on guitar. On the piano, the major and minor second intervals that crop up often in Evans's chords are played on adjacent keys. On a fretboard, however, these intervals often require challenging stretches. Despite his small hands, Lenny had an astonishing reach on the fretboard, which his splayed little finger increased. Through the use of taxing stretches, Lenny was able to realize some of Evans's voicings, but reproducing his tight, extended voicings, or clusters as they are commonly called, was often simply not possible. For example, Evans might play an inversion of a D-flat-major 7th chord voiced A♭-C-D♭-F—a configuration that a beginning piano student can play easily. On the guitar, however, this voicing with its interval of a minor second between the C and D flat is unachievable through usual means. But Lenny found that he could play this type of close-voiced chord by raising its bass note with an artificial harmonic, as he explained to Mona Coxson from *Canadian Musician Magazine* in 1981: "I had to invent the style where I could play a Bill Evans chord without working too hard, so I play a chord and then I put a harmonic on the bottom [note] of the chord . . . [that] raises it up an octave and it gives you a cluster—what I call an impressionistic chord."[14] For example, while playing a D-flat-major 7th chord, voiced D♭-A♭-C-F, Lenny would pick the top three notes of the chord with his middle, ring, and pinky fingers (Lenny had begun using all his right hand fingers early on in his study of Evans's style) while simultaneously using his thumb and index finger to play an artificial harmonic twelve frets above the D flat in the bass. This produces a D flat note an octave higher, placing it beside the C in the middle of the chord and creating a tightly voiced cluster. Lenny worked on this technique throughout his life, applying it to dozens of chord shapes and, especially in ballads and introductions, creating whole progressions using these clustered voicings.

Lenny also routinely used open strings in his chords to duplicate Evans's voicings. For example, he often played a tightly voiced A major 9th chord with the following intervallic structure: A-G♯-B-C♯-E-bass to treble. The inner voices are fretted on the D, G, and B strings—a considerable stretch in itself—while the outer voices are played on the open A and E strings. However, open string voicings are relegated to one position on the neck, which makes their use highly specific and limited to certain keys, and for this reason many jazz guitarists generally eschew them. Chords using open strings work best in the keys of C, D, G, A, and E, which contain notes of many of the guitar's open strings. Few open string chords work easily or well in the flat or "horn" keys—E flat and B flat—favored by jazz musicians. This meant that Lenny, particularly when playing solo, favored keys often avoided by jazz guitarists.[15] (He could play in any key and when working with a band, often dumbfounded the musicians by choosing unusual keys for tunes on the spur of the moment.) Where most jazz musicians would play "My Funny Valentine," for example, in its original key of C minor—a flat key which has little potential for the use of open strings—Lenny used Am, a key containing chords in which all the open strings of the guitar can be used. Thus, his open string voicings and the "unusual" keys he played in to realize them became identifiable traits of his style.

Lenny's fascination with pianistic chord voicings kicked off a lifelong interest in extending the range of his instrument to more easily realize them on guitar. Ironically, the first instrument he found with an extended register was not some futuristic creation, but rather an anachronism: a 1905 Gibson harp guitar, which Lenny bought after he found it gathering dust in the stockroom of a local music store.

The harp guitar, popular in North America in the late nineteenth and early twentieth century, is essentially a modified, large body six-string guitar with a harp-like frame holding ten bass strings attached to its headstock and upper bout on the bass side. Plucking one of these strings with the right hand produces a low bass note that sustains under fingered chords that the guitarist strums or plucks immediately afterward on the fretboard of the instrument. "It was wonderful to hear Lenny play the harp guitar; so beautiful," Ron Halldorson says. "He would play ballads on it, just hit a drone bass, let it ring and then play a chord over top of it. He'd muffle the bass note and then play the next one followed by another chord. It was like having a bass player because the notes were an octave lower than the ones on the guitar portion of the thing. Of course you can't play very fast; even Lenny only had one hand on each arm." Accordingly, Lenny rarely used the instrument on stage and then only to play arrangements of hymns and country tunes.

In September 1961, Lenny began playing with Ray Moga and a drummer in the lounge of Winnipeg's Viscount-Gort hotel. "The job was all right and we could play all the jazz we wanted," says Moga. "But for Lenny, it was a short-lived thing and I knew it would be. Everyday I'd come to work with the feeling that Lenny was going to tell me he was going to quit. I knew that one day he'd say, 'Ray, I'm leaving.' I expected that because Lenny was too great to stay in Winnipeg for long."

Moga's prescience proved correct. Within the month, a meeting with another talented young artist would set in motion the events that would take Lenny and his music to the heart of Canada's music scene and beyond.

Out of Nowhere
November 1961—May 1963

4.

"Don Francks has a voice that is just unbelievable, so soulful. He has a brilliant mind. He's a genius and I don't mean it lightly. Together, him and Lenny were like rocket ships."

—Joey Hollingsworth

Joey Hollingsworth, a young African-Canadian dancer from southern Ontario, was already familiar with Lenny's reputation when he came to Winnipeg in October of 1961 to play a two-week engagement at the Town and Country Inn. The summer before, he'd met Ray St. Germain in Toronto where Lenny's brother-in-law was trying to break into the city's entertainment scene. St. Germain had regaled Hollingsworth with stories of his brother-in-law's prowess as a guitarist, insisting that he was the greatest player in the world. Hollingsworth was skeptical until he arrived in Winnipeg and dropped into the Stage Door to check Lenny out.

Lenny was playing with Reg and Bob. I was just blown away, just blown away. I knew right away there was greatness there. I introduced myself and in time, we became friends. He was just one of those types of people that I really, really dug: very unpretentious, and as funny as anything. As soon as he'd open his mouth, I'd start laughing. He had an amazing sense of humor. I remember we went to this restaurant in downtown Winnipeg. He jumped into the restaurant and kept jumping up and down as we were waiting to be seated! Then he jumped over to the table and says to the waitress, "H-h-h-have you got any sleeveless sandwiches?" She says, "No, that's not on the menu." He says, "Well, give me an elephant's ear." Stupid things. That was very much Lenny. He was crazy, and he truly made me laugh because he didn't try to be funny. And if he did, it was so childlike. His mind was so different then anyone else's, at first you might think "well, maybe he's a little bit slow" because he didn't say much, but his mind went like a trip hammer, very fast in making associations between things.

Lenny's enormous capacity for disciplined study and work and the pure musical ambition that drove him also amazed Hollingsworth. "He told me he practiced hours and hours every day," Hollingsworth says. "I remember he'd play 'Mary Had a Little Lamb' and 'Three Blind Mice' at the same time, but he'd play one in ¼ time and one in ¾ time so he had all these things going at once. I said, 'Lenny, how long did it take you to learn that?' He said, 'W-w-well, about nine months, five hours a day. Maybe a little bit more.' I said, 'Well, why? Most people will hear two tunes but they won't hear two time signatures.' He said, 'I know.' I said, 'Well, why would you take nine months to learn it?' He said, 'Because nobody else can do it!'"

Hollingsworth's manager was a German-born, prairie-raised lawyer/entrepreneur named George Sukornyk, who had co-founded Harvey's, a successful Canadian restaurant chain. Sukornyk had sung professionally while in college, and his strong interest in music and the arts in general had led him to make many friends and business contacts in Toronto's entertainment community. In the late 1950s, he'd decided to try his hand at managing select artists and began representing—pro bono—singer/entertainer Juliette, then Canada's most popular female singer and show business personality. "I've always had an affinity for music and entertainment but never with the view of trying to make money with it," Sukornyk says. "Never collected a dime from Joey or Lenny or anybody. I just really enjoyed being with them and doing what I could to help." Under Sukornyk's management, Hollingsworth's career had taken off. At the time he met Lenny, he was well on his way to becoming recognized as one of the greatest tap dancers in the world, and within the year would be performing on *The Ed Sullivan Show*.

After hearing Lenny play, Hollingsworth called Sukornyk in Toronto. "Joey was very excited," says Sukornyk. "He said, 'Hey, I think you should see this fellow. He's really, really good, a natural talent.' So I said 'OK, I'll come out and see.' I trusted Joey's judgment on it so I got in my car and I drove."

A few days later, Sukornyk arrived in Winnipeg where he introduced himself to Lenny after taking in a few of his sets at the Stage Door. "I said, 'Lenny, you're absolutely amazing. What are you doing in Winnipeg? This is the end of the world!'" Sukornyk recalls. "And he said, 'Yeah, you're right.' I made a snap decision. I said, 'Let me see if I can help you. If you want to come to Toronto, well, come on.' He said, 'I can't afford it.' I said, 'forget about it. Come and stay with me.'"

The offer was tempting. Lenny was not oblivious to his own abilities and potential, and knew that he had reached the limit of what Winnipeg could offer him in terms of new playing experiences, job opportunities, and recognition. Toronto was the epicenter of Canada's entertainment and broadcasting industry, and a magnet for the country's best musicians and entertainers. It was also a huge step for a man barely out of his teens who was struggling to support his family. Lenny, faced with his first real career decision, was stymied until Sukornyk suggested a plan. There was no need for Lenny to immediately relocate for the long term, Sukornyk said. Why not stay at his home in Toronto for a month to get a feel for the city and see what it had to offer him? Afterwards, he could talk it over with Valerie and make a decision based on this experience. When Lenny explained this plan to Erlendson and King, both men were encouraging and agreed to use temporary substitutes for Lenny in their bands. If things did not work out in Toronto, he would have work waiting for him on his return.

When Lenny arrived in Toronto in early November 1961, Suko-rnyk immediately began to spread word of the wunderkind he had brought from Winnipeg among his music contacts in the city. One of these was pianist Oscar Peterson who had employed guitarists Herb Ellis and Barney Kessel in his trio. Peterson agreed to meet Lenny at the club where he was playing but the encounter between the men, Sukornyk says, was not auspicious. "Oscar began playing very quickly and he wouldn't give Lenny an opportunity to play. He just rattled off a lot of jazz, and Lenny sort of looked at him like 'what are you doing?' It was really short. Oscar was very impatient, in fact rude. Then he turned to me and said, 'He'll never make it.' I remember that very clearly."

Undaunted by Peterson's prediction, Sukornyk continued to seek work for his slightly crestfallen but resilient protégé. Knowing that Lenny had played a few CBC sessions in Winnipeg, Sukornyk took him to the network's studios in downtown Toronto. "I had some connections down there," Sukornyk recalls, "so I arranged for Lenny to sit in on a paid recording session for a commercial with CBC house musicians. But, lo and behold, when we got there, I found out he couldn't read music. That shocked me; I was really quite floored that he couldn't read." Unlike CBC staff in Winnipeg, Toronto producers had no time for unschooled musicians and another door was closed in Lenny's face.

Sukornyk decided that a demo tape of Lenny's playing might help him find work. On the advice of Ronnie Hawkins, a popular rock and roll singer and bandleader from Arkansas, Sukornyk booked time at Hallmark Studios in downtown Toronto. At the first session on November 11, Lenny recorded six solo tunes on an inexpensive nylon string guitar that Sukornyk had bought for him.

Lenny was apparently seeing stars by this time and decided to take the stage name "Lennie Martin," perhaps after the famous acoustic guitar company, and this moniker appears on the tape boxes from the two Hallmark sessions. The name makeover was short-lived, however, and Lenny went back to using his given name after the second Hallmark session, which took place on November 28. This time around Lenny was eager to record a jazz set with other musicians, and he and Sukornyk considered bringing in Reg Kelln and Bob Erlendson for the session. This idea was deemed impractical and instead Lenny teamed up with Rick Danko and Levon Helm, members of Hawkins's group, who would later go on to international fame with The Band. The trio recorded seven tunes, mainly jazz standards, a few blues numbers, and an original country-flavored piece.

The tapes of these two sessions would languish in Sukornyk's wine cellar for forty years before Art of Life Records remastered and issued them as *The Hallmark Sessions* in 2003. This CD is a testament to Lenny's astonishing development as a jazz guitarist after less than three years of seriously studying the style. His single-note solos on "It Could Happen to You" and "I'll Remember April" illustrate how remarkably his knowledge of chord/scale relationships had improved under the tutelage of Bob Erlendson. At times he has a tendency to recycle the ideas of which he is fondest, and when ideas occasionally fail altogether, he falls back on riffs that suggest a hybrid of Coltrane's "sheets of sound" and the fast, slurred licks that Chet Atkins liked to inject into his tunes. The best of his single note playing on *The Hallmark Sessions*, however, at least approaches— and often surpasses in terms of phrasing, tone, and articulation—the guitarists from whom he learned his craft. Lenny is also using, in nascent form, several of his signature techniques. He plays the melody of "It Could Happen to You," with a tremolo—a technique assimilated from flamenco and classical guitar that became a signature of his style—and uses 3rd/7th dyads to support the tune's head. The tune also features his first recorded example of chordal harmonics, a technique that involves playing an arpeggiated chord with alternating natural notes and artificial harmonics to produce a chiming, harp-like effect. His inspiration for this technique, Lenny explained to Walter Carter, came from his first guitar icon. "I got the idea for the chime tones from Chet . . . I started using it in jazz. Nobody else was doing it and I just developed it."[1] According to Atkins historian Craig Dobbins, the first recorded example of Atkins's use of chordal harmonics was on his arrangement of "White Christmas" from the album *Christmas with Chet Atkins*.[2] RCA released the album less than two months before Lenny recorded the Hallmark sessions, which means that Lenny had learned the technique just prior to the studio date and was already using it in a jazz context. Guitarist John Knowles, a longtime professional and personal friend of Chet Atkins, says "Most of the tunes Chet used [chordal harmonics] on had standard chord progressions. . . . What Lenny did was to figure out how to fret the left hand to make really odd patterns. He would finger a B♭7♭9♭5 chord on the first fret and then apply the alternating harmonic-fretted technique to produce this effect that you hear more in jazz and impressionist music."[3] Lenny made a lifelong study of the technique and used it in myriad ways, often entwining it with slurs, trills, and scalar patterns to play melodic passages. It remains his most immediately identifiable and widely copied technique.

Lenny played a few well-executed flamenco pieces on the sessions and included an excellent rendition of Brazilian guitarist Luiz Bonfa's polyrhythmic tune "Batucada." A version of Travis's "Cannonball Rag" and his original "Lenny's Western Blues" indicate that, despite his extensive jazz studies, Lenny had not turned his back on his country roots. Lenny also did some fine jazz/blues playing on "D minor Blues" and the original "Oscar's Blues," a musical reference to his failed audition with Peterson. (Lenny modelled the tune after Thelonious Monk's piece "Rhythm-A-Ning," a gently humorous jab at Peterson, Lenny explained to Hollingsworth, whose elaborate keyboard style was the antithesis of Monk's.) Solos in both of these pieces show the influence of Kenny Burrell, whose blues-based playing Lenny greatly admired. But, as *The Hallmark Sessions* recording illustrates, while Lenny was still developing his own musical voice and the bebop concepts on which he had modeled his playing were still the foundation of his playing, he was no longer slavishly imitating his influences. The playing of Farlow, Burrell, and Kessel informs his single note solos on *The Hallmark Sessions*, and he refers to Johnny Smith's harmonic style in sections of "My Old Flame" and "It Could Happen To You," but by 1961 Lenny Breau was well on his way to becoming a singular voice in the realm of jazz guitar.

Neither this demo tape nor Sukornyk's promotional footwork yielded work for Lenny. He returned to Winnipeg in December unconvinced that a permanent move to the big city was the right step, especially after the Breaus' son was born on January 7, 1962. Fulfilling the vow he had made to Valerie early in their courtship, Lenny named the boy "Chet Sabicas" after two of his guitar idols. Time would show that Chet, also dark-eyed and fine boned, possessed an innate musical talent that would lead him into a life as a professional guitarist and highly regarded teacher.

A week after his son's birth, Lenny bussed to Edmonton to play bass on a two-week gig with a jazz quintet led by drummer Terry Hawkeye at a venerable Canadian jazz club called The Yardbird Suite. The University of Alberta's CKUA radio did a remote broadcast from the club on the quintet's opening night—January 15, 1962—and recorded the band doing two hard bop numbers: "Blue 'N' Boogie" by Dizzy Gillespie and Cannonball Adderley's "Spontaneous Combustion." The acetate survives and is the finest extant example of Lenny's bass playing. He drives the band with rhythmically precise yet swinging walking bass lines, locking in tight with Hawkeye's stick work. "Lenny's bass playing was just beautiful—the kind of feeling someone gets playing a left hand bass line on a B-3 organ," says Hawkeye. "All the guys in the band were just blown away by it." The highlight of Lenny's performance is his solo on "Spontaneous Combustion." Lenny begins by playing short phrases using strong left-hand vibrato and then builds to a series of blazing, slightly dissonant riffs that fall into the "sheets of sound" category. He alternates these fast passages with wry, sustained notes and patches of space until he suddenly returns to a walking bass figure, prompting the band to return with the head as the audience bursts into cheers. This bravura solo was not simply a piece of astonishing technical work: its guitaristic concept presaged an approach to bass that would become cutting edge ten years later and supports the great Canadian jazz bassist/pianist Don Thompson's assertion that "Lenny Breau was ahead of us all on bass."

While in Edmonton, Lenny met the late Frank Gay, a musician and luthier who had built guitars for a number of country musicians including Webb Pierce and Johnny Horton. He was also an excellent flamenco guitarist and had once played for Carlos Montoya following a concert that the great *flamencoista* presented in Edmonton. Montoya was impressed with Gay's playing, but not by his instrument, and he arranged for Gay to buy a Ramirez guitar—one of the world's finest classical instruments—owned by the widow of a guitar-playing friend of his in Spain. Through this connection, Gay became the first distributor for Ramirez Guitars in western Canada.

Until Sukornyk bought him a cheap classical guitar in Toronto, Lenny had been doing his flamenco playing on his Martin steel string. Lenny found both instruments unsuitable for the style and placed an order with Gay for a Ramirez model A-1 flamenco guitar, which he received about two months later. Lenny was always newsworthy in Winnipeg, and Jimmy King mentioned his new acquisition in one of his columns that spring.

> [Lenny] recently acquired a $1000 Spanish guitar made by famous guitar-maker Jose Ramires [sic] Classical and flamenco artists such as Segovia, Carlos Montoya and Sabicas have identical instruments. And Lennie has the same flawless technique and imaginative conviction in flemenco [sic] as he has in jazz.[4]

Lenny not only acquired his guitar from Gay, he also appropriated from him the story of its origin, regularly telling friends, fans, and journalists that Carlos Montoya had heard him play and was so impressed that he procured the guitar for Lenny in Spain. Over the years, Lenny put various spins on this story, including one in which Montoya, after hearing him play, gave him his own guitar on the spot. Ray Couture recalls another version where Lenny claimed that he had flown to Spain to pick up a guitar that Montoya had selected for him. In fact, Frank Gay sold Lenny two and possibly three Ramirez A-1 model guitars over the next few years, and although Lenny did meet Montoya in a CBC Winnipeg studio in the early sixties, those present say that Lenny did not play for the Spaniard. Throughout his life, Lenny was never above a little self mythologizing, particularly if the anecdote had a romantic slant to it.

In March 1962, Winnipeg pop/country singer Ted Rivers (aka Theodore Botcho) hired the Stage Door house band to back him on a recording for the Winnipeg label, REO. The group—with Ron Halldorson on steel guitar—laid down a dozen cuts for the album, *Introducing Ted Rivers*, which ranged stylistically from country to pre-Beatles rock. There are a few interesting spots on the recording where Lenny and Halldorson trade hot country/swing solos but the overall quality of this album is such that its out-of-print status shouldn't sadden fans of Lenny Breau.

In coming years, Lenny would play on many rock and roll sessions around Winnipeg, but had no affinity for the music, says his then sister-in-law, Judy St. Germain: "He thought rock and roll was garbage," she says. "In fact, he was very concerned because I was listening to rock and roll. I was going through that stage and he said, 'You know, Judy, you've got to stop listening to that rock and roll. It's no good for you.'" Valerie confirms this and says there was not a single rock album in Lenny's now sprawling record collection.

After Chet's birth, Valerie and Lenny resumed their discussion of the pros and cons of moving to Toronto. In Winnipeg, Lenny was a known and respected musician. While the Breaus were far from wealthy, Lenny had steady work in clubs and on casuals, and he was slowly working his way into the studio scene at CBC. Giving this up to scuffle in a large city where he was unknown and had already spent a month looking fruitlessly for work was an enormous step. As a young mother with two infant children and a strongly interdependent relationship with her family, Valerie had her own special concerns about moving to Toronto. Still, she says, "The offer sounded really good because Sukornyk would pay our fare up there, and we could stay with him at his house. I thought it would be a really great advancement for Lenny. But he felt he wasn't ready for it. I said, 'Honey, you're the greatest guitar player in the world,' and he looks up at me and goes 'Yeah, I know, but you're the only other person who knows it. You know what? I'm scared.' I said, 'I'm scared too. But let's go and try it.'" Lenny reflected for another moment, nodded his head tentatively, and the decision was made.

When Lenny broke the news to his friends, they were generally encouraging, Bob Erlendson recalls. "All the musicians who hung out at the Stage Door said 'This is wonderful Lenny. If it all works out, it'll be really great for you. We're all really behind you.'" Not everyone was convinced that he was making the right move, however. "He was as innocent as a newborn babe," says Jack Shapira, "and I figured he should stay here and be with his mentor Bob Erlendson for at least a couple of years." Mary Nelson shared some of Shapira's concerns.

> Lenny was so far ahead of all of us that you knew that somebody strong was going to take him on and you prayed that it would just be the good guys. We knew that Lenny would be the kind of person that people could easily exploit because of the shyness in him, the introversion, the complete absorption in music that drove him. The ones of us that knew this—and I'm always surprised to find that

I'm really close in age to him because he was like a little brother—
were always so protective of him. We knew that the world had hard
edges and Lenny couldn't handle hard edges. He couldn't handle
them personally: as a musician, as a father, as a husband, as a
friend. It wasn't that he didn't want to; he just couldn't.

Still, Nelson and Shapira joined the rest of the Stage Door crowd
in wishing Lenny well, if a bit uneasily. In late March 1962, George
Sukornyk got a phone call from Winnipeg. It was Lenny on the line
and he said simply, "OK, I'm comin' out." On May 11, 1962, an
article in a Winnipeg newspaper noted Lenny's relocation with pre-
dictions of great things to come.

> Lennie Breau is good, very, very good. And he's an artist. This week
> he packs his guitar and with his wife and two babies, heads for
> Toronto [where] recognition is waiting for Lennie. He can't miss.
> He's going to be one of the greats . . . I have absolutely no doubt
> whatever about his future . . . I think Lennie will make it—big.[5]

George Sukornyk had more than enough room to billet the
Breaus in his large estate home in the city's exclusive Rosedale neighborhood. "The house was such that although Lenny lived in the
basement, it was a complete walkout because it was built on a
ravine," says Sukornyk. "He had his own bedroom, bathroom and
that sort of thing, and this was next to a recreation room and a bil-
liard room." For the next several months, Sukornyk would live with
the sound of Lenny's practicing drifting up to him from his guests'
living quarters below. "I heard him play everyday and it was the
most fantastic experience of my life," says Sukornyk. "He would
play four, five, six hours a day. I would do some work at home and
go to the office and come back and he'd still be playing. I used to
watch him doing his nails, putting enamel on them to strengthen
them, and filing them. This was a ritual done every day to make sure
he was in shape. It was quite a chore, but he really wore them out."
Union regulations requiring new musicians in town to wait three
months for a local card restricted Lenny's employment possibilities.
Without his card, he could only play three consecutive nights a week
at a particular job, which meant that he was not able to take steady

work with any of the six-night-a-week house bands around town. While waiting out this time restriction, he sat in with musicians at small, jazz-oriented clubs like the House of Hambourg, the lounge of the Edison Hotel, and George's Spaghetti House. It was through buzz generated by dates of this sort that word of the new kid in town first reached Ed Bickert, one of jazz guitar's most celebrated masters. At the time, Bickert was doing session work in various Toronto studios and working jazz clubs in the evening. On the advice of a musician friend, Bickert dropped by a popular Toronto nightspot called The First Floor Club to see Lenny play with a trio. "My first reaction was a combination of jealousy, envy, admiration—things like that—because he was so good and so original," says Bickert. "I thought 'Oh my God. This guy is light years ahead of me and so many other people around here.' So, in that respect it was kind of scary because if I had to try to catch up with him, I would have been in big trouble. He was using most of the techniques he became known for. He had the country and flamenco stuff and the jazz and was putting it together in a wonderful way. He had all that going the first time I saw him."

Lenny's only regular paying work during this period was with Joey Hollingsworth. The pair had first appeared together on a CBC variety show called *Parade* a week after Lenny arrived in Toronto. "It was just an interview," Hollingsworth says. "Lenny told me, 'You do the talking, OK? Because if they ask me anything other than my name and what I play, I'm d-d-done for!'"

Over the next few months, the men performed around Toronto and the southern Ontario region. Lenny learned by ear all the songs that Hollingsworth used in his dance routines, and would sit on a stool playing "Bye-Bye Blues," "Whispering Sleep," and other songs with his Ramirez providing the rhythms for Hollingsworth's skillful footwork. Every night, Hollingsworth would turn the stage over to his guitarist for a fifteen-minute solo set that would sometimes include Lenny's idiosyncratic humor along with his guitar playing. "He absolutely floored the people," says Hollingsworth. "We did one show at the Royal York Hotel [an upscale Toronto hotel] where I brought him out and gave him a big introduction. I said 'Ladies and gentlemen, this is one of the finest guitarists in the world today, and I'm speaking of none other than Lenny Breau.' And he sits on the stool and he looks at the people and he sings 'I'm Back in the Saddle Again' like Gene Autry! I was thinking, 'Come on Lenny. Don't do this to me!' and the people were looking dumbfounded. Finally he laughed and started playing. He just had such a weird sense of humor."

As Lenny observed Hollingsworth's act night after night, it occurred to him that the dancer could incorporate into his routine some of the same polyrhythmic principles that he was absorbing into his guitar work from flamenco and the playing of Bill Evans. One night while staying at Hollingsworth's house, Lenny explained to him exactly how this could be done.

He said, "Have you ever thought of doing multiple rhythms? It's not that hard, man. What you do is break one rhythm down and you break another rhythm down and you intermix them. You don't think of them as two different rhythms; you think of them as one." It was so simple for him. Tap dancing is all in the balance and Lenny understood all of that. He understood rhythm patterns so he understood tap dancing. He worked out a rhythm pattern for me and I knew what he meant instantly, but it was so hard. He said, "It would take maybe a year to get it, but nobody else could do it." That's the way he thought. [LAUGHS]. But I wasn't going to spend nine months doing something nobody else could do—not eighteen hours a day like he did. But that's what made him a genius, so different, so unique. His creativity was at a different level than mine, far different, and it was just wonderful to stand there and be in awe of it.

That July, Sukornyk and Lenny took a week-long trip to New York City to visit several of the city's jazz clubs. At the Metropole, Lenny played a guest set with a Dixieland band called the Dick Ruedebusch Septet and later when he introduced himself to Philly Joe Jones, who was holding court at Birdland, the legendary drummer invited him to sit in. Sukornyk and his protégé also took in the Village Vanguard where Lenny's icon, Bill Evans, often held court. Lenny would have been shocked had he known that in less than a year, he would be back in the Big Apple with his own band, making his first album on this very stage.

Just before Lenny and Sukornyk left for New York, Valerie returned to Winnipeg to visit her family and reflect on the problems that were beginning to trouble her marriage. Prior to coming to Toronto, Valerie had run the Breau household and looked after her husband almost as she did her children. "He was a child," Hollingsworth says. "Valerie would have to make sure he had the right socks on, that they weren't mixed. I mean, she literally dressed him and directed him, like 'OK, Lenny, here's where we're gonna move to.' It was just wonderful to see, but it was sad too. I thought 'She's got a child on her hands, but she loves him so much.'" Valerie believed that Sukornyk was purposefully trying to usurp this role with the intention of destroying the Breaus' marriage and leaving Lenny free to pursue his career unencumbered by family responsibilities. She wrote to Sukornyk from Winnipeg expressing these complaints and accusing him of exploiting her husband for financial gain. In his reply, Sukornyk stated that he had no financial interest in Lenny and simply wanted to see him succeed. Jimmy King then intervened and sent a scathing letter to Sukornyk. He claimed that by creating a situation in which the Breaus—Lenny in particular—had become dependent on his good will, he had aroused in Valerie "a sense of indebtedness and frustration." King charged Sukornyk with encouraging Lenny to turn his back on his family responsibilities and stated that if Lenny did not send money by the end of the week, Valerie would be forced to go on welfare. He insisted further that Sukornyk provide her and her children with airfare back to Toronto.

While his handlers were arguing over his welfare, Lenny suddenly found himself in the midst of a career dilemma when he was simultaneously confronted with two very different professional opportunities. Tony Bennett, one of the world's most popular jazz/pop crooners at that time, was in Toronto to play the O'Keefe Center and Sukornyk used his contacts to reach the singer and persuade him to give Lenny a listen. "[Bennett] said 'OK, come on down,' says Sukornyk. "He was just finishing up his show and going back to LA. Lenny came down and there was Tony Bennett and his pianist. The pianist started rattling stuff off, and Lenny picked right up. Tony listened and said 'I'd like you to join me.' Lenny said, 'We-we-we-well, I'll think about it.' Tony was in a hurry to get to the airport and I volunteered to drive him. On the way, he told me that he wanted Lenny to tour with him. But when I hooked up with Lenny later, Lenny said, 'No, I don't want to go on tour with Tony.' Turned him down with no regrets. Lenny was just free and easy and always confident that he could make a go of things but not really ambitious. If he had been ambitious he would have taken my advice and gone with Bennett. I said 'Listen, just go with him for a year. You'll be exposed to top quality musicians, and then if you want to strike out on your own, hey, you've got it.' But he said no."

The biggest factor influencing Lenny's decision was a man he had met a week or two earlier. Don Francks, born in Vancouver, British Columbia, in 1931, was already well known in the Canadian entertainment industry as an extraordinarily talented if slightly eccentric actor, singer, and writer for television and radio. In 1962, he was writing a radio piece with Hollingsworth when the dancer mentioned Lenny and his astounding playing. Francks (then known in some circles as "Don Francksinatra") had been singing professionally for over ten years and had just parted ways with his guitarist, Ian Tyson: later to gain international fame as one-half of the 1960s folk act, Ian and Sylvia. Hollingsworth's description of Lenny's abilities piqued Francks's interest, and he asked Hollingsworth to introduce him to his friend. The two musicians met a few days later at Sukornyk's home and Francks was stunned by what he heard. "I was—phewww— just knocked out, just absolutely knocked on my ass," he says. "He would start to play something and I would start to sing. I said, 'would you like to do something with me? What if we get a bass player and try it on for size?' He said OK and that's how we came to form the group called 'three.'[6] Right off the bat. We were at work almost immediately." In fact, the group eventually known as "three" would be another month in the making. What was immediate, however, was the powerful affinity that arose between the two men during their initial meeting. Despite the differences in their personalities—Francks's worldliness, street savvy, and self-assured verbosity contrasting sharply with Lenny's naiveté and diffidence—the men shared a passion for creative musical innovation. Lenny's love of artistic adventure would always overshadow his interest in financial gain and career advancement, and he turned down Tony Bennett's offer without a thought in order to explore the exciting potential he sensed could be realized in a partnership with Francks.

His choice disappointed George Sukornyk, who felt that Lenny's career would benefit from a tenure with Bennett, but he continued to support Lenny and was deeply involved with the trio that Lenny and Francks would form.

Lyrical digression was (and remains) the cornerstone of Francks's approach to singing jazz. "When you play jazz on any instrument, you extemporize on the time and melody." Francks explains, "You extend the chord structure with 9ths, 11ths or 13ths or whatever you're gonna put in. So with a vocalist, if he's gonna sing jazz, it behooves him to extemporize on the words!" Francks would explore and refine this concept with "three" but it was already a component of the group's sound when—performing as the Don Francks Trio—the men did their debut in August of 1962 at the Purple Onion, a popular Toronto nightclub. The day before the show, Francks contacted Eon Henstridge, with whom he had worked previously, to play bass on the gig. (Lenny lobbied for a drummer as well, but Francks wanted a level of dynamics and rhythmic flexibility that he felt would preclude most percussionists.) For reasons now forgotten, a CBC remote crew was on hand to record the show and later gave Sukornyk the resulting tape, which he stored along with the Hallmark sessions tapes for the next four decades. In 2004, Art of Life Records released the tapes as *Live at the Purple Onion*, which captures in nascent form the raw chemistry that already existed between Francks and Lenny. Francks—sounding like a diabolical cross between Frank Sinatra and comedian Lenny Bruce—ad libs a few comedy skits and sings extended versions of blues and jazz standards while Lenny and Henstridge improvise in a more or less straight-ahead jazz vein behind him. The show wraps up with Lenny backing Joey Hollingsworth's vocals on Nat Adderley's "Work Song," followed by a dance routine on which Lenny plays a speeded up version of his own "Oscar's Blues." The set is unpolished and at times slightly plodding, but it's clear even in this very early performance that the group had its own unique direction. In terms of musical energy, imagination, and a willingness to take creative risks, Lenny had found a stimulating kindred spirit in Don Francks.

Shortly after this gig, Lenny was the subject of a *Toronto Star* article by Ralph Thomas. The piece detailed the arrival of the "small baby-faced young man"—as Thomas called him—in Toronto and his struggle to survive in the music scene there. After giving Lenny's birthplace as Malta, Thomas mentions that Lenny is working with Francks at George's Spaghetti House. Lenny relates his invented tale about receiving his flamenco guitar from Montoya, and also tells Thomas that he had just turned down a job with the Dixieland band with whom he had played in New York. (Oddly enough, he does not mention the far more prestigious offer from Bennett.) Lenny is concise when it comes to his musical goals. "My ambition is to make the guitar sound like a piano," he says, "like it's being played with two hands. . . . Usually a guitarist has to play with a group or other instruments. Here I have a chance to develop." The article concludes by saying that after a short tour of Ontario with Don Francks, Lenny will return to Toronto "to hold down a steady television job on 'Country Hoedown' as soloist and member of the band . . ."[7]

CBC's *Country Hoedown* was a nationally televised variety show featuring country-oriented music and square dance routines. (Folk/pop singer Gordon Lightfoot began his career on this show in 1960 as a dancer.) Details of Lenny's actual involvement with the show are vague. One of the show's vocalists, Marjorie Hames, claims that Lenny worked on *Country Hoedown* regularly for at least one full season but Tommy Hunter, the show's host, says that Lenny only subbed occasionally with the show's band and was never a full-time member of its staff. (No detailed records of the show's staff records have survived.) It's likely that Lenny worked on the show briefly in the fall of 1962. Apart from this, Lenny did no session work during his year in Toronto. His playing was confined to occasional casual dates at small clubs that paid $20 or $25 a night and he relied heavily on loans from George Sukornyk to supplement his meager income.

While Lenny's finances were low, when it came to media attention his cup was overflowing. In early September, the National Film Board included the Don Francks Trio, as it was still called, and two other jazz groups in a documentary called *Toronto Jazz '62*, which Francks narrated. The documentary shows one of the trio's early performances at George's Spaghetti House and captures them in rehearsal at Sukornyk's home as they work on a jazz arrangement of a Bach piece with lyrics that Francks was in the process of writing. (The arrangement was never completed and all that Francks can recall of its lyrics is the cadential line, "Seek the sun and steal the spark and try to light the dark side of love.") This was an example of the eclectic musical territory that "three" was aiming for. As Francks says in the documentary, "We have a different aim than most jazz groups. We feel that there are many facets of jazz. . . . There are many things in jazz we're trying to strive for. A freedom in jazz, especially vocal freedom is something I want to try and get. We want to break out of that restriction . . ."[8]

The realization of this goal took a huge stride forward when Francks discovered a way to create a foundation for his stream of consciousness peregrinations while still allowing the group the freedom they sought. His description of this discovery sounds very much like one of his vocal extemporizations:

> I was coming home from rehearsing with Lenny at Sukornyk's place. Lenny loved "My Favorite Things"[9] and for some strange reason I said to myself, "these are a few of my favorite things" and then I said "these foolish things remind me of you. [lyric from the standard "These Foolish Things."] They both deal with things and so do other lines from jazz tunes like 'It don't mean a thing if you ain't got that thing. What is this thing called love? It's a many splendored thing.'" So I thought if anything can be a thing, that means nothing can be a thing that means that everything can be a thing. That means that [jazz standard] "The Things We Did Last Summer" is just some things. In my mind I started humming "Favorite Things." Then I said, "OK, keep that in your skull-bone and now do 'Foolish Things,' and they sort of went together." I said, "that's interesting. Now what happens?" So what happens if you sing the words to "My Favorite Things" to the melody of "These Foolish Things" and vice versa? I tried it and I phoned Lenny and said, "I've got to see you almost immediately. Go to sleep and I'll see you in the morning."

Francks's epiphany led to the unique hybrid arrangement, "Favorite/Foolish Things," that appeared on three's first album, and would inform much of the trio's other material. Using his own brand of extemporaneous logic, Francks would deconstruct and reassemble familiar jazz standards and link them to other songs via a common fragment of lyric or simply invent new lyrics on the spot. This cut and paste approach was a defining aspect of "three's" sound and the group applied it to many arrangements including a surreal version of "Bye, Bye Black Bird" and a piece that ingeniously combined "Isn't it Romantic," "A Fine Romance," and "My Romance."

That October, the group polished these pieces during a short tour that included dates in Hamilton, Ontario, and Montreal. In the latter city, they recorded an acetate for CBC Radio that featured readings of "God Bless the Child" and "Nobody Knows You When You're Down and Out." (The acetate was never released commercially and was used as between-program filler on CBC stations. There are no known copies of this recording extant.) A week before Halloween of 1962, the trio performed at Le Hibou in Ottawa, Canada's oldest and most venerable coffee house until its demise in the seventies. A reviewer from *Variety* magazine was present and described the show in pseudo-hipster jargon of the era.

> Bring together three capable performers with solidly scripted material and you can't easily miss. That's what happened with the trio logically and simply called Three. It's one of the slickest acts to play L'Hibou [*sic*] and would be clicko in any room. Don Francks, one of Canada's ablest performers, chants, thesps and does comedy with equal expertise. Guitarist Lenny Breau works magic with his instrument both in solo and with the trio. Bassist Ian [*sic*] Henstridge is par with the others in ability. They raced comfortably through a string of satirical items, spliced into socko, solo and serious bits to big mitting [clapping]. There's a spoof on CBC recital shows, Music Hall in turn gets a going over, cowboy and Western shows are kidded. On the serious side, Breau gives an impressive handling with a flamenco solo and the Three provide a weird but exciting arrangement of "Bye, Bye Blackbird." Throughout, the stint is structurally solid and designed for the utmost impact. While the stanza moves more freely in a coffee room such as L'Hibou, with minor refinements it might be nice for nighteries and television.[10]

As this review suggests, "three" was not a typical jazz group in terms of its material, arrangements and, particularly, its presentation. In an era where jazz musicians often did not even acknowledge their audiences, "three" was always conscious of entertaining its listeners and worked hard to connect with them. "I used to say 'When we go out on the stage, Lenny, always offer the audience a bon-bon,'" says Francks. "'A bon-bon for being so good, for listening to us do fifteen yards of solos.' That's where his harp guitar came in. He'd play a little, simple country thing on it, "We Shall Gather at the River" or something, which the audience loved. There was always room for Lenny to play. There was always room for everybody."

There was little room for Lenny's family during this period, however. Valerie and the children had returned to Toronto in August and settled into an apartment that Francks had found for the Breaus. She was relieved to end her contact with Sukornyk, but soon formed a similar antipathy towards Francks. Not only was she displeased with the apartment that Francks had found for the family, which she says was shabby and dilapidated, she was upset by the influence that Francks's bohemian lifestyle seemed to be having on her husband. "We went over to Don Francks's house," says Valerie, "and Lenny took me to the back to see his garden and it was all marijuana. I'd never even heard the word 'marijuana' before. I didn't know what it was. But I found out, and then learned that Lenny was smoking marijuana." Francks denies that he was cultivating pot, but says that he and Lenny often smoked a joint or two while cruising up and down Yonge Street and talking music in one of Francks's vintage cars. These were almost certainly Lenny's first experiences with marijuana and, as Bob Erlendson says, "He liked it; he really liked it a lot."

The couple eventually moved to a better apartment but marital tensions continued to run high as Lenny spent every available moment practicing and hanging out with Francks. These tensions finally boiled over one day when Valerie went to an appointment and left the children in Lenny's care. She returned a few hours later to find that her husband had gone to visit Francks after depositing Chet and Melody with some neighbors. Melody had managed to get out of the building and her distraught mother eventually found her under a wire fence, roughed up by some older children and requiring medical attention. "I told Lenny 'that's it. I'm leaving you,'" Valerie says. "I'm tying things up, taking my babies and leaving." Lenny's pleading did no good and a few days later, Valerie put her children in a taxi and left for the airport. "I never expected to see Lenny again," she says.

As Lenny's marriage foundered, his professional life took an upswing. In 1961, Francks had signed with the prestigious William Morris Agency while doing a play called *The Warbirds* in New York City. After the advent of "three," Francks used his contacts at William Morris to persuade them to arrange an audition for the trio. The group, dressed in matching leather suits that Francks had designed, drove to New York and did a successful audition for the agency. This led to a booking at a highly esteemed New York cabaret called the Blue Angel, where the band was scheduled for a five-week stay beginning in late March. The trio was jubilant over their good fortune as they left the city with this prime gig marked on their calendar.

On their way back to Toronto, the men took a detour through Maine to visit Lenny's mother who had retired from music and was working in a box factory in Auburn to support herself and her three sons. Francks hit it off well with Betty, and she taught him the Ray Couture-penned tune "Dear Brother," which she'd recorded for RCA in the fifties. Several months later, Lenny and Francks would record this song on "three's" first album in a straightforward country arrangement with Lenny singing high harmony as he had once done with his mother and father.

Back in Toronto, the trio played a sold-out performance on January 17, 1963, at the Ontario College of Art and received further exposure when CBC televised the documentary *Toronto Jazz '62* a month later. In late February, the men learned that two important events had been added to their itinerary in New York: a live recording date at the Village Vanguard and an appearance on the ABC network program, *The Jackie Gleason Show*, one of the top-rated variety shows in the country at the time. Suddenly, "three's" future was beginning to look very bright indeed.

The trio drove to New York in their vocalist's vintage hearse, and put up at the apartment of an absent friend of Francks's a few days before they were to open at the Blue Angel for singer Georgia Brown on March 26. The event was noted in *The New Yorker* magazine's calendar section but only Francks was mentioned, described in the short blurb as "just down from Canada where he is deemed a way out humorist."[11] Accounts of "three's" opening night vary. According to Francks, the audience loved the trio and gave them an enthusiastic reception. The only problem, Francks says, was their leather suits, which Blue Angel management said would have to be replaced with tuxedos. However, George Sukornyk, who was in the audience, tells a very different story. "On their opening night the place was really packed because the word was out that this was really a great act. Ed Sullivan's son-in-law, who was his producer, was there. But when the band came out, the show was an absolute disaster. Don was so rude and crude, telling the women they had leather bras on and stuff like that. It was awful—immediately. I was just beside myself. They were canned." Joey Hollingsworth, who heard about the gig from Lenny, confirms Sukornyk's version of events. "In those days Don Francks was a bit of a rebel," he says. "You just couldn't harness Don." Francks refutes this story, and the next four issues of *The New Yorker* listed Francks as being in residence at the Blue Angel (describing him in one listing as "a leather-jacketed missioner from Mars" and in another as a purveyor of "humor deep in surrealism"[12]) so it may be that Sukornyk and Hollingsworth are confused about the date of the incident.

On April 23, the trio appeared on Jackie Gleason's show and performed their idiosyncratic version of "Bye, Bye Blackbird" for a national television audience. "We were allowed to do 'Blackbird' because Jackie loved where it went," Francks says. "But when I wanted to do the other tune I'd chosen—I forget which one it was—they said 'no, we've got to bring it back to middle America somehow,' and I had to do a Broadway show tune without the guys."

A week later, the group was back in Toronto to appear on a CBC-TV program called *Parade* and soon afterwards returned to New York to play a one-night booking at the Village Vanguard. The Kapp Jazz Label, a subsidiary of Decca, recorded this performance and later released it as *Jackie Gleason says—"No One in This World Is Like Don Francks."* The tight, exuberant and well-paced set recorded that night shows how far the trio had come since their first gig at the Purple Onion eight months earlier. It also documents the extent to which Lenny's playing had evolved in the year and a half following the Hallmark sessions. His bebop-influenced solo on "Come Rain or Come Shine" has a focus and economy of line lacking on much of his playing on *The Hallmark Sessions*. He uses dyads as a comping device on "Favorite/Foolish Things" with far greater adroitness and confidence than on the earlier album, giving the tech-

nique a sparser, more syncopated application in the manner of Bill
Evans. Throughout the set, he is completely attuned to Francks and
complements beautifully the singer's madcap digressions at every
twist and turn.

With an appearance on one of the top variety shows in the
country, a recording date in a legendary jazz club and several weeks
at a top New York bistro—all in a two-month period—the trio
seemed to be on its way at last. But as Joey Hollingsworth says,
"You can't harness Don Francks." Just as the trio appeared to be
taking off, Francks opted to leave the group and remain in New
York to pursue his acting career.[13] His decision, he says, did not
appear to disappoint Lenny. "There was lots of work for him in
Toronto," Francks says. "By then, he was well known there and
was a really in-demand player." Lenny may not have exhibited any
ill feeling over the break-up of the band, but, in reality, he had no
real employment prospects in Toronto beyond the twenty-dollar-a
night jobs he had been playing since arriving in the city a year earlier. The idea of returning to Toronto and continuing to hustle these
low-paying gigs was not appealing, particularly after a taste of the
sweet life in New York. He also desperately missed his family. During the past few months, Valerie had corresponded with Lenny regularly, imploring him to return to Winnipeg so they could begin to
repair their damaged relationship. Compared with his currently
bleak prospects in New York City and Toronto, the security and
comfort that Winnipeg and his family offered him were irresistible,
and he finally decided to go home. There was a snag, however;
Lenny was broke. To keep afloat, he had pawned in quick succes-
sion his Gretsch, Martin D-28, Ramirez, and finally, his Gibson ES-
125. (The harp guitar remained at Sukornyk's house where Lenny
had stayed since Valerie returned to Winnipeg.) Valerie was unable
to help with airfare and in a panic, Lenny called Bob Erlendson. As
luck would have it, the pianist had been fronting a band six nights
a week at the Town and Country Inn and was in desperate need of
another musician to fill out his band when Lenny called. "He said
'Li-li-like, is there any way you can get me out of New York?'"
Erlendson says. "I said 'well, it just so happens that I need a fourth
man for the band. Do you want the gig?'" Lenny jumped at the
offer and Erlendson wired his friend money for airfare.

Lenny then returned to Toronto to pick up items that he had left at Sukornyk's house. There are two versions of what transpired between the men at this meeting. Lenny would later claim that Sukornyk had pressured him into signing a contract on his twenty-first birthday that entitled the manager to 30 percent of his earnings as well as reimbursement for expenses—including room and board—incurred while Lenny stayed at Sukornyk's house. Lenny later insisted that when he went to Sukornyk's house to pick up his instruments, Sukornyk presented him with a bill for $15,000, threatened legal action, and seized his guitars for partial payment of the bill.

Sukornyk vehemently denies the story. There was never any contract, he says, and his assistance was "absolutely gratis": never did it cross his mind to charge Lenny to stay at his home. He insists that while he did make substantial loans to Lenny, he saw little prospect of repayment and would never have considered charging Lenny to stay in his house. It was Lenny, says Sukornyk, who brought up the issue of the loans when he came to his house before returning to Winnipeg. "He said he was broke and would pay the money in time," Sukornyk says. "He wanted me to take his harp guitar as collateral but I didn't want it. What was I going to do with it? He insisted, and I kept it for about twenty-five years. I sent him some letters in Winnipeg telling him to come and get it but he never responded." Lenny told friends that these letters were legal threats to garnishee wages from gigs and session work if Lenny did not repay his loan.

Under scrutiny, there are significant flaws in Lenny's claim of managerial tyranny. By the time Sukornyk took Lenny on as a client, he had already managed—without recompense—two well-established, profit turning major acts: Juliette and Joey Hollingsworth (who still refers to Sukornyk as "the most honorable man I ever knew.") One wonders why Sukornyk would sign an unknown with limited financial prospects to an outlandishly exploitive contract when he had already represented two proven money earners without charge and with no motive except to be, as Francks puts it, "a really, really good patron of the arts that people said only good things about." Also, considering Lenny's habit in years to come of offering his guitars as security to friends who had lent him money, and then failing to reclaim them, Sukornyk's assertion that Lenny insisted on his taking the harp guitar as collateral for his debt rings true.

Artifice may not have come naturally to Lenny Breau but he did have a lifelong inclination to shift responsibility for his failings to others. Great things had been expected for Lenny when he moved to Toronto, and now he was returning to the city with, as he viewed it, nothing to show for his time away. His charge that Sukornyk had unfairly burdened him with an enormous debt and seized his guitars (which Lenny told Erlendson and others that he had pawned), thereby stripping him of his means for making a living, provided him with an unimpeachable motive for returning prematurely to Winnipeg, no better off than he had been when he left. Not everyone accepted Lenny's story. "Lenny told me some things about why he came back to Winnipeg, but whether I believe them or not is something else," says Gary Gross. "I think they were simply face saving, dignity protective statements." Many of Lenny's friends accepted his story verbatim, however, and Lenny stuck by it throughout his life, often citing it to explain his reluctance to work with a manager.

Sukornyk saw his former "client" only once more. When Lenny returned to Toronto in the late sixties, he gave Sukornyk a friendly call, chatted him up, and invited him to a downtown club where he was playing. Sukornyk was pleased to hear from him and dropped by the club but found Lenny in such a drugged state that he left without saying hello and never saw him again.

Lenny may not have lived up to Anne Henry's prediction that he would become "one of the greats" in Toronto, but his sense of failure was harsh and ill founded. During his year in Toronto, he had wowed the city's best players, performed on an American national network television show with a group that had turned important heads in the Big Apple, and made an album at a New York City club in which his idols worked regularly.[14] These were impressive accomplishments for a young man who less than three years earlier had been playing community centers in far-flung, northern Saskatchewan villages. Lenny had every reason to view the past year as a success or at least a harbinger of great possibilities to come, which indeed it would turn out to be.

5.

Workin' Man's Blues
June 1963—December 1967

"He took the jobs at CBC so the kids and I could have a good life. Not that he wanted to be a studio guitar player; he didn't. But he did that for his family."

—Valerie Breau-St. Germain

"He seemed different when he came back from Toronto. He seemed to be in a different world like . . . more locked in than being wide open. Before it was like everything was 'yeah, yeah!' He came back from Toronto and it was like he was scared and turned inward. It seemed like he'd had a bad experience and he kept it to himself. To deal with that he played more outwardly to release whatever was upsetting him inside."

—George Reznik

Lenny returned to Winnipeg with little more than his leather suit and a recently acquired hipster patois heavy on expressions like "dig it," "like man," and "cool." Valerie was now living in an apartment on Jamison Street, a few miles from downtown Winnipeg, and that's where Dave Shaw brought Lenny after picking him up at the airport one afternoon in late May. After a few words with Valerie and hugs for his kids, he and Shaw left to meet Erlendson at the Towers Restaurant in the Town and Country Inn. The men greeted each other warmly and the pianist gave Lenny a new Gibson ES-125 guitar to use on the gig with the understanding that he would pay him for it when he was able.

The two men would be the core of what Erlendson refers to as "the best bloody band in the world" with a rhythm section that initially comprised bassist Dave Shaw and a drummer named Wayne Finucan. The Towers advertised the group as a dance band, but the room's large dance floor was rarely used, Finucan says. "We played from eight to one in the morning: a five-hour gig. We'd do an opening set, do the show [usually backing out of town singers and entertainers] and then we were supposed to play a whole bunch of dance music. But this was the hilarious thing about the T and C: the manager thought any time anybody danced, they weren't drinking and he wasn't selling alcohol. So we would have to stop and break into a jazz tune that was too fast to dance to. Some of those tunes would last twelve to fifteen minutes. We would be playing "Going Home" or "Nardis" and we would go on and on. I think we even played some 5/4 stuff in those days." Lenny, says Erlendson, loved the gig and used it to hone the concepts he'd been refining in Toronto. "He was into new things after he came back from New York," says Erlendson. "All the stuff that we'd talked about and had been working on: building chords, understanding how fourths work, voicing them on the guitar, all that stuff. He'd just run with it."

After his gig at the Towers, Lenny would rush home to his family to enjoy the domestic scene he'd missed for the past year. Judy St. Germain spent much time at her sister's apartment, and recalls that Lenny would arrive home at 2:30 or 3:00 a.m. with milkshakes, fries, and foot-long hotdogs from a nearby restaurant. "He'd wake Val and me up and say, 'You've got to eat with me. I can't eat alone.' He'd be all high and ready to take on the world kind of thing and happy just to be home with Val and the kids."

The couple's money situation was tight, and Lenny was constantly hustling for work in and out of town. In early 1964, he played a two-week gig at the Yard Bird Suite in Edmonton and, during his stay there, reconnected with Frank Gay. He ordered a new Ramirez and also discussed with the luthier an idea he had for a new and novel guitar. The instrument Lenny envisioned would have three extra strings—a low bass string and two treble strings above the high E—to allow him to achieve piano-type chord voicings on the fretboard. Gay agreed to build the instrument on the condition that Lenny provide an electric guitar body to which he would splice a custom-built neck. On the advice of Bob Erlendson, Lenny gave Gay Erlendson's ES-125 and ordered a new one to use as his working guitar. (Erlendson would have a half share in Gay's creation.) When the new Gibson arrived, Lenny sent Erlendson's guitar back to Edmonton to be modified. Erlendson describes the results.

> It was tuned as a regular guitar with an extra [bass] string on the bottom that Lenny tuned to a B and [there were] two extra treble strings—an A and a D—on top. But it was tuned too high for the strings [causing them to break] so Lenny tuned the whole thing down a tone to A-D-G-C-F-A-D-G-C. He didn't have a problem using that set-up. He had already been working on making use of strings lower than E with those extra strings that were on the harp guitar and, when he added the low A, he learned to use it really fast. The high G string was no problem because the D to G was another perfect fourth so he got used to that quickly, too. The guitar sounded pretty good even though the electronics never worked very well. The ES-125 body had a good sound on the low string and the other strings were OK.

Lenny struck an endorsement deal with the LaBella String Company who provided him with the thick bass string—an .062 gauge—required for the low A. He was pleased with his new instrument, but found that the strings were too close together to make the guitar comfortably functional. However, he continued to experiment with the invention, revising its tuning several times before selling his half to Bob Erlendson in 1971 without ever having used it on stage. (Erlendson still owns it.)

The Breaus' gloomy economic situation began to brighten in early 1964 when Lenny started doing occasional sessions at CBC. Lenny's longtime friend, Jim Pirie, a versatile guitarist with superb jazz and reading chops, had been the first-call guitarist at the station for the past few years. But as work increased and Lenny's name got around, various music directors and producers began using him as well, particularly on jobs where reading skills weren't crucial.

One of these was the late Bob McMullin, a talented sax player, arranger, and conductor. As one of the most respected members of

CBC's musical staff, McMullin was free to use any local musician he wanted for his projects and hired Lenny for hundreds of CBC sessions over the coming years. His regard for Lenny and his talents is obvious in this excerpt from a 1967 CBC interview in which McMullin profiled the young guitarist.

> Musicians that know him often say that he doesn't really know how good he is, how much talent, how much technical ability, how much playing ability he has . . . I think here in Winnipeg he's really influenced every musician who has ever worked with him. He'll bring things into it a lot of other musicians have never thought of. The same applies to any kind of music that he plays. He is in this, for lack of a better way of saying it, this little world of his own. Not because he likes to shut himself off but music is, I guess, his whole life, his whole reason for being. People refer to him as a genius, some people even think he's a little kooky because of, not his mannerisms, but because he's an individual. This individuality shows through everything he plays and everything he does. He has a commercial sense in that he can play music for all kinds of people. His whole personality shows in his playing, through the guitar and through the way he is: the way he says hello, the way he eats those cheese and onion sandwiches . . . with the mustard.[1]

Lenny's first gigs with McMullin were on the arranger's own show, a program that featured mainly Percy Faith-style arrangements of pop tunes. While other musicians in the orchestra were expected to read their parts on sight, Lenny's weak reading chops made it necessary for McMullin to give Lenny his parts a day or two before the show so he could have them ready for the session. Lenny's reading ability would develop during his years as a studio musician, although as he later explained to Lee Major, his ears and knack for playing exactly what was required of him remained his greatest strengths: "All the experience I had in the CBC studios was great for me because I learned how to read: I had to learn how to read because a lot of times there's a time limit and you have to get things done within a certain time and if you don't read, you don't get it done. But luckily I got a good ear so even when I didn't know how to read, if I heard the part once, I'd memorize it anyway."[2]

One of Lenny's first regular gigs on CBC-TV was a Saturday evening show called *A Song For You* on which Lenny and bassist Dave Young backed Jose Poneira, a pianist fond of playing standards with a slightly stodgy Latin feel. Jack Lyttle, the show's producer, often allowed Lenny to take solo spots on the show where he could play, within reason, music of his choosing. One such show, broadcast on May 23, 1964, featured Lenny in a guitar trio with Ron Halldorson, by then an excellent jazz guitarist, and Jim Pirie. "Each of us contributed arrangements," says Pirie. "I wanted to do a classical thing and Lenny said 'Well, there's one that I already know.' So I thought, 'Well, OK, that's probably going to be easier than having to teach it to him.' He said 'This is the part I know. Can you play the other part?' I said 'OK.' So we got to one passage about halfway through and I said, 'Whoa! That doesn't sound quite right.' He said, 'Oh yeah. Well, I changed that.' I said, 'Well, this is Bach. You can't change it.' He said, 'Well, OK, but I like mine better.' I said, 'Well, I might too but I don't think we can do that because the counter melody that I was playing doesn't fit with what you're playing.' He said, 'OK, we'll go back to what's written. No problem, but it's kind of vanilla though.'"

The Bach piece was vetoed, and instead the trio played "The Song is You," "Billie's Bounce," and "The Days of Wine and Roses," a tune that would have a special place in Lenny's repertoire for the next twenty years. The arrangement of the piece that Lenny put together for the Poneira show was intricate and complex. Pirie and Halldorson were required to play harmonized counterlines behind the melody and use chords that were superimposed over one another to form large, extension-filled harmonic structures recalling Bill Evans's piano voicings. "That arrangement was really weird at the time," Pirie says. "There were chord progressions in there where I thought 'where the hell is this going?' And the thing is, nothing was written down! He taught us our parts out of his head, which is mindblowing. Now, either he was making it up on the spur of the moment, which I doubt, or else he'd already worked out all of the voicings for the whole arrangement in his head. But he taught every bar to us. So I just wrote it down as he was doing it and I think Ronnie did the same thing. Then we just went home and learned it."

The trio to which Lenny was giving most of his attention at this time was his group with Halldorson and Kelln, who had replaced Shaw and Finucan as the rhythm section of the Towers band. There was no precise moment when the classic Lenny Breau Trio came into being, and in its earliest incarnation, it did not even have a specified leader, Reg Kelln explains. "Lenny wasn't really the leader then. We might go by his name or maybe Ronnie's name or my name or who-ever got the job. Lenny didn't care to be a leader. He didn't want all the stress of all the phone calls. He just wanted us to play."

Lenny's approach to learning and developing material, however, prevailed in the group and was as loose as the inception of the trio, Halldorson says:

Lenny rarely called tunes. He'd just start playing and he'd leave it to me to figure out what key he was in and what tune he was going to play. I don't have perfect pitch so I'd put my finger down some-where and slide it around until I figured out what key he was play-ing in. And Reg would be swishing away on cymbals just making some sounds, waiting to feel it out. Lenny just wanted to feel that it was free, that it was not coming out of any kind of structure or for-mat. All the shifts of tempo and things just happened. They could come from any of us but they were little triggers that we all got to know. Lenny would set something, start playing maybe a 6/8 feel against a 4/4 and then he'd jump into a 3 feel at a different quarter note tempo so it was a related rhythm but was different. We got to know these things that we'd hear each other do, but they were never talked about much. They mostly just happened. And once you've done those things, they'll happen again because they're neat. His repertoire just came out of the ether, so to speak because it was never planned, it just developed. Lenny didn't want arrangements so nothing was ever arranged. Of course, we played a lot of these tunes over the years many times so they did develop and grow. Each time we would play "Stella by Starlight," there would be things that we liked, things that we did maybe every time or came to be a regular part of playing that piece but it was never permanently set where the arrangement became like "OK, this is how we do it." A few things sort of fell into arrangements but they were created out of spontaneity and elements of the arrangement that were originally spontaneous ideas and were repeated because he really dug it. You would try things and some things you would sort of retain and they would become like a regular part of the playing of the piece. Other things you would try and then discard and you would be looking for other stuff. It was evolving but certain parts of it would remain: a time feel or a certain chord change or an interlude or space.

The trio's first gigs were mainly in small, no-frills clubs spawned by the early sixties folk boom. These clubs were often simply rooms in a church or YMCA basement, and bore names like The Wise Owl and The Black Spot. Audiences consisted of young people who were usually more familiar with Bob Dylan than Charlie Parker. Lenny, by now a solid fan of Dylan, would often play "Freight Train" and "Don't Think Twice" and other folk-flavored tunes to break the ice with these audiences, as he explained to Lee Major:

I enjoy working in a coffee house even though they're young kids that come there. But they come there to listen and their minds are really open. I know what they like so I'll play what they like and then I'll play what I like and then they're ready for it, you see. Otherwise if I went out and played a jazz tune right at the beginning of the set, it wouldn't be interesting enough, see what I mean? I have to build up so I'll open with a folk tune, maybe a tune written by Bob Dylan because they know Bob Dylan and they can associate with the melody and eventually I lead into my own things.[3]

Lenny had clearly taken to heart Francks's advice to "Give the people a bon-bon for being so good." He reached out to his audience, enticing them into his music through a process of musical acclimatization—a singular precept for a jazz musician of the time. There were other precepts from his tenure with Francks that had shaped Lenny's developing musical approach as well. Jazz standards were the backbone of the Lenny Breau Trio's sets, but like Francks, Lenny saw no reason to be stylistically exclusive and played folk, pop, and country tunes, as well as flamenco and novelty numbers. As Francks had done in "three," Lenny would run through several apparently incongruous musical styles in the course of a single tune, taking a number like "Freight Train" from jazz to country to flamenco. This would become another signature of his style, later epitomized by tunes like "Taranta" and "The Claw" with their shifts in tempo, mood, feel, style, and long sections of other tunes embedded into their basic structures. Lenny absorbed this concept directly from Francks, and its effectiveness was proven by the response of the young audiences for whom the Lenny Breau Trio played in the mid to late sixties.

His church basement gigs paid little, but Lenny's income was climbing. During the fall of 1964, CBC hired him to work full-time on two weekly national television shows. The first of these was *Red River Jamboree*, a program featuring country music and choreographed square dancing. *Red River Jamboree* had been on the air for four years when Lenny replaced Jim Pirie as its staff guitarist in 1964. (Pirie moved to Toronto to work on *Country Hoedown*.) Once Lenny was aboard, he lobbied the show's producer, Dan Waters, to take on Ron Halldorson as steel guitarist with the ten-piece band. Waters complied, and as Reg Kelln was already the show's drummer, the Lenny Breau Trio was now the musical heart of one of Canada's most watched television shows, albeit playing a very different style of music than that for which they would become best known.

The *Jamboree*'s cast rehearsed three times a week to prepare for the Wednesday night show, so the trio had to find substitutes for their Towers Restaurant gig on that night. This rankled the hotel's manager, and he demanded that the men choose between the Towers job and their CBC date. Money from the hotel gig could not compete with CBC wages and the trio quit.

Lenny could afford to let the Towers job go because he was now also the guitarist on a new, nationally broadcast CBC TV show called *Music Hop*. The original *Music Hop*, a rock-based Toronto program first broadcast in 1963, was so successful that CBC decided to create similarly formatted shows in various cities across Canada. Each had its own theme, but all were youth-oriented and employed a core of crack, local musicians. CBC Winnipeg chose a young producer and folk music buff named Ray McConnell to head up the local show and allowed him to choose its theme. "When they asked me what type of *Music Hop* I'd like to do, I automatically went for a Hootenanny format," says McConnell, referring to the impromptu folk music jams popular in the fifties and early sixties. "Then I auditioned singers to put together a group modeled loosely on [popular sixties commercial folk group] the New Christie Minstrels." *Music Hop*'s musical cast comprised six singers split evenly along the gender line and backed by Lenny on guitar, Dave Young on bass (replaced by Werner Franck after the first season), and Wayne Finucan on drums. Ray St. Germain was the show's host and lead vocalist.

As usual, Lenny relied on his ear to learn the folk, country, and light rock numbers that were arranged by Bob McMullin, the show's music director, or taken directly from records. "Of course Lenny could listen to a cut just once and then he'd do fills they hadn't even dreamed of when they were actually making these recordings," says McConnell. "I think the fact that he didn't have the restraints of the more traditional background in music gave him this incredible freedom." Lenny was allowed one or two solo spots on each show and played "Freight Train" and an instrumental version of "Washington Square" on *Music Hop*'s first broadcast on October 7, 1964. The program was a great success from the night of its début, and would provide Lenny with steady employment and a high profile for the next three years.

With Jim Pirie gone, Lenny was now first call guitarist at CBC. By early 1965, he was spending six to eight hours a day in the CBC studios, taking only a short afternoon break to return to the Breaus' new apartment on nearby Banning Street to change his clothes and have a quick bite to eat. He practiced constantly during session breaks in the studio or while having a snack in the station's cafeteria. As other musicians relaxed and chatted, Lenny pored over his instrument looking for new riffs and progressions and heralding his discoveries with a loud, enthusiastic, "Like, man; dig it!"

Wayne Finucan, also busy with CBC sessions, took Lenny under his wing and saw to it that he received the maximum union benefits for his work at CBC. "I'd fill out all his forms and act like his bookkeeper," says Finucan. "We used to get five dollars to put on makeup, and if you carried your own instrument, you'd fill out a form and you'd get $3.50. It all meant filling out paperwork so I'd fill it out and say 'here Lenny, sign this.' It was union scale for shows based on whether they were national or regional. We were getting national rates for *Music Hop*. I think it was $175 a show and that was with a full day of rehearsal. It wasn't a lot of money but it wasn't bad in 1965."

Lenny sometimes played twenty-five and more shows a week for fees that ranged from $35 to $175 per show, making his average income between 1965 and 1967 close to $35,000 a year, a considerable salary for a musician at that time. Lenny and Valerie were able to send Melody to an exclusive girls' private school and purchase a brand new, top-of-the-line Studebaker (in which Lenny, who never obtained a driver's license during the course of his life, was content to be a passenger). Lenny was also able to indulge his high-toned sartorial tastes regularly. According to one widely repeated anecdote, Lenny once visited an upscale Winnipeg clothing store and was shown a new suit just in from New York. Unable to decide between the six available colors, he ordered a suit in each shade. Weeks later when the suits were ready, the haberdashery called Lenny to discover that he had completely forgotten about his order, but would be right down to pick it up. It isn't known how Valerie, who still handled money matters and picked up Lenny's check at CBC each week, responded when she received the haberdasher's bill.

Lenny was chronically insouciant with money, spending it freely and rarely giving much thought to financial commitments—an attitude that would create long-term problems for him. CBC did not deduct income tax directly from his weekly check, and he was required to put aside enough money to cover the amount he owed to Revenue Canada at year's end. Long-term financial planning was an alien concept to Lenny, and his failure to file with Revenue Canada between 1964 and 1969—the highest income period of his life—would come back to burden him at a time when his income was a small fraction of what it was in his glory days at CBC.

Most of Lenny's work on CBC was confined to mundane material, but occasionally he would be hired to play a show on which he was able to do what he did best. One of these was *A Touch of Jazz*, featuring jazz/pop vocalist, George La Fleche with a back-up band that included Lenny, Bob McMullin, Wayne Finucan, and Dave Young. A segment of one of these shows, broadcast March 2, 1965, is included in full in the 1999 documentary *The Genius of Lenny Breau* and provides an excellent example of Lenny's evolving harmonic concepts. A trio made up of Lenny, Finucan, and Young plays a mid-tempo version of "Georgia on My Mind." After stating the melody over top of simultaneously played chords, Lenny takes two choruses during which he turns the song inside out harmonically. At one point, he plays a rising chord sequence as a turnaround between the repeated A sections of the AABA form. Instead of resolving this figure when he arrives at the first bar of the second A section, where typically a turnaround would end, he continues it for several more bars, successfully and effectively blending it into the tune's harmonic structure. Several bars into the A section, he finally resolves the turnaround by dovetailing it into harmonic material more closely aligned with the original progression. This type of tangential harmonic thinking would become more and more prevalent in Lenny's playing over the years, keeping band mates not familiar with the complex and sometimes arcane logic of his harmonic conception on their toes.

CBC cancelled *Red River Jamboree* in the spring of 1965, but the Lenny Breau Trio had not yet finished its association with country music. In May, CBC Toronto hired its members to back Tommy Hunter, the Hames Sisters, and other key members of *Country Hoedown*'s cast on a three-week western Canadian tour. The group kicked off with a date in Brandon, Manitoba, and then hit the highway for a series of one-nighters that took them as far west as British Columbia before doubling back to Edmonton to perform for two weeks at the city's Klondike Days celebration. Lenny, says Reg Kelln, filled the long hours on the road practicing and picking the brains of his fellow musicians.

I'd sit in the back seat with my drumsticks practicing on the back of the front seat or on a leg or towel and Lenny would be sitting there practicing too. He had himself a little board with strings on it and would practice flamenco patterns. He'd sit there and go "whirrrrr," just steady rolling on the [right hand] fingering. I'd be doing something and he'd say, "Hey Reg, what are you doing? A paradiddle? What's a paradiddle?" I'd explain and he'd say, "OK, just a minute . . ." He'd pick two strings with two different fingers and he'd play "tic to-tic tic to-tic to to" and he'd play a paradiddle as if he was playing drums: two different fingers being like two different hands playing the rhythm. He'd get that down and say "that's neat. I like that." And then I'd say, "well, here's a paradiddle-diddle. There's six beats in it." He'd say, "Oh?" and he'd play it back. Now he'd incorporate all this into his playing: three against four, six against four, you know, by using different fingerings. So I was showing him a lot of drum movements and he kept saying, "Wow, show me some more." So we'd practice in the back seat for an hour and a half sometimes and after awhile that stuff was all through his playing because when I showed it to him, he'd have had it down right quick, playing musical lines with these paradiddles or paradiddle-diddles. I'd say, "Lenny, what are you doing?" And he'd say, "oh, just messing around." But it sounded great right away.

Lenny loved being back on the road, and played brilliantly on stage and afterwards when the trio would jam in their hotel room, says Marjorie Hames. But this changed once the tour arrived in Edmonton where they were part of a stage show that included the Rosemary Clooney band. "Suddenly, there was a big change in Lenny," says Hames. "I don't know whether he connected with somebody in Rosemary Clooney's band or what, but he became less reliable and more distant. We didn't know what happened, but he was just not Lenny. Whatever it was, it threw his playing. The rest of the tour, he'd been right on the ball."

Lenny's mysterious transformation, as Hames implies, was likely the result of his increasing drug use. It's not clear exactly when and how Lenny was introduced to drugs. He once told his brother Bobby that he had used uppers (amphetamines) to stay awake during long nights of playing and practice in the Stage Door years. However, Bob Erlendson and others strenuously deny this, saying that drugs of any sort were virtually unknown in the Winnipeg music scene at that point. Lenny was, by all accounts, immaculately clean and sober during this period, and did little more than sip a beer in social situations. There's little doubt that Lenny had his first experience with marijuana in the company of Don Francks in Toronto and continued to smoke pot regularly after returning to Winnipeg. In 1964, the Lenny Breau Trio played behind a rising Canadian poet at a reading in Winnipeg. After the show, the poet gave Lenny a quantity of LSD, which he ingested with his friend, trombonist Barrie Tallman, and another musician who has asked to remain nameless. This musician recalls, "I was on the floor and could hardly move, but Lenny wanted to go out and score some pot!"

Lenny's affinity for LSD and pot was hardly anomalous among the demographic group to which he belonged. Tens of thousands of young people around the globe were at that time beginning to explore alternative lifestyles in which experimentation with psychedelics was almost mandatory and carried with it a cachet denoting spiritual awareness as well as countercultural hipness. Lenny showed some interest in the alleged spiritual and consciousness expanding effects of LSD and other psychedelics, claiming that drugs enhanced his creativity and opened his inner "doors of perception," a notion popular with many LSD crusaders of the time. In the late 1960s, he devoured Carlos Castaneda's books on the possibility of attaining spiritual awareness through drugs, and was fascinated by Castaneda's peyote shaman, Don Juan. However, most of Lenny's friends agree that his taste for psychedelics had far more to do with the childlike glee he derived from their hallucinogenic, Alice in Wonderland-ish effects than a passion for the spiritual insights or bursts of creativity that mind-altering drugs ostensibly provide. In any case, by 1966 Lenny's drug use had become a significant factor in the problems that were undermining his marriage. Valerie did not like the distancing effect that drugs seemed to have on Lenny, nor did she appreciate his tendency to leave drugs around the house where his children could stumble on them. She confronted Lenny about this many times and each time he would promise to clean up, disingenuously as it would turn out.

The marriage was being tested in other ways as well. Initially, Valerie kidded Lenny about his indiscreet interest in other women, and, in jest, gave him the tag, "Rubber Neck Breau." But in time, she began to lose her sense of humor about her husband's proclivity, and with good reason. "Lenny was not so much a partier, but he would end up in a love situation easily," Wayne Finucan says euphemistically. "Lenny liked women and if he met one, he'd just take off. Many times, I had to bail him out of hotel situations. A lot of times, I'd have to find out where he was, get his act together and get him back to CBC. I'd come by and say, 'Lenny, it's time to go to the show.' This was around the time that he and Val were almost finished." Lenny did not seem to grasp the distress he was causing Valerie, says Bob Erlendson. "Lenny's trouble in general was that he just didn't understand personal relationships very well at all," Erlendson explains. "He didn't understand what his marriage needed. He talked about that a little bit with me, and I would try to be as understanding and advice filled as I could. But he just didn't get it and the responsibilities required." Considering Lenny's paternal role model, it's little wonder that this was so.

In the spring of 1965, a Winnipeg pianist named Mike Lewis and two partners took over a coffee house called The Establishment (where Lenny had often played) and turned it into the Jazz A Go-Go, a club/restaurant with an exclusive jazz policy. Lewis asked Bob Erlendson to put together a house band to play six nights a week at the club and the pianist obliged by forming a unit of musicians that had played together often at the Stage Door: Lenny (on bass and guitar), Reg Kelln, trombonist Barrie Tallman, and the band's arranger, Pete Thompson, on tenor. Thompson suffered a nervous breakdown a few weeks into the gig and left the band.

The band began its first set at midnight on May 8, 1965, and soon the club had become Winnipeg's hottest jazz spot. A few months on, however, crowds began to dwindle when Lewis was unable to procure a liquor license for his enterprise. Desperate to fill seats, he began to bring in well-known, out-of-town musicians to play with the club's house band. One of these was multi-sax man and flautist Moe Koffman, who, after Oscar Peterson, was perhaps Canada's best-known and most commercially successful jazz musician. Lenny and Koffman had crossed paths briefly in Toronto a few years earlier, but their first formal gig together took place on December 15, 1965, when Koffman arrived in Winnipeg to play a four-day stint at the Jazz A Go-Go with Lenny, Dave Young, and Reg Kelln. (Bob Erlendson had moved to Toronto a week before Koffman's appearance and was replaced by a pianist whom Koffman fired in rehearsal.) Local music writer Ted Allan described the musical meeting between Koffman and Lenny in an article biased heavily towards Winnipeg's hometown hero. Describing the band's performance of the tune "A Taste of Honey," Allan writes only that Koffman "played a wistful solo." His prose is considerably more inspired and dense when writing about Lenny's playing on the same song. Allan calls Lenny's choruses "a revelation" and writes that he "sort of glanced into his solo, as is his wont, in an obtuse [sic], introspective manner dallying with stop-time chords and choppy phrases. Then building to a climactic release, he jumped into a string of flashing, funky-butt phrases that fell like smooth pebbles." Koffman's solo on his jazz hit "Swinging Shepherd Blues," gets barely a nod from Allan who writes that Lenny's solo on the piece "assembled a riotous, yet logical composite of guitar effects, unorthodox single line phrases, smooth chord sequences, flamenco-like strums and the bisection of a particular phrase he found interesting." Lenny, Allan declares, has evolved "from a man possessed with a formidable technique to a consummate artist, belonging to no particular stylistic compartment. He is, as they say, his own man. . . . He maintained a consistently high degree of invention in all his solos, each a masterful mélange of wit, contrast and strikingly effective phrasing." Not surprisingly, the last lines of Allan's review are directed, however obliquely, at Lenny rather than the show's headliner: "to hear [Koffman] stimulate Lenny Breau as he did Thursday is something no clear-thinking music lover should miss."[4]

Allan's breathless review likely brought many a "clear-thinking music lover" to the club during Koffman's four nights' residence there, but it was a case of too little too late. Lewis still had not been able to procure a liquor license for the club and business continued to drop off sharply. In February of 1966, the club hosted one of its last shows when the great Canadian vibes player Peter Appleyard did a weeklong stint with the band. Thirty-five years later, Appleyard recalls the gig enthusiastically. "In jazz, I've worked with Joe Pass, Barney Kessel, Bucky and John Pizzarelli, and Ed Bickert," he says. "They're all marvelous, of course, but none of them came near the style of Lenny Breau. That struck me the first time that I played with him in Winnipeg." Once again, reviewer Ted Allan sang Lenny's praises: "much of the credit for the strong, persuasive jazz the quartet plays must go to guitarist Breau. As he did when Toronto reedman Moe Koffman played here Breau quite unintentionally took the play away from the featured artist Appleyard."[5]

The club shut down shortly after this gig—a closure that coincided with the denouement of Lenny's marriage. Valerie had already given Lenny several ultimatums about his drug use when one day a package decorated with hand-drawn flowers arrived for Lenny in the mail. Her instincts alerted, she opened the package and discovered that it contained hashish. "That night Lenny came home and I said 'I thought you were finished with this,'" says Valerie. "Lenny started really crying. I said, 'Goodbye. I can't do this anymore. I can't keep on pretending. It's over.' At that point, I told him to leave and he moved out of the house." Lenny left his family and moved in with his friends Maggie and Barrie Tallman, with whom he would stay for the next several months.

Lenny and Valerie were legally separated on April 22, 1966. Lenny was distraught over the separation but evidently felt relieved to be free of domestic pressures. "I got married too soon," he told writer David Baines in 1973. "I couldn't worry about home and the guitar at the same time."[6] The couple continued to be close friends, even after difficult divorce proceedings five years later, and Lenny maintained a close relationship with Chet and Melody until his death.

Lenny was by now one of the city's most popular musicians, largely through his ubiquitous presence on CBC radio and TV. It seemed natural enough that when the network wanted a personality around which to build a six-week summer replacement music show with "youth appeal," the twenty-four-year-old guitarist's name would come up. "The concept for the *Lenny Breau Show* was my idea," Ray McConnell says. "[CBC administration] said to me, 'Look, we've got six weeks to fill late evening. Can you bring us in a show for those six weeks?' And because I'd been working with Lenny and Bob [McMullin], I wanted to build a show around them and take advantage of Lenny's jazz playing."

When the idea was put to Lenny, McConnell says, he instantly agreed to host the show that was to air nationally on Fridays beginning on August 12, 1966. Among the musicians backing Lenny on the show were Reg Kelln and Ron Halldorson who had just returned to Winnipeg after a year of working with a country band in Toronto. Once again the Lenny Breau Trio had a national audience, although Lenny's rhythm section was rarely shown on camera. Winnipeg singer Yvette Shaw was the first of three young female vocalists McConnell hired for the show. The other two singers—Karen Marklinger and Judi Singh—were brought in from Edmonton to provide fresh faces for CBC Winnipeg audiences. Marklinger had worked

for a few years in Edmonton's clubs and on CBC radio, as had Judi
Singh, an eighteen-year-old, Afro/Indo-Canadian with a rich, sultry
voice. The women arrived in the city in midsummer to begin rehearsals for the show, both excited to be working with Lenny.

McConnell wanted *The Lenny Breau Show* to feature music
exclusively with no dialogue. This was an unusual format but an
ideal one for Lenny, who—because of his stutter—was not eager to
be called on to speak on camera. "Lenny always seemed to me to be
at ease on camera, always at ease playing" says Marklinger. "But he
didn't speak much nor would he have wanted to at the time. His personality didn't really come across on camera. It didn't for any of us.
We were all very young and just developing presence."

McConnell says that the show's cast chose the material, but
Marklinger refutes this. "We were given the songs and had to learn
them even though we didn't want to do some of them," she says,
referring to tunes like Petula Clark's "Downtown," which the singers
performed with obvious distaste on the opening show. "We didn't
have a lot of say. Even Lenny was basically told what to play. Not
how to play but what to play. He got to suggest a few songs for the
show and did a few things that he would do in clubs. But by and
large, we were all relegated to what was picked by the producer."

Still, the jazz content on *The Lenny Breau Show* was high. Lenny
and his off-camera band would play a few standards on every show
and always romp through an up-tempo jazz/blues instrumental or
two. Lenny also played solo instrumentals—a flamenco piece or an
arrangement of a pop tune like the Beatles' "Yesterday"—and would
usually do a duet with one of the women. Various guests dropped by
to perform including Moe Koffman who signed off one show dueting with Lenny on a seven-minute-long jazz rendering of "The Bat-
man Theme."

Just before the series got under way, Lenny's Gibson ES-125 was
stolen at a gig and he went to see his old friend Eddie Laham, then
manager of Croft Music, to see about replacing it. Laham had no
Gibson ES-125s in the store and suggested that Lenny try the new
Baldwin guitars that Croft's had recently begun carrying. Baldwin
guitars, originally built in England, had just started to make inroads
into the North American guitar market which Fender and Gibson
dominated. When Lenny showed some interest in a couple of Baldwin

instruments, Laham convinced the store's owner to arrange an endorsement deal for Lenny. This was the beginning of Lenny's five-year association with Baldwin, during which time the company supplied him with a few guitars—both electric and classical—and possibly dozens of amplifiers, which Lenny had a knack for losing or leaving behind in clubs. Lenny's first Baldwin was an electric/acoustic Virginian model with a built-in pickup—hardly a standard jazz instrument—which he used on his show. A few months later, he replaced this with a Baldwin Vibraslim model, the guitar that he would use on his first two albums and in hundreds of sessions in Winnipeg and Toronto between 1967 and 1972. Lenny's new Baldwin Vibraslim had a very different sound from the Gibson ES-125s he had been playing for the past several years. The Gibsons were true hollow body instruments, characterized in part by their rapid note decay. The Baldwin was a semi-hollow body; that is, while the body appeared to be completely hollow, it had a large piece of wood running down the center of the interior of its body. This extra wood mass considerably enhanced the guitar's sustain. In tandem with Lenny's amp settings, the Vibraslim's rich sustain allowed his lush chords to hang in the air like sonic clouds and his melody lines to ring on while he changed chords beneath them. The latter reinforced the impression of separation between simultaneously played chords and melody that Lenny had worked so hard to achieve. The broad, spacious tone of his guitar now recalled at times a piano with its sustain pedal pressed to the floor. This would become a sonic fingerprint of Lenny's sound and for the rest of his life, he would choose his guitars, mainly solid body instruments, largely for their sustaining capabilities.

The Lenny Breau Show received high ratings during its six-week run and there was talk of turning it into a regular season program. This did not come about, but the show was in many ways a great success for Lenny. He had proven that he could step out of a sideman's role and into the limelight on a major television program and win over his audience solely with music rather than the skits and dialogue that most hosts used to engage their audiences. Lenny enjoyed the experience but, Judi Singh says, the success of the show didn't put stars in his eyes. "I'm sure he'd been happy to do the show but he wasn't concerned with the idea of making it," she says. "He was just too engrossed and preoccupied with music to worry about things like that. He didn't view it as 'Oh, I'm getting my name out there, I'm famous.' He was not concerned about those kinds of things, not at all."

By this time Judi Singh was close enough to Lenny to divine his feelings with some confidence. There had been a strong mutual attraction between the two from their first meeting, and by the time the series ended, they had developed an intimate relationship. "Just like every other female I found him very cute," Judi laughs:

> There were always women around him wanting to protect him and save him, but I didn't want to mother him. He was just this great, wonderful personality that I was attracted to because he seemed so free in his own right. Lenny had the guts to play what he wanted to play. He always played from the heart and he never pretended anything when he was playing, never tried to impress. He didn't buy into the bullshit. There was just total honesty all the time and that was why he was so special. Didn't matter who was around, he was continually himself. He didn't know how to do anything else or be anything else. That's one of the reasons I loved him so much: he was always, always true.

The couple began living together that fall in an apartment in the St. Boniface area of Winnipeg, and spent most days working separately and together on various CBC TV and radio sessions. On days off, they often visited Winnipeg's art galleries where Lenny, now sporting a beret in the manner of a dapper Parisian, would indulge his growing passion for French Impressionist painting. "He was very into Monet," says Singh. "He liked that very soft, watery impressionistic painting very, very much and he was very visual in his playing. It was about playing different feelings as opposed to the music itself: the instrument becomes a paint brush." Over the next decade this notion of "painting with sound" would come to preoccupy Lenny more and more.

Lenny and Judi worked together occasionally in coffee houses and clubs around Winnipeg, sometimes with Halldorson and Kelln. "Lenny was a great accompanist, always very supportive and knew how to lead singers into singing something that would surprise them," Singh says. "He'd play a line that would suggest something or play softer or play something different time-wise. Subtle things, but at the same time giving the singer a lot of space. He never tried to upstage a singer. He knew what singing was about and understood the mechanics of singing. He was very aware of phrasing and time. Together we did things like 'Shadow of Your Smile' and 'Once Upon a Summer Time,' and 'A Taste of Honey.' We did that tune a lot."

Many nights, the pair would stay at home and listen to records while Lenny provided insightful commentary. "He'd say, 'Do you hear that?' and point out all these things in the music," Singh recalls. "He would teach me lines that I would scat but outside of ordinary scatting. He would play different chord changes and then he would play me scales that worked with those chord changes. Then he would say 'OK, if I change this note in the chord that means that you can sing this scale.' He was trying to develop my ear, and it worked. If we were listening to Indian music, he would sing the scale to me and say, 'Can you hear this? Can you hear that?' He was born an artist and spent his whole life in that space. That's where he lived and that's what he talked about, not politics or things that other people would talk about. At the same time he was extremely liberal, liberated, and very just and kind; always willing to share his art. I was really lucky to have had that."

Singh was also lucky enough to hear Lenny's best-known composition at the moment of its conception. One morning, she woke just before dawn to hear Lenny singing softly over a minor chord progression underpinned with a slow bossa nova beat. Occasionally he would stop, as he searched for a voicing or worked out a cascade of chordal harmonics. Intrigued, Singh got out of bed to ask Lenny what he was playing. "He told me he couldn't sleep and was woken by the bells of St. Boniface Cathedral and was trying to write a song using the sound of the bells," she recalls. The piece was his poignant "Five O'clock Bells," which ends with a coda evoking the tolling of church bells. The tune became a staple of Lenny's repertoire, and would provide the title of his "comeback album" in 1978.

Buddy Spicher and Lenny had kept in intermittent touch over the years, and when Spicher came to town as part of country singer Kitty Wells's band in the winter of 1966, he called Lenny and invited him to the show. Barrie Tallman accompanied Lenny and says that Wells, a colleague of Lenny's parents in Wheeling, invited Lenny on stage to play a few songs with her, to the great delight of the audience. Afterwards, Tallman and Lenny went back to the band's motel where Lenny jammed with Wells's guitarist, Paul Yandell, who worked often as back-up guitarist for Chet Atkins. Yandell was astonished by Lenny's playing and the two guitarists became friends during the band's weeklong stay in Winnipeg, drawn together as much by their shared love of fingerstyle guitar as their mutual admiration of Chet Atkins. "Lenny was the greatest," Yandell says, "after Chet, of course." One night Lenny dropped by Yandell's room with a demo tape for Yandell. "At that time, he'd had his own CBC television show," says Yandell, "and he gave me a tape of a recording of that show. He said 'Could you take this down to Nashville and give it to Chet, so I might get a record deal?' I said, 'Sure, OK.'" This is an anomalous example of Lenny acting in a practical, self-promotional mode and his action would result in some life-changing consequences within the next year.

On New Year's Eve of 1966, Lenny was in Toronto to do a CBC variety television show called *In Person*. Performing on his Ramirez, Lenny played an original flamenco/jazz fantasy that was a mixture of Spanish sounding arpeggios, jazz runs, and quartal harmony with an occasional quote from the Miles Davis tune "Milestones." The piece is clearly an early version of "Taranta," which Lenny would record on his first album eighteen months later. A drummer and bassist joined Lenny as the piece segued into the Toots Thielmans jazz waltz, "Bluesette." The version here is similar to the one he would play on his 1969 album, *The Velvet Touch of Lenny Breau. Live!*, although with less improvisational development and no extended single note line solos. It's a wonderful performance, and an early glimpse of the unique, complex style that Lenny would soon unveil on his first two RCA albums.

Music Hop was now in its last season, and had become so rock and pop oriented that Lenny bought a wah-wah pedal—the only effects box he would ever own—to reproduce the solos on the contemporary rock tunes the show featured. Lenny no longer harbored the antipathy towards rock music that he once had and admired the Beatles, Jimi Hendrix, and Eric Clapton among others. Still, he was beginning to find the Top Forty musical content of *Music Hop* something of a grind, says vocalist Chad Allan, who had joined the show's cast after a stint as lead singer for The Guess Who.

> He was floating there in jazz land and *Music Hop* was very pop-oriented. Hate is too strong a word but Lenny didn't like most pop music or rock and roll. We'd do the show and when we were finished taping a particular song and on a break, the guys would start jamming on a jazz tune. You could tell that Lenny was thinking "Okay, we've done the pop stuff now, let's do the real thing." He'd start playing these fast jazz riffs and say, "Like, what do you think of this?" Then the floor director would say, "OK, We're ready to tape," and everybody would go into the pop mode and we'd play "Everyone Knows It's Wendy" [*sic*].[7] I remember thinking this must be torture for Lenny, absolute torture. He didn't say it in so many words but you could tell. But he was getting paid quite well and at least he was doing music. I know he had a good time playing with us but you could tell this was not where his heart was. Not so much against the label "pop music," but just its lack of creativity.

Lenny's dwindling interest in *Music Hop* was also becoming obvious to Ray St. Germain. For three years, preparation for the show had followed the same schedule, St. Germain says: rehearsal on Wednesday with taping for the following week's show done on Thursday. One week during the third season, Lenny made the Wednesday night rehearsal, but failed to show up the next day. Panicked, St. Germain called him at his apartment. "I said, 'Lenny, what are you doing at home?' and he said, 'Well, like I'm practicing, man.' I said, 'Yeah, but today's Thursday. What have we been doing for the last three years every Thursday?' [He answered], 'Uh, I dunno.' I said, 'We've been doing *Music Hop*!' He said, 'Oh yeah, oh, it's today?' I said, 'We just rehearsed yesterday like we've done for three years, followed by the taping of *Music Hop*.' He'd completely forgotten, just completely wrapped up in one of those all-day practice things he got into. So we sent a cab for him.[8]

As he grew increasingly frustrated with the studio scene and its lack of jazz opportunity, Lenny began subbing out his scheduled CBC sessions to other players. Ron Halldorson took many of these dates and bassist Bob Jackson, who also played guitar, recalls that Lenny asked him to fill in at the last moment on ten of thirteen Jose Poneira shows. But it wasn't just the studio scene that was holding Lenny back from playing jazz. Since the Jazz A Go-Go had gone under, Winnipeg no longer had any serious jazz clubs where he could try out his ideas on the bandstand. He sat in with bands at supper and dance clubs around town, but his playing would often perplex audience and musicians alike. "He'd drop by and play a few tunes, but he'd lose us completely," says Jackson, who fronted a dance band at a Winnipeg supper club. "We had to stop asking him to sit in because the people would get mad. They couldn't dance to what he was trying to do, you know. He'd get into some far-out thing and people would say 'C'mon! Play "Yellow Bird!"' And he'd say, 'I am playing "Yellow Bird"!' Didn't sound like 'Yellow Bird.' It was apparent by then he didn't know what kind of job he was on. Unless it was a jazz job, he didn't fit in. This was strictly a commercial job, but he didn't seem to realize that. It was strange, especially for a kid coming from country roots. It wasn't attitude. He didn't mean to be mean. He'd just sit down and get carried away."

Lenny's confusion about the type of gig he was on may also have been exacerbated by the same substances that had contributed to the end of his marriage. He was now taking daily doses of LSD and smoking pot regularly in an attempt to alleviate the pressures that were mounting in his life, as he told writer James Marck.[9] "I had a lot of emotional problems during those times—my marriage, money—those kinds of things that are hard to deal with—and I looked on the various drugs that I was using as being almost a therapeutic thing—I'd use them to ease my mind so I could play. I didn't take drugs because I thought they made me play better but because they made me feel better." His LSD use was constant, as he later explained to journalist Bart Testa, and not relegated to after hours recreation. "I took acid every day but it didn't show in my playing. I was hiding it, in fact, and doing TV shows—the CBC, serious music shows where I played Bach. But I was out to lunch."[10]

"Out to lunch" or not, Lenny continued to play a few CBC Winnipeg shows until he left the city in 1968, and would later do infrequent radio and television sessions in Toronto. However, his career as a full-time studio musician effectively ended in the late spring of

1967 when CBC cancelled *Music Hop*. For Lenny, this was a release and a relief as he explained to Brawner Smoot several years later. "I eventually learned that those things [CBC studio sessions] really weren't what I wanted to do by doing them. . . . Studio work took up too much time. While it paid good money, I wasn't playing my own music. It was like I was always under the gun to play something. Since my reading wasn't that good, I was always nervous. I always had a pain in my neck."[11]

His days as a session musician were not quite finished, however. On a trip to Edmonton in 1967, Lenny agreed to play on a record with a country singer named Hank Smith. Lenny had been trying out guitars at Smith's music store when Smith mentioned that he was doing a country album for Point Records, a subsidiary of Decca. Lenny volunteered to play on the record, but Smith balked, explaining that he didn't have the budget to pay him properly. Lenny, never one to let low pay stand in the way of an interesting gig, offered to do the session for a hundred dollars and the next day recorded half a dozen tunes with Smith for an album called *Ten Golden Years of Country*. Hal Lone Pine would have been proud of Lenny's playing on the album. Except for one altered dominant chord that Lenny used tastefully on a cadence in "He'll Have to Go," there isn't a jazz lick in sight. On "Oh Lonesome Me," Lenny reels off a solo lifted note for note from Don Gibson's original recording of the tune. When the session wrapped up, Lenny promised to return the next day to record tunes for the second half of the album, but failed to show up, says Smith. "That was him; dependability was not his forte. He was the greatest guitarist in the world but the most undependable businessman."

Lenny was now exploring a musical style far removed from that he had played with Smith. It's not clear when Lenny first heard Indian music, but Don Francks recalls that he was already familiar with the realm of ragas and tablas by the time he came to Toronto in 1962. By the mid-sixties, Lenny—like many young jazz musicians of the time—was trying to bring Eastern musical influences into his playing, although as Wayne Finucan explains, it was more the spirit of the music than its letter that intrigued Lenny. "We listened to a lot of Ravi Shankar," says Wayne Finucan. "Lenny was trying to get these feelings and these emotional phrases in there, to get the passion that he heard in it. But he never really copied riffs or licks from Eastern music. It was more about capturing the feeling of it. I don't know if it was a spiritual thing with him but it fed him. It inspired him." A *Winnipeg Free Press* column in the fall of 1967 briefly noted the newest chapter in Lenny's relationship with Indian music: "Lenny Breau, Winnipeg's guitarist for all seasons, has purchased his first sitar and is woodshedding his picking fingers to the bone to be ready to at least present one sitar selection at his Oct. 17 noon concert at the Mezzanine Theatre."[12] How well Lenny fared with his "sitar selection" is unknown but in one 1967 CBC session he demonstrated that he was no real threat to Ravi Shankar.[13] On this four-minute, multi-tracked piece Lenny strummed modal sounding melodic fragments on the principal and sympathetic strings of the sitar over top of his own twelve-string guitar work. The result has little to do with Indian classical music and is more of an interesting wash of sound that evokes a dark, mystical mood. Lenny experimented with his sitar for the next few years but played it only rarely and never really advanced on it. Considering his love of harmony and voice leading, it's little wonder that the sitar—essentially a melodic, single note instrument—would not hold his interest long. However, during the late sixties in particular, Indian modal phrases popped up regularly in Lenny's music, particularly in his more free form playing.

After returning to Nashville, Paul Yandell had been true to his word and turned over Lenny's tape to Chet Atkins. In an interview many years later, Atkins recalled hearing the tape for the first time.

> It was the freshest, most exciting thing I had heard in years. . . . So I said, "Who is this guy," and Paul kept telling me, "Lenny Breau," and then I happened to remember I used to work with his mother and daddy. We did a tour once with Hal Pine and Betty Cody [RCA Caravan, 1954] and their last name was Breau. They used to tell me about their son, Lenny, who was eleven years old [Lenny was twelve at the time] and could play so great. [After hearing the tape] I was highly impressed. I'd never heard such great technique in so many different areas of music. You know, he played great flamenco guitar also in those days and then he played electric and he had taken the harmonics that I had kind of developed, he had taken

them so much further than I ever had and was doing things that I never dreamed of. It was one of the greatest days of my life, the first day I heard Lenny.[14]

It would also turn out to be a great day for Lenny, whose tape had won him the advocacy of one of the most powerful men in the music business. Not only had Atkins's records sold millions of copies and garnered countless industry awards (including a few Grammys), as a talent scout and producer for RCA in the '50s and '60s, Atkins had discovered and/or produced some of country music's biggest stars including Waylon Jennings, Willie Nelson, and Don Gibson. In 1968, when Atkins became vice president of RCA Records, he had already been for many years the most powerful force in shaping Nashville's music scene and country music in general as well as a major figure in the North American record industry. Yet, while Atkins approached his career with great professional commitment and focused ambition, he was also a kind, empathetic man known for his personal warmth and generosity. A benevolent patron to talented young musicians, he often bucked commercial odds to sign musicians like Jerry Reed and Argentinean classical guitarist Jorge Morel who had been rejected by other labels because of their apparent lack of marketability. Although Atkins was aware that a jazz guitarist, especially one with Lenny's idiosyncratic style, was not likely to garner a wall full of gold records for RCA, he was, says Yandell, ready to sign him to a recording contract immediately upon hearing Lenny's tape. Finding Lenny, however, was no simple matter. He had been floating between addresses when he met Yandell, and Atkins did not have the number for the apartment that he now shared with Judi Singh. It would take a fortuitous coincidence set in motion by an intermediary to bring the two men together.

Winnipeg broadcaster Lee Major had been a friend and admirer of Lenny's since coming to CBC Winnipeg in the early sixties. In the fall of 1967, CBC brass asked Major to do a feature on Nashville, focusing on the city's International Music Disc Jockey Convention. On a whim, Major asked Lenny if he'd like to go along for the ride and attend the convention with him in the guise of a CBC music librarian. Lenny was interested, but said he would have to meet

Major in Nashville a day late due to a CBC gig he was scheduled to work. Major agreed and arranged to pick Lenny up at the airport the following Friday.

A few days before the trip, it occurred to Major that an interview with Chet Atkins would fit well into his piece on Nashville, and he called Atkins to see about setting up a meeting with him. Atkins rarely granted interviews and initially balked at Major's request. However, a light went on when he realized that as a CBC Winnipeg employee Major might be acquainted with Lenny Breau. When he brought up the subject, he was shocked to learn that not only did Major know Lenny, but was bringing him to Nashville within the week. "Chet went, 'Phfft! You get him down here and bring him to this office as soon as he gets here. I want to meet him,' Major recalls. "Chet said, 'If you bring Lenny, I'll give you an exclusive interview.' I said 'OK.' It was sort of like blackmail, but I'll never forget the look on Lenny's face when I told him that he was going to meet Chet Atkins. His jaw dropped and his eyes flew wide open."

Major left for Nashville on Oct. 5, 1967. The following day, he went to pick Lenny up at the Nashville Airport, but found that he'd missed his flight. Major, surmising that Lenny had simply forgotten about the trip, returned to his work at the convention center. Several hours later, however, he bumped into Lenny, who had arrived on a later flight and found his way into the city. Major hustled him into a cab and made for Atkins's Music Row office where he witnessed the meeting between Lenny and the man who would become one of the most important figures in his life.

> Chet and Lenny just smiled and hugged each other. Lenny was in tears because he was meeting his idol. They immediately sat on the floor and started playing guitar. Lenny started picking away and Chet said, "Hey, man. I've never heard that before." Lenny says, "Well, li-li-li-like, I got it from one of your records." Chet said, "I used another guitar player for half of the lick that you're playing." He just flipped out. Now Lenny is sitting there teaching Chet what he just did. And then they went back and forth swapping notes and this went on for about an hour and a half. There was a sitar on the wall that Ravi Shankar had given Chet and Lenny says, "Can I play it?" Chet took it down and Lenny started plunking away. At that

point, Chet says, "Where are you staying?" And Lenny says, "I'm not staying anywhere. I haven't checked in yet." So Chet says, "You're staying with me at my house." I got my interview with Chet and said goodbye but Lenny stayed on with Chet.

This happy meeting was the first scene in a relationship that would change the lives of both men. The stable, straightlaced, and generous older man would become the empathetic, accepting father to Lenny Breau that Hal Lone Pine had not been. Motivated by a deep affection and respect for Lenny, Atkins did all he could to guide Lenny professionally and personally. For his part, Lenny adored Atkins and turned to him often for support and advice that—while dispensed freely and unconditionally—was seldom heeded.

The men spent a few weeks together jamming and picking one another's brains, although in truth, Atkins had little to show Lenny at this point. It's likely more than a coincidence that Atkins's album *Solo Flight*, recorded a month after his first meeting Lenny, includes two pieces—"Mercy, Mercy, Mercy" by Joe Zawinul and the pop hit, "Music to Watch Girls By"—that had been part of Lenny's repertoire for the past year or more. Atkins's arrangement of the latter bore little resemblance to the version Lenny recorded on his first album, but his arrangement of "Mercy, Mercy, Mercy" is too close to Lenny's to be accidental, although Atkins eschewed the improvisational twists and turns that characterized Lenny's rendering of the tune. Lenny's influence is also heard on Atkins's version of "When You Wish Upon a Star," an arrangement built on a complex intertwining of slurs with chordal harmonics, a technique that is straight out of Lenny's bag of tricks. Atkins was always candid about borrowing ideas from Lenny and pleased to give credit to a guitarist who had in essence been his student for decades. He told Lee Major a few months after meeting Lenny, "Yeah, he plays a lot of my licks, but he's modern with them. I'm kind of old fashioned and square, you know. But he plays the harmonics that I do. I originated that but he does it a lot better than I did."[15] It was a classic case of student surpassing master and Atkins, proud to be the inspiration behind so much of what Lenny had accomplished, graciously accepted this.

During Lenny's stay in Nashville, Atkins offered him a recording contract and was mystified when Lenny turned him down. Ron

Halldorson, however, was not surprised by Lenny's reluctance to sign with Atkins and RCA.

> For quite awhile we'd talked about doing his first album and then he said, "Chet wants me to come down and do an album, but I don't feel ready." Lenny had this vision of the guitar trio and the guitar techniques that he was working on that were more pianistic. That was all being developed. He didn't want to record until he had that up to a certain level, though the level he had it to by 1962 was something that most of us would hope to get to in a lifetime. Also, there was some thought in Lenny's mind about whether he should record with Chet or whether he should get a contract with some jazz label like Verve or Blue Note so that he could place himself in the jazz spectrum. He was concerned that it wasn't too cool to do this album in a country environment and have it put it out by Chet who wasn't really known as any kind of jazz freak.

Atkins was not easily put off, however. During November and early December, he continued to talk with Lenny and a few weeks before Christmas, Ron Halldorson got a phone call from his old friend who was now singing a very different tune. "Lenny said, 'Chet wants me to come down and do an album and I'm ready. I'm finally ready,'" Halldorson recalls. "He'd decided it was OK to record with Chet because he didn't really want to be lumped in with all the other jazz guitar players." Lenny explained that Atkins had agreed to let him use a rhythm section of his own choosing on the date, and he had naturally decided on Bob Erlendson, Reg Kelln, and Ron Halldorson. Atkins gave the nod to Kelln and Halldorson but nixed Erlendson's participation in the session for fear that a keyboard would conflict with Lenny's pianistic guitar style. Lenny may have been disappointed that Bob was left off the session but considering that he would be recording with two of his closest friends under the guidance of a man he had idolized since childhood, there was little that could significantly dampen his spirits.

The recording session was scheduled for late April of the following year and Nashville would loom large in Lenny's thoughts during the intervening months. But another city lay in his more immediate future. Lenny had left Toronto five years earlier with a sense of failure and defeat, rebuffed—as he saw it—by a city that had promised much and delivered little. But time had dulled the sting of Lenny's first disappointing experience there and when an opportunity to return to the city presented itself in early 1968, he felt ready to take it. This time, Toronto would swing its doors open wide in welcome as Lenny blithely entered a period of his life that he would forever remember as his halcyon days.

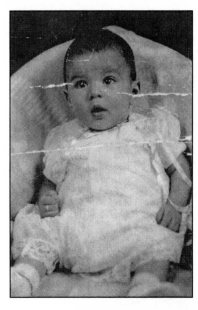

Above: Lenny Breau's christening photo, Auburn, Maine. *Courtesy of Valerie Breau-St. Germain.*

Below: Promotional photo with parents, Auburn, Maine, 1946. *From the author's collection.*

"Lone Pine" & Betty Cody
& "Lone Pine Jr."
1946

Above: Promotional photo at age 15.
Courtesy of Al Hawkes.

Below: With Joey Hollingsworth, 1962.
Courtesy Valerie Breau-St. Germain.

three   don francks
             lenny breau
             eon henstridge

Promotional photo of "three," 1962. *Courtesy George Sukornyk.*

Event Records. *Courtesy of Al Hawkes.*

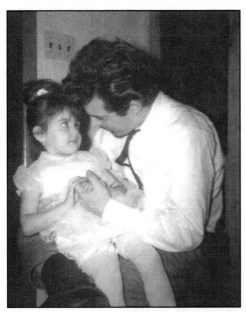

Above: With daughter Melody, 1963. *Courtesy Valerie Breau-St. Germain.*

Below: With Reg Kelln at the Establishment, Winnipeg, 1965. *Courtesy Archives and Special Collections—University of Manitoba.*

With Ron Park, Jerry
Fuller, and Don Thompson.
(The Ron Park Quartet at
George's Spaghetti House,
June 25, 1969).
Courtesy Mark Cohen.

With Bill Evans at Town Tavern, Toronto, March 29, 1971.
Photo by Barrie Tallman. Courtesy Maggie Tallman.

At Jazz A Go-Go with Bob Erlendson, Pete Thompson, Barrie Tallman, and Reg Kelln, Winnipeg, 1966. *Courtesy Archives and Special Collections—University of Manitoba.*

With No Tomatoes owner Peter Balis, Auburn, Maine, 1978. *Courtesy Peter Balis.*

At Donte's, Los Angeles, 1979. *Courtesy Valerie Breau-St. Germain.*

With Tal Farlow, Sea Bright, New Jersey, 1980. *Courtesy Lorenzo DeStefano.*

Above: Trying out Kirk Sand's
7/10 template, Laguna Beach,
California, 1984.
Courtesy Kirk Sand.

Below: Jewel in album photo.

Rooftop pool at Langham
Apartments.
Courtesy Brian Berge.

Langham Apartments
from the street.
Courtesy Brian Berge.

Guitar star found dead

BREAU'S STORMY LIFE ENDS IN L.A. SWIMMING POOL

By JOHN CRUST
Sun Staff Writer

Lenny Breau, the star jazz guitarist who got his start on Winnipeg radio and in city night clubs, died on the weekend. He was 43.

Breau, who celebrated his birthday on Aug. 5, was found at the bottom of his apartment block's swimming pool in central Los Angeles.

Bob Dambacher, of the Los Angeles County coroner's office, said Breau was pronounced dead at 11:10 a.m. Sunday. Although it appeared Breau drowned, Dambacher said the cause of death is pending further investigations which could take "a couple weeks."

Breau's wife, Jewell, said her husband was drinking Saturday night. But she said he slept it off and was working on his music by the swimming pool when she left the apartment that morning.

Betty Cody, Breau's mother living in Maine, said she received a telephone call from her son early that morning before he died. She said he sounded depressed.

Breau's sudden death shocked his peers and fans in Winnipeg and across the continent yesterday

"I still can't believe it," said Winnipeg musician Ray St. Germain, who grew up with Breau and performed with him. "The musicians in Winnipeg are in a real shock. He could play anything. He was the most respected guitarist."

Renowned Nashville guitarist Chet Atkins dubbed Breau as "the greatest guitar player in the world."

"Almost all the guitar players I meet ask me about my association with Lenny," said city musician Ron Halldorson, who with fellow city drummer Reg Kelin played with Breau in the 60s and recorded two albums together.

"He was an underground hero. He wasn't a household name. But in the guitar world he was very well known."

St. Germain, whose sister Val was Breau's first wife, said Breau was working on a new album and performing at Los Angeles night clubs.

"His music's going to be missed, his playing is going to be missed, he's going to be missed," said Carey Leverette, who last night had to find an alternate performer at his North Hollywood night club, Donte's, to replace Breau. Breau had been at the club every Monday night since January.

Breau was born in Auburn, Maine, to country-and-western performers Cody and the late Hal Lone Pine. The eldest of four sons, he took up the guitar at 8, and joined the family act as "Lone Pine Junior, the Guitar Wizard."

In 1957 they settled in Winnipeg to become regulars on CKY radio's Caravan, a country-and-western show.

Breau's family soon moved on, but he stayed in Winnipeg where he performed at long-gone city night spots as the old Stage Door on Fort Street, the Royal Alexandra Hotel and the Cafe Jazz A Go Go.

Despite his greatness, however, in the late 60s and early 70s he was addicted to heroin. The addiction lasted 12 years. In 1972 he was granted a two-year conditional discharge in a Winnipeg court for a charge of possession of heroin. In 1978 he came out of a drug rehabilitation program free of drugs.

Breau's first wife, Val Breau St. Germain, and their two children — Chet, 22, and Melody, 21 — still live in Winnipeg. She and the legendary guitarist was a special person.

"We met when we were both 16," she said. "We grew up together. We loved each other very much.

"He left behind his beautiful music for the whole world to enjoy. Lenny was a very tender, very loving person. He loved everyone he met."

She said a memorial service is scheduled at 1 p.m. on Friday at the Holy Rosary Church Parish at 510 River Ave.

Guitar wizard Lenny Breau got his start in Winnipeg.

Winnipeg Sun clipping, August 14, 1984.

Jazz guitarist Lenny Breau, found dead in a pool Sunday, died from injuries consistent with strangulation.

Guitarist's death not an accident

Autopsy indicates jazz great Breau was murdered

By Nicole Yorkin
Herald staff writer

Jazz guitarist Lenny Breau, who was first thought to have drowned accidentally in his apartment house pool Sunday, was murdered, police said yesterday.

Results of an autopsy performed Monday on the 43-year-old guitarist showed the cause of death as "asphyxia caused by compression of, or to, the neck," according to Bill Gold, county coroner's spokesman.

He said Breau's body had "certain injuries about the neck ... consistent with those found in strangulation."

Breau, a musician whose unique, melodic style won the acclaim of jazz guitarists everywhere, was found floating in the pool early Sunday by a tenant of the apartment in the mid-Wilshire district, said Detective Larry Bird of the Los Angeles Police Department's major crimes division.

Originally, Bird said, the death was believed to be a drowning. According to Detective Richard Aldahl, authorities later received some "independent information" that caused them to return to the apartment complex Monday for further investigation.

"Then, we received the information from the coroner's office and knew, in fact, that we had a homicide and not an independent drowning," he said.

Authorities yesterday would not say if Breau had been strangled — or had died — before entering the pool, but early reports on the death said Breau had been dead for about an hour before his body was discovered.

Police have no suspects yet in the murder, but Bird said the victim's neighbors have been "very helpful."

The news that Breau, a Maine native who had been living in Los Angeles for the past year, had been murdered came as a surprise yesterday to those who had known and played with him over the years.

"I just got the news that he was strangled and it really shocked me. I was overwhelmed," said guitarist Louis Lee II, a friend and student of Breau's. "Lennie was a very good friend of mine and I loved him. I know justice will prevail.

"He was a great individual ... a quiet man totally devoted to his music," said Carey Leverette, owner of Donte's, a jazz club in North Hollywood where Breau was featured every Monday. "He was really an experience to hear ... but as a person he was troubled."

Police yesterday would not comment on whether the guitarist had any known enemies or had been involved in any disputes before his death. Police did say that Breau was not performing the night before he was murdered.

"The investigation is definitely progressing," Bird said, "but we can't give any information out as to which way its leading. We're hopeful we'll come to some conclusion soon."

A memorial benefit to raise money for Breau's wife Jewel and 3-year-old daughter Dawn Rose Marie will be held Monday at Donte's. The benefit will feature such jazz greats as guitarists Joe Pass and Herb Ellis, vibraphonist Red Norvo and drummer Shelly Mann, Leverette said.

Portland Herald clipping, August 15, 1984.

Days of Wine and Roses
January 1968–September 1972

*"Here's a jazz ballad that I've been playin' for quite a few years.
It brings back old memories of when I was living in Toronto and
everything was, like rosy. And it was, like, all wine. And roses."*
—Lenny Breau introducing "Days of Wine and Roses" in 1976

Judi Singh, long restless with Winnipeg, moved to Toronto in late 1967 on the understanding that Lenny would soon follow. Lenny had made several trips to the city during the past two years but because of his past experiences there had qualms about relocating permanently to Toronto without promise of steady work. These concerns were assuaged when on a trip to Toronto in the late fall of 1967, he met Doug Riley, an arranger, composer, and brilliant pianist and Hammond B3 organ player. Riley had produced a number of major acts including Ray Charles, and ran his own music company that specialized in arranging and recording music for commercials, jingles, and films. When he met Lenny, Riley had just begun working with Malka Himmell, who for many years had been one-half of Joso and Malka, a popular international folk music duo with several albums to their credit. In late 1967, the Israeli-born singer split from Joso and asked Riley to work with her in a folk act updated with contemporary, popular material. "I could have done it," says Riley, "but I was totally busy doing a million different things. So I picked Lenny because he was like an orchestra. He could do anything and play any style. It was a great opportunity to get him to move to Toronto so we called him in Winnipeg, and he said he was into it and came out."

On January 12, 1968, Lenny did a CBC Radio broadcast from the University of Winnipeg with Halldorson, Kelln, and Karen Marklinger, and then flew to Toronto to rehearse with Himmell for a club date in Montreal on January 24. According to *The Winnipeg Free Press*, a number of high profile dates were to follow.

> Lenny Breau, the finest guitarist this city has ever produced, has temporarily joined Malka, the singer who has parted company with Joso to go solo in show business. Malka calls Lenny "an artist" and offers are already flowing in for the pair including one major booking from the Sheraton chain in New York.[1]

Malka, who remembers Lenny as "a wonderful man and musician who could play anything by ear," says that these bookings never materialized and the duo split a month after its inception.

However short-lived, the act had served to bring Lenny to Toronto. He and Judi stayed with Bob Erlendson and his wife Jackie for a time before moving into an apartment in a Toronto neighborhood known as The Annex. This funky, older residential area abuts both the campus of the University of Toronto and Toronto's Yorkville district, then the center of the city's music scene. Lenny had become familiar with Yorkville during his first stay in Toronto and had worked there often at various music establishments. But in the intervening years, Yorkville had changed from an area frequented mainly by artists, writers, and jazz musicians into the hip nucleus of Toronto's youth culture and nightlife. By 1968, the area was rife with folk and jazz clubs that included the legendary coffee house, The River Boat, where Neil Young, Joni Mitchell, and many others played in the early part of their careers. Lenny would perform often in these clubs over the next two years, perfecting the style on which he'd worked so long and, in the company of other young, brilliant players, pushing the parameters of his music in an atmosphere supportive of experimentation and originality.

Not long after returning to Toronto, Lenny reconnected with Don Francks. The singer/actor's career had taken off since the mid-sixties and he was in town visiting from England during a break in the filming of *Finian's Rainbow*, in which he had a major role. The two men had kept in touch since the break-up of "three," but had seen each other only rarely in the intervening years, a period during which Lenny had changed very little, says Francks. "Lenny was still right on the money," he says. "He felt like Lenny to me: quite the same, just the same plain brilliant as ever." After jamming together a few times, the two men decided to reprise "three" using Dave Young (a Toronto resident since 1966) on bass to replace Eon Henstridge who had committed suicide the year before. The trio began a week-long booking on January 31 at the Castle George, a jazz room above George's Spaghetti House. The audience responded enthusiastically to "three's" mix of new and old material, but not everybody was impressed. The next day in a *Toronto Star* review titled, "Franks [*sic*]: His Super-Hipster Bag Obscures Talent," pop music critic Peter Harris slammed Francks's monologues and criticized him for not "just stepping up to the microphone and singing. . . ."[2] He had an equally critical opinion of Lenny, who he claimed sardonically "fuzzy-fingers his way through such deeply significant works as 'Shadow of Your Smile.'" Dave Young, one of the most respected jazz bassists in the country by this time, was never mentioned in the article. Typically, Francks took a perverse delight in the review and the writer's failure to grasp the gist of his act. He persuaded the Castle George's owner to place an ad in the *Toronto Star* for the group's remaining shows, which read "Castle George presents super hipster, over-rated Don Francks with fuzzy fingered Lenny Breau (and bassist)."

During Lenny's brief tenure with Malka, she had introduced him to her manager: a transplanted American named Dee Drew who had run a janitorial firm in Los Angeles before coming to Toronto to get into the music business. Drew was impressed with Lenny and persuaded him to become her client. Despite the exploitation that Lenny claimed had taken place at the hands of his first manager, George Sukornyk, he apparently had no misgivings about signing a contract with Drew. She promptly took over all of his business affairs and personal finances, and found him a weekly gig in the lounge of the Colonnade Hotel where she ran her business from the hotel's penthouse suite. Drew had lofty career plans for Lenny, Judi Singh says, ones that had little to do with Lenny's own wishes. "Dee Drew was into the LA 'I'm-gonna-make-you-a-big-star' syndrome," Singh says. "She didn't recognize who or what Lenny was; she saw dollar signs. She saw him as a meal ticket. He tried desperately to communicate with her, to tell her that it didn't matter to him if his name was up in lights, that it was not his goal, not his priority. She just didn't hear him."

On February 16, Lenny did his first Toronto recording session. The album on which he played, *Soft and Groovy*, was the brainchild of pianist/arranger Jimmy Dale and CBC producer Dave Bird, and featured Lenny, Ed Bickert, and iconoclastic Coltrane disciple and musical mystic, Sonny Greenwich. Each guitarist played an instrumental of his choosing, around which Dale built an ensemble arrangement using eight violas and a rhythm section. Lenny contributed "Music to Watch Girls By," playing the tune on an inexpensive acoustic Framus twelve-string guitar that he had equipped with a soundhole pickup. He starts the piece solo and is joined first by bass and drums before the strings sweep in behind him. The performance, on which another unlisted guitarist (possibly Ed Bickert) backs Lenny, doesn't quite work largely because Dale's breezy, Klaus Ogerman-like string arrangements are at odds with the dark, mysterioso ambiance that Lenny creates. Although not credited, Lenny also plays with Sonny Greenwich on "The Look of Love," setting the tune up with some chordal harmonics, and possibly—no information is provided—contributes a solo to "Norwegian Wood," another of Greenwich's choices.

Lenny was now gearing up for his Nashville recording date and beginning on March 27, Lenny, Halldorson, and Kelln did four nights at the Castle George before moving on to Nashville to lay down tracks for Lenny's first RCA album.

The trio members were not the only Winnipeggers on hand for the date. Atkins, seeking to promote Lenny's début album, had called

Lee Major and asked him if CBC would send a reporter to cover the sessions. Major and CBC producer Dale Nelson went one step further and arranged to make a documentary for CBC of Winnipeg's hometown boys making good. This documentary, *One More Take*, in combination with an hour of out-take material that Major recorded at the first night's sessions and later broadcast on CBC radio as "The Kid From Canada,"[3] provides a remarkably detailed account of the making of Lenny Breau's groundbreaking début album, *Guitar Sounds from Lenny Breau*.

The first session got under way at 6:00 p.m. on April 2, and Atkins did his best to make the young musicians feel at home, says Reg Kelln. "Chet was a super guy, so nice," he says. "He'd say, 'Well guys, how do you feel? Everything all right?' Lenny says, 'No man, like, it's too bright in here.' So they sent a guy in with a big ladder and he climbed up and screwed in a red light bulb and then they turned off all the lights in the studio. Lenny said that was better and Chet said, 'Well, whatever you need: coffee, beer, whatever.' He really tried to make us feel relaxed." True to form, the trio had nothing planned or rehearsed, Kelln says. "When they were ready to roll, Lenny looked at me and said, 'What do you want to start off with?' I said 'I don't know Lenny. What do you want to play?' So then Lenny asks Ronnie 'What do you want to play?' Ronnie says, 'I don't know. It's your album, Lenny.' Finally he picked a tune and as usual, there was no counting in, and no worked out intros or endings. We just started and hoped it would come out all right."

The trio began with the jazz standard "Time after Time." Lenny took several bop-flavored solos over a vamp that he fashioned from a portion of the harmonic structure of the tune, a device he and the trio used often. This was followed by a version of "Hard Day's Night," one of the three contemporary pop tunes the trio recorded for the album. The tune fell apart after the first chorus, apparently due to the nervousness that Atkins induced in Lenny, as Atkins recalled in an interview three decades later. "He was recording and he was having a little trouble, and I thought, 'He needs an audience.' So I went out and sat by him and said, 'Lenny, would it help if I sat here by you and encouraged you along with my expressions?' He said, 'Well, like man, it's an experience.' He didn't want me in there. Hell, he didn't want me in the same building."[4] Lenny, calmer now, began the tune again, and delivered a considerably straighter version than the first aborted run through. This became the album's second track. Lenny followed this with an original—a minor key, hard-bop blues called "Comin' Home" which segued into "Summertime." The next piece, "King of the Road," a country/pop hit for its composer Roger Miller a few years earlier, was the suggestion of the session's co-producer, Danny Davis. Along with Atkins, Davis—a trumpeter who fronted the Grammy-winning band, The Nashville Brass—was one of the architects of the new country sound that some called "Country-politan Music." This precursor to the pallid "New Country" sound of the nineties featured lush, Percy Faith-like string arrangements and anodyne back-up vocals, ostensibly to make it palatable for pop audiences. This was not an option on Lenny's first album, but Davis freely admits that he was there to make the album as commercially viable as he could. "We wanted Lenny to do his own thing," he says, "But Chet was all for me trying to commercialize Lenny. What was left of the legitimate musician in me was very entertained by Lenny's sound, but at that time I was thinking much more like a commercial producer than a legitimate musician. I was thinking, 'If I could only get something that had just a little commercial edge to it, maybe I could get some disc jockeys interested in playing it.' So I talked him into doing 'King of the Road.' We did one take and he was all over the instrument, I said, 'Lenny, just on this one take, give me the first eight bars of the melody and then go.' But he couldn't. God, he was funny." Major's out-take recording tells a slightly different story. In an obvious attempt to please Davis and Atkins, Lenny played the melody straight in the first two choruses and never strayed far from it even in his improvisation. Davis's strictures were apparently too narrow for Lenny; the tune fell apart a few verses in and a second take was required the next night.

The trio continued with a tight, Latin-flavored version of "Call Me," and then moved on to the Hank Williams tune "Cold, Cold Heart." Ron Halldorson says this was the most difficult piece of the session to get right. Lenny had just worked out the arrangement, which the bassist says, "moved in some funny ways." Still, the trio recorded it in one take, jumping from its opening rubato statement of the melody into an up-tempo hard swinging groove without a hitch. Atkins, ever the perfectionist, gave a qualified thumbs up to "Cold,

Cold Heart," saying, "Very good, Lenny—except for a couple of squeaks on the strings there."[5] The band then moved on to an up-tempo "Too Close for Comfort," the closest thing in the sessions to straight ahead bebop.

During the first take of "Georgia," which was captured on the out-take tape, Lenny barely acknowledged the melody and simply used the chords as the basis for a long improvisation. It was an inspired performance but when Lenny had finished, Atkins told him that the tape was not rolling and that the men in the control booth had thought he "was just rehearsing." Stunned and obviously disappointed, Lenny responded incredulously, "Really!?"[6] Atkins then asked for a second take of the tune with more melody and less improvisation. Lenny agreed obediently and then played a version of the tune that had a stronger blues feel to it than the first take. "Georgia" is one of the gems on the album, jumping from a mid-tempo ballad feel into a swinging, up-tempo rave up. Lenny overdubbed the intro at another session, one of the few edits on the recording.

The next tune, "Music to Watch Girls By," was a vehicle for some of the ideas from Indian music that Lenny had been exploring. He plays the piece on his twelve-string guitar, possibly using an altered tuning in which the G string was tuned down to F$^\sharp$. The first and only take pleased the producers although not everybody was satisfied. The out-take tape catches Ron Halldorson saying, "We didn't get like as wild with it as we usually do. The feel was different." Lenny defends the take. "Well, no, but it felt pretty good," he says. "We can do it another time." But Atkins was content with it as it was and there was no second take.

The first session ended with "My Funny Valentine," also played on twelve string. He begins with a beautiful, rubato chord intro before the band builds to a steady groove. Lenny seamlessly shifts the mood from dark and dreamy to whimsical and blithe, but is always faithful to the structure of the tune. He also plays several phrases using Wes Montgomery-style octaves, his only recorded example of this technique.

Since purchasing the Framus twelve-string guitar in 1964 or '65, Lenny had routinely experimented with a number of different string set-ups on the instrument, but consistently used single B and E strings rather than the standard doubled octaves. This allowed more space between the treble strings and made right-hand playing easier as well as creating more tonal distinctiveness between bass string chords and melody. The following year Lenny would tell Lee Major that the tracks he recorded with the twelve string on *Guitar Sounds* were among his favorites, stating that the instrument might well become his main axe in the future.

> I liked the stuff I did with the twelve-string guitar because [it] has a whole new sound. . . . It can sound like a sitar, it can sound like a guitar. It can also sound like a harp, it can sound like a piano or you can play octaves on it like Wes Montgomery does. . . . I feel that the twelve string guitar is going to be the biggest thing for me 'cause I can see a lot things on it that haven't been done and I can't do them but I think that if I get down to it, if I do a little practicing, I'll be able to do it in a couple of years.[7]

Lenny continued to play twelve-string guitars from time to time during the next decade and used the instrument on his second RCA album but it did not loom nearly as large in his future as he predicted in the interview above. In late 1969, he purchased an Espana acoustic double neck six/twelve string which he played occasionally at solo gigs in Toronto before discarding it and his Framus twelve string in 1972. He used a Fender electric twelve string on a session with George Hamilton IV in 1971 and later bought a Hagstrom electric twelve-string that he converted to a six string before pawning it in 1974. In 1979, Chet Atkins gave Lenny a double-necked Ibanez electric 6/12 string that he pawned a week later. By then, Lenny was committed to a non-conventionally strung instrument of a very different sort and his interest in twelve strings had long since faded.

Prior to the next day's session, Lee Major interviewed Lenny in his hotel room for the CBC documentary. Lenny, looking healthy and elfinly handsome, is eloquent and self-possessed. Asked to describe his music, Lenny smiles and says reflectively, "Well, if I had to say something fast, I'd have to say, it's just music. But it's a combination of all the different kinds of music that I learned: all the country music years, and the flamenco records I listened to, and the East Indian records. It's a combination of all that I like to inject into my jazz playing. So it would be hard to have one name for it, you know what

I mean?" Later in the interview Lenny admits, "There was a time when I would have been afraid to record in Nashville because I wanted to be known as a jazz player. . . . But now I don't really care what I'm called as a player 'cause I feel that it's just music now. I don't have to be tagged as any kind of player, as a jazz player or a country player. It's just a combination of everything I'd like to be known as, you see?"[8]

Lenny's eclectic tastes were clear at the second session, which he kicked off with his original jazz/flamenco hybrid, "Taranta." Lenny later told the host of CBC's *Sunday Suplement* that this was his favorite cut on the album and described how the tune had evolved in the studio.

> I was playing a flamenco tune and right in the middle of it, I brought the bass and drums in and I started to play jazz. But it didn't lose the mood; it melted in. And after that, I went back to the flamenco again, you see. So I was mixing two things and that's what I like doing, 'cause I'm trying to prove a point there . . . it was a spontaneous thing although we had a structure, they didn't know what I was gonna play or how fast I was gonna play it. . . . I was gonna give them a nod and when I felt the time was right, I went like this [strums guitar] and we knew what we were gonna play on 'cause we had a set of chords but there were no notes written down. And it happened on the first take. So I was very happy with that take.[9]

In fact, the strong similarity of the version of this tune on *Guitar Sounds* to the piece that Lenny played on CBC's *In Person* in 1966, indicates that the studio recording was not quite as spontaneous as Lenny suggests. However, the latter version is greatly extended with jazz and flamenco sections overlapping and segueing smoothly into one another. At one point, he plays the entire opening theme of Miles Davis's "Milestones" before drifting into a modal jazz fantasy that quotes "Fascinatin' Rhythm" and winds up with more flamenco themes and material. While it may not have been the spur-of-the-moment creation that Lenny describes, he was entitled to be pleased with the tune, which stands as one of his most successful recorded marriages of jazz and flamenco.

Flamenco influences also crop up on his extended version of "Freight Train," which begins with a series of variations on the simple theme of Elizabeth Cotton's venerable folk tune. Each variation highlights some aspect of Lenny's stylistic palette: straight ahead Atkins-style playing, 3 over 2 meter, jazz balladry, and a segment of rhythmic flamenco. After these variations, the trio joins Lenny and begins what might be described as a country/bebop section. He concludes with a two-part coda consisting of a short baroque sounding figure followed by a Charlie Christian-type riff with a bass counterpoint line. In 1977, Lenny recorded an "original" piece he called "Ba De Da-Da" which used the latter riff as its theme. But Lenny was not quite original with either of these figures. The mock baroque device was taken directly from Barney Kessel's incongruous intro to "When the Red, Red Robin" on his *The Poll Winners Ride Again* album and Lenny lifted the concluding riff of the coda from a Kessel tune called "Easy Like" from *Barney Kessel Vol. 1.*

Lenny's version of "Don't Think Twice" bears little resemblance to the original, which Lenny had learned note for note from Bob Dylan's second album in 1963. In the first verse, he jumps from a simple folk feel to a flamenco tremolo and then into a jazz progression before the band joins him. The swing feel improvisation that follows is some of the best soloing on the record. Lenny also broadens the harmonic construction of the tune with extended chords obviously influenced by Bill Evans. He leaves the form behind a few times, but Halldorson predicts his deviations and follows his flights of fancy perfectly.

The session wrapped up with a jaunty version of the pop hit "Monday, Monday" that—while slightly more tame—was not dissimilar to one the trio had played at their CBC concert in Winnipeg a few months earlier.

All the tunes the trio recorded on the second night were done in one take and the session ended early. Atkins announced that they had more than enough material for the album and canceled the session he had scheduled for the next night. RCA paid the musicians for three full sessions, with Kelln and Halldorson each earning $225.00 for their work while Lenny—paid double scale as bandleader—walked away with $450.00.

A few days later the trio were in Winnipeg to play a homecoming date before moving on to Toronto where on April 9, they did a series of gigs at the Riverboat. (A few glimpses of these dates are included in *One More Take*.) *Variety* magazine gave one of these performances a short but enthusiastic review which read in part: "Breau hunches over his guitar bringing out the music, a whirl of classical, folk, jazz, country and flamenco. A standard like 'Too Close For Comfort' under Breau's brilliant playing becomes a work of art, one that can be savored. In short, Breau at 25 [Lenny was 26] displays a feel of his guitar rarely seen and heard. Breau teases the music, coaxes it and makes an evening with Breau a true excitement."[10]

When the gig ended, Lenny's rhythm section returned to Winnipeg. Great things seemed to be in the offing, but for now they were content to bide their time until RCA released the album and firmed up further plans.

Lenny continued to be busy through the summer. His projects included sessions on a pop/folk album with Canadian folk/pop singer Catherine McKinnon and a two-week gig at the Riverboat that began on August 27. He also did some studio work for Doug Riley on an album (*Some Other Kind of Soul*) that Riley produced for an R & B singer named Diane Brooks, with whom Lenny occasionally played gigs around the city. On October 10, he recorded three songs for a Reader's Digest compilation record, a session that Atkins had arranged for him. Lenny did two effective flamenco numbers on the album, one of which was marred by voices drearily muttering "Ole" during his performance, apparently for the sake of someone's misguided sense of authenticity. He also recorded an excellent performance of "Lullaby of Birdland" with an unlisted rhythm section that was not, contrary to common belief, Kelln and Halldorson. (Beyond the date, Reader's Digest has no information on this session and it's not clear whether it was done in Toronto or Nashville.)

Lenny's second daughter, Emily Lisa Singh, was born on October 20, 1968. Named for her parents' favorite jazz ballad, thirty years later Emily would chronicle her absent father's life in her award-winning documentary, *The Genius of Lenny Breau*.

Various problems, including a mysterious hum detected in its first pressing, held up the release of *Guitar Sounds* until a few weeks before Christmas. While Lenny was pleased that the album had finally been released, he was disappointed that Atkins had left off the straight-ahead jazz tunes in favor of the more commercial, radio-friendly numbers like "King of the Road" and "Monday, Monday." Lenny also found Atkins's choice of takes questionable, says Bob Erlendson. "He really wasn't happy about it. Lenny wanted a different set of tunes, not entirely, but with some changes. He also said he would have programmed it [sequenced the tracks] differently. They'd promised him they would fly him down and he'd be able to go over it with them before they released it. But they didn't. When Lenny heard the album, he said, 'We did three takes of each tune so why did they pick that one?[11] It wasn't the best one we did.' He was intimidated by the whole thing and didn't really assert himself because he loved Chet so much. But his attitude was 'Well, it's my ticket. I've gotta flog it.'"

Lenny was characteristically critical in his judgment of the album. In fact, there are sublime moments on *Guitar Sounds* despite its lack of pure jazz content, as writer John Burke noted in a perceptive review of the album in *Rolling Stone* magazine. Burke described Lenny's playing as "tender" and "understated," and wrote that it contained "a muscularity and quiet power reminiscent of jazz pianist Bill Evans." He says "part of the fascination in hearing an imaginative player like Breau lies in how he reinterprets each song so that you hear it as if for the first time. Breau—while he's still in the process of defining his sound/style—has that gift." Burke concludes by saying "This LP satisfies in a way most of [Wes] Montgomery's—which also used pop/rock songs—failed to. Montgomery too often curtailed his immense talent (on record) in the hope that a diluted product would appeal to the greatest number of consumers. Breau's direction is just the opposite. Within the pop/country, rock/jazz frame he has set for himself, you feel Breau extend himself to the fullest. A handsome first effort."[12]

Lenny was also getting attention from music critics closer to home. In early February 1969, he did a date at a Toronto jazz club called the Pornographic Onion, and received a review from *Globe and Mail* music critic Alastair Lawrie on February 14. Impressed by what he heard, Lawrie wrote, "[Lenny's music is] a sheer delight to the ear, which places Breau among the best musical talents to which Canada could lay claim . . . Breau stands on the brink of great things." He compares Lenny to vibist Gary Burton on the basis of the innovative sensibilities they shared as well as their "facility for coordinating simultaneous lines of musical thought." Lenny, he says, "has learned to coax from his instrument the full range of its expression. Sometimes he calls upon its full power; sometimes his hand shimmers over the strings like the beating wing of a dragonfly." Lawrie also gives credit to Lenny's bassist that night, "a young man called Bill Meryl [sic] whom he had met only recently . . . Meryl, with a minimum of rehearsal, showed the kind of musical instincts that augur well for his future with Breau. . . ." (Lenny had actually met Billy Meryll a few months before the date and developed such an affinity for the talented but troubled young musician from Montreal that he often declared Meryll his favorite bassist.) Lawrie ended his article with a blessing for both: "The promise is there, however, and I expect to hear a great deal from both of them in the near future."

A few months after this gig, Lenny was off to Los Angeles to record his second album for RCA. Atkins had set the project up, but would not be on site during the recording, apparently to spare Lenny the nervousness that he had incurred in his friend during the Nashville sessions. Instead, he sent Davis and RCA engineer Ronnie Light to record the trio at Shelly's Manne Hole, a much-loved Hollywood jazz club where they were booked to play three nights beginning on April 28, 1969.

Lenny traveled first to Winnipeg to do a warm-up gig with Kelln and Halldorson at a restaurant called the Birch Cove. Despite not having played together for over six months, a tape of the event shows that the trio clicked immediately and treated their hometown audience to a night of inspired, raw, high-energy jazz. Halldorson says that while Lenny was playing as well as ever, he was not quite the same man he'd recorded with the year before. "Lenny was in good shape for the Hollywood sessions although he'd changed a fair bit from when I'd seen him the last time in Nashville," says Halldorson. "Then he'd seemed still sort of happy and innocent. In Hollywood, he wasn't quite so innocent, not quite as starry eyed as the first time around. But he was still in good shape."

The trio arrived in LA the next day and checked into their rooms at the appropriately named Players Motel. The following afternoon, they went by the club and after meeting and talking with Shelly Manne, did a sound check for Davis and Ronnie Light who manned the console in the RCA recording truck parked behind the club. A few hours later, the men took the stage in front of a full and enthusiastic house. Carol Kaye, then LA's premier session bassist and author of several books on her instrument, was one of the many musicians in the audience that night. She had become friends with Lenny the month before while in Toronto at Doug Riley's bidding to record with the rock band Motherlode. Kaye says she was pleased to see Lenny in Los Angeles, as were many of the city's best-known guitarists who had been floored by Lenny's first album.

> If you had dropped a bomb on the place that night you'd have wiped out all the guitar players in the world. They were all down there, from Howard Roberts to George Van Eps to Joe Pass, and LA studio guys like Dennis Budimir and Al Hendrickson. Everybody I knew was down there. We were all just so happy that he'd come down to play his wonderful music for us. He conquered Hollywood because we all loved him as a player and we loved him as a person. When he got up on stage, he got you so involved in the music. He had so much love for the music that he just got you into it and he was so wonderful to watch because he had all these beautiful sounds coming out of him. I remember Lenny and George Van Eps meeting and George kept saying to him, "What a player, what a player!"

Lenny typically opened the trio's shows with a solo set, but perhaps due to nervousness, he did his first set at the Manne Hole with the trio. He welcomed the crowd and announced "The Tuning Tune," a piece in which he tuned his guitar with chordal harmonics as his rhythm section limbered up behind him. The leap from "The Tuning Tune" into "No Greater Love" is not quite as spontaneous as it sounds on the album. Ronnie Light later spliced "The Tuning Tune" from the first night's performance onto the group's apparently superior version of "No Greater Love" performed on the second night—one of the very few edits on the album. Several tunes that made it to the finished album were taken from the first night's session including Jerry Reed's up-tempo country/jazz number "The Claw" into which Lenny embeds an entire chorus of pianist Bobby Timmons's tune, "Dis Here" before segueing into some laid-back blues and a gentle, ballad-like section. Lenny also recorded "That's All," on opening night. He had learned this piece from a Merle Travis album in his Event Records days and performed it in many forms since then, often using it as a vehicle for his own particular brand of scatting, which he said was inspired by Miles Davis's trumpet playing. The trio's opening night performance of "A Taste of Honey" also made it to the album. Much could be said about Lenny's brilliant playing on this piece, which he infuses with a dark, wistful beauty that characterizes much of his most affecting work. Suffice it to say that hearing this piece of inspired musical poetry made this author an immediate and lifelong Lenny Breau fan.

At the end of the night, Davis told the trio that he was pleased with the performance in general but there was a problem. The shortest tune of the evening had been "The Claw," which, at well over four minutes, was well beyond radio friendly length. Couldn't the trio do a two-and-a-half minute number, he asked, something in the vein of "King of the Road" from *Guitar Sounds*? Lenny agreed to give it a shot, and at rehearsal the next day the trio worked out a truncated version of "Sweet Georgia Brown" on which Lenny would take a one-chorus solo and trade fours with Halldorson before ending it. "We rehearsed it just fine," recalls Halldorson. "That night we went into Shelly's and it was fourteen minutes long! I remember Danny shaking his head, and Lenny saying to him, 'Well, geez, man, you know, I mean, uh,' muttering some excuses about why it was not the little tid bit it was supposed to be. That was the last time Davis asked him to do that." Recalling the incident, Davis says, "Lenny was like a rider on a wild horse going off in every direction."

Two tunes from the trio's second night at Shelly's—"No Greater Love" and "Bluesette"—made it onto the album. Lenny begins his improvisation on the latter with a musing exploration of the form and melody, using notes of long duration that shorten as the piece builds to a rave-up vamp several choruses on. Once the climax of his extemporization is reached, Lenny lets the dynamics of the tune spiral downwards, introducing a brief coda that refers to the melody, and ends on a classic blues figure. "No Greater Love" served as a warm-up for the trio, to get musical blood pumping between Lenny and his rhythm section. Lenny changes the form of the tune slightly as was his wont on certain standards, reharmonizing it and throwing in long patches of fast lines with an Eastern modal flavor.

On the trio's final night at the club, Lenny recorded three solo guitar pieces, all of which appear on the album. "Indian Reflections for Ravi," a piece that Lenny played on his twelve string, was one of these. Lenny incorporated feedback, string bends, and tapping on the guitar's body into this haunting, otherworldly piece of genre-bending music. He also played "Mercy, Mercy, Mercy" taking it from its original R&B/cool funk feel into a dark, almost free section with controlled feedback before returning to the theme.

"Spanjazz" was, as the title suggests, one of Lenny's flamenco/jazz hybrids, combining a Soleas form with a gentle jazz waltz and an exquisitely played tremolo section. Throughout the piece, Lenny shifts in and out of the two genres, masterfully blurring the boundaries between them. The listener is left only with the impression of luminous beauty and poignant expression beyond simple musical categorization, which was very much Lenny's intention in pieces of this type.

By the time the trio ended their last set on their third night at Shelly's, they had given RCA more than enough material for Lenny's second album. Davis took the masters back to Nashville and he, Light, and Atkins began the process of preparing the album for release. Editing, Davis says, was minimal, consisting mainly of eliminating crowd noise and the occasional flubbed note. Several months later, RCA would release the album under the title *The Velvet Touch of Lenny Breau. Live!* but the album is commonly known among Lenny's fans as "Live at Shelly's Manne Hole."

Lenny would later say that he hadn't felt ready to record either of his RCA albums, and Ron Halldorson insists that neither captured the trio at its adventurous best. This may be, but not only does *Velvet Touch* rank among the best of Lenny's recorded work, it is one of the most important jazz guitar albums ever made. Both of his RCA albums evince a unique style that had pushed beyond the parameters of standard jazz improvisation while retaining the traditional matrix of the genre. On the second album, however, Lenny's innovative technique and incorporation of non-jazz influences into his improvisational concepts is less self-conscious and intertwined more effectively with his straight ahead jazz playing. Lenny had proven that he could do intriguing things with three chord pop songs on his début recording, but the material on *Velvet Touch* is more harmonically sophisticated and challenging, giving him more musical substance with which to work. The interplay among the trio's members is also a more crucial part of the performances on *Velvet Touch*. Halldorson and Kelln anticipate and occasionally instigate Lenny's changes in feel and meter with a level of acuity not present on the first album and are more involved with the spontaneous flow of their leader's musical ideas and shifts in mood. This was a challenge because while the prevailing character of *Velvet Touch* is pensive and brooding, Lenny gives voice to a full and constantly shifting palette of moods. In the course of a single tune, dark introspection will suddenly erupt into exuberant, childlike joy and then segue into poignant wistfulness. Lenny's ability to draw on and communicate spontaneously such a broad range of emotions is a defining, essential aspect of his best playing. None of his albums capture this essence better than *The Velvet Touch*, a recording that confirmed the arrival of a huge talent on the jazz scene and changed forever guitarists' notion of what was possible on their instruments.

Halldorson and Kelln left for Winnipeg a few days after their final gig at Shelly's, but Lenny stayed on at the home of a recently acquired friend. A few days later, he called John Pisano, a guitarist who had introduced himself to Lenny during a break at Shelly's. Pisano was one of LA's stalwart session guitarists, often performing with Joe Pass and much in demand in LA clubs and studios. Over the next few weeks, he and Lenny got together several times to talk music and jam. In early May, Carey Leverette—owner of Donte's, one of LA's most popular jazz clubs—called Pisano to see if he was available to do a two-week stint at his club at the end of May. Pisano was already booked and suggested that he hire Lenny who was already known to Leverette, having played at the club informally the week before on their weekly guitar night with drummer Dick Berk and bassist Ray Neopolitan. Naturally enough, when Leverette agreed to book Lenny, he asked Berk and Neopolitan to back him on the gigs.

Pisano brought a tape recorder to one of these dates, and, while sitting at a table with seven-string guitar master George Van Eps, captured one of Lenny's sets. In 2000, String Jazz Records released this performance as *Live at Donte's* (with a cover photo of Lenny that was shot at Donte's in 1979). Lenny's playing on this recording is markedly different from the thoughtful, measured work he'd done with his hometown trio at Shelly's a few weeks before. He counts in "Too Close For Comfort" and "Time after Time" at very fast tempos, and wryly warns the club's patrons not to try to dance to "All Blues," which he takes at warp speed. His solos are comprised of long, elaborate bebop lines with little breathing space or nuance and behind him, Berk and Neopolitan often sound as though they're struggling to keep up. "I think he probably felt freer [than on his dates at Shelly's]," says Pisano, "and was more able to do what he wanted." Perhaps, but one wonders if the opposite were not true. Lenny plays as though he has something to prove to his audience and—atypically—seems intent on impressing his listeners with his astonishing technical facility in the bebop idiom, which was a side of his playing rarely heard in his performances at that point in such a pure form. When Lenny heard this tape in 1983, says Pisano, he was incredulous. "He said, 'Wow, did I play that?'" Pisano recalls. "I'm not sure exactly what impressed him about it."

Lenny was now staying with Carole Kaye and her fiancé. Kaye had been an excellent jazz guitarist before giving it up to become the First Lady of Fender Bass, as she was known, and she and Lenny spent many evenings jamming together. Several years later, Lenny told colleagues in the Anne Murray band that at one of these jams, he and Kaye co-wrote an original called "Meanwhile Back in LA," a staple of Lenny's sets for the next several years. Kaye insists she has never heard the tune and does not recall writing it with Lenny. "We probably sat down and jammed and invented a tune together, just came up with something. But he was that type of guy who would give credit like that, very typical of him because he was just beautiful." Kaye, however, did not receive writer's credit for the song when Adelphi released it on Lenny's *Last Sessions* album.

Lenny's stay with Kaye was cut short when his host learned that her fiancé had died suddenly while on a trip to Mexico City. "Lenny was very sweet and nice to me and tried to help me," Kaye recalls. "But then I began grieving pretty bad, and he found someone else to stay with out of respect for me. When he left my house, I remember that he was very, very up. He'd conquered Hollywood and it had been very exciting for him to come to Los Angeles and be the king of the town."

Lenny's high spirits did not last long after returning to Toronto where his relationship with Judi Singh was rapidly deteriorating. The couple's first year in the city had been an exciting and fulfilling one, devoted to making new friends and indulging themselves fully in the city's thriving music scene. But there was another less healthy scene thriving in Toronto. "Everybody was using drugs at that time," says Lenny's old Edmonton friend, drummer Terry Hawkeye, who had moved to Toronto in the mid-sixties. "It was all through the Toronto scene and beyond. I lived in Montreal and in Vancouver and it was pretty much the same all through Canada. It definitely wasn't just Lenny." Drugs were easily available and Lenny seldom passed up an opportunity to get high or higher. Judi became increasingly intolerant of Lenny's drug use, particularly after Emily's birth, and, just as Valerie had done, she insisted that he either lighten up on his chemical consumption or she would end the relationship. Lenny's attempts to clean up were half-hearted and short-lived, and not long after he returned from Los Angeles, Judi demanded that he move out. Badly shaken by the split, Lenny took refuge with Terry Hawkeye, Billy Meryll, and his girlfriend in their apartment in the Beaches area of Toronto. Desperately wanting to continue his relationship with Judi, Lenny would straighten up for a time and return to her, but his periods of abstinence usually lasted only until he ran into a friend who was holding. Finally Judi had had enough. "He was using drugs and gone all the time, and I was starving with Emily," she says. "Then [celebrated Canadian jazz pianist and bandleader] Tommy Banks called and offered me a job and I took it." Judi returned to Edmonton with her daughter and it would be another three years before she saw the father of her daughter again.

In July 1969, a tenor sax-playing friend of Lenny's named Glenn MacDonald introduced Lenny to bassist Don Thompson who had just arrived in Toronto. Thompson, one of Canada's most celebrated jazz musicians, had spent his career in Vancouver, except for a year-long stay in San Francisco where he played bass with the John Handy Quintet. Thompson had heard the 1962 CKUA recording of Lenny playing bass with Terry Hawkeye, and was stunned by his facility on the instrument. "He was the best electric bassist ever including Jaco [Pastorius]," says Thompson. "He played the best solos on bass that you ever heard. It was ridiculous. Lenny was so advanced on bass that most guys wouldn't even try to do what he was doing because it was light years beyond anything they could ever think about."

During their first face-to-face meeting, however, it was Lenny's six-string playing that grabbed Thompson's attention. "The first or second night I was in town, Lenny came by Glenn's place with his guitar and amp," Thompson recalls. "We wound up playing standards all night and it was amazing. Everything he played was note perfect: every chord and every melody and every tune was like he'd written it. A lot of the stuff we did were Bill Evans's tunes, and he played very much like Bill because he'd gone to so much trouble learning Bill's approach. Back then I really knew those things [Thompson is also an excellent pianist] so he'd play a tune and right away I'd know how he was gonna play it. I mean if he played 'Young and Foolish,' he'd play the verse and chords just like Bill. I knew how Bill played [these tunes] so it was just like we'd been rehearsing."

Soon Thompson and Lenny were working gigs together around Toronto. Although Thompson played bass on many of these jobs, he would often play the drums and turn bass chores over to Billy Meryll. "There weren't a lot of guys playing drums [at that point on the Toronto scene] and if there were, they weren't loose enough to be what Lenny wanted," says Thompson. "I seemed to be able to play loose enough in a trio, especially with Billy Meryll, who was a great bass player. Most drummers would say 'OK, here we go' and would just go dang-danga-dang-danga. Lenny didn't like that because it locked him into something. He liked the way I played because I left him space." Ron Park, a remarkable tenor sax player and sometime bassist originally from Edmonton, often worked and jammed with the men. Lenny had befriended Park in Winnipeg in 1966 when he came to the city to play the Jazz A Go-Go and stayed for a time to work with George Reznik. A devoted musician who was strongly influenced by Sonny Rollins, Park was one of the leading lights of Toronto's jazz scene and at twenty-five years of age was on his way to becoming a legendary figure in Canadian jazz. And a tragic one, as it would turn out.

Lenny was by this time seeing a young woman named Cedar Christie, a free-spirited visual artist with a great love of jazz. After meeting Lenny at a party, Christie began dropping by the apartment he shared with Meryll and Hawkeye, and the two would spend afternoons strolling through the neighborhood. "I remember him walking around in the Beaches wearing an ankle-length Oriental flowered kimono," she says. "He'd go to the store and buy smokes without any self consciousness whatever, saying hi to people on the way by—sort of like a local Buddha type." Later, after Lenny had moved into Christie's apartment, she made him a vest entirely out of feathers, which he wore to his gigs and would absent-mindedly stroke as he spoke to his audience.

Christie often accompanied Lenny to these gigs to watch him perform with various young, adventurous musicians. These players inspired Lenny to push himself and explore more contemporary jazz sounds, says Christie, citing a particular gig on which Lenny played with Park, Meryll, and Thompson at a jazz club called The Cellar.

> Lenny was doing this fascinating music using lots and lots of feedback. While the other guys were doing their solos, he would introduce feedback by putting the guitar close to the amp and making it whine and scream. Don, and to an extent, the other players, energized and challenged him to make a new gesture in his music. They were playing things like "Freedom Jazz Dance" [by Eddie Harris] and a tune called "Toronto" [an alternative name for his original Taranta]—not standards. There were a number of tunes that Lenny was interested in playing at that time that were a little bit more out there. "Vision" was one of those. Lenny was into that tune big time around then.

The modal jazz piece "Vision" became a lifelong staple of Lenny's repertoire, and he often cited its composer, McCoy Tyner, as an important influence. But purely modal jazz in which modes are played over a sparse harmonic foundation would never really become a major aspect of Lenny's work. His exploration of modal playing, says Don Thompson, was more of an attempt to stay abreast of contemporary jazz than a deeply felt and committed interest that challenged his affinity for more harmonically elaborate and dense music. "Lenny told me that the only reason he played modal music was because of Sonny Greenwich," says Thompson, who often played with Greenwich. "He really liked Sonny and he'd come down to hear Sonny a lot. Sonny could really play modes and Lenny would sit there and listen and then he'd try to play that stuff. He once said, 'Every time I hear Sonny, I want to try to play like that' but he could never do it. At that point Lenny's hands actually got in the way because of his classical approach to whipping off scales and stuff like that. Sonny didn't play like that. Sonny was into a different kind of melody thing completely and Lenny was always trying to get that together." (Greenwich and Lenny did at least one public performance together, according to the jazz historian and writer Mark Miller. Miller recalls the men playing an American Federation of Musicians Fund gig at York University, on which Lenny played bass with Greenwich.)

Cedar Christie believes that it was simply in Lenny's nature to want to master all the music that he was hearing around him. "He was challenged by this tremendous appetite to do all this other music, wanting to do all these creative things," she says. "I think a lot of creative people struggle with this, wanting to be everywhere at the same time instead of having more gentility and exclusivity about their experience." She saw signs of this struggle firsthand when she and Lenny attended one of Greenwich's gigs at the Cellar. "Sonny was playing his waterfall of sound stuff," Christie recalls. "Lenny seemed to get quite angry. He walked out and I followed him out to the street. He wasn't articulate enough to say 'I'm angry with Sonny' or anything but I think he was because Sonny was doing things that Lenny wanted to do. I think this was probably always a part of his character because he was so ambitious in his music, had such an insatiable appetite for it. I think that his drug use was also related to those insatiable appetites."

Until mid-1969, Lenny's "insatiable appetite" for drugs had been confined to marijuana and LSD, which he consumed regularly and in astounding dosages. While Lenny's fellow travelers might find their mental limits stretched with one or two "hits" of LSD, Lenny could manage fifteen and still take the stage. But after three years of constant heavy LSD use, Lenny was beginning to suffer the sort of paranoia, confusion, and disorientation that the prolonged and indiscriminate use of psychedelics can produce. Instead of ceasing his use of the drug, he turned to another substance that dulled the serrated edges of his LSD experiences. "[LSD] turned on me," Lenny said in 1979, "and I couldn't handle it. Some musicians I knew were on this new drug. I didn't know what it was, just some orange liquid, but it brought me back to earth."[13]

The "orange liquid" was methadone, a drug developed in the 1950s to cushion the effects of withdrawal from heroin. But it also has a potent kick of its own, especially when mixed with barbiturates and alcohol, as Lenny and many of his friends did regularly. Initially, because Lenny was not a heroin addict, he was not able to get methadone from a treatment clinic and instead acquired it from a doctor in downtown Toronto who was known to have no reservations about writing scripts for drug users for a price. Within the year, however, Lenny would tap into a never-ending supply of the drug that cost him nothing.

Signs that Lenny's drug use was beginning to interfere with his professional life appeared shortly after he began using methadone. Lenny was frequently asked to do guest spots on various Toronto radio and television programs and in October of 1969, he played with Don Thompson and an unidentified drummer on a CBC TV show called *Time for Living*. Ray St. Germain, who had relocated to Toronto, hosted the show and had arranged his brother-in-law's appearance. "I got ahold of him and he did the show," says St. Germain, "but he was wired, live in front of an audience. He went into a shell and just kept playing way past his time. I actually had to poke him on camera, 'Hey, it's time, it's my turn' you know." Over the next year, these sort of incidents would begin to occur more frequently and as a result, television and radio producers became wary of having Lenny appear on their shows.

RCA issued *Velvet Touch* in early November, and to herald its release, Lenny, Kelln, and Halldorson played a two-week date at The Purple Onion followed by a weeklong gig at Le Hibou in Ottawa. RCA and Dee Drew joined forces to arrange an extended North American tour for the trio with the possibility of subsequent European dates. After years of playing catch-as-catch-can gigs mainly in small local clubs in Winnipeg and Toronto, this should have been a heady moment for Lenny. Yet, he apparently wanted no part of Drew and RCA's promotional machinations and failed to show up at scheduled meetings with his manager and record label, says Reg Kelln. As a result, touring plans were eventually dropped.

Drew and RCA brass may have been puzzled by Lenny's attitude but his indifference towards their publicity gambits did not surprise Ron Halldorson.

> Lenny wasn't the kind of person who could be channeled like that. He did feel that being famous was his birthright; his parents were famous and he would be famous too, that's how he saw it. But that wasn't what drove him. He just wasn't ambitious in a commercial sense. Back then I think he just took it for granted that success would come, and in a way it really didn't mean that much. He accepted that he belonged in that strata with other famous artists but being there wasn't what drove him either. He was striving to accomplish what he wanted to do as a player. Lenny did know that he was great, no question. He knew who he was, knew what he was, and knew he belonged with the greats. But as far as doing what needed to done to be commercially successful, he didn't want to think about anything that was just a business plan. Like if we'd said, "Lenny, we've got to put this tour together and do this or that," he'd say, "Yeah, but like man, I'm listening to some Chinese music and these things in 13/16 time and there's a lot of poly-rhythms happening. That's what I want to think about."

After Kelln and Halldorson returned to Winnipeg, Lenny did a series of dates with Moe Koffman at George's Spaghetti House, one of the three Toronto jazz rooms that Koffman booked and regularly played. In December 1969, Koffman took Lenny and a band consisting of Doug Riley, Dave Young, and drummer Dave Lewis into the studio to make the album, *Curried Soul*. "At that time, Moe was really looking for a follow-up to his jazz hit 'Swinging Shepherd Blues,'" says Rick Wilkins who arranged the strings and horns on *Curried Soul*. "He wanted something commercial to put on the hit parade." Most of the material on this album—pop songs by other writers or rock-oriented originals—reflects this aim. Lenny is heard playing guitar on several cuts including "Country Song," a piece he co-wrote with Koffman, but his only notable solo is on "Cantalope Island." With the tone controls of his amp set for optimal sustain, Lenny spins out a two-chorus solo, blending rock elements with modal jazz ideas to create a decent albeit truncated solo. This is the only cut that comes close to making full use of the creative talents of Lenny and the other men on this album.

In January of 1970, Lenny began a three-month, six-day-a-week gig with vibist Peter Appleyard's group (which included, for a time, bassist Dave Young) at a lounge called Stop 33 in the swank Sutton Place Hotel. Appleyard's middle-of-the-road jazz was considerably more conventional than the music that Lenny had been playing with Park and others in Yorkville's small clubs. But Appleyard so admired his guitarist's playing that he gave Lenny license to go in any direction that took his fancy. "Lenny was amazing, one of those people who make you feel like you've arrived," says Appleyard. "It was like when I used to play with Hank Jones or Benny [Goodman] or Mel Torme: the Good Housekeeping Seal of Approval. You stepped up a notch because he made you sound so great. You'd play a melody line with those kinds of changes behind you and it would sound marvelous. He was also physically beautiful besides being such a sensitive, kind individual. One night we were playing and he looked so lovely and played so beautifully that I just went up to him and gave him a kiss on the cheek. So he brought that to the group as well as complete devotion and a genius's talent when it came to playing." The Appleyard group also played on the *Barbara McNair Show* where they covered "Someday My Prince Will Come" on which, Appleyard says, Lenny played a monumental solo. Afterwards, Appleyard procured a copy of this tape and used it to audition for the Benny Goodman Band. Goodman gave Appleyard the gig on the strength of the tape and was also taken with Lenny's playing. "He said, 'Who's that guitarist?'" recalls Appleyard, "and I said, 'Lenny Breau.' He asked if Lenny would be interested in working with us and I said I would ask him, which I did. He said, 'Yeah, sure man' but it didn't come to pass. I don't think he was too well at the time."

Lenny was also working regularly with Don Thompson and drummer Terry Clarke during this period. Clarke had arrived in Toronto from his hometown of Vancouver on New Year's Eve 1969, at the behest of Don Thompson with whom he worked in various situations in Vancouver in the early to mid-sixties. The two men had also worked together in John Handy's band in San Francisco before Clarke joined the sixties pop vocal group, The Fifth Dimension. The two men would become one of jazz's finest rhythm sections, playing together often over the next few decades in many situations including an ongoing gig with guitarist Jim Hall. Playing with Lenny at this time, says Clarke, was often a wild and unpredictable ride.

> He did his own thing. It was like playing with Oscar Peterson. He wasn't playing with you. You played with him. So I had to, as all drummers did, adapt to where Lenny was going because depending on Lenny's consciousness at the time, he may play the A section three times instead of twice. He might play the bridge twice. He might drop a few beats here and there or a whole section of the tune. So you had to be on guard and go with him. He would get lost in tunes fairly regularly. I knew that so I would always approach a gig with Lenny ready for anything. You had to be on your toes because it wasn't always going to be the same every night. You'd play the same tune every night but it could be so erratic depending on how the chemicals were combining in his body, you never knew whether it was going to be a great night or a disastrous night. Nothing was consistent about him.

Lenny had long since lost his shyness on stage and, taking a page from his father and Don Francks's book, loved to entertain his audiences with more than music. He often did a comedy skit in which he would impersonate Johnny Cash singing "I've Got You Under My Skin" or do his "Lenny's Radio" routine, shifting suddenly from one song and musical style to another as though switching between stations on a car radio. The musicians found these antics as hilarious as the audience, says Don Thompson:

> Sometimes Terry and me were laughing so hard we could hardly play. Lenny would play two tunes at once—one in one key in 3/4, one in a different key in 4/4. He'd say, "OK, here it is now and don't nobody try and dance to this." He'd go "1-2, 1-2-3" and then boom! He had an amazing sense of humor. He liked to sing a jazz version of "Back in the Saddle" at his gigs, which cracked people up. He stuttered and sometimes he'd stutter on purpose because he knew people were waiting for it and he knew people would laugh. He would play "I Fall in Love Too Easily" and he would always announce it like "Li-li-like we're gonna p-p-play a beautiful ballad

called 'I Fall in L-L-Love li-li-li-like Too Easily.'" And by the time
he'd get it out everybody would be laughing and he'd be watching
this and make it even worse on purpose. Then he'd play the tune
and it would be so beautiful that people would be crying after eight
bars, just falling apart. He had a real presence on stage.

In late January of 1970, Doug Riley hired Lenny, Clarke,
Thompson, and flautist Jeremy Steig to play behind Beverly Glenn-
Copeland, a young African-American singer/songwriter he was pro-
ducing at the time. Born in Philadelphia, Glenn-Copeland had been a
classical singer and was studying nineteenth-century art song at
Montreal's McGill University when she became interested in contemporary folk music. In 1969, she moved to Toronto where she began
performing her original songs at coffee houses and eventually came
to the attention of Riley. "She blew me away," says Riley. "Her
music wasn't the most saleable commodity but all I cared about
then was what turned me on musically, and Beverly definitely
turned me on." Glenn-Copeland had never heard of the musicians
Riley brought in to back her, but they won her over immediately, she
says, Lenny in particular.

> I was stunned; stunned is the word. Here was this little guy with
> this ready smile who had so much respect for other people and their
> music and was so encouraging about whatever you were doing.
> Completely selfless in that way. Then he picked up his guitar and it
> was like someone from another planet playing—effortless genius,
> just effortless. Totally apropos, no matter what it was. Every note
> that came out of his guitar would be like it was dictated from the
> music muses of the universe. He just totally tuned into what I was
> doing, which is why every one of those takes [on the album] is a
> first take. I just can't explain the effect his music had on me. There
> was no discussion. He'd listen to the music and go "wooowwww"
> and "ahhhhh" and "ooohhh" and his eyes would roll around in his
> little dark glasses a couple of times and he'd get this beatific smile
> like what I was doing was so geniusy or something, and then he'd
> pick up his guitar which was bigger than him and he'd play this
> stuff and go off into LaLa land. As far as I was concerned, I felt I
> had the good fortune to accompany a genius on that album.

Lenny's playing fit perfectly with Glenn-Copeland's ethereal and earthy jazz/folk sound, underscoring her commanding, sinuous voice and rhythmic acoustic guitar work. He added cascades of chordal harmonics to several tunes and took a particularly memorable solo on the song "Ghost House," perhaps inspired by Glenn-Copeland's passionate and astonishingly powerful singing on this cut. Lenny did some of his most interesting playing on the eponymous final cut, the eerie, enigmatic "Erzili." Glenn-Copeland sings one verse before the tune turns into a nine-minute, instrumental jam on one chord. Clarke, Thompson, and Glenn-Copeland create a raging sea of sound into which Steig and Lenny drop jagged, dissonant phrases. Lenny plays fast bursts of modes and altered scales in various intervallic sequences while he mutes the strings with the heel of his hand, evoking an aural image of McCoy Tyner's modal concepts being realized by a *flamencoista*. These sequential note flurries began to turn up in his playing around 1970 and he used (and misused) the device frequently in his soloing for the rest of his life. His work on "Erzili" is the first recorded example of this device.

In early March, Glenn-Copeland and the band played a badly attended album release concert at Ontario Place Center. She and Lenny also played a series of dates at a coffee house on the University of Toronto campus called Meat and Potatoes, a popular hang out for Toronto jazz musicians and fans. Lenny jammed at the club regularly with many of the cream of Canada's young jazz musicians exchanging and honing ideas in conversations and jams that went on into the early morning hours. "We were living the nocturnal life then," Cedar Christie says, "always hanging out and eating lobster and fancy Italian food, and drinking lots of wine. Then we'd go home and start all over again. Lenny played all the time at home but I don't know if I would call it practicing. The guitar was always out in the house and he was always working out lines and listening to things. But it wasn't like 'I'll practice between two and four.'"

These days of wine and roses were not completely carefree, however. Christie had serious concerns about Lenny's increasing drug use and in July 1970, she persuaded him to come with her to her parents' cottage near Pointe au Baril on Georgian Bay, three hundred miles north of Toronto. There, the couple took a drug-free, two-week vacation, passing their days swimming, boating, and fishing. Lenny, who hadn't fished since he was a child, was proud to catch a tiny pike, which he insisted Cedar photograph from a dozen angles. One afternoon towards the end of their vacation, they boated to a nearby village. Stopping into a liquor store to buy a bottle of wine, they ran into Lenny's friend, Toronto drummer Andy Cree, a longtime heavy drug user who—astonishingly—just happened to be visiting the remote area. Cree had an extra bottle of methadone that he passed to Lenny, bringing his two-week hiatus from drugs to an abrupt end. Lenny, it seemed, would always have uncanny luck finding drugs or people who could supply them in the most far-flung and unlikely locations.

Not long after the couple returned to Toronto, Lenny's father came to town to play a gig at a local tavern. Pine had spent the past several years touring a B-level country circuit throughout the eastern states and provinces, and had released a handful of albums of dubious quality on small labels like Rodeo and Banff. Career breaks had been non-existent for him, but on one occasion, Pine had unknowingly been given a shot at the big time. While living and working in Halifax, Nova Scotia, in 1967, he befriended a young folk/country singer and songwriter named Gene MacLellan. MacLellan was excited about a song he had just written and tried to persuade Pine to record it for his next album on the Audat label. Pine agreed to learn the song and carried the words to it in his guitar case for several months, says Gene Hooper, who was traveling with him and MacLellan at the time, but wasn't quite sure if it suited him and finally decided against recording it. Two years later, MacLellan sold the song to Anne Murray who turned "Snow Bird" into one of the biggest Canadian pop hits in history.

Lenny had not seen his father since 1962 when Pine was in Toronto with Gene Hooper to do a recording for ARC Records. That visit, recalls Don Francks, was strained and difficult, and apparently father and son had not resolved the animosity that had persisted between them since their days in Moose Jaw. On this visit, Pine was friendly to his son, says Cedar Christie, but the relationship was still entirely on Pine's terms. "Lenny was very generous about his dad, but I sensed this kind of sorrow from him when his dad was around," Christie says. "Hal didn't come in and say 'Hey son. How are you doing with your music? I'm so proud of you' or anything. Everybody wants acknowledgement from their parents, but Lenny never got it from his dad, and it saddened him. He didn't say anything about it, but I could see it in his body language when his dad was around."

Lenny went with Barrie Tallman to his father's date and joined him on stage for a few songs. In turn, Pine showed up the next night at Lenny's gig at George's Spaghetti House. But as Lenny later told his mother, Pine sat with his back to the stage, talking loudly during Lenny's sets and not acknowledging his son's music with applause. Afterwards, Pine told Lenny that he should break off with Christie, whose independent nature was not a quality he admired in women. Despite the long hiatus in their relationship, Pine apparently still held sway over his son, and Lenny remained aloof from Christie until his father packed his guitar into his Cadillac and hit the road for parts unknown.

In July of 1970, Leonard Feather used "Mercy, Mercy, Mercy" from *The Velvet Touch* in a *Down Beat* magazine Blindfold Test featuring Lenny's one-time guitar mentor, Barney Kessel. Kessel, who had a deserved reputation for being harshly critical of young contemporary jazz musicians, had a mixed reaction to what he heard. While he commended Lenny's playing, he downplayed its originality saying, "It's the kind of artistry that is more extrapolation than innovation." He went on to question Lenny's "taste" and "continuity," and concluded by commenting, "I get a sense of a very fine, excellent, complete guitar player but I don't get a sense of a human being who is making a personal commitment of his own."[14]

Kessel's remarks were virtually the only mention that *Velvet Touch* had received in a major music magazine since its release seven months earlier. Despite the high quality of the album, it was simply too jazz oriented to interest most record buyers at the time. In the late 1960s, rock was the music of choice among a whole generation of young people who had little or no affinity for jazz. Even established, well-known jazz musicians were feeling the pinch and going to great and often lamentable lengths to win over a young audience. Moe Koffman's album *Curried Soul*, with its jazzy versions of pop songs like Donovan's "Sunshine Superman" was typical of the questionable projects that many jazz musicians were undertaking in order to remain relevant in a music industry dominated by rock. Wes

Montgomery, one of jazz's finest guitarists, had a string of Top Forty hits that featured his severely dumbed-down guitar work on facile, insipid instrumental versions of pop songs. Other attempts to blend jazz and rock had similar success commercially with more artistic merit. These included the jazz/pop fusion of groups such as Blood, Sweat, and Tears and Chicago Transit Authority, and—on the other side of the coin—Miles Davis's iconoclastic, 1969 album, *Bitches Brew*: an edgy, raw combination of modal and free jazz propelled by ferocious rock rhythms that would change the course of both jazz and rock. Lenny's delicate, complex music had little appeal for most rock fans, and its traditional emphasis on melody, harmony, and a tendency towards romanticism and introspection were anathema to young jazz/ rock fans cranked up on *Bitches Brew*. In a classic case of bad timing, Lenny's career as a jazz recording artist had gotten under way at a moment when jazz seemed on the verge of becoming an obscure, outdated musical genre with little more than a cult following.

Lenny, however, laid the blame for his albums' lackluster sales squarely on RCA, faulting them for—as he saw it—pushing him into recording prematurely and then putting little energy into promoting his albums. "When I initially recorded, I didn't feel ready—I wanted to practice for another 10 years first," he told one interviewer. "And then the records didn't sell because RCA didn't get behind them."[15] Lenny failed to acknowledge that his indifference to RCA's touring and promotional plans had played a large part in the label's decision to not "get behind" his records, and withdraw promotional support. But in a period when jazz legends like Louis Armstrong and Duke Ellington were pleased to find gigs at county fairs and community centers, even a full-on publicity assault by RCA would have had little effect on the meager sales of Lenny's albums.

Although Lenny had little interest in promoting his recordings, their commercial failure affected him deeply. "I got depressed," he told *Down Beat* several years later. "I felt like there was no way I could play that stuff [jazz] and sell it and so my style of life changed."[16] So too did his drug of choice. For Lenny, the only solution for depression was self-medication, and this time he not only stepped up his drug use, he began using a substance that would finally lead him into full-blown addiction.

After playing on Don Thompson's album, *Love Song for a Virgo Lady*, in the fall of 1969, Ron Park drifted down to New York City where he eventually began touring and recording with jazz organist, Brother Jack McDuff. While with McDuff, he became re-addicted to heroin—a drug he had used on and off since 1965. Strung out, he returned to Toronto in October of 1970, proudly wearing his habit like a jazzman's badge of honor. Lenny, says Cedar Christie, was impressed.

Lenny and Ronnie were close and very competitive in a good way, the way a lot of creative people are. Then Ronnie came back from New York with a heavy drug habit—a habit that he seemed to show off. "Been hangin' out in New York and got a habit." That was like a red flag in front of Lenny because Ronnie had been sitting in with all these heavy people like Jack McDuff. And that's when Lenny started shooting up. There was this thing that happened between them, almost like Lenny putting his head down against another bull. "You think you can do heroin? Well, watch me." Lenny got a habit and then it was into the methadone program because it was available, it was free and legal, and they really loved it.

In January of 1971, Lenny and Ron Park became outpatients at Toronto's Alcohol and Drug Addiction Research Foundation but, as Christie implies, therapy was not uppermost in their minds. Methadone was simply another high for Lenny, one that he would often boost by augmenting it with pills or alcohol. In coming years, Lenny would use the drug therapeutically from time to time—usually when his heroin tolerance made his habit too expensive to support. In the main, however, methadone was for Lenny a cheap and often free recreational drug and just another component in the cycle of substance abuse that would envelop him for the next decade.

Soon after Park's return, he and Lenny formed a band with Billy Meryll and drummer Andy Cree, which Lenny referred to sardonically and accurately as the Junkie Quartet. Although the depth of talent in the band was great, the group found little work because Lenny and Park's habits had become known to Moe Koffman whose policy was not to use known drug users in his band or hire them for the jazz rooms he booked. In February of 1971, however, the quartet (with drummer Dave Lewis subbing for Cree) did a two-week stint in Ottawa at Le Hibou. Lee Edwards, a reviewer for the Canadian jazz magazine *Coda*, had seen Lenny perform at the club with his trio a year earlier and had written of the experience, "[Lenny was] in a rut . . . prone to playing memorized patterns instead of ideas." But when Edwards caught Lenny with the quartet on the night of February 10, 1971, he was impressed and posited, "[Lenny must have] recharged his creative batteries because he now sounds better than ever. Wednesday night was the first time I'd really heard Lenny's ideas catch up with his technique, and the result was stunning improvisation all night." Edwards praises in particular Lenny's work on "Vision," calling the tune "the sort of forward-looking material that was absent previously." In conclusion, he says, "The whole band was . . . taking care of business all night, with Lenny Breau out front, leading the way."[17]

During their stay in Ottawa, Christie and Lenny spent a day perusing the art collection at the city's National Museum where Lenny indulged his passion for the Impressionists.

> Renoir was big time for him. He tried to talk to me about his love of Renoir, but he didn't have that kind of articulation and he'd get very frustrated trying to express what he saw in these paintings, but he loved them, just loved them. There was a huge Jackson Pollock in the lobby of the gallery. Lenny totally freaked out on it. He got so angry that he almost couldn't continue with us through the rest of the gallery. He was just incensed because it was this huge application of bicycle riding stuff—so far from Renoir. But we went in and looked at everything and came out some time later and he actually said "Well, you know, having seen all that stuff, I have a little bit better understanding of where [Pollock] is coming from."

In mid-March, Lenny realized one of his dreams when he sat in with Bill Evans at Toronto's Town Tavern. Lenny had watched Evans in awe three nights running before he summoned the nerve to approach the pianist, says Bob Erlendson. "Lenny finally got over his shyness and introduced himself to Bill on Friday night," he says.

"Lenny talked about sitting in and Bill is like 'Well . . .' you know, should he or shouldn't he? Then he says, 'I'm doing the matinee tomorrow. Why don't you come down and play on the matinee?' He got him up and they did five songs together. It was good. Bill was very generous and seemed to be happy with it. He realized that Lenny Breau was genuine." Not everyone present was equally impressed. "They thought and played so much the same and their comping and voicings were so alike, it didn't work," says Doug Riley. "It was great to be there and see two giants getting together and playing, but there was nothing special happening because they were in each other's way. If a guitar player was going to play with Bill, it had to be someone who just played single notes: Joe Pass, Herb Ellis, or Jim Hall. When Lenny was playing all these incredible solos he always comped. That's what Bill did, and they were bumping into each other. When I played with Lenny, I had to really stay out of his way as much as I could and be more polar. I played down low and up high and left the middle to Lenny." Lenny was euphoric over the meeting, however, speaking of it often over the years (with predictable embellishments) and treasuring a photo Barrie Tallman took of him and Evans playing together.

Not all his experiences in mid-1971 were quite so bracing. His divorce from Valerie became final around this time and while the two would remain friends, the proceedings were not amicable. When Dee Drew took Lenny on as a client in 1969, her duties as his manager included sending Valerie child support payments each month. She apparently hadn't fulfilled this duty and a year prior to the divorce Valerie had called her to ask why payment had not been sent, explaining that she needed money for Christmas expenses. Drew, Valerie says, told her to "f—off." Lenny appeared shocked when Valerie told him about the incident, but did nothing to rectify the situation and continued to let Drew mishandle his affairs. As a result, Lenny was deeply in arrears with his payments even before the divorce was final.

Drew finally dumped Lenny as a client in early 1971 when it became clear to her that he was not the goldmine for which she had hoped. Afterwards, Lenny told friends that Drew had withheld money owed to him, and although he did not state it explicitly, he implied that she had paid him with drugs in lieu of cash—a not uncommon practice in the music business at the time. Christie says that Lenny did go to Drew's office to confront her about money owed but after a few fruitless trips, he gave up, and his second and last formal manager/client relationship ended on a sour note.

These events in conjunction with the poor sales of his RCA albums and his break-up with Judi Singh, added to Lenny's mounting depression. But it was the tragic and unexpected cessation of another relationship that finally pushed him deep into darkness. Ron Park was seeing a young dancer who worked at The Silver Dollar, a round-the-clock Toronto strip bar where Park sometimes played. On May 19, Park met up with this woman after taking a dose of methadone and several valiums, which he chased with rum. They returned to Park's rooming house in the Annex area where Park went to bed and slipped into a drug-induced coma. The next morning his companion was unable to wake him. Not recognizing Park's precarious condition for what it was, she let him "sleep" through the morning. The twenty-six-year-old musician died of asphyxiation sometime during the afternoon of May 20, 1971.

In the days following Park's death, Lenny was "stunned and terrified" says Cedar Christie. Rather than heeding the warning implicit in his friend's death, Lenny began taking suicidally large doses of drugs, sitting for long hours alone in their kitchen, talking to himself and refusing most visitors. As he grew more and more uncommunicative and morbidly despondent, Christie called Lenny's mother, whom she had never met, and explained the situation. It was Betty's turn to be stunned. Lenny took the phone and in tears asked his mother if he could stay with her in Maine for a time. "It was a shock, but I said, 'of course, son, of course you can come home,'" says Betty. "We would never turn him down." In a panic, Betty dispatched Denny to Toronto to retrieve her eldest son. After collecting Lenny and visiting a clinic to obtain several doses of methadone to stave off withdrawal pains for a few days (all of which Lenny downed on the plane home), Denny brought his emotionally and physically damaged brother back to Auburn.

Lenny had paid a short visit to the family in the fall of 1967, but they were not prepared for the son and big brother who arrived home three-and-a-half years later. Lenny, with his long hair and beard, splendiferous robes, tiger balm, and inch-long, lacquered nails was like a rare butterfly landing—or more aptly crash landing—in their midst. Heavy drug use, stepped up sharply during the past few months, had been hard on his body and he now walked with a stiff-jointed shuffle and had difficulty getting up the stairs of Betty's small basement apartment. "I told him, 'Well, just go upstairs on your butt one stair at a time until you're feeling better,'" Betty recalls. What Lenny needed was rest and long-term isolation from the drug culture.

Unfortunately, Auburn would serve as a home base from which he would make forays into the Toronto music scene, inevitably succumbing to the temptation of drugs and wiping out whatever gains he had made. The first of these trips was a midsummer tour with Doug Riley's band Dr. (read "D"oug "R"iley) Music. Comprising eight singers and eight instrumentalists that included Terry Clarke and Don Thompson, the group's sophisticated arrangements of original material encompassed funk, jazz, R&B, and pop. "It was a fusion band, the first one of its kind in Canada," says Riley, "way ahead of its time." Lenny was one of the band's three guitarists, and Riley gave him license to add whatever he wanted to the band's sound.

> Lenny couldn't read music so I'd just show him the song and he'd add things to it. Lenny contributed all kinds of solos with all those colors he could play. If the horn section played a certain tight voicing thing, Lenny might float this angel dust [chordal harmonics] over top of that. Lenny had free rein once he knew the arrangement to do whatever the hell he wanted to do. And very seldom would I have to say to him "I don't think that works." He just had such an innate sense of what was right and wrong that whatever he did just added to it. Whether he was just adding ambiance or sounds or if he took a solo in a more jazz type tune, that's what he did. He had the fingerpicking stuff happening so they'd be playing the high James Brown voicings with the ninths up high and Lenny would do a single note thing underneath and it would just sound incredible. His ears were so good that when he knew the arrangements he could just do whatever he wanted and add these incredible things. Lenny could be a chameleon, and to me that was one of the wonderful things about him.

The tour began in Calgary in mid-July and then moved to Edmonton where the band played at a club called Zorba's on the city's university campus. Lenny still had an adoring following in Edmonton and his friends and fans turned out in droves to hear him. Dr. Music had played only a couple of tunes before the audience began to chant Lenny's name. The band members drifted off the stage one by one until Lenny was left alone with his guitar and, weaving precariously on a stool, proceeded to play the rest of the evening solo for the reverent crowd.

The band reached Winnipeg on July 23 and played at Centennial Concert Hall for an audience of about 1,100 people. This time Lenny opened the show with Don Thompson and Terry Clarke. Susan Janz reviewed the concert for the *Winnipeg Tribune,* and reported that "Mr. Breau, with hair much longer than when he left Winnipeg about five years ago, got a warm welcome from the audience." However, she says, the set, which included "Summertime" and "Milestones," "didn't really get off the ground . . . Don Thompson seemed unsure and appeared to hold the other two back at times." Janz concludes by saying that while some members of the audience seemed to enjoy Lenny's music "many of the younger listeners found his playing too esoteric, perhaps because they were not familiar with the jazz idiom."[18] Riley agreed with this assessment and in subsequent gigs did not give the trio a solo spot.

Lenny had resumed his old habits virtually from the moment the tour got underway, beginning with LSD in Calgary and branching out into heavier substances as the tour went on. He arrived back in Auburn a month later strung out once again, but determined to overcome his dependency. However, he faced an enormous hurdle. Le Hibou had booked him for a week in September, but as the date came into view he was still in fragile condition and worried that revisiting old haunts would mean a return to drugs. Still, with money tight, he did not want to miss the gig. He resolved this dilemma by asking Betty to accompany him on the trip, an idea that the club's owner John Russo expanded on by suggesting that Betty be Lenny's opening act. "I remember when we were in the airport in Ottawa," says Betty with a laugh, "Lenny had his arm around me, holding me close like I was his girlfriend or something." The audience enjoyed Betty's singing and yodeling and responded well to the mother/son duo. Betty says she was amazed at how closely the audience listened to her son and their obvious high regard for his playing. But by the third day Lenny was suffering, she says. "He was having trouble sleeping, and then one day, I went to his hotel room and he was crying and said he didn't think he could make it. So we went to see the club owner and he gave Lenny some medication to help him sleep and calm him." Lenny managed to make it through the gig and when the week was done, Lenny, still clean and sober, returned to Auburn with his mother.

Back in his hometown, Lenny hung out with old friends, dropped into Shorty's Diner for his daily meatball sub and stayed up into the early morning hours reading and rereading his favorite novel, *Don Quixote*, until, says Denny, "his eyes were spinning in his head!" He also filled in occasionally for his brother Denny—by now an excellent guitarist in his own right—in a general business band that included Steve Grover, a sixteen-year-old drummer and budding composer who would eventually win the prestigious Thelonious Monk Award for Jazz Composition. Lenny was unfamiliar with most of the Top Forty material the band played but had no trouble winging it. "His ears," says Grover, now a New England-based music educator, performer/composer and recording artist, "were unbelievable. The bass player would whisper the changes to, say, 'Wichita Lineman' during the first verse. The second time round he'd do the same thing, but Lenny would whisper back, 'Yeah, man. That's nice, but check *this* out!' and he'd play some wonderful, unbelievable chord that was just beautiful."

In late October of 1971, Lenny returned to Toronto to play with Beverly Glenn-Copeland on a CBC TV show called *Music to See*. The pair did several songs from Glenn-Copeland's album before Lenny, wearing square, rose-colored glasses, white bell bottoms and a startlingly bright tie-dyed T-shirt, played a version of "Don't Think Twice" on his Ramirez. The jazz content in this rendering is far less rich than in the version on *Guitar Sounds* and his stylistic flights of fancy sound forced and do not flow. He had also grown his right-hand nails to a length that most players would consider unmanageable, which may account for the rough tone he draws out of his classical guitar on this performance.

Lenny then flew to Winnipeg in December for an uneven gig at the Fort Garry Hotel with Erlendson, Halldorson, and Kelln. He returned to Maine to celebrate Christmas and then spent three weeks with his boyhood friend, Shep Spinney, in New Hampshire. A month later, against his doctor and family's advice, he decided he was ready to return permanently to Canada. In late February of 1972, he took a plane from Boston to Ottawa for a two-week-long solo gig at Le Hibou, where his opening act was a West Coast experimental folk duo called Ptarmigan. The duo's guitarist, Monte Nordstrom, says that Lenny was in excellent shape during his first week at the club, playing for standing-room-only audiences who lined up in sub-zero temperatures hours before the show to see him. Lenny, says Nordstrom, played a selection of material from his albums as well as pieces like "Days of Wine and Roses," "Five O'clock Bells" and his own very obscure composition, "The Waves are Angry," a piece in a minor mode for which he had written lyrics. Only Nordstrom and Judi Singh seem to recall this song, which apparently disappeared from his set list sometime in the early seventies.

During the second week at Le Hibou, says Nordstrom, Lenny spent much of his fee on a large amount of LSD and hashish. "He gobbled it for the rest of the week," says Nordstrom. "His ability to communicate was definitely distorted but it didn't deter his ability to perform the songs well even though he was having trouble getting to and from the stage. But once he got in his zone musically speaking, there was this intense channeling of energy and intellectualism and pure spirit."

Lenny spent the following month with friends on a farm/commune not far from Ottawa. In early April, he was back in Toronto where he heralded his return to the city with an appearance at an after hours club called Dave Caplan's Jazzland. Columnist Alastair Lawrie was delighted to see him back in the city and wrote in his *Globe and Mail* music column, "Lenny's back! This crisp bulletin has run swiftly through the ranks of Toronto's music colony with a seismic effect that pays tribute to the talents of Lenny Breau. . . . Toronto has missed Lenny Breau. . . . Quiet-spoken, placid and unassuming, he nevertheless occupied an important place [in Toronto's music scene]."[19]

Another music writer, however, thought Lenny's return was much ado about nothing, and took an Emperor's New Clothes slant in his review of Lenny's gig at Jazzland. Pop music writer Peter Goddard insisted that Lenny was "the type of jazz musician whose appearances are always overshadowed, confused, and preceded by his reputation. Nothing he does could possibly be as good as what his fans think he can do, as was made evident [at the Jazzland date]." He withholds all details of this apparently sub-par performance except to say that Lenny's "technical skill, taste, and feeling for his music are sometimes hindered by a lack of imagination," and then dismisses him with the comment that "one doubts if he could play as well as his 'best' is supposed to be."[20]

Lenny received considerably more praise from Alastair Lawrie for a short gig he did with Clarke and Thompson a few weeks later at Toronto's venerable Massey Hall on a bill with the Toronto Symphony. The trio opened with a version of "Bach's Bouree," which Lenny had used as springboard for jazz improvisation since the mid-sixties. Lawrie describes how Lenny played the tune through "with the measured grace appropriate to the great master" before Thompson and Clarke—"very delicately, and still with considerable dignity"—joined him on the second chorus. Lawrie wrote that the trio then took the piece into a territory that "could not be defined as anything but jazz." Lenny followed the Bouree with an original called "Song of Love"(a piece even more obscure than "Waves are Angry") and the set ended with an up-tempo version of "Taranta." Although most of the 1,500 members of audience were there to hear the symphony, Lawrie says the crowd "rendered unstinting appreciation as Breau, an engagingly shy character, nodded and smiled."[21]

Apart from these and a few other low-paying gigs, there was little work for Lenny in Toronto, and he soon found himself in desperate financial straits. This indigent condition led him to accept an offer to play with rising Canadian pop star Anne Murray whose band was staffed largely with musicians from the Toronto jazz community. A year earlier, under the urging of her bass player, Skip Beckwith, Murray had agreed to hire Lenny to play on her premier CBC television special, *Bring Back the Love*, which had aired on June 1, 1970. In February of 1971, Lenny had again played with the band sans Murray when they were hired (along with Canadian pop/folk star Bruce Cockburn) to play on country singer George Hamilton IV's RCA album *North Country*. The following year, when Anne Murray was gearing up to do her first international tour, Beckwith—

by then the musical director of the band—asked Lenny to become a full-time member of the group, joining drummer Andy Cree, sax man Don "DT" Thompson, Billy Speers (later replaced by Pat Riccio, Jr.) on keyboards, and singer/songwriter Brent Titcomb on rhythm guitar, harmonica, and percussion. For Lenny, who had been leading a hand to mouth existence for the past year, the offered $350 a week salary was too tempting to pass up and he took the job.

Beckwith called the band "Richard" and was proud of its musical depth. But, as it turned out, some of the band's musicians had depths he hadn't been aware of when he'd hired them. Many years later in the documentary *The Genius of Lenny Breau*, Chet Atkins recalled in an interview how Anne Murray had told him that Lenny had turned her entire band on to drugs. Both Beckwith and Thompson scoff at this claim. "It's not true," says Thompson. "We all knew a lot about drugs a long time before Lenny came along."[22] But what the men did not know was that Lenny, Cree, and Speers were all hard drug users in various stages of addiction. Beckwith says that this was not an issue during the first few dates of the tour that kicked off in Winnipeg on June 1, 1972. But a few days later in Edmonton, Beckwith and the group caught a disturbing glimpse of what was to come. Murray's opening act was Celtic singer John Allan Cameron for whom Richard also served as back-up band. "There was a tune that John Allan used to sing called 'Anne,' which was meant to bring Anne on," recalls Beckwith. "It was always a great tune for Lenny to play because it was up-tempo and Lenny had so many chops. Lenny was supposed to take a guitar solo, but when it came time for the solo this night, there was nothing. Lenny was nodding out. So I looked at Cree and Cree pokes him with a drumstick. Lenny jumps into the air and starts playing this solo that had nothing to do with the tune, not even in the same key or anything. Things went downhill from there." There would be a number of similar incidents throughout the tour including Lenny's passing out in an elevator in Chicago and nearly drowning in an Atlanta swimming pool while high on methadone and LSD.

Lenny's performances with Richard varied in quality, but some nights he received more praise from reviewers than did his employer. One writer who was not impressed with Murray's "unremarkable voice," compassionately referred to Lenny as "an accomplished, versatile musician evidently fallen on hard times. He was surely an embarrassed accomplice, though he managed to unroll a few fine riffs among the open spaces of the uncultivated potato patch."[23] *Toronto Star* writer Ian MacDougall echoed similar sentiments in a review he did of one of Murray's concerts later that summer, observing "jazz guitarist Lenny Breau seemed a little wasted on the relatively simple pop tunes Miss Murray sings."[24]

The band dipped into the United States to play a series of dates in Chicago, New York, and Boston where Betty Cody attended the show and met Murray backstage. "Anne Murray said back when I played with Hal in [Murray's home town] Spring Hill, Nova Scotia," recalls Betty, "that her mother and father used to take her to my shows and she'd say, 'boy, someday I'm gonna sing like that and I'm gonna yodel!'" After a few more gigs in the southeastern US, including a stop in Nashville where Lenny visited briefly with Chet Atkins, the band returned to Toronto to play at the Canadian National Exhibition on August 25. Murray then gave the band a three-week vacation, part of which Lenny spent at Skip Beckwith's Toronto home. Brent Titcomb recalls having an intriguing conversation with Lenny after dropping by for a visit and finding him practicing in Beckwith's backyard, which bordered a treed ravine.

> Lenny began talking about music and sharing some of his experiences. He had a guitar in his lap and he would punctuate some of the things that he would say by breaking into playing different passages. Then he became aware of the soundscape of the city and nature sounds because the yard was by this ravine so there were a lot of birds. I could see his attention shift to hearing everything and I went there with him, suddenly locked into what he was hearing or how he was hearing it. He knew that I was there with him and he started playing and riffing with the sounds of the city and nature. It was a very profound moment for me and revealed to me that as great a talent he was, he was limited by the instrument to some degree. We were only hearing a small fraction, just a portion of what he really heard in his mind. He was so receptive to the world around him in ways—a very, very sensitive person. Sometimes the world is just too harsh for a person like that.

In the second week of September, Lenny returned to Winnipeg to play two dates with Halldorson and Kelln. The first of these was an eighty-minute show in the Augustine United Church which reviewer Susan Janz said was full of "good vibes all around." The group played two sets of material that included "Hard Day's Night," "Autumn Leaves," and "Vision." Janz wrote, "[Lenny] demonstrated further his ability to take any emotion and translate it into music. His introspective themes are treated with subtlety and when he tears into a fast number, he plays circles around it. He's able to take a theme as far as it can go, and bring it all back home again without ever losing direction."[25] Lenny played two new guitars on this gig. His Baldwin had been stolen from a club in Chicago, and after trying several newer Baldwin models that didn't satisfy him, he purchased a solid body Gibson—model unknown—along with a new Yamaha Concert Classical to replace his Ramirez. Lenny had insisted on using the flamenco guitar as collateral for a loan from Toronto bassist Gary Binstead the year before and had never reclaimed it. At about the same time, he had sold his share of his Frank Gay nine string to Bob Erlendson who still owns it at the time of this writing.

After doing a second Winnipeg gig at the University of Manitoba's University Center on September 18, Lenny performed a few dates in the western United States with Anne Murray before returning to Toronto where he and Richard backed John Allan Cameron on his second album, *Lord of the Dance*. On Thursday, September 28, Lenny appeared with Anne Murray on *The Ian Tyson Show* and a month later performed with her at the National Arts Center in Ottawa. Capitol records recorded this performance and used material from it on Murray's 1973 album *Danny's Song*. Lenny is buried in the mix and the little that can be heard of his playing is generic and uninspired.

This would be Lenny's last performance with Anne Murray, but he was not yet finished working with her band. In early November, he laid down tracks with Richard for an unreleased album of Murray's hits that DT Thompson had arranged as funk/jazz instrumentals. Lenny played several excellent solos on the recording, particularly on "Bidin' My Time," where his lyrical nylon string phrases reveal depths not plumbed in Murray's version of the tune. He also recorded a beautiful acoustic rendition of "Meanwhile Back in LA" backed by Beckwith and Cree. Unfortunately, while Capitol had funded the project and was pleased with the album, they were horrified with the title Beckwith insisted on giving it. "The band's name was Richard," laughs Beckwith, "so I thought it should be called *Anne Murray Loves Dick!*" Capitol washed its hands of the project and the album was never released although a 45 from the session with the novelty tune "Dracula is Coming to Town" received some radio play.

During the last two weeks of November, Lenny played a few gigs with Beckwith and pianist Pat Riccio, Jr., at the Purple Onion in Toronto. Capitol had arranged a European tour for Murray and her band to begin in the New Year, but Lenny's contract with the group was not renewed. DT Thompson, a man with deep respect and affection for Lenny admits, "We just got tired of taking care of him all the time."

Lenny's tenure in Richard was a minor footnote in his career: more a signifier of his dire financial situation than a meaningful musical experience. Still, his parting of the ways with Murray marked the beginning of a severe downswing in his career and personal life. Contrary to the dark, pervasive mythology that has its origins in this period and frequently supplants the factual narrative of Lenny Breau's life, his career did not end at this point nor did his guitar skills atrophy and permanently vanish. However, he would never again have an association with a major recording label or garner the sort of industry attention that had briefly been his while recording for RCA. For the next five chaotic years, he would eke out a hand-to-mouth existence playing mainly in small, low-paying clubs and restaurants as he wandered aimlessly from one city and one dilemma to another. This downswing in his circumstances had everything to do with depression and a drug problem that had spiraled out of control, precluding any possibility of advancing his career or instrumental skills, and leaving all in a state of disarray.

7.

Turn Out the Stars
December 1972—July 1976

"I stopped progressing in a business sense when I started on drugs. I wasn't playing as much and not at the bigger places, but I still feel my mind kept on learning. I could always play things in my mind."

—Lenny Breau[1]

After leaving Richard, Lenny returned to Winnipeg to visit his children. On December 13, in search of heroin, he connected with a drug dealer in a downtown tavern, and the pair took a cab to a drug house in Winnipeg's North End. Lenny scored and returned to the cab, but as the vehicle pulled away, it was stopped by the police who had been watching the house and had seen the buy go down. Lenny was frisked, arrested, and taken to jail where he was charged with possession of heroin. Valerie covered Lenny's bail, and the court remanded him until January 8, 1973.

News of Lenny's arrest spread quickly through the city, fuelled by articles in local papers detailing the bust. Lenny had not lived in

Winnipeg for five years, but he was still a hometown celebrity and his public, while aware of his eccentricities, was shocked to find out that he was a heroin user. Melody and Chet were taunted at school while the parents of their tormentors shook their heads in disgust. "The attitude was like 'Hometown Boy Wonder Disappoints Winnipeg,' sort of thing," says Valerie.

When Lenny appeared in court in January, the judge set his trial date for March 21, and Lenny returned to Toronto for a date at George's Spaghetti House with Montreal bassist Michel Donato and drummer Claude Ranger. *Globe and Mail* critic Jack Batten wrote that the trio's sets were comprised of "good, swift inventive jazz" played for an audience largely made up of "dazzled and envious fellow musicians."[2] Lenny's lawyer had his trial date pushed ahead to May 10 and Lenny remained in Toronto, working frequently with Billy Meryll. Meryll's girlfriend was then working in Vancouver and she arranged for Lenny and her partner to come to the city to play a two-week stint in early April at a jazz club called The Nucleus. They opened on April 5, using a local drummer named Al Weirtz and received a glowing review in a local newspaper, which read in part, "[Lenny's] crisp and articulate style is a mellow pleasure for the ear, the mark of a craftsman whose constant inventiveness should delight guitar aficionados of all persuasions."[3]

A few weeks later, Lenny returned to Winnipeg for his hearing, justifiably concerned that a conviction would earn him the sort of stiff jail sentence typically handed down by the courts in Canada at that time for possession of heroin. Fortunately, his lawyer managed to persuade the judge that Lenny had turned his life around in the months since the bust, and presented him with an affidavit from a Toronto clinic to prove that he had been enrolled in a methadone program since January. This apparently swayed the judge, who handed down a two-year conditional sentence after telling Lenny, "you must not indulge in this sort of thing because you are just destroying yourself."[4] The ruling included a proviso stating that Lenny must report regularly to a probation office and continue his methadone treatment at a certified clinic in whatever town he happened to be. This was an enlightened and anomalous sentence at a time when possession of heroin was usually punished with lengthy jail time. Still, it did little to help Lenny with his problem, which despite his lawyer's contention, had not disappeared. In fact, audience members at the Nucleus gig say that while Lenny played well during his string of dates there, both he and Meryll were obviously stoned on heroin some nights. Therapy was not part of treatment in most methadone clinics; addicts were simply given a supply of the drug and told to move along after little more than a pep talk. Nor did clinics monitor their clients, which explains how Lenny could be using heroin in Vancouver while being officially registered in a methadone program in Toronto. The judge had, in effect, given Lenny a state-sanctioned license to procure methadone—a drug that he had used almost exclusively for recreational purposes for three years—with great ease in any city in Canada.

Lenny returned to Toronto where he did another gig at George's that was covered once more by Jack Batten who called him "one of the principal glories of the Toronto jazz scene."[5] It was not a glorious time for Lenny, however, who spent most of the next nine months scoring drugs and living with friends or putting up in seedy boarding-houses until he was evicted for non-payment of rent. He began to carry a knife in his boot, a dubious self-protective measure motivated by his low rent haunts and the dealers—often motorcycle gang members who now controlled Toronto's drug scene—from whom he scored his drugs. He played a few usually disastrous gigs but lived mainly on the charity of friends including Chet Atkins who kept in touch with him as best he could and pleaded with him to clean up his act. "He'd say 'Chet, I'm trying,'" Atkins later told an interviewer. "He was always dreaming. He was always saying that he would straighten out but he was never able to bring that about."[6]

In November of 1973, Lenny returned to Winnipeg and moved in with a female companion. He worked with a series of musicians that included Kelln and Halldorson, often at a coffee house called the Ting Tea Room. Here he alternately thrilled and embarrassed the musicians with whom he played, depending on how severely drugs and—increasingly—alcohol had affected his motor skills that night. He often dropped by a supper club called Chan's Moon Room to sit in with Kelln and Halldorson who had a steady gig there with Ray St. Germain, but quickly wore out his welcome. "Lenny was a mess," says Halldorson. "He was drinking with methadone and was always really messed up, crude, and loud. It got to be a real drag. We loved

Lenny, but it was just awful when he'd come by and want to sit in."
One night at the club, Lenny, in worse condition than usual, played
one note on the bass over and over again. St. Germain kept his cool,
but after the show, he blew up at Lenny and accused Kelln and Halldorson of turning a blind eye to Lenny's behavior. "Lenny and I
never really saw much of each other after that," he says.

Lenny stayed in Winnipeg for several more months, keeping
body and soul together with money procured from giving lessons
and playing low profile gigs at weddings, restaurants, and coffee
houses. In the summer of 1974, he returned to Vancouver to play at
The Nucleus with Billy Meryll and Al Weirtz. Singer/guitarist Eugene
Smith, who opened for the trio, recalls that Lenny fired Weirtz on
the first night of the gig and a few nights later took the same action
with Meryll. "They weren't getting along on stage," says Smith.
"Billy was really messed up and it made things worse for Lenny who
was stoned too. But Lenny was just phenomenal—at least for the
first set. In the second set, he'd just start nodding out and it would
be disastrous."

Coincidentally, Judi Singh was visiting Vancouver at the time and
dropped into The Nucleus one night when Lenny was playing there.
She and Lenny spoke for the first time in over three years and
although she was pleased to see him, she did not like the changes that
she saw. "He was just right out of it," Judi says. "He'd changed. It
was all about the drugs now: drugs, drugs, and more drugs. Great
losses and terrible waste."

Lenny remained in Vancouver for a few months, living with a
woman in a boardinghouse in the city's Kitsilano area. He gave up
playing entirely and spent most of his time availing himself freely of
the cheap, strong heroin for which the city was then known. Cedar
Christie, who was also living in Vancouver, ran into Lenny during
this period and recalls that "he seemed dark and very unhappy."

Lenny then pulled up stakes and traveled to Edmonton where he
played a weeklong gig at The Hovel coffee house. For the past year,
Lenny had been using a Hagstrom twelve-string guitar from which
he had removed the octave strings. Having pawned this instrument
after his second Nucleus gig, he arrived in Edmonton without a guitar and had to borrow one for his date at The Hovel. Despite the
unfamiliar instrument and three-month musical hiatus, Lenny played

well enough at the Edmonton gig that the club's owners offered him further work. Lenny was happy enough to remain in Edmonton, but his reasons for staying were motivated less by performance opportunities than affairs of the heart. Lenny had never been able to put his feelings for Judi Singh behind him and after seeing her in Vancouver, he was determined to resurrect the relationship that seemed to have ended irrevocably three years earlier. Singh, recalling their final difficult days in Toronto and Lenny's toxic condition at The Nucleus gig, initially refused to even consider reuniting with the father of her daughter. But when she learned that Lenny had enrolled in a methadone program in Edmonton and seemed to be genuinely trying to overcome his addiction, she agreed to give the relationship another chance on the condition that Lenny obey to the letter the strictures of his methadone program and gain control over his drug problem. Lenny accepted these conditions and appeared determined to honor them.

Singh was not yet ready to have Lenny move in with her and Emily, so for the next few months, Lenny shared a house with Gary Koliger, a musician he had met at The Hovel. Koliger was astounded by Lenny's facility not only on guitar but on a number of other stringed instruments as well. "Lenny was an excellent five-string banjo player," Koliger says. "He sounded like [virtuoso banjoist] Bela Fleck. I had my pedal steel guitar set up and Lenny could play the shit out of that too. He had a holographic memory for notes on any fretboard, which is why he could play anything so well."

Lenny was giving his creative impulses free rein during this period. In performance, he would often forgo standard repertoire in favor of playing spontaneous compositions—"stream of consciousness things," as Koliger describes them—made up on the spur of the moment. He also began experimenting on stage with African thumb pianos, various types of percussion, and autoharps that he placed on stools beside him, strumming the instruments with one hand while fretting his guitar with the other. He acquired a set of tubular bells that he would hang close to him on stage so he could strike and blow into them while playing his guitar. These musical experiments likely stemmed from his desire to capture the *musique concrete* he heard in the world around him—the sort of natural soundscape he had described to Brent Titcomb in Skip Beckwith's backyard two years earlier. "Lenny could hear harmony in traffic," says Koliger. "He'd be in the car when I was driving him to the methadone clinic and he'd hear a car horn and say 'li-li-li that's a sharp nine.' The cars, the wind. It was like what they say about dogs, that they smell the same way we see. It was eerie." At one point Lenny sewed small silver bells onto his long Afghan coat. When a puzzled Frank Gay asked him why, Lenny told him that the sound of the bells jingling around him as he walked gave him physical sensations that inspired him musically.

One afternoon while jamming with his friend, Gaye DeLorme, later a renowned guitarist and composer of international reputation, Lenny came across a book called *The Mysticism of Sound and Music* in Delorme's guitar case. The book's author, Sufi master Hazrat Inayat Khan, posits that music is the highest and most spiritually compelling of all the arts. It has, Khan contends, not only a powerful healing effect on body and soul, but is the source from which all life springs. "Before its incarnation," writes Khan, "the soul is sound. It is for this reason that we love sound."[7] The book and its message intrigued Lenny and he borrowed it from Delorme. When Lenny next saw his friend, he told him that the book was his bible, an assertion he would repeat many times to other friends over the coming years. This was not a sudden conversion experience, and it's unlikely that Lenny ever considered seriously practicing Sufism. Music had simply been the center of Lenny's universe since childhood and Khan's conception of music as the essence of life coincided with his own perspective. Until the last years of his life, Lenny carried with him a well-thumbed copy of Khan's book and often took solace in its words.

In September 1974, *Guitar Player* magazine published the first major article ever written on Lenny. In the article, titled "Atkins Style Jazz on a 6-string 12" in reference to the Hagstrom he had owned at the time the article was written, Lenny touches on a number of subjects including his preference for solid body guitars and his respect for guitarist John McLaughlin. He lauds the current music scene but asserts that jazz musicians have been held back commercially by the huge popularity of rock. "It just seems to me that the main thing is to not mention that it's jazz and then you can sell the album," he says. Curiously, he says "I'm really happy about the popularity that I've got out of [my first two albums]."[8] He tells the interviewer that he's anxious to get back into the studio and do a new album and wants to get out of the small club scene into concert-type venues where the money is better and distraction from the audience is not a factor.

At the time the article appeared, Lenny was a long way from realizing these goals. In Edmonton, he took work where he could find it: club and restaurant dates, a few CBC shows, and a recording session with Canadian pop star Terry McManus for a never-released album. In October, he returned to Winnipeg to play with Halldorson and Kelln at a concert for Winnipeg's Festival of Light. CBC broadcast and recorded this date on which Lenny played another obscure original called "The Message," an up-tempo minor/modal blues. Halldorson and Kelln tear the tune apart, sounding far more aggressive and adventurous than they do on either of Lenny's recordings. Lenny's playing, however, was routine and flaccid, and the tone of his guitar—a new Guild SG copy that he had bought in Edmonton—is thin and trebly.

On November 14, he was back in Edmonton to play a date at the city's SUB Theatre, leading a group that included Pete Thompson, who had been part of the original Jazz A Go-Go house band. Lenny was, according to a review published the next day "in fine fettle . . . tanned and fit and in great spirits. . . ." The first set was an hour and half long and included a thirteen-minute version of "Days of Wine and Roses," "My Funny Valentine," and a solo performance of Bill Evans's "Two Lonely People," which had become a staple of Lenny's repertoire. The reviewer says that this tune "demonstrated the sureness and deftness with which Lenny handles the instrument." During the second half of the concert, Judi Singh joined the band for a forty-minute set, which kicked off with "Stella by Starlight." Her presence, notes the reviewer, "bolstered an already impressive array of instrumentalists. . . . ."[9]

Leery of Lenny's drug problem, Judi Singh had twice turned down his proposals of marriage. However, by November of 1974 Lenny seemed to have gained control over his addiction and when he proposed for the third time, Judi accepted on the condition that he remain in the methadone program and continue to work on his drug problem. Lenny eagerly agreed to this condition and the couple began to plan their wedding.

Lenny was now living at the Singh household. This was five-year-old Emily's first recollected contact with her father and she was in awe of him, she says, watching him closely as he played his guitar for her in the family's living room. Sadly, the relationship would be short-lived. Lenny was becoming discouraged with his methadone treatment and the clinic's complete lack of support and encouragement. "There really wasn't any help, serious productive help," Judi says. "Anybody who was strung out was looked at as the scum of the earth. There wasn't a positive attitude like 'you can do this.' The therapist told Lenny that he needed to go to church and *that* was going to save him; this was coming from a counselor at a clinic! Then he'd come home from the clinic and he'd be so zonked that I couldn't wake him up. A bomb could have gone off and it wouldn't have disturbed him. That's how stoned he was on methadone."

Methadone's lethargic high was no longer enough for Lenny. He began using heroin again and a few days after Judi's wedding shower, she stumbled across Lenny's used syringes in the garage of her home. She immediately cancelled the engagement, ordered Lenny to leave her house, and permanently ended her relationship with him. Although the Singhs would occasionally receive cards and letters from Lenny, they never saw him again.

Devastated, Lenny returned to Winnipeg. For the next few months, he taught and played sporadically while living in one of the city's most notorious drug houses. In January of 1975, he contributed a mediocre solo to a track on singer/songwriter Len Udow's CBC-sponsored album. "His musical intellect wasn't all that playful the night of the recording because of his drinking," explains Udow, who had known Lenny and admired his playing since the early sixties. "He usually had such a fine sense of discovery, this delight even when he was somewhat stoned, but this session was disappointing because he didn't even come up with that."

In the throes of chronic addiction and estranged from friends and family, Lenny fled to Toronto in February of 1975 but could not outrun the darkness that had pursued him for the past three years. For several years, Billy Meryll had struggled with a drug and alcohol habit that surpassed Lenny's. Not long after Lenny returned to Toronto, Meryll's demons finally overcame him and he took his life in the kitchen of the apartment he shared with his girlfriend. Lenny was distraught over this news and, as he had done after Ron Park's death, ratcheted up his drug use another dangerous notch. He virtually quit playing, and was soon destitute and dependent upon friends and newly made acquaintances for shelter. While staying at the home of Bill Evans's former drummer Marty Morell and his wife Craggy, Lenny wandered into a nearby convenience store. Stoned and disheveled, he aroused the suspicions of a clerk who called the police. When they arrived, Lenny gave them an angry lecture on the plight of the American Indian—a favorite subject of his when he was high—and the police frisked him. They found the knife he kept in his boot, arrested him for possession of a concealed weapon, and took him to jail. Frantic, Lenny called Don Thompson who in turn contacted Glenn MacDonald. MacDonald took charge of the situation and was able to persuade the police to release Lenny into his custody.

MacDonald and his wife Lynn were then living near Killiloe, a small town west of Ottawa. Years earlier, MacDonald had had his own struggles with drugs, and in 1970, he and his wife had left Toronto to join the then popular "back to the land" movement. The couple built a two-story, twelve- by twenty-four-foot log cabin with no indoor plumbing or electricity on a several-hundred-acre tract of land, and their sylvan home soon became a retreat for many of their city dwelling friends. After rescuing Lenny from jail, the MacDonalds elected to take Lenny back to the farm for an extended period of time and, armed with a ten-day supply of methadone obtained from a Toronto clinic, help him defeat his habit once and for all. When he and his hosts arrived in Killaloe, Lenny appeared to be exhausted and was put to bed in an upstairs room. A few hours later, however, when he was sure the McDonalds were asleep, he stole downstairs and swallowed his entire methadone supply for one last body and mind numbing high before sobriety. "We were left," says Lynn Mac-Donald, "with an itchy, scratchy Lenny who was trying his best to crawl out of his skin."

Over the next month, Lenny sweated out his toxins and his health began to return. MacDonald gave him a nylon string Yamaha guitar, which Lenny clung to like a life preserver while those around him carried out the endless day to day chores that needed to be done. MacDonald ran a contracting business that did demolition and restoration of old buildings in the Killaloe area. Obviously, Lenny was not predisposed to work of this sort, but he insisted on contributing musically to the morale and spirit of the workers, says trombonist John Capon, a Toronto-based session musician who played with the Toronto symphony and Rob McConnell's Boss Brass big band. "I remember once Glenn got a call to pull down an old building close by," says Capon. "So Lenny says, 'well, I'll come along and help, but I think I'll bring my guitar just in case.' It was so hot—August hot: sticky, buggy, sweaty, and it was a big, heavy, dusty, dirty job. Lenny said, 'hey guys, I'm gonna play.' So he stood around with his acoustic guitar right beside us while we were lifting these big old logs. The day went by like that. His guitar playing was so beautiful that we didn't even notice the pain and the sweat and the heat because he'd just be right in our faces, virtually touching our ears with his instrument as he played, and we were totally focused on this."

These idyllic days were not entirely carefree, however. For the past few years, Revenue Canada had been pursuing Lenny for a $15,000 tax bill that he had amassed during his days at CBC Winnipeg and in the years following. Lenny's income since leaving Anne Murray had been negligible and he had been unable to pay down the bill, which continued to rise as penalties were added. This debt load was compounded by several years' worth of unpaid child support payments. MacDonald, whom many friends describe affectionately as a born hustler, hit on a plan to alleviate Lenny's financial problems and open some career doors for him in the process. He explained to Lenny that he would record a demo tape of his solo work and shop it around to record labels in hopes of garnering him a recording contract and a large cash advance that could wipe out his debt. MacDonald then purchased a reel-to-reel tape recorder and a generator to power it with a grant from the Canada Council of the Arts. He set up the generator in the barn and ran a cord from it to the tape recorder in the granary where Lenny would play. Bob Erlendson, a regular visitor to Killiloe, describes the results of the sessions.

> They made [the tapes] over a period of six weeks, slogging away and getting a little bit here and a little bit there. But playing it back was so disappointing. The sound of the generator had leaked onto the

tape and there was so much distortion that whatever good playing there was on it was ruined. Lenny was not happy with it either. The first part of it was just him noodling around and then he started getting his head working a little bit better towards the end and they had some examples of stuff that wasn't all that bad but it was just badly recorded. So in desperation they came down to Toronto to record at Don Thompson's home studio.

Thompson managed to record only a few tunes before the session bogged down. A confirmed chain smoker, Lenny was unable to play without puffing his way through a steady stream of cigarettes, something that Thompson—a militant non-smoker—forbade him to do in his house. The men moved the session to Gary Binstead's home where Lenny used his old Ramirez, still in Binstead's possession, for the second half of the recording. The recorded sound on these sessions was superior to those he'd done at the farm, but Lenny was not pleased with his playing and refused to allow the recording to be sent out to record labels. MacDonald had no choice but to reluctantly box and shelve the tape.

Twenty years later, MacDonald approached Guitarchives Records with a tape of Lenny that he said had been recorded on the farm, a detail that he apparently felt gave the recording an element of romantic mystique that made up for Lenny's aimless playing. With no reason to doubt MacDonald, Guitarchives bought the tape and released its contents on a CD titled *Cabin Fever*. However, Thompson, Binstead, and Erlendson all insist that this is the recording Lenny made in Toronto and the whereabouts of the tape of the failed sessions at Killiloe are unknown. Whatever the actual location of the *Cabin Fever* sessions, it's little wonder that Lenny was not happy with his performances on the recording. Although his technique and tone are laudable, and there are moments where Lenny seems about to take off, the CD is not much more than a rambling, unfocused practice session. Lenny noodles half-heartedly through a few standards and fragments of unidentifiable tunes for which Guitarchives contrived names such as "Celtic Dream Stream" and "Lenny's Mood" (actually a mistitling of the standard "Why did I Choose You?"). Lenny often felt pressured in studio situations, particularly when recording unaccompanied, and this CD captures the uninspired results of one such session.

Except for occasionally sampling the weak pot that MacDonald grew on the farm, Lenny spent the late spring and summer entirely drug-free. His mental and physical health had improved considerably and although he confessed to John Capon that after years of being high on stage he was uneasy about performing straight, he was eager to begin working again. His first gig was a performance with Don Thompson and Marty Morell at the Riverboat in mid-July. In a review of the gig in *Down Beat*, jazz journalist Mark Miller addressed a rumor about Lenny's death that had been circulating during his absence from Toronto, announcing "Lenny Breau is very much alive." Miller goes on to say that Lenny began each night "playing carefully . . . drawing his improvisation out of a wash of chords and working, in a roundabout way, towards a chorus or three of spectacular lines. Later on he would play more spaciously, almost editing the thoughts that he might have had earlier, and riding high, deliberately, and assuredly on Thompson and Morell." Miller finishes the article by noting Lenny's rising confidence and pleasure in his playing. "The two years off have had their effect," Miller concludes, "but he still has the magic. It's White Magic, of course, starting to shine again."[10]

On his trips to Toronto, Lenny often stayed with John Capon, who says that he was pleased and honored to put Lenny up at his apartment despite their very different lifestyles. Lenny would wake up midday, says Capon, light a cigarette and begin to play his guitar while still in bed. He recalls that at this time his houseguest was working intently on voice-leading chords built from modes and diminished scales.

> He was running modes in three-part parallel lines. For example, he would start with a diminished scale and use it to build a little three-part chord, a diminished triad or a minor second, minor third thing. Then he'd run it up the fretboard in parallel motion—all in that scale. He was just obsessed with that idea and practiced it constantly to get them flowing because if you could do it you could play these beautiful things over top of ordinary chords, diminished harmonies and whole tune harmonies, using these as melodic patterns. For example, he'd take a B-flat 7th chord as his basic chord and run a diminished scale [half step-whole step] over it. He'd take

that scale and create a little three diminished triad, say B♭-D♭-E, and run them up while sticking to that scale. The whole resulting texture works over a B-flat 7th chord. Because of the huge difficulty of getting this down, he was spending lots of time trying to work it out, trying to do the fingerings, trying to ingest it so it flowed for him and would happen spontaneously during moments of improvisation without thinking.

Lenny had been using similar constructions in his playing since about 1971, often in the form of arpeggios that he would drop into his single-note solos. Originally, these were memorized sequences, but Lenny's goal, as Capon points out, was to use the device in spontaneous improvisation. It's difficult to know precisely when it began to appear in live performance but the technique turns up on his recordings after 1977, particularly in modal tunes like "Vision."

In late October of 1975, Glenn MacDonald and Lenny came to stay at Capon's house with, unbeknownst to the trombonist who was not a drug user, a pound of low-grade, homegrown pot to sell to friends in the city. MacDonald did his transactions surreptitiously while Capon was at work, and by Halloween night, there was only a small amount left of his wares. Capon was out at a party, and Lenny and MacDonald were relaxing in Capon's living room when the police entered the apartment with—according to Lenny—guns drawn. As MacDonald and Capon later discovered, a police surveillance team had been staking out a building nearby and noticed the comings and goings of MacDonald's customers, one of whom the police detained when he/she was leaving the building. The customer confessed to buying pot at Capon's apartment and on this evidence the police managed to obtain a search warrant. Tipped off by the customer they had rousted, they went directly to the closet where MacDonald had stashed the remainder of the pot, arrested Lenny and MacDonald, and charged them with possession of marijuana with intent to traffic. The police then contacted Capon who hurried to the station where Lenny and MacDonald were being held. After a short discussion with the police, he was taken into custody when he refused to testify against his friends. The next morning, the police released the men, and Capon and MacDonald drove in a rush to Killaloe, fearing that the police might search the farm. Lenny stayed behind, convinced that his second bust in three years would earn him a stiff jail sentence. That evening he phoned Bob Erlendson from the Toronto airport and in a panic-stricken voice told him that he was returning to Maine. Erlendson tried to calm him, but Lenny would not be placated and, with only the clothes he was wearing, boarded a plane to the United States.

In discussing this event in later years, Lenny portrayed himself as a falsely accused, innocent bystander who was unfairly stuck with the rap and forced to run. The charge against him, he insisted, arose from MacDonald's refusal to confess ownership of the pot that police found in Capon's hall closet. "He wouldn't admit it was his so we all got charged with the same thing," Lenny complained in a 1981 interview. "Plus, I didn't show up in court because my dad was dying in the states so it made me look like the guilty one . . . like the guy who had the big two pounds and wanted to sell it. So I had to take the rap."[11] Not only was Lenny's father reasonably hale and hearty at the time, MacDonald had in fact deflected all blame from Lenny, confessing to the police that the pot was his alone. This admission was moot because the police quickly realized that they had not busted a significant dealer and didn't even bother to show up for MacDonald's hearing. His charge was lowered to simple possession and the judge levied a small fine. However, because Lenny did not appear at the proceedings, the charge against him stood. The judge had no choice but to issue a bench warrant for his arrest and at that moment Lenny became a fugitive in the eyes of the Canadian justice system. This would preclude his entering Canada for the next six years, during which time the landed immigrant status he had held since the age of sixteen lapsed and was revoked. At least as a resident, Lenny's twenty-two-year relationship with his adopted country was over and he would never live in Canada again.

As he had done four years earlier, Lenny returned to Auburn to stay with his mother. Betty had revived her singing career and done a tour with Dick Curless, who had scored a major national hit a few years earlier with "A Tombstone Every Mile." After leaving Curless's band, Betty began singing regularly at a resort in nearby Poland Springs, a job she would hold until the early eighties. She had also reluctantly played a few dates with her erstwhile husband, more out of compassion for Pine than any interest in reviving the Lone

Pine/Betty Cody duo. Pine, now a chronic alcoholic, was still performing around New England, playing mainly in seedy bars that he would not have set foot in five years earlier. Jeannie Ward had left him and returned to Winnipeg, and Pine was now seeing Bernice Possounier, a Lewiston resident who was also struggling with alcoholism. Lenny reconnected with his father shortly after arriving back in Maine and visited him often at Possounier's apartment in a rough area of Lewiston between the taverns of Lisbon Street and the waterfront mills. "Lenny used to make my home his home," she says, "which I didn't mind because he was very close to his dad, very close." Unfortunately, father and son did much of their bonding over endless drinks in run-down Lisbon Street bars where they soon became a familiar and sometimes pathetic sight. During a visit to Toronto in 1981, Lenny told Cedar Christie that his father taught him how to drink during this period. Considering that Lenny's habit of mixing alcohol and methadone seems to have begun in 1972, this is another example of Lenny's tendency to bend the truth into his own design. Still, there's no doubt that Lenny became a chronic binge drinker under his father's guidance. Possounier says that Lenny's drugs of preference at this time—mainly pills and potent cough syrup—distressed Pine and he pressured Lenny to change his vice to a substance that he deemed safer and healthier. Ironically, alcohol had a far more devastating effect on Lenny's nervous system than any other drug he used, including heroin. A few drinks were often enough to completely sabotage his coordination, and his most egregious performances were the result of drinking. It was also the one substance that Lenny would never entirely give up.

While Auburn and Lewiston's robust music scene kept Top Forty bands like Denny Breau's working six nights a week, there was little call for a jazz guitarist in the region, even one of Lenny's stature. However, not long before Lenny returned to Maine, a local entrepreneur named Peter Balis had opened up a club in Auburn called the Cellar Door, and began to hire musicians to play the small room. "I was having single and double acts at that time," says Balis. "One day, this gentleman showed up, an agent, nobody local. [This may have been Rusty Scott who was Pine's manager for a very short period in the '70s] He left me a picture of Lenny and played him up as a premier guitar player. Everyone knew who Hal and Betty Cody were, but I had no idea who Lenny Breau was. I listened to him and I couldn't understand what he was doing," admits Balis. Still, Balis recognized his talent and hired him to play at the club where Lenny would be a fixture on and off for the next five years.

Between January and May of 1976, Lenny also played several performances at the University of Maine in Orono, gigs organized by graduate students Andrew Periale and Mike Hughes. Although the men were aware of Lenny's substance abuse problem and had some concerns about his reliability, Periale says that this was never a problem at any of the shows. "He'd do a little bit of this and a little bit of that and be pretty wasted by the time of the concert but his playing was amazing," Periale says. "Once he sat down and focused on the music, he was fine. He went over really well. You couldn't hear him without being stunned by what he was doing whether you were a musician or not." This is borne out by a recording Periale made of one of Lenny's Orono concerts, probably in April 1976. Lenny played two sets on his nylon string that included "Five O'clock Bells," "Days of Wine and Roses," "Emily," (which he dedicates to his daughter in Edmonton) and a beautiful rendition of "Theme from Spartacus," an exquisite piece that Bill Evans recorded in the mid-sixties. He also did his crowd-pleasing two-key/two-time signature novelty tune and sang his trademark set-closer, "Back in the Saddle." Considering the drug inflicted physical trauma of the past four years, his technique was remarkably good despite some clams and general stiffness.

At the Orono concert, Lenny was in a congenial, outgoing mood, joking and kibitzing articulately with his audience between tunes and if he were high, his condition did not seem to interfere with his playing. At the Cellar Door, however, it was common for him to play a woozy ten-minute set before taking a break and heading for the bar. Some nights he would wander into the club hours late or not show up at all. Maurice Hebert, who had opened his jazz record collection to Lenny in the fifties, did his best to look after Lenny and keep his drinking to a minimum. "He palled around with his dad quite a bit then and went out of his way to be friends with him, probably a little too much," says Hebert. "Lenny would have a few drinks and he'd tell me 'I want my mom back with my father.' This was long after they'd left each other for good, but it was still in his mind after all

those years." Lenny would spend days at a time bar-hopping with
Pine, sometimes playing for drinks in a shabby tavern called the 20M
Club, a "social club" to which Pine belonged and the site of his marriage to Bernice Possounier that August. "Lenny and his dad went on
such a binge," says Betty. "I'd say, 'you're killing yourself' and he'd
say nothing." Betty was frightened and decided that the only way to
end Lenny's relentless alcoholic juggernaut was to get him away from
Auburn and his father's influence. Lenny was not eager to leave but
Betty finally persuaded her son to call Chet Atkins to see if there
were any opportunities for him in Nashville. Atkins sensed the
urgency of the situation and immediately wired Lenny money for a
plane ticket with a promise that good things were awaiting him in
Music City.

In mid-May, Lenny finally boarded a southbound plane at the
Portland airport, but his destination was not Nashville. Instead, on a
whim Lenny decided to fly to Wheeling to visit his old friend, Ray
Couture, whom he had not seen for nearly twenty years. He gave his
former guitar mentor no warning that he was coming to Wheeling,
and, unprepared for the visit, Couture was initially at a loss when
Lenny greeted him outside the radio station where he now worked as
a sales representative. "There was this guy with really long hair and
this long coat, a hippie. His teeth were real bad: brown and rotten,"
recalls Couture. "Then he says, 'Hi Ray,' and I looked at him for a
minute and said, 'Lenny, is that you?'" Despite the changes in his old
friend, Couture was delighted to see Lenny, and he and his wife welcomed him into their home. Lenny, Couture recalls, spoke little
about his present situation, preferring to recall old times with Ray
and the family band in Wheeling, Maine, and New Brunswick. Couture says that his plans for the future were vague and although Lenny
mentioned that Atkins had summoned him to Nashville, the city and
its opportunities seemed to hold no real interest for him. "Lenny did-
n't seem to know what he wanted to do with his life. So I says, 'here's
what you do. When you land in Nashville, you tell Chet that you'd
like to be sideman on the RCA label. The first year you play there,
you'll make $150,000.' All he had to do was work for a few years
like that and he'd be set and he could play whatever he wanted
then." Lenny, Couture says, nodded and looked thoughtful, and then

told his old friend that what he really wanted to do was to go to Spain and rub shoulders with some *flamencoistas*.

Lenny spent his days in Wheeling aimlessly: checking out music stores, occasionally jamming with some of Couture's friends and still drinking heavily. The latter activity began to fray his hosts' patience and they arranged for him to bunk on a couch in the apartment of their daughter, Darlene, who lived in nearby Bridgeport, Ohio. Lenny played occasional gigs in Wheeling, usually drinking to quell his nerves before going on stage. One day, during an afternoon of alcohol consumption with one of Darlene's neighbors, Lenny stumbled and fell through a glass coffee table. Couture's daughter had to administer first aid to her inebriated and bloody house guest as he joked about winning his fight with the neighbor's furniture. Shortly after this incident, Lenny moved in with Doc Williams, who had been responsible for bringing his parents to Wheeling in 1953 and was still active as a performer.

In late June, Atkins came to town to play a concert at Wheeling's Ogilvie Park. He and Lenny spoke after the performance and Atkins once again tried to persuade him to come to Nashville. Lenny balked, but Atkins was not ready to give up. About a week after the concert, he called Doc Williams's home asking for Lenny. When Williams told him that he was not at home, Atkins left an explicit message for his friend, Williams recalls. "Chet told me, 'Well, when he gets back, tell him I want him to come to Nashville. Tell him that I'll send him $400 and I want him in Nashville as soon as possible. Tell him that I have some plans for him.'" Williams relayed the message to his guest but Lenny seemed to take it more as threat than an invitation. "Plans" were something that Lenny had been trying to avoid for the past four difficult years. Since leaving the Murray band, he had drifted on impulse and without purpose, seeking relief from depression and the slightest pressure with whatever substances were at hand. The thought of trying to rebuild his professional life was terrifying to a man who had been hard-pressed to maintain even a healthy career. Wheeling offered him little beyond the companionship of a few old and dear friends who were happy to serve as his caretakers and reminisce with him about the golden years of his childhood. But the town provided sanctuary, as Auburn had done, from the weighty commitments that he sensed would be involved in putting his life back together. Still, Lenny regretted the hard, reckless, and unproductive living of those lost years, less for the damage it had inflicted on his career than its deleterious effect on his art. He had managed to maintain his skills at—considering the abuse he had heaped on himself—a surprisingly high level, but his technique had suffered and his playing had not evolved significantly. "It's like a painter who goes through five years or so of confusion," he said of those years to one interviewer. "He's just trying to feel a specific thing, or maybe develop a certain technique. And possibly those years will go by and he hasn't really done anything he's proud of. It's something like that I went through."[12] Lenny would never be entirely free of the problems that had wreaked havoc on his life during the past half-decade. Still, the next several years would be far more productive ones for him than the chaotic and punishing period that had begun when he was ousted from the Anne Murray band. His decision to finally obey Atkins's summons to come to Nashville was the first step in salvaging a life, a career, and a gift that a few years earlier had seemed on the verge of being irrevocably damaged.

8.

Back in the Saddle Again
July 1976—May 1980

"I always felt I could go down [to Nashville] and rub shoulders with Chet and my inspiration would come back."

—Lenny Breau[1]

This time around, no film crews greeted Lenny in Nashville as they had when he'd arrived in the city as the *enfant terrible* of guitar eight years earlier. Even Atkins, who was tied up with business, was not on hand to meet him when his plane touched down at the Nashville airport one day in early July 1976. Instead, Atkins had sent his pianist Randy Goodrum to pick Lenny up and keep him overnight at his home. The next day Goodrum took Lenny to Chet's office at RCA where the two guitarists, who had not seen each other since Lenny had visited Nashville briefly with the Anne Murray band in 1972, greeted each other happily. On hand to witness the reunion was guitarist/arranger John Knowles, a Texan with a doctorate in physics who had given up a position with Texas Instruments to come to Nashville to work as a guitarist. There he formed a close working and personal friendship with Atkins and provided him with several arrangements that became staples of Atkins's repertoire.

Atkins placed the responsibility of getting Lenny settled in Knowles's hands and sent the pair out to investigate a small apartment he'd found for Lenny in a motel-like complex not far from the RCA building where Atkins had his office. After helping Lenny complete the rental deal, Knowles drove him to Nashville Electric to open an account, a chore that stymied Lenny for whom the act of completing any official form was an agonizing one. Atkins would always make sure the rent was covered on Lenny's apartment but, many times, friends would drop by to discover Lenny playing his guitar by candlelight, less for the ambiance than as a result of his having ignored a series of disconnection notices from Nashville Electric.

Atkins had found Lenny a six-night-a-week gig at Ireland's Restaurant on 21st Avenue South: "a sort of family steak and biscuit house" as Knowles describes it. On the night of Saturday, July 17, musicians, music industry movers and shakers, and fans packed the place to watch Lenny do four sets on a guitar supplied by Paul Yandell who was also present. Atkins had made sure that a reporter from Nashville's daily paper, *The Tennessean*, was on hand to do a review of the show and he peppered his portion of the interview with accolades about Lenny's prowess. "I think he's one of the greatest players I've ever known—and I've known a lot of them," he told the reporter. "I listen to Lenny and I go home and practice for about three hours." The article continues with a bio of Lenny and a description of his style before addressing his drug problem, which Lenny claims is in the past and was brought on by "the pressures of show business and the break-up of his marriage." "Drugs are a downer," he says. "They'll get you in the end—like alcohol." (Years later, Lenny disingenuously blamed this article for trumpeting his drug problem to local dealers who, he claimed, came to Ireland's to pressure him into taking up his old habits.) The article concludes with Lenny saying, "It's nice to be alive again. . . ." an appropriate line considering that many of his fans in Nashville had been surprised to learn that Lenny was still among the living.[2]

One of these was twenty-two-year-old guitarist, Stephen Anderson, who two decades later would write *Visions*, the definitive book on Lenny's guitar style. Anderson was a rock guitarist just edging into jazz when a friend of his, the son of Lenny's first producer Danny Davis, gave him Lenny's two RCA albums. "I was in shock after hearing those records," he recalls. "Nobody ever made an impact like that on me, and I had an immediate and incredible respect for him." Anderson assumed that Lenny was dead or had long since faded from the scene, and was naturally skeptical when a friend told him that Lenny was playing at Ireland's. He dropped by the restaurant the next night, and arrived just as Lenny was shuffling up to the small stage to begin his set. Anderson didn't recognize Lenny as the guitarist who graced the cover of his prized albums until he played the first notes of the set. "I knew for certain then that it was him, and he was fantastic," says Anderson. "He played with his eyes closed and at one point he opened them and I was sitting directly in front of him. He saw me and started smiling that incredible smile that he always had. After the set was over, he came over and sat down." Lenny and Anderson talked until Lenny returned to the stage and played several songs Anderson had requested from the RCA albums as well as "Here's that Rainy Day" and Bill Evans's "Waltz for Debby."

When the gig ended, Lenny asked Anderson for a lift home and invited him inside when they arrived. The two men spent the entire night talking and listening to Lenny's small stash of records, which included *Workin' with The Miles Davis Quintet* and Sonny Greenwich's *The Old Man and the Child* on a cheap record player Lenny had bought with funds from Atkins. "We just talked about everything," says Anderson. "He told me about Lone Pine and his mom and that he'd almost given up playing after his first two records. But when I asked him why, he didn't seem to remember much of what had happened."

Anderson returned to Ireland's nightly to listen to Lenny, talking with him between sets and inevitably driving him home. Soon the men were spending afternoons together hanging out in downtown Nashville. "It was like we were looking for Hank Williams's footsteps," says Anderson. "I think he expected there to be a lot more of the old Nashville than there was. He loved all that stuff, all that old country thing. There were a lot of snobs in this town who would put down that whole trip, but Lenny was never like that. He always had a great deal of respect for Chet and Merle and that whole tradition."

As close as Lenny became to his new friend, Anderson says that Lenny kept him at arm's length from his friendship with Atkins whom he saw almost daily at his RCA office. "Their friendship was very private," Anderson explains. "I didn't have to be told that; I knew it. Lenny's girlfriends couldn't even go with him when he met Chet. It was an interesting thing, but Chet would come by sometimes when Lenny was really down and Lenny would pick right up. Chet would hardly stay in the apartment. He didn't like it much so he would take him to lunch and then go by his office and spend the day."

Atkins was a busy man, but never too preoccupied to spend a few minutes jamming with Lenny (and other members of Nashville's inner circle of guitarists) who dropped by regularly to say hello and swap licks. As Atkins related in his book *Me and My Guitars*, more often than not, these jams would turn into impromptu lessons.

> [Lenny would] come by my office almost every day and try to teach me things, and I would always put on a tape because I knew I wouldn't remember it. He showed me some different chord positions that made certain rolls [fingerpicking patterns] and arpeggios possible, and were especially helpful for playing alternating bass and melody. He played with all five fingers on his right hand, and some of his licks I couldn't get because I never really learned to use my right little finger. His depth and freedom of expression were amazing to me.[3]

Lenny was eager to record again, but there was no possibility of returning to RCA, and a deal that Atkins had tried to swing for Lenny with A&M records failed to get off the ground. For the time being, Lenny's only recording experiences took place in the studio Atkins had built in the basement of his suburban Nashville home. The first of these was a duet version of "Sweet Georgia Brown," which Atkins included on his 1976 album, *The Best of Chet Atkins and Friends*. The duo plays an arranged opening chorus with chordal harmonics in harmony before Atkins turns the show over to Lenny who takes several solo choruses on the old chestnut. Lenny's playing is competent, but his ideas are routine and his guitar sound is thin, particularly in comparison to Atkins's fuller, richer tone.

Lenny was acutely aware that his playing had suffered during the past few years and desperately wanted to regain and surpass his former élan, Anderson says.

> He was trying to get it together and bounce back right then. Sometimes he'd say that he didn't play well, and that he really needed to get down and do some work. And that's exactly what he did, too. He practiced constantly. It seemed to me when I heard him play that first night, he played great but at that general time he had not made the mental and spiritual commitment to playing at the level he knew he could play. At times it was like he was winging it and was maybe only giving 50 percent. That's all he could muster. It's not that he wasn't into it but he didn't feel like he was quite there yet to do what he knew he could do. He would express to me at times that he needed to get it together and was excited about working on his technique, getting into new material as well as keeping up his old material.

A month or so into his gig at Ireland's, Lenny began a relationship with twenty-year-old Sinde Shubert, a budding musician who sang and played a smattering of guitar and bass. Neither a drinker nor a drug-user, Shubert had a subtle knack for dissuading Lenny from overindulging in his vices, says Anderson. "Lenny hated to be pressured and told not to drink," Anderson says. "He'd react to that and Sinde understood that. A couple of times when he might have had a little too much, she'd say something about it, say it again, and then she'd stop. She'd know he was gonna do it and she'd stay with him anyway and help him home when he was done and that was the end of it. She wouldn't be happy about it, but she wouldn't bitch about it either. She'd just say, 'OK let's go.'" Atkins was also pleased with Lenny's new mate, and once told an interviewer, "Cindy [sic] has been a stable influence on Lenny. . . . She's been real good for him and I think he loves her a lot."[4]

Shubert was not able to keep Lenny from drinking on the job at Ireland's, however. Lenny had abstained during his first month at the restaurant, but he was still not comfortable performing sober, and Anderson says that he often appeared nervous and on edge. Playing four sets a night to a roomful of family diners and struggling to be heard above their conversations and the clatter of dishes while in this condition was apparently too much for Lenny. He began fortifying himself with alcohol before and during the gig and many evenings he was unable to play his third set. One night, Anderson recalls, a group of record executives dropped in to check out the new phenomenon in town. Lenny was in rough shape after a few too many and the executives loudly mocked his performance before leaving. Soon, the only people showing up to hear Lenny play were a handful of Nashville guitarists who were often disappointed by his erratic playing. Less than two months into his gig at Ireland's, even Atkins's influence could not stop the restaurant from letting Lenny go.

Despite the missed income, Lenny was not unhappy to lose the gig at Ireland's and soon found work in a club better suited to his music. Mississippi Whiskers was a popular restaurant/club with a regular clientele that came to listen to the musicians who performed on its small stage, rather than to talk over them, as been the case at Ireland's. Lenny would play here regularly over the next few years, often in the company of other Nashville musicians. One of these was the late Richard Cotten, an excellent swing guitarist and owner and manager of the highly respected Nashville music store that still bears his name. In 1972, Atkins had introduced Cotten and Lenny when the latter was passing through Nashville with the Anne Murray band. When Lenny returned to the city in 1976, the two quickly became close friends and began playing together as a duo with Cotten on bass. Neither Cotten nor the other musicians—a group comprised largely of Nashville studio players—with whom Lenny played at Mississippi Whiskers really challenged him musically, but they became a close, friendly circle and this camaraderie was important to Lenny. Legendary country/jazz guitarist picker Jimmy Bryant was a marginal member of this crowd for a time and although he usually disdained fingerpickers, he greatly admired Lenny's playing. "The first night Bryant saw Lenny," says Anderson, "he couldn't believe what he was hearing and couldn't figure out how Lenny was doing it. He thought it was a trick or that Lenny was using an open tuning or something. He was amazed."

Lenny's mood improved further in August when he received a visit from his daughter and son, now sixteen and fourteen respectively. Chet and Melody stayed with Lenny in his cramped apartment, but despite the overcrowding, he was elated to be with his children. "Lenny really changed around his kids," Anderson says. "Suddenly he was very happy, warm, and very up, joking and laughing all the time. It helped to get him out of that down phase and he was drinking way less." During their visit, Lenny's children went often to Mississippi Whiskers to watch their father play. Unencumbered by drugs and liquor, Lenny was in fine form night after night and his children were given the opportunity to see their father at his best, musically and otherwise.

Unfortunately, shortly after Chet and Melody returned to Winnipeg, Lenny veered sharply off the path that he had walked during their visit. Anderson had been a heroin user prior to meeting Lenny, but while the scars of old needle tracks on Lenny's arm tipped him off, he had never broached the subject of drug use with his friend, who had not used heroin regularly since early 1975. But Lenny apparently intuited Anderson's familiarity with the drug because in mid-September, he admitted to him that while walking through the housing project behind his apartment, he'd met a dealer and bought a fix. This admission opened the door for the two men to begin using heroin together, and they were soon taking full advantage of Nashville's abundant supply of cheap, strong junk. By early spring, both were badly strung out and enrolled for treatment at a local methadone clinic.

Back in Maine, Lenny's father and Bernice Possounier, his wife of nine months, were also struggling with addiction. After Pine returned from a short tour of Connecticut with Gene Hooper in early March 1977, he and Bernice checked into a detox center near their home. Bernice completed "the cure," as she calls it, before Pine, for whom long-term sobriety was a remote and fading hope at this point. She was back at work in the Bates Mill (where Pine had worked briefly) when on the morning of March 26, Pine left the clinic and walked to Lisbon Street. In one of the area's many taverns, he met a friend: an ex-prize fighter who was also an alcoholic. The men bought two quarts of vodka and rented a room at the Manoir Hotel, a notorious Lewiston skid row dive. Both were inebriated when Pine's friend left him alone in the room for a time in the late afternoon. When he returned a few hours later, he discovered Pine's lifeless body crumpled against a radiator. At 6:35 p.m., attending medics pronounced Harold John Breau dead. According to the physician's report, death was immediate and caused by a coronary occlusion.

Bernice had Pine interred in a cemetery in nearby Togas, Maine, and to help pay funeral costs, she sold his mid-fifties Gibson J200. Through a long, convoluted route of buyers and sellers, the guitar became the property of country music queen Emmy Lou Harris who donated it to the Country Music Hall of Fame in Nashville where it still hangs.[5] This is as close as the lifelong "singer of Western ditties" would ever come to being immortalized by the country music world to which he'd committed his life.

Lenny had no phone in his apartment and did not hear about Pine's death until a few days later when he made his weekly call to his mother from a phone booth near his apartment. Betty was singing at a resort in Florida and it was left to his Uncle Leonard to tell Lenny of his father's death. Lenny took the news hard and immediately called Chet Atkins who advised his friend not to attend his father's funeral, fearing that the experience could precipitate another binge. Lenny agreed reluctantly, but did return to Lewiston in mid-April to visit his father's grave and perhaps reflect on old songs and sweeter, simpler times long passed.

Back in Nashville, says Anderson, Lenny remained deeply stricken by his father's passing.

> Hal's death affected him really intensely. He just went into a deep depression for several days and everybody was so concerned because he took it so hard. He didn't play for a while and when he did, it was not with the same enthusiasm. Later, he came out of it but he never got over it. He'd break down and cry and talk about his dad and how he'd let him down, sometimes during gigs. He'd been expected to follow in Hal's footsteps and he felt that he'd disappointed his dad for not being his little sidekick, for not staying as little Lone Pine, Jr., for making that split.

Not long after arriving in Nashville, Lenny had reconnected with his friend Buddy Spicher, then one of Nashville's busiest musicians.

Besides touring with country legends George Jones, Hank Snow, and others, he had played on countless non-country sessions with such diverse artists as Linda Ronstadt, Henry Mancini, and the Nashville Symphony. Spicher had continued to develop his jazz playing and he and Lenny spent many hours jamming together at Spicher's farm outside of Nashville.

Spicher did his best to help Lenny get back on his feet. Besides arranging for Lenny to teach at his wife's music school, he often drove him to the Nashville methadone clinic for his daily dose. One day, Spicher decided to expose Lenny to therapy of a different sort and brought him to a local church service. Afterwards, the minister noticed the musicians and introduced himself. "He could see that we were new there," Spicher says. "He asked Lenny about his relationship with God and I'll never forget it: Lenny said, 'music is my god.' But he went to church with me rather than hurt my feelings by saying no. Still, he didn't worry about hurtin' this fella's feelings when he said music was his God. It kinda broke my heart to tell you the truth. Still, Lenny was a beautiful soul."

Lenny sat in regularly with Spicher's group, The Nashville Super Pickers, a conglomerate of some of the city's best session players who held court at a downtown club called the Pickin' Parlor where they played jazz and jazzed-up country music. "One of the things that I loved about Lenny's playing," says Spicher, recalling these sessions, "is that he didn't always try to play real fast, but he was always real tasteful. He'd kind of squint his eyes, listenin' for that line, that extra, above average lick. He was always reachin' for it and most of the time he would come up with somethin' nobody else would or could get. It's the same with all the greats."

While Lenny's connection with Atkins would have made it possible for him to find steady work in the busy Nashville studio scene, he steered clear of session work for the same old reasons: too much pressure and uninspiring music. (Not long after Lenny returned to Nashville, Atkins had arranged a session date for Lenny with country/pop singer Kenny Rogers, but Lenny failed to show up for the gig.) However, he was always happy to do sessions with friends if he found the project interesting enough and in early May 1977 he accepted an invitation from Spicher to play on an album the fiddler was recording for Direct to Disc Records.[6] The label derived its name from a recording process in which musicians recorded directly to a master disc lathe that served as the source for further copies rather than first recording on tape. Eliminating this step produced a fuller sounding recording, but the direct-to-disc process had its disadvantages. An entire side of the acetate disc had to be recorded at one pass with no mistakes because the process precluded overdubs and splicing to cover players' errors. Musicians also had to move from one tune to the next in complete silence to keep extraneous sounds from being etched onto the master disc between tracks. These factors made for a level of tension far greater than found in most sessions, Spicher says, and this had a palpable effect on Lenny. "We were waitin' between cuts and there wasn't a sound," recalls Spicher. "Suddenly there was this noise. I looked around and it was Lenny holdin' a piece of paper on his music stand and his hand was shakin' so bad it was makin' this rattling sound!"

Lenny's contribution to *Buddy Spicher and Friends* was neither extensive nor, for the most part, inspired. His finest moment comes on his original instrumental ballad, "I Remember Lone Pine" (listed as "I Remember" on the album), which Lenny had just written. Anderson says that Lenny played this tune often in performance throughout 1977 and 1978, after which—as was the case with most of his originals—it seemed to disappear from his set list. (The piece "Lone Pine," which Lenny recorded for his second Adelphi Records release *Mo' Breau* in 1977, is actually a mistitled "I'll Remember April.") "I Remember" is a wistful, lilting waltz with a simple melody and an ABC structure that modulates to the relative minor key for the B section. Lenny's solo is beautifully constructed and uses slurred double stops that recall the country guitar style he played for so many years behind his father. This lyrical performance, with its restrained and delicate poignancy, is the highlight of an album that Spicher now dismisses because of the stiffness of his own playing, which the tedious recording situation caused.

A few months later Spicher used Lenny again on *Buddies*, a collaborative project with steel guitarist Buddy Emmons. Lenny plays brief solos on two cuts: "Uncle Pen" and "Magic Swing." Either of these generic solos could have been played equally well or better by any number of session players.

Lenny also played on Chet Atkins's album *Me and My Guitar*, dueting with Atkins on "Long, Long Ago" and "You'd Be So Nice to Come Home To." On the latter, Lenny plays bass in one section and then switches to nylon string to play a progression of Brazilian-type chord voicings with a bossa nova rhythm. Atkins plays a very straightforward reading of the singsong melody of "Long, Long Ago" on his resonator guitar while Lenny supports him with some exquisite chords. This cut is a stylistic precursor to the duets the men would record on the 1981 RCA release, *Standard Brands*.

Since losing his Baldwin, Lenny had used a string of guitars that never quite measured up to his standards. This changed in June of 1977 when Richard Cotten approached his friend, luthier Tom Holmes, about building a guitar to Lenny's specifications. Holmes agreed to take on the project, asking only for Lenny's endorsement in lieu of payment. Lenny was not particularly articulate when it came to guitar-speak, but with Cotten's help he managed to explain to Holmes that he wanted a solid body guitar with a long, extra wide neck that would permit him to play chords easily on the upper frets. Lenny's nylon string at the time was a cheap Japanese copy of a Spanish Barbaro guitar that Atkins had lent to him. At Lenny's request, Holmes replicated its long scale, 665-millimeter neck on his custom-built instrument, which had an ash body and maple neck and was outfitted with Holmes's own handmade pickups. Lenny was initially a bit overwhelmed by the result, says the builder. "I don't think he adapted to it immediately," Holmes recalls. "But about two weeks after he got it, he said he fell in love with it." Still, his affinity for the instrument wasn't enough to deter him from pawning it a few days after taking possession. "He hocked it," says Holmes. "Richard [Cotten] went out and paid fifty bucks to get it out of the hock shop so he could play a gig on it. That was really hard for me to deal with. It didn't matter that I, being pretty broke at the time, had spent all my time building this guitar and then he just decided that he wanted to get high and would just hock it. That probably has something to do with the fact that I charged him $600 for the next one. We remained good friends even though."

Lenny was playing this guitar one evening in late June of 1977 at Mississippi Whiskers when Gene Rosenthal came into the club.

Rosenthal, a Maryland resident, owned and operated Adelphi Records, a small recording company he'd started in 1964. Folk music and blues had been his primary interests but by the '70s, he had branched out into jazz and was recording upcoming young jazz lions like David Murray and Arthur Blythe on his Adelphi Jazz Line. Rosenthal was in Nashville on business and had some spare time on his hands when an associate told him to check out Lenny at Mississippi Whiskers:

> I was nursing a beer when Lenny got up on stage and my mouth just hit the dirt. I sat there mesmerized. Never heard him; didn't know the name. He finished the set and I went and talked to him. I found out a little—that he knew Chet and not much more. But what I did know was that I'd never seen anybody play a guitar like that. I stuck around for the next set and then gave him my card, my number, and a little background on the label. If I'd had a contract in my pocket, I'd have had him sign it right there. I told him I was leaving the next day. He told me that he was shortly heading for New York. I said, "Ok, when you're in New York, call me and/or call my friend Dan Doyle who lives in New York." But Lenny was pretty blasé about it all.

Lenny was jaded enough at this point to take Rosenthal's offer with a grain of salt. But Rosenthal, who left Nashville the next day doubting that he'd ever hear from Lenny again, meant every word he'd said and would prove it to Lenny before the year was over.

A few weeks later, Lenny and Cotten attended the annual NAMM (North American Music Marketers) convention in Atlanta. Jazz guitarist George Benson, representing Ibanez guitars at the convention, was riding high with the hit guitar instrumental "Breezin'" from his hugely successful disco-oriented album of the same name. Benson had never heard Lenny play although he knew his name through his mentor and idol, Wes Montgomery, who had told Benson years before, "forget what I'm doing. There's this kid up in Canada. . . ."[7] Benson was looking for jamming partners in the Ibanez booth when Lenny introduced himself and asked to sit in. The men jammed on a few standards and blues, and meshed well together despite their very different styles. Benson enthusiastically praised Lenny's playing, and Stephen Anderson recalls that when Lenny returned from the convention, he seemed elated by Benson's kind words. "Lenny told me that George was really into his music," he says. "He was surprised that he even knew who he was and knew his music. He said that Benson asked him all kinds of questions about his playing and said, 'I can't believe Benson would be into the kind of playing I'm doing.'"

Back in Nashville, Lenny had the opportunity to play with another jazz guitarist of a very different stripe. After stints with Chico Hamilton and Gary Burton in the mid- and late-sixties, Larry Coryell had become a celebrated jazz/fusion guitarist with a pyrotechnical approach that owed as much to Jimi Hendrix as it did to Wes Montgomery. He was touring as an acoustic solo act in 1977 when he was booked to appear at a Nashville club called The Exit/Inn and was excited to learn that his opening act would be Lenny Breau. "I'd loved his [RCA] records but I'd first heard about Lenny from Gary Burton when Gary was forming that first quartet of his [in 1967]," says Coryell. "He had consulted Chet Atkins about guitarists and Chet had sent him one of Lenny's records.[8] But Gary decided not to hire Lenny and he hired me."

Coryell has not used drugs since the early 1980s, but admits to having once had a substance abuse problem that rivaled or surpassed Lenny's, and does not remember much about the Nashville gig. However, Stephen Anderson recalls that Coryell, astonished by Lenny's opening set, cut his own set short after only a few tunes and invited Lenny back up to jam with him for the remainder of the evening. "I'll never forget it," says Anderson. "Lenny proceeded to play flawlessly in Larry's basic style: that is to say, Django-esque. At one point Larry just stopped and walked off the stage in a very humorous, dramatic fashion, throwing up his hands in mock exasperation. It was really something—special for the uniqueness of the entire night as much for the music." A surviving tape of the evening bears this out. Lenny does an astonishing job of matching and complementing Coryell's hard driving style and although a bit rough around the edges, the men's supercharged and often playful duets on tunes like Coltrane's "Impressions" encompassed some very fine and sensitive jazz playing.

Afterwards, Coryell and Lenny went to a friend's house to jam and share techniques. "He showed me a trick on how to improvise on [the John Coltrane tune] "Giant Steps," and also how to do his artificial harmonics thing," says Coryell. "I worked the harmonics into my playing with some practice." Coryell was then writing a monthly column for *Guitar Player* magazine and a few months after meeting Lenny, wrote a piece called "Lenny's Lesson" for the January 1978 issue of the magazine explicating Lenny's chordal harmonics. Coryell's column was responsible for finally revealing the mechanics of Lenny's mysterious and beautiful technique to many guitarists.

In the early fall, Lenny and Richard Cotten did a series of week-end gigs at Nashville's Bluebird Café. Cotten, who played bass on the gigs, taped these shows and after his death, his wife Darci gave the masters to the Guitarchives label who released on CD two sets that the men recorded on September 23 and 24, 1977. The CD—*Pickin' Cotten*—has its share of good guitar work, especially on "Nardis" and Bill Evans's "The Two Lonely People," but Lenny's playing lacks a cohesive flow of improvisational ideas and is constrained by Cotten's limited bass playing. Several times, Lenny is heard counting the beat aloud as he tries unsuccessfully to get Cotten to switch the feel and meter of various tunes.

During the gig, Lenny surprised his audience by announcing that he was leaving Nashville for New York City to see "what's out there in the world." Other motivations he may have had for relocating to New York City a few days later are unknown. Sinde Shubert, who accompanied Lenny on his move north, does not recall what precipitated the move or how long it had been in the works. It was not done on an impulse, however. Lenny had a teaching position waiting for him at a music store in the Jackson Heights area of Queens, where the couple stayed with friends whom Lenny may have met in Nashville. He'd also been booked at a jazz club called Sweet Basil's for a four-night gig that was, according to *New Yorker* magazine, scheduled to start on October 4. Sweet Basil's was then one of New York's most popular jazz clubs and often booked young, upcoming jazz musicians like John Scofield and Randy Brecker. It was a beautifully timed opportunity for Lenny. Not only would it herald his arrival in the city's jazz scene, the gig could have provided him with badly needed exposure after years of being buried in out-of-the-way venues. This was not to be, however. Lenny, depending on which version of events he related to friends, lost the gig before or during his first night at the club. He claimed that Sweet Basil's insisted he work with the bassist, drummer, and pianist from the club's house band. Lenny gave thumbs up to the bassist and drummer but said he was concerned that a piano would interfere with his harmonic concepts and demanded the keyboardist sit out the date. In one telling of the story, the club refused to honor his request and Lenny left before setting foot on stage. In another, he stated that he played one set before quitting in frustration. Neither story has the ring of truth about it. Piano did not blend well with Lenny's style, but he had worked willingly with pianists dozens of times over the years, and could easily have come to some kind of arrangement with any competent keyboardist. Even if he had had concerns about working with a pianist, one wonders why Lenny—usually so passive and undemanding—would decide to play the prima donna at this crucial show. It's likely that the pressure of a date of this magnitude spooked Lenny and he decided not to show up for it. Whatever the motivation, Lenny's balking on the threshold of what would have been his most significant club appearance in many years effectively killed his chances of working at any of the city's more prominent clubs. (Lenny later did a few gigs at a small Manhattan club called The Tin Palace where David Murray and Arthur Blythe often played. The details of these dates are sketchy, but it appears that Lenny failed to show up for several gigs and was not rebooked.)

A few days later, Lenny called Gene Rosenthal in Maryland to see if his recording offer still stood. Surprised and pleased to hear from Lenny, Rosenthal assured him that it did. He told him to sit tight and flew to New York the next day where he signed Lenny to a three-album contract. In the agreement, Lenny stipulated that his share of royalties from album sales would be sent directly to Valerie Breau, who had received little in the way of child support payments since the early 1970s. The contract also specified that Adelphi would publish and register whatever original material appeared on the albums.

Lenny did his first midnight-to-six a.m. Adelphi session towards the end of October at Blank Studios in Manhattan. Rosenthal says he wanted the session to be as loose and informal as possible with no musical constraints imposed on Lenny. "I kept saying to [engineer] Bob Blank, 'don't turn the tape off,'" recalls Rosenthal. "'Keep rolling it. Roll the f—g tape because he doesn't know from 'OK, start the tune.' He'll be noodling around and he'll just get into the tune. So just roll the tape.'"

The next day Rosenthal was called away to a session at Muscle Shoals Studios in Alabama and turned the session over to his colleague Dan Doyle, a young producer who had recorded several artists for Adelphi including sax man, Arthur Blythe. Doyle says he had never heard of Lenny prior to this assignment. "I went and got some of his records and I thought, 'Well, he can play, but these are wretched records,'" Doyle says. "Then he played for me and it was great. I went to the apartment in Queens and we'd hang out and he'd play stuff and I'd say 'I like that, I can do this one and I can do that one.' I had him play at every kind of tempo, standards, free improv. I had him sing and just really tried to push the envelope with it. But I wasn't interested in getting other musicians in because I did not want to see Lenny's day taken over by some New York jazz rhythm section before I knew who he was."

Lenny did five or six sessions for Adelphi over the next two and a half months, finishing his last one on a cold, snowy afternoon in early January. When this session ended, he asked for and received a loan from Doyle. Doyle had work to do in the studio and asked Lenny to meet him later at his fiancée's loft, which was several blocks away. Lenny left and Doyle, after completing his chores, followed about forty-five minutes later. A few blocks from the studio, Doyle came across a police cruiser and an ambulance driver tending to an unconscious figure prone in the snow. "There laying on a snowbank was Lenny Breau," says Doyle. "He'd scored, and by the time I'd helped clean the studio and signed the time sheets and all that sort of thing, he'd overdosed. They took him to Bellevue so I had to go see him in the hospital. They took care of his immediate needs and let him go." What Lenny had "scored" were several drinks and possibly some pills in a neighborhood bar. Lenny was still taking daily doses of methadone and during his time in New York regularly mixed alcohol and pills with his therapeutic doses of the drug. It was this toxic cocktail that landed him unconscious in the snowbank where a NYPD officer discovered him partially buried by the blizzard.

Coincidentally, Canadian journalist Bart Testa arrived in New York to interview Lenny for *The Globe and Mail* the day after this incident and learned that after initial treatment at Bellevue hospital, Lenny checked into a drug treatment center. "Lenny was in an isolation clinic at a detox center in Brooklyn for his drug and alcohol problems and I couldn't see him," Testa says. "I spoke to him on the phone at length and that's how I got the story. He was certainly in good spirits. He said something like 'I'm sorry this happened but everything's OK now. I'm getting it all squared away. I think I'm going to do this.'"

After checking out of the treatment center in mid-January, Lenny returned to Nashville with a ticket that Richard Cotten provided. His sojourn in New York had seen peaks and valleys but he had at least left Rosenthal with a large amount of recorded material that he would release on three albums over the next several years. The best of this material is arguably from Rosenthal's first session with Lenny, which Adelphi released in 1979 as *Five O'clock Bells*. Lenny once said that this recording "shows a little bit of darkness—echoing the mood I was in."[9] His mood may well have been dark during this period, but "languid and bittersweet" might better describe the prevailing ambiance of *Five O'clock Bells*. Only on "Visions" (as it is listed on the album), "Little Blues"—a sprightly jazz/blues original— and segments of "My Funny Valentine" does he push the pace above mid-tempo. Five of the album's eight tunes are originals of varying quality. "Toronto" (a revised "Taranta") is less successful than the version on his début album, but has some engaging moments. "Other Places, Other Times" is an unfinished idea that rambles along at a lugubrious crawl before it lumbers to a close not a second too soon. An original dedicated to "Cinde" [*sic*] but inexplicably titled "Amy," is a short piece based on an unremarkable chord progression. Except for "Toronto," these pieces were probably either improvised at the session or written shortly beforehand because Lenny obviously does not feel comfortable enough to stretch out on any of them. (Danny Davis would have been pleased to see that "Amy" is less than two and a half minutes long.) "Five O'clock Bells" is by far the most successful of the originals. Lenny's singing is not strong, but is effectively poignant within the context of the song. He builds the tune through an astute and creative use of dynamics until it reaches a striking crescendo with an instrumental, polyrhythmic paraphrase of the tune's singsong refrain.

The two standards on the album—"Days of Wine and Roses" and "My Funny Valentine"—have their moments of fine playing. Lenny's performance of the former is among his most expressive on the album, but he loses his place in the tune and the piece loses momentum and falls apart. He artfully covers this with a rubato section segueing into a non-sequitur modulation that goes nowhere. The album ends with "Vision," one of Lenny's four recorded versions of the McCoy Tyner tune that was something of a musical anthem for him and a springboard for his most elaborate modal explorations. While a decent performance, the version here tends to meander and has neither the flow nor intensity of later recorded performances of the tune.

John Knowles puts the unevenness of this and the other Adelphi albums down to their producers' lack of familiarity with Lenny's work. "It was recorded by people who didn't know what Lenny's playing was at its best," he says. Still, *Five O'clock Bells* is of a considerably higher quality than the two Adelphi releases that followed. On most of *Mo' Breau*, released in 1981, Lenny's playing is stiff, detached, and bland. "Emily" and ". . . But Beautiful" are the highlights of the album, although neither are exceptional performances by Lenny's standards, and McCoy Tyner's "Ebony Queen" conjoined with Lenny's original, "Pam's Pad," features some imaginative, well-realized playing. "Autumn Leaves" is mere filler and one of Lenny's most staid and unremarkable recorded performances on any of his albums. Adelphi listed four of the album's tunes as originals, but in fact Lenny penned only one of these: the wistful vocal number "New York City." Two are well-known jazz standards—"I'll Remember April" and "Beautiful Love"—and the third is a medley comprising two country standards. Doyle says that Lenny duped him by claiming authorship of these retitled tunes. Lenny's playing on these pieces is merely competent.

In 1987, Adelphi released the material from Lenny's final New York session on the album, *Last Sessions*. Lenny is in slightly greater technical control of his material than on *Mo' Breau*, but his playing is, for the most part, equally bland and uneven. The CD's one original, "Paris," an apparent attempt at Keith Jarrett-like spontaneous composition in which Lenny was interested at the time, is little more than a pastiche of recycled and unrelated phrases and tricks from Lenny's bag of tricks. The album is memorable only because it is the sole recording of Lenny playing his original "Meanwhile Back in LA," but his performance of the tune here is lackluster.

The Adelphi albums had a mixed response from Lenny's fans. While a new release from Lenny, who hadn't recorded an album under his own name since 1969, was cause for celebration, those of Lenny's fans who had been waiting for a reprise of the materials, approach, and format of his RCA recordings were disappointed with the albums. Lenny himself was not satisfied with the Adelphi recordings, says Stephen Anderson. "He wasn't really happy about those albums, especially about the material they ended up releasing. . . . He felt like it was really rushed and said the guy was always bitching about studio time. He gave me the impression that he was really unhappy about the whole experience. They didn't know how to make him comfortable and being comfortable was real important for him."

To be fair, Rosenthal and Doyle had Lenny's best interests at heart, and went out on a limb to record and promote him at a time when his career had been stalled for many years. Lenny was not an easy musician with whom to work and his substance abuse problem further complicated the situation. In fact, his drug use was likely responsible for the emotional flatness—an effect of methadone—and lack of focus evident on much of his playing on the Adelphi sessions. While these flawed but listenable albums did not represent Lenny at his best, they heralded the fact that he was still playing and recording, and gave his career a boost at a time when it was badly needed. They have also remained consistently in print since their release and have been responsible for creating many new fans of Lenny Breau despite their inconsistencies.

Several months after Testa's interview with Lenny in New York, he talked again with his subject who told him that the snowbank incident had been a wake-up call and said that his treatment at the Brooklyn detox center "left me drug free for the first time in twelve years."[10] Unfortunately, this condition was short-lived. After leaving the clinic, Lenny returned to Nashville where he recorded a few solos on guitarist Bucky Barrett's jazz/rock album, *Killin' the Wind*. Within days, he was bingeing heavily on drugs and alcohol, and when this behavior began to alarm Sinde Shubert, she persuaded him to return to Maine where she said she would join him later. Lenny complied and went north to stay with his mother and brother but his drug and alcohol use continued. His family quickly realized that they could not handle him, and in desperation, Denny turned to his friend Tom Rowe. Rowe—a sax/bass player whom Lenny had first met in 1971—and his fiancée Donna, offered to put Lenny up in a spare room at their old farmhouse a few miles outside of Auburn, and the next morning Denny arrived with his brother in tow. "He was wrecked," says Rowe. "He showed up in the late morning and it wasn't until evening that he could even get out of the chair."

With the Rowes' help, Lenny had recovered dramatically by the time Shubert arrived in late February. He was now playing solo gigs at the Cellar Door and the newly opened No Tomatoes, a restaurant that Peter Balis had built on the upper level of the building that housed the club. Lenny worked in the restaurant backed by Dan Hall, the Portland Symphony's principal bassist at the time, and Hall's roommate, Steve Grover, who had worked with Lenny in Denny Breau's group in 1971. This latest incarnation of the Lenny Breau Trio played regularly in Balis's establishment as well as other clubs and restaurants throughout northern New England.

Hall says that the trio's sets typically included "Funkallero," John Coltrane's up-tempo blues tune, "Mr. Night," "I'll Remember April," and "Impressions," but says that Lenny would often call other numbers depending on his mood. "He had a lot of stuff scratched out for bass players," Hall says. "He'd use penciled charts with chord changes or quasi lead sheets, and every so often he'd pull out something else." Lenny did little solo guitar playing at this point, but would sometimes ask either Grover or Hall to sit out so he could, as Hall puts it, "change the texture a bit." Interplay was encouraged, says Hall, unless Lenny was stoned, which would often cause him to slip into an isolated and sullen state. This happened less and less as time went on and, with a few lapses, Lenny was sober on the bandstand.

Lenny and Sinde continued to put up at the Rowes' house where on a typical night, a group of reverent guitarists could be found sitting in the living room, listening to Lenny and peppering him with questions far into the early morning hours. The living room was immediately under the Rowes's bedroom and the music and general chaos below would often wake Lenny's hosts. Weary of the nightly hubbub below, Tom Rowe decided that the couples would switch rooms so that he and Donna would be at the back of the house away from the furor below. Shortly after the switch was made, an incident occurred that was more disturbing than the cacophony from Lenny's all-night lecture/jams, says Rowe.

> Donna woke me up in the middle of the night. She said, "I just saw the weirdest thing." I said, "What the hell is Lenny doing now?" She said, "It wasn't Lenny. It was some guy standing at the foot of our bed." I said, "A guy?" She said, "I think I saw a ghost. He looked like a cowboy. He was wearing a fancy fringed shirt and he had on this big tall white hat." A few weeks later she was in Lewiston and saw a picture of Hal Lone Pine and she said, "That's the guy I saw in our bedroom." She swears to this day that Hal—the ghost of Hal— was in our room that night. I've often wondered how many visitations Lenny got from Hal before we switched rooms.

Pine had been dead for almost a year, but was far from forgotten by his faithful Maine fans. In fact, the picture that Donna Rowe had seen after the "visitation" was likely advertising Pine's upcoming induction into the Maine Country and Western Music Hall of Fame, which was to take place on Sunday, April 30, 1978. The event's managers had asked Lenny to accept the award on his family's behalf, a request that Lenny said he would honor although apparently with mixed feelings. The day before the induction ceremony, Hall and Grover came to the Rowes' farmhouse to take their leader to a gig at the restaurant of a Vermont resort. Lenny, however, had disappeared earlier that afternoon without a word to the Rowes. The men waited for nearly an hour before he returned, precariously high and upset. "I asked him what was wrong and he said he'd been over at his aunt's place looking at scrapbooks of his father," recalls Grover. "He said he got really down and went through the medicine cabinet. He found a bottle of pills and ate the whole thing. Instead of going to the hospital, he just got really high and was pretty much in the bag. I guessed he'd made a half-hearted attempt to commit suicide. I said, 'Well Lenny, that's too bad, but we have a gig to go play tonight,' and he says, 'No! Really?'"

Lenny's condition had improved by the time the trio and Sinde Shubert reached the restaurant and the gig went off without a hitch. Lenny seemed calm and in reasonably good spirits when the band bedded down for the night but a few hours later, when his companions were asleep, Lenny slipped out and somehow—at 2:00 a.m. in a remote Vermont village—managed to buy a supply of marijuana and pills. He then broke into the restaurant's bar where Grover and Hall, alerted by Shubert, found him drinking shots of vodka, says Grover. "He turned to us and said, 'you cats think you're gonna keep me straight? Well, good luck! Ha-ha-ha-ha-ha.' From what had happened the day before, I knew it was because he was thinking about accepting the award for his father. He felt guilty about his dad, maybe because he didn't attend his funeral."

The next day, the trio played a short noontime gig in Bath, Maine. Lenny was tired and withdrawn but played well enough, says Hall. "He got into his Jimi Hendrix mode, tied a bandana around his head and was doing this anguished kind of stuff. He was kind of a mess because the drive to Bath didn't do much to sober him up. After that gig, we drove him down to Portland to the Italian Heritage Club where the ceremony was and the whole thing got very tearful."

Al Hawkes was at the ceremony and recalls that Shubert had to physically support Lenny. Despite this condition, Hawkes was delighted to see his old friend from the Event Records days and made plans to talk with him after the ceremony. But Lenny left part way through the presentation and when Grover and Hall returned to the Italian Heritage Club, they found him "staggering around in the alley," Grover says. They drove to Auburn where they played one set at the Cellar Door before Peter Balis sent Lenny home. Afterwards, Lenny never explained or referred to the incident and his friends knew better than to bring it up.

As was often the case immediately after one of his drug and alcohol catastrophes, Lenny pulled himself together and entered what Grover refers to as "a relatively stable period," consistently showing up for gigs straight and sober. He and Sinde decided to move out of the Rowes' farmhouse and with Steve Grover's help, found an apartment above a store in Lewiston. "I visited him one day," says Grover, "and he'd put up these pictures by the Impressionists. He'd also bought a record player at a pawnshop along with six records, and he'd transcribed every note from every one of them. He had this Bill Evans record called *Alone Again* and there was a tune called "Make Someone Happy" and he was trying to pull some voicings off that. He said, 'Man, if I can learn a couple of voicings every day, I'm happy.'"

By now, word of Lenny's residency at the Cellar Door and No Tomatoes had spread throughout the New England guitar community and beyond, says Peter Balis. "Out of the blue, I'd get calls from all over the United States: New Hampshire, Montana, Canada—all over. People saying, 'you got Lenny Breau playing there?'" One of these callers was a Los Angeles guitar/sax player named Scott Page who had been a fan of Lenny's for several years. Page was working with the folk/pop duo Seals and Croft when he ran across a brief reference to Lenny's gigs at the Cellar Door in *Guitar Player* magazine. As luck would have it, Seals and Croft was booked to play a show in Portland in late August and when Page arrived in the city, he called the club to confirm that Lenny was playing there. "They said 'yeah, Monday, Tuesday, and Wednesday' and it was Thursday!" recalls Page. "I said AHHH! I had the whole next day open and didn't have to be back until the evening so I said 'can somebody get ahold of him and [tell him] I'll come and take a lesson and I'll pay him whatever he wants.'" Balis agreed to act as a liaison between Page and Lenny (who had no phone in his apartment) and arranged the lesson. The next day Page arrived in Auburn armed with two guitars, an amplifier, and a tape recorder.

> I knock on his door and here's this little guy dressed in this white sort of guru robe. He had a cigarette in his hand, and I remember how beautiful his hands were. Those long fingernails and his hand was so soft and perfect. He said hello in this voice that always sounded like Peter Lorre. I go in and right away he's showing me all this stuff and I'm saying, "how do you do this? How do you do that?" He's really cool and we're having a great time and there's a knock on the door. It's Lenny's mom and two nieces. It was funny because Lenny is like my god, my guru, and they come up and they can hardly speak to me because I'm with Seals and Croft! I'm like "wait a minute. You've got this all wrong. This is Lenny Breau and you're bowing down to me?" I thought. "if they only knew!" They

were so close to him they didn't understand. So we sit down and Lenny tells me about his mom and says, "C'mon, mom, let's sing some tunes." They did two tunes. One was a yodeling tune and the other was this country song with Lenny doing all this stuff and I'm just about crying it was so beautiful.

Page invited Lenny and his kin to the Seals and Croft show in Portland the next night. When the concert ended, Page spoke with Lenny and made a proposal that eerily paralleled the one George Sukornyk had put to him many years before. "I said, 'Lenny, you've got to come to LA and stay with me,'" says Page. "I told him, 'I'll be on the road for another three months, but when I get back, you come out to LA and it'll be rockin',' man. There'll be gigs, teaching, and you can make some records. They'll love you out there so come out and we'll make it happen.'" Lenny accepted Page's offer on the spot. The men shook hands and Page gave Lenny his number in Los Angeles with instructions to contact him in September.

Earlier that summer, Lenny had received a call from pedal steel guitar virtuoso Buddy Emmons about doing a duo album for Flying Fish Records. Since meeting on the *Buddy Spicher and Friends* sessions, the two men had become friends and jammed together whenever Emmons's busy schedule allowed. Like Lenny, Emmons had worked in country bands throughout his teens, playing with acts like Little Jimmy Dickens and Ernest Tubb. But he also had a deep love of jazz and proved that he had the technical skills to play it on the 1962 bebop-flavored album, *Steel Guitar Jazz*. In 1978, producer Mike Melford of Flying Fish Records asked Emmons, who was signed to the label at the time, if he would be interested in doing a jazz-oriented album with Lenny Breau. Emmons agreed, but only on the condition that he be listed as a "guest" on the album with Lenny designated as headliner and leader on the session. Emmons also wanted Lenny to choose the tunes, "to better serve his musical vocabulary" as Emmons puts it. Melford agreed but apparently did not relate Emmons's conditions to Lenny who arrived at Emmons's house the night before the recording session without having chosen a single tune for the album. Emmons says that they worked until midnight drawing up a set list and running over Lenny's composition, "Minors Aloud," which would be the title cut on the album, and began the first session the next morning (August 7) at 10:00. Melford had hired a rhythm section for the duo made up of Nashville session scene stalwarts Randy Goodrum on piano, bassist Charles Dungey, and drummer Kenny Malone. The band gelled quickly and this and the following day's sessions went smoothly with few second takes required.

Lenny was in excellent form and played with great fire and clarity on the sessions, contributing particularly notable solos to "Secret Love" and "Scrapple from the Apple." The band does Lenny's reharmonized arrangement of "On a Bach Bourree" as a slow, dreamy 6/8 jazz waltz and both men take exquisite solos on the tune. "Minors Aloud" is an up-tempo minor jazz blues built on a descending minor scale sequenced in fifths, and Lenny and Emmons's playing on the tune brings to a mind a very updated duet between Jimmy Bryant and his musical partner, steel guitarist Speedy West. *Down Beat* writer, Pete Welding, referred to the album's material as "mellowed out bebop" and wrote that Lenny's playing, "crackles with fire and invention just about every time up . . . for guitarists, the LP is a must simply for its principals' technical command and empathetic interplay."11 Ignoring Emmons's request that he be given second billing on the project, Flying Fish designed the album cover to promote Emmons over Lenny. Above a caption that reads "Buddy Emmons with Lenny Breau," Emmons's image dominates the cover with Lenny's photo appearing in a small inset that seems almost an afterthought. In any case, neither name helped sell the album. It lapsed into out-of-print status within a few years of its release. (In 2005, Art of Life Records remastered and released the album on CD.)

Lenny remained in Nashville for a few weeks, headlining at the Exit/Inn on August 17 and 18, and doing some recording in Chet Atkins's home studio for a solo album that would be released the following year. He then returned to Auburn where he and the trio continued to work throughout northern New England, driving miles of highway and back roads in a car packed with musical equipment just as Lenny's parents had done so often thirty years earlier. Over the next few months, Lenny played on an album that his mother recorded for EAB Records and contributed a solo to a recording by his old friend, guitarist Shep Spinney. He also began working with a local clarinetist named Brad Terry who had begun playing Dixieland as a teenager, moved into swing and, by the time he encountered Lenny, was a first-rate bebop player. "I'd never even heard of Lenny, but the [Augusta Jazz] society knew me and they knew Lenny and they just put us together," says Terry of his first meeting with Lenny in 1976 at an Augusta, Maine, club called Hazel Green's. "We played a little bit of duo stuff and just locked in immediately and had a tremendous sense of communication right off the bat."

Terry knew little music theory and relied wholly on his astonishing ear. He was capable of playing anything he could imagine, and when playing with Lenny, he says, his imagination was always in overdrive.

> We would do key changes, modulations, tempo shifts, and all kinds of stuff. It was just a matter of listening. And he found out very quickly that right in the middle of my solo he could go into 3/4 time and I was going to follow him right into the bushes, right into the swamp. He couldn't lose me, so we had a lot of fun chasing around that way. My face would hurt after we played; not from playing but from grinning. I'd be looking at him and I'd have to push my face back together.

Over the next few years, Terry would record many of these performances on his reel-to-reel tape recorder, setting it up at gigs and informal jams in the living room of his home in Brunswick, Maine. These performances and several others would eventually provide material for two of Lenny's most deservedly celebrated albums.

In September, Lenny and Scott Page finalized plans for his trip to the City of the Angels and on October 10, Lenny (dressed for the occasion in a black jumpsuit) and Sinde Shubert arrived at LAX where they were met by Page and the late Ted Greene, an exceptional jazz guitarist known for his series of guitar instruction books and classic fingerstyle jazz album, *Ted Greene, Solo Guitar*. Greene had first heard Lenny in 1969 on *Guitar Sounds* and was not, he says, an immediate convert to his style. "I just didn't get it at first. I knew the guy was playing great stuff but it just wasn't for me," Green says, adding, "When it finally was, I became an addict."

Page's close friend Dan Sawyer was also on hand to meet Lenny on his first day in Los Angeles. Sawyer, a session guitarist who had played behind Barbra Streisand, Diana Ross, and other well-known pop acts, had admired Lenny's playing for nearly a decade. Seeing Lenny's technique up close was an eye-opening experience, he says.

I was shocked the first time I saw him play because his technique was so different from anybody I'd ever seen. I understood why Chet called that album *The Velvet Touch* because it really did look like he was just tapping his fingers on a piece of velvet, just stroking it. The movements he would make with his right hand were so small, so controlled and so light. It was incredible to watch and he was also playing with very light strings, what I would call rock and roll strings. That's something you never saw because jazz guitarists never play with light strings. But Lenny was able to completely control them because his touch was so light.

When his guests were settled in, Page, an entrepreneurial dynamo to the present day, wasted no time in setting up gigs for Lenny. His first two dates were guitar clinics held on October 13 and 14 at Valley Arts Music Center, a music store that was then a popular hang-out for many top-notch Los Angeles guitarists. These clinics, Page says, were instantly sold out, as was a gig played before a standing-room-only audience on October 25 at McCabe's, another well-known Los Angeles area music store. According to a *Down Beat* review of the gig, the concert was "less than sensational,"[12] probably the consequence, Dan Sawyer says, of Lenny's nervousness in a new environment. "Lenny was kind of stiff in those early gigs," he says. "His manner was stiff when he was around people or talking in the mic. I think he was in his own little world or uncommunicative so he might have come off as stiff. Sometimes he'd play so brilliantly and people would just clap politely because it was like he hadn't made a connection with them or wasn't bothering to communicate. Sometimes he was painfully shy, but he wasn't really capable of playing badly."

Page next tried to convince Donte's—the jazz club where Lenny had played during his first trip to LA—to hire Lenny for a weekly gig, but the club refused to pay the minimum that Page demanded. "So I went to this club called The Sound Room," he says. "The guy there had no idea who Lenny Breau was, but I said, 'Man, we'll split the door because this place is gonna be filled up.' But I had no idea that it was gonna fill up like it did. We did several weeks there and the place was sold out two shows a night for weeks on end. Every guitar player in LA showed up: Joe Pass, Larry Carlton, Lee Ritenour, Jay Graydon, Joe Diorio—everybody lined up to get in and see him." This was Lenny's first gig with drummer Carl Burnett, then a member of Freddie Hubbard's band, and *Tonight Show* bassist Joe Di Bartolo. Reviewer Lee Underwood wrote that the trio's playing on their first Monday night gig was "a bit tense, constricted and self-conscious." By the trio's fourth appearance at the club, however, Lenny had apparently acclimated to The Sound Room and was playing, Underwood says, "the kind of music the guitar players in the SRO audience had come to hear." The trio did "Days of Wine and Roses," "Funkallero," "Billie's Bounce," and "Don't Think Twice," with Lenny's glib rendition of "Back in the Saddle" finishing off sets—an indication that he was beginning to unwind and enjoy himself in his new environment. They also performed what Underwood called "a terrifyingly speedy version of John Coltrane's 'Impressions,' playing as a poised and dynamic team." He goes on to say, "aside from his awesome Autry-to-Coltrane diversity, Breau is also an accomplished improvisational stylist of rare originality and taste. He's back in the saddle again, hopefully for the long, enjoyable and prosperous ride he so well deserves."[13]

During Lenny's stay at his house, Page recorded hundreds of hours of Lenny playing solo guitar in his living room or home studio and jamming with some of LA's top guitarists including Joe Pass, Ted Greene, and Larry Carlton. But he and Sawyer wanted to get Lenny into a professional facility to record material for what they intended to be his next album. In December, the pair rented time at California Sound Studio, and hired drummer Steve Schaffer and a bassist (name now forgotten) to back Lenny on these sessions, which Page and Sawyer would engineer and produce. They gave Lenny a free hand to play anything he choose, but Page suggested that he throw in some material that would be appropriate for commercial radio. "I got him to cut some pop tunes," says Page. "One was that great tune 'Reminiscing' [by '70s pop group, The Little River Band]. We were going to try to go the George Benson-ish pop route 'cause he could play great over that stuff though he'd never really done that before."

The session went badly from the moment the tape began to roll. Lenny was unable to focus and would stop playing in the middle of a song without explanation. As he grew more perturbed and restless, he made the first of several phone calls to Chet Atkins to ask for advice, but if Atkins had any suggestions for Lenny, they didn't help. Lenny continued his directionless playing, sometimes halting in the middle of his lackluster solos to suggest that they visit the bar next door. "Lenny would play a chorus or two and then he'd just stop," Sawyer remembers. "Nobody knew why. He'd say 'I don't know what to do.' And we'd say 'Lenny, just finish the tune. Even if you don't like it, keep playing so we can see what we have.' But it was very hard to get him to do that or decide on what to play or anything. I got the feeling that he was used to having Chet Atkins tell him what to do in the studio. He just wasn't feeling it." Page says Lenny was able to complete only a few intros and rhythm tracks, and while there were moments when he seemed about to take off, the day ended without a single decent performance or usable start to finish track. The next day's session also failed to yield any fruit, and Sawyer and Page, both of whom had their hands full with other work, reluctantly decided to shelve the project.

Lenny's LA album never became a reality, but these were not unproductive days for him, Page says. Lenny was working constantly: teaching, performing, and holding masterclasses throughout LA. These activities generated a steady income and while he was glad to be pulling in some decent money after years of penury, his increased earnings presented Lenny with a new problem. Lenny had never had a bank account in his life and routinely kept his money in his boot or shirt pocket. After a month or so in LA, his bankroll had simply become too big for this cavalier treatment. "So we went down to American Pacific Bank and opened an account," says Page. "I had to show Lenny how to write a check. He had no idea. At one point, after a few months, he had about $5000 in his account, probably the most money he'd ever had at one time."

Lenny, as was his tendency with his handlers, became completely dependent on Page who arranged gigs, provided transportation, set up jam sessions and lessons, and in general played both a managerial and—along with his wife Wayne—a provider/housekeeper role for Lenny. This situation affected Sinde Shubert in much the same way as

Lenny's dependency on George Sukornyk had done with Valerie a decade and a half earlier "After a while, she started getting really uptight because Lenny and I became such good buddies," says Page. "She started to feel like I was pulling him away from her because she had been basically taking care of him." The Pages soon overheard her expressing these dissatisfactions in the loud verbal skirmishes emanating from the guest room where the couple stayed—rows that were often fueled by alcohol. Lenny was drinking again, and the Pages were receiving complaints from friends—including Ted Greene's grandmother—whose prescription drugs were disappearing from their medicine cabinets during Lenny's visits to their homes. Adding to these tensions, says Page, was his guests' complete disinterest in doing any housekeeping. Finally the couple gently suggested to Lenny and Sinde that after two months of living on top of each other in the Page's small bungalow, it was perhaps time that they found their own home. Lenny and Sinde were amenable to the idea and in January 1979, the Pages helped them move into an apartment on Van Nuys Boulevard.

Lenny saw little of the Pages in the following months but continued to play at The Sound Room and do clinics around the city. These included a few masterclasses that were organized by John Pisano who now worked with Herb Alpert and the Tijuana Brass and taught music at Valley College. "Lenny played a lot of the solo things like 'Freight Train,' explaining different styles and influences," says Pisano. "He was good in those situations, and always cracking himself up. He'd play something that amused him and you'd hear that little cackle." Pisano says his friend had changed little since the late sixties, but recalls that he still seemed troubled by his father's death. "We were at my house once," Pisano says, "and at about four in the morning, after a lot of drinking, he started telling stories about his past, growing up, and his parents. He got very emotional and actually started crying."

While Lenny was adjusting to life in California, Adelphi producer Dan Doyle and Direct to Disc Records owner Joe Overholt were busy setting up a recording session for him in Nashville. Overholt had wanted to record Lenny since hearing him play on the Spicher session, and when he learned that Lenny was under contract to Adelphi Records, he worked out a deal with Doyle and Rosenthal.

The men agreed that Direct to Disc would cover all expenses for the session including Lenny's advance and fees for back-up musicians. All royalties would go to Direct to Disc (although publishing mechanicals would be property of Adelphi), but Adelphi would be allowed to release a conventional recording of the session taken from Overholt's master at a later date.

Lenny and Doyle had discussed the recording before Lenny went to LA, and Lenny suggested hiring Don Thompson and Claude Ranger for the session. Doyle agreed and arranged for both men, who were then working with Sonny Greenwich, to come to Nashville on February 18. Lenny landed in the city a few days before his rhythm section to prepare himself for the session. Lamentably, part of these preparations involved using Overholt's advance to buy $1500 worth of Dilaudid, a powerful synthetic form of heroin. He then holed up in Nashville's egregious Anchor Hotel where he shot the drug continuously for two days while he practiced his guitar virtually around the clock. "That's what it took for him to feel ready," says Stephen Anderson. "Otherwise if he hung out around a lot of people, he'd feel scattered and couldn't get focused. He felt like junk helped him focus, and the thing is that it does. I'm not saying it's a good thing, but that's why it's so attractive to some musicians."

The night before the session, the trio played a scheduled date at Mississippi Whiskers and—without any rehearsal—gelled beautifully, says Don Thompson. "If we'd recorded the gig the night before we would have had a fantastic album," he says, "but it turned out sounding awful." Part of the problem, he says, was the delay that the painstaking direct-to-disc set-up caused. Hours went by as studio hands arranged and rearranged the placement of the musicians and their equipment. Finally the trio was able to record, but the first finished side was junked when engineers discovered a technical error caused by malfunctioning equipment. The musicians grew more and more restless as the session reached its sixth hour with no tunes recorded. By this time, the trio was not only impatient, but two of them were drunk, says Thompson.

> [The producers] brought in a whole bunch of beer to make us relax because they figured "wow, the guys will really like that!" Being a direct-to-disc record, they took all day to get a sound they wanted.

So of course Lenny and Claude just drank all day and by the time we got to record they were so out of it, they couldn't play—either one. They couldn't get through anything. It was ridiculous. The first run through was all right but every time we ran through anything, it would just be worse the next time and being direct-to-disc and getting the whole side at once, we had to be really together and it took a lot of rehearsing and a lot of time before the engineers knew what they were doing. By the time we actually recorded it, neither one could play. And it sounds like it.

Thompson's criticism reflects his very high musical standards. There is, in fact, some well-played music on the album although certainly less than one might expect from musicians of this caliber. Lenny's playing is clean and fairly adroit but throughout the album he sounds dogged by Ranger's busy, heavy-handed stick work and propensity to dictate the groove at Lenny's expense, leaving him with little room to move. On "Don't Think Twice," Ranger uses brushes to create a swinging, muted groove behind Lenny. By the second chorus however, one can hear Lenny stiffening as Ranger's playing becomes louder and busier, allowing little breathing room and pushing the beat. Lenny sounds rattled, and his solo is disjointed and contains little improvising of merit. Instead, he uses the stock, rapidly played sequences that turned up in his playing when his fingers were racing ahead of his ideas. His solo on "Mr. Night" uses the same riffs, and towards the end of the tune, he loses his place and muffs the head before bringing the tune to a premature stop. The second side opens with "Neptune," a piece that Lenny had co-written with Stephen Anderson in a somewhat different form. "There's a tuning that I use a lot that's a drop D tuning but I tune the G string up to A and Lenny really dug that," Anderson says. "Lenny took those two changes at the beginning of the tune and used them and put that little melody line on top. Then a little later he put in these changes that are really cool. He named it 'Neptune' and he would play it live and did some beautiful versions of it. But in that session it just didn't go right." The version here sounds like a sluggish, protracted introduction to a tune that never begins. "Claude (Free Song)"—the cut that follows—is even more directionless and ponderous: the jazz trio equivalent of an orchestra's pre-concert tune-up.

The best-played piece on the album is a duet with Lenny and Chet Atkins backed by Thompson on Randy Goodrum's song "You Needed Me"—a hit for Lenny's one-time employer, Anne Murray. The piece sounds out of place on the album, as much for its non-jazz flavor as for its laid-back interplay, which the rest of the recording lacks. Lenny told interviewer Walter Carter soon after the session that he was particularly pleased with this cut: "That's gonna give the album an extra zing . . . a lot of people know that song, but I'm still doing some stuff. See, I played what I wanted to play in it. I think the secret is to play something people know, but do it your way. Instead of playing a real far out tune where two or three people say 'that's really far out' but that'll never get played on the radio."[14]

Overholt released the album in June 1979 and *Down Beat*'s Pete Welding reviewed it several months later.

> [Lenny's] playing treads a fine line between display and content, but far too often the former assumes a primacy that, however interesting to other players of the instrument (who are in the best position to appreciate the extent of his technical accomplishment) overshadows the purely musical aspects of his work . . . his solos consist of one startling phrase after another, each a jewel of conception and execution, strung together on the song's structure but developing no sustained ideational relationship to one another . . . without this, his music for all its technical wizardry fails to resonate in the mind's eye once it's over.[15]

The problems plaguing the session didn't end when the musicians played their last notes. Overholt admitted he was nearly broke and unable to cover Doyle's personal and business costs. His attempt to withhold the musicians' fees provoked an angry confrontation with the hard-nosed Ranger. Overholt managed to come up with half of the $2400 owed the musicians and promised to send the rest to Toronto, but never followed through on this guarantee, says Thompson. Nor did Overholt provide Adelphi with the master of the session. Eventually the company made a master tape from a new copy of the direct-to-disc album and released it a few years later.

Lenny remained in Nashville for the next two months. After a mini tour in late April with Buddy Emmons, during which the men played at the Cellar Door in Washington DC (on a bill with guitarist Danny Gatton), Lenny returned to LA and began playing regularly on Wednesday nights at Donte's. Initially, Lenny played these gigs solo on a nylon-string guitar but soon began working with bassist Bob Magnussen (later replaced by John Heard) and drummer Joey Baron. Baron, one of the most brilliant and creative drummers in contemporary jazz, has played with his share of great guitarists including John Scofield, Bill Frisell, and John Abercrombie as well as working behind Carmen McRae, Dizzy Gillespie, Chet Baker, and many other jazz greats. His association with Lenny, he says, was a highpoint of his career. "Playing with Lenny was the most influential thing that happened to me in LA along with meeting and playing with John Abercrombie for the first time. Lenny was one of the most generous people I ever knew and one of the first to help me find my voice." Baron knew nothing about Lenny before Donte's owner asked him to do the gig, but he was impressed with Lenny from the outset of the date. "As soon as we started 'No Greater Love,'" Baron says, "I thought 'wow, this guy is great!'" Baron says that Lenny treated him and Magnussen not as sidemen, but as "equals," welcoming their input and ideas, an atypical attitude in the LA scene of the time, says Baron. "LA is not a nurturing place for creative musicians. LA nurtures accounts, money made from jingles and movies. It's sedate and non-challenging and has nothing to do with artistry. Lenny always wanted to take risks and we were always raw and emotional. The way he played, the interaction was always encouraged and that's what I was modeling. It took a lot of guts for him to play that way and I looked forward to Wednesday night more than anything else I was doing." Donte's was a hangout for many of LA's top musicians who often came to schmooze rather than listen. With Lenny, however, the audiences were attentive and respectful, says Baron, who remembers Pat Metheny coming by one night and watching Lenny with "his mouth hanging wide open." Lenny seemed to be in a consistently good frame of mind, Baron recalls. He occasionally dropped by Lenny's apartment and would spend afternoons with Lenny hanging out by the building's pool. "He was with Sinde then, and he seemed very happy and had so much zest for living, such a playful spirit. So many people lose that playful spirit, but he never did. Everything he did musically came from that place."

Baron's gig with Lenny came to an end in October when Lenny and Sinde returned to Nashville without a word of farewell to anyone, says Dan Sawyer. "Lenny didn't say goodbye. I don't think it would have even occurred to him to ever get on the phone to let somebody know what he was doing. He just didn't have those kind of social skills." Despite the kindness of his hosts and the amount of work he had found there, Lenny did not leave the city with fond memories. In an interview in Maine two months later, he confessed that he had found the city "plastic" and "not real enough" and told the interviewer "a lot of people were trying to get me to play Disco. It's not me."[16] His relationship with the city was far from over, however.

In Nashville, Lenny and Sinde moved in with guitarist Terry Wedding and his wife B. J. Wedding had met Lenny in Nashville in 1976 and later moved to the city to become "a professional student of Lenny's" as he puts it. He also played in a number of Nashville bands, and in 1979, was fronting a group called The Terry Wedding Explosion, which was the house band at a popular Nashville nightspot called Faisson's. Lenny sat in with the band regularly and, according to Wedding, he relished the chance to play material that was outside his usual musical metier. "We were doing cover tunes of the day plus some jazz standards," says Wedding. "It wasn't a disco band, but it was a disco scene with people dressing up and there were a lot of disco songs played. Like Donna Summers. She did songs that had some chord changes to them and Lenny just ripped that stuff up. He loved that band and had a good time because he never got to play like that." Lenny later told an interviewer that there was nothing special about his playing with The Explosion saying, "I just took off and played what I usually play, only with a disco beat."[17]

Although his guitar work had been confined to six string exclusively since the early 1970s, Lenny had never given up on the idea of owning a guitar with an extended range that would increase the melodic and harmonic possibilities available to him. He'd discussed this idea often with guitarist Jerry Roberts. Besides teaching guitar at Nashville's Blair College, Roberts ran a small guitar business procuring and selling high quality and difficult-to-find instruments to Chet Atkins and other Nashville players. In the fall of 1979, Roberts discovered that an Illinois guitar distributor named George Dauphinier was importing a line of seven-string classical guitars from the Aria company in Japan and marketing the model under the name "Dauphin." Roberts procured one of these instruments for Lenny and agreed to sell it to him at cost, half of which Lenny covered in trade with an Ibanez Artwood steel string guitar that Atkins had managed to secure for him as a possible endorsee for the company. (The balance owing remained outstanding, as Roberts says he knew it would.) The extra string—made from a piece of thirty-pound-test Stren fishing line— did not hamper Lenny's quick mastery of the instrument, Chet Atkins told *Vintage Guitar* magazine in July 2001. "See, [Lenny] had already given so much thought to this seven-string guitar that when he picked it up for the first time, he already knew how to play it. He said, 'I've been rolling it over and over in my mind and this is what I want.' And he truly was amazing. He could use that high A and get all kinds of stuff going."[18] Within six months, Lenny was using the guitar on gigs, and the instrument would be an essential part of his musical explorations for the rest of his life.

In the fall of 1979, a small, ad hoc Nashville-based label finally released the recording that Lenny's fans had eagerly awaited for nearly a decade. Lenny had recorded the album, *The Legendary Lenny Breau . . . Now*, in Chet Atkins's home studio during August/ September 1977 and late August 1978. The sessions usually took place in the morning after Lenny had spent the night at Atkins's home, insuring that he was clean, sober, and ready to play. Atkins's presence in the studio, says John Knowles, had everything to do with the high quality of the album. "Lenny's different recordings all seem to reflect where Lenny was in his life at that particular time: whatever musicians he was with and even his production environment," Knowles says. "On the recordings in Chet's studio, you hear Lenny playing in a more structured format as though he's being influenced just by knowing Chet's in the other room." This recording is free from the sometimes diffuse and mechanical playing that marred the Adelphi albums. Instead, Lenny plays with an economy and restraint that give his ideas greater focus and clarity and thus more expressive power. His lyrical single-line solos on "I Love You" and "Our Delight," on which Lenny duets with himself via overdubbing techniques, evolve naturally out of melodic phrases that Lenny finesses to logical but unpredictable conclusions. The incongruous and tedious patches of rehearsed intervallic sequences are absent, and his improvisations have a fresh, spontaneous quality. His harmonic ideas are also well developed, particularly on the Hank Williams classic "I Can't Help It" and the standard "It Could Happen to You," in which he uses an ingenious modulation device to introduce a new key partway through the tune. His performance of "Ebony Queen" is more refined than his earlier version on *Mo' Breau* and a highlight of the album. The middle section of the tune, listed as "Pam's Pad" on *Mo' Breau*, is built on a series of intricate right-hand arpeggios that create a light etherealness contrasting the tune's darker main theme and evoke a musical terrain where McCoy Tyner embraces the spirit of Debussy. The album ends with an exquisite, near cathartic performance of "Vision" in which Lenny segues from a long section of dizzying modal lines and quartal chords played over a pedal tone into a beautiful tremolo section that leads seamlessly back to the tune's theme. This is perhaps his definitive recording of a piece that he once said was "about visions: whatever you see in your head, you try to play."[19] Judging from this performance, Lenny's inner eye was particularly keen and bright on this session.

The Legendary Lenny Breau . . . Now stands as one of Lenny's finest albums, and also one of his most rare. John Knowles released the album on his own Sound Hole Records—a label with a catalogue of two. (The other album on the label is John Knowles's guitar solo album, *Sittin' Back Pickin'*.) The album, never distributed in record stores, was sold through ads in the back of guitar magazines and its meager sales totaled between two and three thousand, Knowles estimates. "That's about how many people probably own the album," he says. "Anyone else who has it probably has a cassette copy." Paul Yandell shot the picture of Lenny that graces the cover of this album at Ireland's in 1976. The guitar Lenny is holding in the photo is Yandell's Electra X310, which Lenny eventually pawned.

Shortly after Knowles released the album, a guitar society in Fort Worth, Texas, asked him to do a concert at the Fort Worth Community College for about 100 people. Knowles took the gig and managed to persuade the guitar society to hire Lenny as his opening act. Lenny was in fine form for the date, and ended his set with an extraordinary rendition of "My Funny Valentine" that, Knowles says, provoked a mystifying reaction from the audience.

Lenny played that tune a lot, but that particular night he took it way out there like I had never heard it any other time, [inserting] key changes and big impressionist sections before coming back to the tune. It went on for four or five minutes and then he stopped . . . and no one applauded. The room was frozen. And so he stood up like he was going to take a bow or something. Nothing. Still the room was frozen. And then a little girl, maybe three years old, got up out of her seat and ran up to him and hugged his legs. And then everybody started applauding. Now what was that little girl hearing? What made her do that? She didn't know him. What was he broadcasting? What was he telling us with that performance? It's one of the most remarkable things I ever saw.

In November 1979, Lenny flew to Maine with Sinde to attend his mother's marriage to her second husband, George Binette, and stayed on at the home of Brad Terry in Brunswick, Maine afterwards. Lenny was welcomed back to the Cellar Door where he did several gigs over the next few months, often sharing the stage with Brad Terry and occasionally his mother. Lenny was always news in central Maine and a few weeks after he'd arrived back in Lewiston, he was the subject of an extensive article in *The Maine Times*. In the piece, Lenny joked about possible career alternatives. "I think I could have been a good gunfighter," he says. "You know if I had been born a hundred years ago, I think I could have really gotten into it . . . the fastest gun in the West . . ." Lenny was having fun, but later in the interview he put a more serious and telling spin on the gunfighter slant. "Really making it," he says, "scares me a little. People say weird things about you. You go into a strange town and some guy says 'hey man, I hear you're the greatest guitarist in the world.' It's weird, man . . . like being a gunslinger or something."[20] Considering the timing, this may well have been a reaction to a piece in the October 1979 issue of *Frets* magazine in which Chet Atkins was quoted as saying "Lenny is the greatest guitar player in the world today."[21]

Lenny had always taken quiet pride in his abilities, but was never comfortable with the—as he viewed them—excessive superlatives that others heaped on his playing. This stemmed from a very real sense of modesty as well as an abhorrence of having to live up to expectations, as he explained to Terry Wedding after an incident that occurred in Nashville in mid-January of 1980. One afternoon, Wedding says, he and Lenny dropped by a music trade show where Buddy Emmons was preparing to play for a large audience when the pair walked in.

> Emmons was sitting on stage talking and as soon as we walked in, he stopped and said "Ladies and Gentleman. I'd like to direct your attention to the back of the room where the greatest guitar player in the world has just walked in. Mr. Lenny Breau." Everybody gasps and gets up and gives him a standing ovation. Lenny panics and turns to me and says "We gotta get outa here!" He waves and says "Be back in a minute." As we leave, Lenny says "Gotta find a drink, man. Gotta find a drink." So we went to a bar and he told me that he felt real vulnerable. He said "you don't know the pressure involved with everybody saying you're the best that there is. I get up there to play and sometimes I feel like I just can't do it. You play a couple of bad notes and people say you're less than you're supposed to be. That's such a hard thing."

Lenny had come face to face with this attitude many times since the 1971 review in which Peter Goddard had glibly posited that "one doubts if [Lenny] could play as well as his 'best' is supposed to be." Lenny was not above playing to impress on occasion but generally had no stomach for musical competition of any sort. The stress of having to prove himself provoked in him a feeling of dread and panic that would be responsible for some of his most disastrous performances during the remaining years of his life.

In an extensive *Winnipeg Tribune* article that was published shortly after Lenny and Sinde returned to Nashville from Maine in January, writer Joan Sadler made much of Shubert's role in Lenny's ostensible victory over substance abuse. She also noted the couple's devotion to one another and reported that they were "contemplating marriage."[22] In fact, the couple's relationship was in its final days. Shubert had done her best to help Lenny overcome his substance abuse problem, and the relationship had been one of the longest and most stable of Lenny's life. However, it had always been volatile, particularly during Lenny's binges, and not long after the *Trib* article came out, Shubert left Lenny and returned to California.

Lenny became depressed, and began showing up at performances in a state of alcohol induced oblivion, says Terry Wedding. "At Whiskers one night, he was ripped out of his mind. He got up on stage in front of about five diehard Lenny fans and couldn't play anything except maybe two chords. He started telling his life story while he was strumming away and crying: 'yeah, my daddy was Hal Lone Pine and he used to set me up on his knee.' Clang-clang, bang- bang on the guitar. 'Then Betty Cody sang' Then he'd hit another chord. Bam. Bam. Finally I said 'Let's go, man. It's over for the night.'"

Not long after Shubert's departure, Wedding and Lenny were visiting Chet Atkins at his office when Atkins's secretary buzzed him to announce a visitor in the waiting room. "Chet told her to wait a minute and then tells Lenny that it's a woman he knows," recalls Wedding. "He says, 'she's available and if you want, I'll introduce you.' Lenny said, 'That'd be cool.' So she comes in and Chet introduces us. Lenny was on the rebound and he starts tripping all over himself." Lenny chatted with the woman and before he left, he asked her for her phone number and promised to call her the next day. There was nothing in this meeting to suggest that it was anything other than an encounter between two mutually attracted adults. In fact, the innocuous scene marked the beginning of a toxic relationship so characterized by hostility and violence that Lenny would spend much of the remainder of his life desperately trying to flee it.

The woman that Lenny met that day in Atkins's office refused this author's request for an interview and the details of her life remain sketchy. What is known is that she was born Joanne Deborah Glasscock in Bryan, Texas, on January 12, 1952, to an American-born father and Lebanese-born mother.[23] At some point in her childhood, she and her family moved to Stockton, California, and she would live in the small farming community on and off to the present day. She appears to have spent some time in Las Vegas and Los Angeles, and during this period was arrested on a prostitution charge. It's not known if she was convicted of this charge. She trained as a nurse but was singing professionally by her early twenties, and claimed to have worked as a back-up singer with Little Richard's band. Acquaintances say that Glasscock often boasted that she was a close personal friend of Elvis and Priscilla Presley. She recorded two albums for A&M Records—*Lady Jo* (1974) and *Joanne Glasscock* (1975)—the latter being a collection of songs by the late songwriter and children's author Shel Silverstein, who plays on two cuts. Chet Atkins played guitar on this album by invitation of Silverstein and was introduced to Glasscock at the session. When she arrived in Nashville in 1977 or 1978, possibly with Silverstein, Atkins arranged for her to record an album for Sky-Lite Records, a small Music Row label specializing in Country Gospel music. Glasscock, now claiming to be a born-again Christian, released one album—*High on Jesus*—for the label under the name Jewel Olivette Taylor.

Lenny was immediately taken with Glasscock—a voluptuous, pretty woman with dark, expressive eyes and a tendency to imbue her voice with a shy child's breathy cadence—and the couple began dating soon after their meeting in Atkins's office. It wasn't long, however, before Lenny began to have reservations about Glasscock that were reinforced by an incident at Faisson's when Lenny played the club in early March. "Jewel was in the audience," says Wedding, "and suddenly she got really ticked off. The waitress was being friendly with Lenny, not doing anything out of the way, but like 'Can I get you a drink, sweetie?' Well, Jewel yells, 'you bitch! Leave him alone. That's my man.' She grabbed a heavy table and turned it over. I mean just threw it out of the way to get to Lenny and she was screaming at him 'you're egging her on. You're bringing this on yourself.' Lenny was pleading with her and saying, 'I'm not doing anything' but she keeps charging at him. We ran out the back door and slammed it. Lenny said to me 'get me out of here, man. Get me out of here!' He was so scared that he left his guitar."

Perhaps in retreat, Lenny returned to Maine a few days later to visit his mother and stepfather in their home in Lisbon Falls, a few miles east of Lewiston. He apparently planned an extended stay because a few weeks later he called Atkins in Nashville and asked him to ship the Dauphin north. Somehow Glasscock came into possession of the instrument and in early April, Betty says, she arrived in Maine, guitar in hand, and prepared to stay. What transpired between the two over the next month is not known for certain. Lenny later told Flo and Gene Hooper that Glasscock had claimed she was pregnant and pushed him into marriage. Lenny's son, Chet, says his father admitted that he had simply caved in after months of

Glasscock's haranguing him to make an "honest woman" of her. Whatever the motivation, on May 18, 1980, Lenny Breau married Joanne Glasscock on the veranda of his mother and stepfather's home. Denny Breau recalls that Lenny, dressed in a suit borrowed from Terry Wedding (the same suit in which he was buried) drank so heavily that he had to be supported while slurring his way through his vows. The news of the marriage came as a shock to many people, not least of all Chet Atkins who did not hear about it until Lenny and Jewel returned to Nashville for a visit shortly after the wedding.

> I didn't want Lenny to get married a second time because I was concerned about his ability to support a wife and handle all the responsibilities of family life. I made him promise he would call me before taking the plunge. A little later I got in from a few days on the road and Lenny came by my office. He was laughing. "Well Chet, I tried to phone you, but you were out—so I went ahead and got married."[24]

Whether or not Atkins could have halted the marriage is a moot point, but during the remaining years of his life he often admitted to friends that he could never forgive himself for bringing the couple together.

9.

Cold, Cold Heart
May 1980—November 1983

"Sometimes Lenny'd meet a woman who just wanted to mother him to death. Other times he'd meet . . . a nemesis."

—Don Francks[1]

At the time Lenny was learning Tal Farlow's licks in the late fifties, Farlow had become so soured on the dreary machinations of the music business that he retreated from the jazz scene at the height of his fame. While he played the occasional date and made a few records during the 1960s and '70s, Farlow generally kept a low profile and worked as a self-employed sign painter in Sea Bright, New Jersey. In the late 1970s, a budding young filmmaker and student of jazz guitar named Lorenzo DeStefano sought Farlow out and persuaded him to be the subject of his first professional feature, *Talmage Farlow*.[2] DeStefano wanted to include a contemporary jazz guitarist in the movie and asked Farlow if he had any preferences.

"Tal immediately suggested Lenny and I said, 'Yeah, Lenny Breau,'" DeStefano says. "So we went after him and after a little back and forth Lenny was booked to do it. He and his wife flew down from Maine to New York and we had them driven up to Sea Bright." The couple arrived on May 21 for their two-day, de facto honeymoon for which Lenny was pleased to receive $400 and a few nights at the local Sandy Hook Motel.

The actual meeting between Farlow and Lenny is not shown in the documentary because DeStefano did not want to intrude on the moment, but he says that the men greeted each other genially and with obvious mutual respect. "They got on great right away," says DeStefano. "Tal had heard him a lot so it wasn't like Lenny was just another adoring student. Tal knew Lenny was special. Lenny understood the tradition Tal was part of—52nd Street, BeBop, Bird—and you could see in Lenny's eyes when he looked at Tal that he saw all that. Lenny knew that tradition. He hadn't been part of it, but he knew this guy in this room was there."

Farlow and Lenny talked and jammed through the afternoon and that night played together at a club called The Sign of the Times. DeStefano recorded this set, which Guitarchives released on CD in 1997 as *Chance Meeting*. Throughout the set, the self-effacing Farlow tended to defer to Lenny who never really caught fire, and the recording is more of an interesting, highly listenable historical chronicle than mandatory listening for fans of either man. However, meeting and playing with Farlow was profoundly significant for Lenny, says Ron Halldorson. "You could see that when that scene [in which the men play together] started, Lenny was in rough shape," he says. "Then they play a tune and there's this look of triumph on Lenny's face that says 'man, I may be messed up, but I just played my ass off here with Tal and I feel really good.' When I saw that, it just made me feel so good because I know that look and I know what it meant. It was an expression of his own kind of success. Tal was one of his greatest influences so to do that was a great moment for him."

Before Lenny left Sea Bright, he and Farlow discussed the possibility of further performances and perhaps doing a joint recording. The latter never materialized, but the two guitarists would play together again before the year was out.

Lenny and his wife returned to Maine where they rented an apartment on Deering Street close to downtown Portland. Lenny landed a weekly solo gig playing his seven string at a local coffee house/restaurant called the Café Domas and later formed a trio with bassist Les Richards and drummer Phil Verrill. The three began working regularly in the area, often at a Portland tavern called the Hour Glass. One night while playing at this club, Lenny was approached by a young guitarist named Bob Thompson who had moved to the area from Connecticut the year before expressly to find and study with Lenny. Lenny agreed to teach Thompson and took his number, promising to call him to arrange a lesson. The next day, Thompson was sitting on the front stairs of his building practicing a few of the techniques he had picked up from Lenny's albums in anticipation of the lesson. "There were some bushes between my building and the one next door, and suddenly Lenny and Jewel emerge from these bushes!" says Thompson. "Lenny said 'Gee, I guess you *have* been working on my stuff.' I was aghast. I asked what he was doing here and he said he lived next door. In some very cosmic, fortuitous way I'd ended up moving in right next door to him!"

Thompson spent time regularly with Lenny over the next year but took only one formal lesson from him. This was enough, he says, to provide him with several years' worth of study material.

> He talked in very concise and clear terms about altered, melodic minor, harmonic minor and diminished scales. He knew his theory inside out. One thing that opened up my musicianship was his thinking about chords as motion; what a particular texture says to you and using it in that capacity. Not just playing it because a voicing is a theoretical constant in a certain place in a tune, but because several chords will create a certain emotion or certain color. These are going to be different for certain people because that's the interpretive beauty of it. His ideas about interpretive values really opened up my mind. He often talked about the color of chords and voicings and how they were evocative.

Lenny had been describing his music in terms of visual art since at least 1969 when he told a journalist, "I use silence as the Japanese artists use space in their prints, where a delicate drawing fades into mist."[3] (This brings to mind Bill Evans's essay "Improvisation in Jazz" from the liner notes of *Kind of Blue* in which Evans compares jazz improvisation to a type of Japanese visual art. The essay may well have instigated Lenny's interest in art, considering the enormous influence Evans had on his music.) In interviews from the late seventies onwards, Lenny often brought up the subject of visual art and the Impressionists in particular when speaking of his music, as he did in a discussion with writer Joan Sadler in 1979.

> Now I'm really starting to get inspired by looking at paintings. I look at some of the old French Impressionists and [they give] me ideas. I sort of relate music to painting and color. I'd like to play sounds you can see if you've got your eyes closed . . . I think of myself as a colorist, adding different colors and shades by using different techniques and touching the guitar in certain ways. I think if you close your eyes, maybe you can see those [things], you can see visions . . .[4]

Lenny found Impressionist art so stimulating, he told writer Dan Rooke, that he carried reproductions of Renoir's paintings in his guitar case. "When I open [the case] up at night, I see a Renoir," he said, "and right away I'm inspired. It gets me into the right state of mind."[5] He also found inspiration in Impressionist composers such as Debussy and Ravel who had had such a strong influence on Bill Evans's reharmonization concepts as well as his own wistful, reflective compositions like "Time Remembered" and "Peace Piece." Thompson says that Lenny was then working on arranging many of Evans's pieces for solo guitar. "He showed me how he was evolving a whole bunch of Bill Evans tunes," Thompson says, "changing the keys to make the positional access more available on the fret board. He was looking for different ways to rebuild some of the voicings and reharmonizing things to make them more accessible and create some interesting colors."

Thompson relished these discussions, but some evenings—especially if Lenny were drinking—they could take a dark and disturbing turn. One night, Lenny appeared at Thompson's door with his guitar in one hand and a bottle of cheap wine in the other. As Lenny drained the bottle, Thompson saw a shocking shift in his usual amiable personality.

> He went beyond maudlin and, as the night wore on, got really pissed off. He stopped playing and started talking about how frustrating it was that he couldn't crack into the upper echelon of jazz guitarists. He said "I can't believe that these bastards"—other guitarists he knew—"are famous and making money and selling records." He said "Chet Atkins goes around saying that I'm the best goddamn guitarist in the world and here I am playing for fifty dollars a night! What kind of shit is that? Sometimes it just makes me want to quit and go do something else." He just launched into this tirade about the frustration of his career. It ripped my heart out because I agreed with everything he said except that I thought he probably needed to look inside himself to see why his career really wasn't taking off.

Thompson was also surprised to see evidence that all was not well between Lenny and Jewel. In public, he says, they were affectionate and doting, often walking the streets of Portland entwined in one another's arms. But Thompson caught a glimpse of the marriage's darker side when Lenny woke him at three o'clock one morning, underdressed for the cold December weather, and desperate to be admitted to Thompson's apartment. "I let him in and he just launched into this thing like 'I've gotta get away from that bitch!' And I'm going 'wait a minute, it's like you're joined at the hip!' But he went on and on saying, 'She's crazy, out of her mind. I can't do anything around there.' I'd seen some tensions over there a couple of times—bickering and the like. But this was a total shock to me."

Lenny did not "get away" from Jewel except to host an occasional workshop in Boston or play his gigs at the Cellar Door and No Tomatoes where he still worked with Les Richards and Steve Grover. At a Cellar Door gig in mid-September, Grover took Lenny aside to tell him some sobering news. "Bill Evans had just died," says Grover. "I'd read it in the paper, but Lenny didn't know about it and I didn't want him to find out from someone else who didn't know who Bill Evans was. I wanted to be the one to tell him. I just said 'Lenny, Bill

Evans died.' He didn't break down or anything. He just said, 'oh wow, oh man!' It was almost like he'd expected it."

It was Grover who drove Lenny to his gig with Tal Farlow at Sandy's Jazz Revival in Beverly, Massachusetts, in the fall of 1980. "It was only one night," Grover says. "Tal seemed very nervous. He deferred to Lenny a lot, and played bass lines almost all the time using that homemade octave divider he had on his belt. He just wanted to listen to Lenny more than anything else. Lenny was very respectful and really enjoyed the opportunity. He was in fine shape and seemed to want to make the most of that gig. He came up to me on a break and was very pleased, obviously enjoying himself."

Later that fall, Lenny was in Boston to do the first of several workshops organized by Bill Hill, a Berklee School of Music professor who had befriended Lenny at one of his Cellar Door shows. These workshops took place in a participant's home and were attended mainly by Berklee students who paid a fee that went in full to Lenny. One of these students was Garrison Fewell, a guitarist who would go on to teach at Berklee and make several CDs with the likes of Cecil McBee and Fred Hirsch, as well as teaching and performing internationally. He calls Lenny "a generous teacher" and considers these workshops among his most important learning experiences. Lenny, he says, had a remarkable knack for making his often complex techniques seem accessible to the class.

> The things he showed us in those workshops were things we'd never come close to playing in our lifetime. There was this one chord that he showed me: a G altered chord. You go from the bottom of the guitar: G on 6, B on 5 and then with his fourth finger he would bar a D flat triad on the sixth fret, A flat, D flat and F. [This is a formidable stretch on guitar even for a large hand.] And to hear him play that, because he had the ability to play with all five fingers [of his right hand], the thing sounded so beautiful. I worked on that for years and still had trouble doing it. [Another] of his examples was playing a 2-5-1 progression in the key of C. For the 2 chord—D minor—he'd play a C triad—G-C-E—with a D bass note so he'd have D-G-C-E and that would serve as the D minor chord. Then he'd go down to a G altered dominant chord with a G on bottom and the C triad moved up half a step to creat a D♭ triad, so he'd

have G-A♭-D♭-F. Then he'd go to the 1 chord using a C bass note and shifting the triad on topdown to a B triad so that he'd be playing C-F♯-B-D♯. So his triads would be moving chromatically—C-D♭ and B—while the bass was playing the regular 2-5-1 progression and that's about as far as you'd get and he'd say, "Yeah, like this" and he'd play something that would blow your mind. He had a way of making you believe you could do it: you just had to work on it. "Practice: you can get this stuff. It's hard but not impossible." Very inspirational, like his relationship with his instrument was so inspiring to him that you would leave feeling "wow, I'm really going to do this!" Until you got home and tackled the stuff!

In 1979, Lenny and Chet Atkins began recording tracks for an album that RCA would release in 1981 as *Standard Brands*. Much of the recording was done in 1980 with Mike Poston—Atkins's personal recording engineer—presiding. "Chet would call me and say, 'Yeah, we're gonna work on this project with Lenny Breau,'" says Poston. "Because of the way Lenny was, we had to get him while the mood was right because you never knew what kind of shape Lenny would be in. Chet would call and say 'this morning is going to be a good morning. C'mon out and let's go for it.'" Sessions would start around 10:00 a.m. and cease not much later than noon. Poston says that while the men may have gone over some of the material the night before, little was carefully worked out simply because of Lenny's disinclination to stick to arrangements.

Chet was such a meticulous worker in the studio that he probably thought about what he was going to play for days before he actually played it, but Lenny would never play anything the same way twice. Chet would adapt because he was capable of it, but you could see the expressions on his face when Lenny would do something unexpected, like "holy shit, where'd he get that from?" It seemed to frustrate Chet a little bit simply because he was so organized and always knew where he was going. So Chet needed to have some ideas and direction because you had to put reins on Lenny. Chet knew where he was going and how he was going to get there. With Lenny, he'd start driving down the road without a clue where he's going and where he winds up is where he winds up. In Chet's really diplomatic way, he'd try to shape and guide him and try to keep him on the track a little bit; that was Chet as a producer. Sometimes Lenny would surprise himself with some of the things he would play. They'd be playing along and this big grin would come up because he was going down a road he hadn't gone before. Sometimes between takes he wouldn't shut up. He'd tell these endless stories about nothing. But once you got him picking, everything'd be fine.

Atkins gives Lenny the spotlight on several tunes including "Polka Dots and Moonbeams," and "Taking a Chance on Love," allowing his friend room to follow his flights of fancy while—for better or worse—managing to keep his divergences to a minimum. On a stunning version of "Going Home" from Dvorak's *New World Symphony*, Atkins does little more than play a chorus of melody on his resonator guitar, leaving Lenny to do most of the piece as a beautifully reharmonized solo. Lenny dusted off "Batucada," the Luiz Bonfa piece he'd included on *The Hallmark Sessions*, and made the most of the cross rhythms available to him with Atkins keeping a solid ground beat. The men also dredged up "Cattle Call," the old Eddy Arnold tune on which Lenny had first harmonized with his astonished parents in their rehearsal barn nearly forty years earlier.

Lenny's name precedes Atkins's on the cover of *Standard Brands*, a detail that Atkins insisted on, says Poston. "It wasn't a 'Chet and guest' album or even a 'Chet with Lenny Breau album.' It was more of a 'Lenny Breau album with Chet as a sideman.'" Prominence of name placement aside, the historical collaboration between two of the world's most accomplished guitarists was apparently too jazzy for many of Atkins's audience and not adventurous enough for most of Lenny's fans. *Standard Brands* sold poorly and was soon relegated to record store deleted bins with so many of Lenny's previous albums. In the past few years, however, it has become a highly coveted album and justifiably so.

In early 1981, the Breaus left Portland and relocated to Jewel's hometown of Stockton, California, so that she could be close to her family during the last months of her pregnancy. Not long after arriving in Stockton, Lenny was contacted by Jim Ferguson, then editor of *Guitar Player* magazine, who asked him to do a monthly instructional column for the magazine. Ferguson wanted to meet with Lenny every few months and record what would be essentially a marathon lesson in which Lenny would discuss various facets of his style and technique. Afterwards, Ferguson would organize and polish the raw material from this session into a concise, readable column. Lenny was delighted with this idea and the first of these columns—an introductory lesson on chordal harmonics—appeared in the magazine's May 1981, issue. Over the next two years, the men would co-create about two dozen of these columns, which constitute the first in-depth study of Lenny's style.

Jewel gave birth to Dawn, the couple's first and only child, in mid-March. She would be the inspiration for her father's poignant composition "Lullaby," written and performed for the first time eighteen days after her birth in the city that Lenny had once celebrated in his wistful song, "New York City" with the lines, "I find that lately I'm missing old Toronto/Where basses strum and drums are full of fire." The machinations that allowed Lenny's return to Toronto had been in the works for over a year and were precipitated by Bob Erlendson with whom Lenny had kept in sporadic touch since fleeing the country in 1975. Paul Grosney, who in 1958 had helped Lenny obtain his first Winnipeg union card, now lived in Toronto and managed Bourbon Street—the city's most popular jazz club at that time. Bob Erlendson was a good friend of Grosney's and suggested that he book Lenny to play at the venue. Grosney was willing, but when he looked into arranging a performer's visa for Lenny, he discovered that his old drug charge and problems with Revenue Canada would result in his arrest the moment he entered the country. At this point, Don Francks stepped in and hired the services of lawyer Austin Cooper who had successfully defended Keith Richard on a possession of heroin charge in the city a few years earlier. When Lenny landed at the Toronto airport in late March, Cooper and Francks were on hand to meet him and drive him directly to Toronto police headquarters where he turned himself in. The court reduced his 1975 trafficking charge to simple possession, as per an arrangement Cooper had made before hand, and Francks covered the $1000 fine. Later that day Francks also paid off $5000 of Lenny's $15,000 tax debt to stop Revenue Canada from garnisheeing Lenny's performance fees. In a single day, all the barriers that had kept Lenny from returning to the beloved city of his halcyon days were removed. This not only opened the door for a two-week gig at Bourbon Street, but a short cross-Canada tour that included a sold-out show in Winnipeg. Lenny was jubilant, but sadly, his return to his adopted country would not turn out to be quite the triumphant experience it was augured to be.

Lenny played his first night at Bourbon Street on Monday, March 30, with Don Thompson and Claude Ranger. The club was packed, but as jazz journalist Mark Miller wrote in his review of the gig, "only the sound of the [club's] door opening and closing broke the spell the guitarist was weaving." Miller goes on to say that Lenny "dazzled with his technique, impressed with the breadth of guitar music . . . and intrigued with the boundless imagination that he brought to his inventions." Miller's one criticism of Lenny's performance was that at times his prodigious facility "interferes with his imagination by making available another path to go follow when inspiration wanes . . . breaking up the flow of his solos and giving them an episodic quality." But, Miller continued, "His lines are never less than clear and concise, with wedge-shaped chords to open up a tune further to exploration . . ." The writer was less enthused by the rhythm section of Thompson and Ranger, noting that Thompson seemed "very subdued" and Ranger's "playing became less adroit than usual and less sensitive to Breau than the guitarist's music requires."[6] Lenny apparently agreed with this assessment; on his second or third night at Bourbon Street, he fired Ranger and brought in Terry Clarke for the remainder of the gig.

Thompson says flatly that Lenny's playing during the first week at Bourbon Street was "the best I ever heard him." This changed, he says, when old friends began showing up and inveigling Lenny to relive old times with various substances. Francks, with whom Lenny was staying, had foreseen this possibility and, along with Grosney and other close friends, formed a ring around Lenny to block old contacts from providing him with drugs.

Their efforts were only partially successful, as a tape made by an attendee of a guitar clinic that Lenny taught at George's Spaghetti House on Saturday, April 5, indicates. After kicking off the workshop with a few bars of music, Lenny suddenly launches into a ten-minute monologue on the importance of music in his life, delivering it with a rapid fire, peripatetic verbosity that is clearly driven by a chemically supercharged mind. "You have to love [music] to the point where it means everything to you," he says. "You have to be not only obsessed by the music but you have to be . . . *possessed* by the music too. The music has to *own* you to the point where it's got you by the balls!" He then counsels the group to have something to fall back on—teaching or running a music store—while devoting themselves to their craft. "Not do like I did," he says, "just float around and practice all the time." Still building up steam, he segues into a fevered explanation of how music connects him to God.

> To the musician who's really serious, it's the fastest route and the fastest way to God . . . it makes me feel close to God and I don't have to go to church and kneel down and praise God because this is my way of praising. This is a gift from God, so when I play, I'm playing for the people, but I'm playing for God because he gave me this gift, so I go home and I feel complete because I played for God. So when you're in music that way, it means that you're in it as a religion, not because you're going to make a million dollars . . . you're in it because you love it. You don't mind taking ten years to do it. . . . I've been playing for twenty-five years and I feel like I'm just starting to develop my own style. I copied Bill Evans for years, this guy for years, but now I'm starting to play stuff that "hey, I think that's mine, man. I don't think I ever played that before." But the reward is a long time coming, like twenty years later. And it probably would have come a lot sooner if I hadn't got caught up with drugs.[7]

The realization that this torrent of words was obviously delivered under the influence of drugs gives it a tragic irony augmented by the note of almost hysterical desperation in Lenny's voice. He sounds less like a self-assured guru imparting truisms to his inexperienced acolytes than a frightened, anxious man fervently trying to reassure himself that his devotion to his art to the exclusion of all else has had meaning and worth. It's as though a deeply personal, inner monologue that Lenny had long used to keep self-doubt at bay during many dark nights of the soul had suddenly burst from his psyche before a roomful of strangers. What is so poignant about this painfully candid monologue is that Lenny sounds woefully unconvinced by his own words.

By the beginning of his second week at Bourbon Street, Lenny was getting high before and during his shows, and disappearing afterwards. "People I didn't know would come in and I'd see Lenny take off with them," says Thompson. "Around the beginning of the second week, his playing began to taper off, by the middle of the second week it wasn't very good and at the end of it, he couldn't play. It was just awful. He didn't apologize, but I know he felt really awful about it because he always tried to be on his best behavior around me."

When Lenny's gig at Bourbon Street ended on the April 11, he remained in Toronto for a few days to take possession of his new Tom Holmes seven-string guitar. Lenny had commissioned Holmes to build this instrument in the fall of 1980, and the luthier had put the finishing touches on it during Lenny's first week in Toronto. Lenny sent $600 of his first week's pay from Bourbon Street to Holmes, and his new instrument arrived from Nashville a few days later. The guitar was essentially a seven-string version of his first Holmes guitar, but with a smaller, single cutaway body and a darker finish. Lenny was pleased with the guitar despite a design flaw that he discovered when he tried to string the instrument: the neck's long scale made it impossible to tune the high A string up to pitch without its breaking. Lenny got around this by tuning the instrument down a whole step and capoing the neck at the second fret. Evidently he felt sufficiently comfortable with this set-up to decide to use the seven string for the rest of his Canadian tour and gave his Holmes six string to the late Toronto guitarist, Peter Harris.

Lenny flew out of Toronto early on the morning of April 15 to play a sold-out show at the 1500-seat Playhouse Theatre in Winnipeg with Ron Halldorson and Reg Kelln. This show was, at least in symbolic terms, the crucial event of the tour. Not only was it the largest venue that Lenny had ever headlined in his career, but he would be playing in front of a crowd of fans and friends who knew him from his glory days in Winnipeg and had come to cheer the return of their hometown hero and exalt in his success. In short, it was a situation that may as well have been specifically designed to make Lenny choke. Lenny stayed up drinking and taking pills during his last night in Toronto and was already in rough shape when his plane touched down in Winnipeg that morning, says Ray St. Germain, who picked him up at the Winnipeg airport. "He hadn't slept and he was bombed on Valium and rum," St. Germain recalls. "I took him to the Fort Garry Hotel and told him to get some sleep and said that I'd come back later in the morning." When St. Germain returned, he found a city sheriff serving Lenny with papers, which Valerie Breau-St. Germain had filed, demanding $100,000 in unpaid child support. The show would not go on until the money was paid, the sheriff explained. St. Germain called his sister and pleaded with her to negotiate with her ex-husband, and then took Lenny to the office of Valerie's lawyer. There she and Lenny reached an agreement in which the amount owed would be reduced to the $3000 fee Lenny was to earn from the show that night. Despite this agreement, Lenny was still badly shaken. He spent the day wandering around the city, visiting his children and old friends while cadging drinks and ingesting whatever pills he could find. At the Playhouse Theatre, Kelln and Halldorson waited in vain for Lenny to appear for the scheduled three o'clock soundcheck and rehearsal. When Lenny finally arrived, he embraced Halldorson and began to cry. It was decided that the rehearsal and soundcheck would not go ahead and Lenny was deposited in the green room. Ross Porter, currently one of Canada's best-known radio journalists, arrived to interview Lenny and found him reasonably coherent and willing to talk. In the interview that followed, Lenny railed against the evils of drugs, describing them as being "like a seductress,"[8] and in a slurred voice told Porter how they had ensnared him and destroyed his life. Chet Breau arrived soon after and stayed with his father until show time. In the presence of his son, Lenny finally relaxed and dropped into a deep sleep. He was woken just as his name was announced to the Playhouse audience and was still in a fog when he took the stage for his opening solo set. After the tumultuous applause died down, Lenny rambled incoherently for several minutes before attempting his first tune, which collapsed after a few bars. He began singing a Johnny Cash song but that too came to a sudden halt. When it became clear that Lenny was incapable of even rudimentary playing, some angry audience members booed and shouted "burn-out" and "asshole" as Kelln and Halldorson watched in horror from the wings. In an attempt to salvage the show, they came on stage before their scheduled time and began playing behind Lenny. There was a noticeable improvement in his playing but it was short-lived and an intermission was called prematurely. Lenny remained on stage for a few minutes arguing loudly with irate fans in the front rows before he shuffled into the green room. One old "friend" offered him marijuana and was physically dispatched by Ray St. Germain. By the time Lenny returned to the stage, the theatre had emptied except for some distraught family members and tenacious fans. Many audience members were now outside demanding refunds, and when they discovered that the show's promoter had left the building with the night's receipts, a riot ensued and the theatre's front windows were smashed. The curtain came down shortly afterwards. Lenny left the theatre with some friends for a small party at which, Ron Halldorson says, he seemed remarkably straight and in good spirits, as though the disaster at his homecoming concert had never happened.

Promoters in Edmonton, Calgary, and Regina who caught wind of the Playhouse debacle were less hasty to dismiss Lenny's behavior, however, and cancelled his shows. Lenny took a short trip to Edmonton to look up Judi Singh and his daughter, but the pair was out of town. He then continued to Vancouver for a show at the Granville Island Arts Club Theatre where this author saw Lenny reprise his Winnipeg performance. The west coast audience was considerably more sympathetic than the one in Winnipeg, and urged Lenny to relax and take his time. Once or twice, Lenny seemed on the verge of pulling himself together but as he candidly described his financial difficulties to his audience between bungled attempts to get a song underway, he became increasingly upset and began weeping and praying aloud on stage. Beyond simple inebriation, he appeared to be in the midst of an emotional and mental breakdown. Lenny returned for a second set, although only a few very optimistic fans remained in the theatre. Finally the promoters ended the show and took Lenny, now completely disoriented, to the hospital. While waiting in the emergency room he surveyed his surroundings and humbly thanked his hosts for bringing him to such an upscale hotel. The next day he boarded a plane back to Stockton and returned to Jewel and his infant daughter. This would be his last performance in western Canada.

Paul Grosney had scheduled Lenny for a return performance at Bourbon Street in mid-June, but after his catastrophic western Canadian tour, this date was dropped as were scheduled appearances at the Edmonton and Montreal Jazz festivals. However, on August 11, Lenny returned to Toronto to play another two-week gig at Bourbon Street. Stories of Lenny's problems during his last visit to Canada did not deter fans from filling the club to capacity every night to hear him play with a rhythm section that, depending on the night, was made up of bassists Dave Young and Don Thompson, and either Terry Clarke or Buff Allen on drums. Once again Mark Miller wrote an enthusiastic albeit brief review of Lenny's opening night at Bourbon Street noting that while Lenny's solos were sometimes unfocused, more often he "worked his way logically and inventively toward a stunning conclusion."[9]

A few days later, Lenny spoke with Ted O'Reilly on his CJRT-FM radio show, *Jazz Scene*. Relaxed and lucid, Lenny explained that his music had become "more introspective" and says that the various styles he once played—classical, country, and flamenco—as entities unto themselves, were now "all wrapped up in the jazz thing . . . I just let those influences come out where they want to." Lenny talks at length about his plans, saying that he wants to do a book and video on his style, and perhaps open up a school for fingerstyle jazz players. He says he would like to "get with a big label," play concert halls instead of clubs, and tour Europe. This reflects his new attitude towards his music, he says: "I've decided that I may as well start playing for money one of these days because it is a business. When I was younger I played just for the love of playing, Ted. I played just because I loved to play. But I'm starting to realize that you can make money doing this too if you handle it right." Lenny states this with much gravity, which he then undercuts when O'Reilly somberly agrees that making money is good if one is interested in purchasing a house or a car. "Or, like—a spaceship!" Lenny interjects gleefully, following his remark with his trademark machine-gun laugh. O'Reilly brings up the subject of fusion music, which in the lexicon of the time referred to jazz/rock. Lenny, however, saw other possibilities for the genre. "If I ever do a fusion album," he told O'Reilly, "I think it would be like country jazz—like country songs with jazz chords to them. That would be like my kind of fusion . . . to play a good Hank Williams tune and use some good jazz chords with it, maybe with a funky feel . . . it's something I'd like to do one day." O'Reilly raises the issue of Lenny's drug problems to which his guest replies quickly with his by now stock line on the subject: "Yeah, but that's all over now."[10]

During his second booking at Bourbon Street, Lenny did manage to stay clean, largely because of Jewel's presence. Grosney installed the family at the nearby apartment that Bourbon Street leased for its performers and when the couple was at the club, Jewel watched her husband carefully, both off and on stage. Those who knew of Lenny's problems understood her protective hovering, but there were other aspects of her behavior that alarmed some of Lenny's friends. Barrie Tallman says that one night he arrived at the apartment to take Lenny to the club and found Jewel and Lenny arguing. Suddenly Jewel pushed her husband and punched him in the face. Lenny, typical of spouses in abusive relationships, later downplayed the incident and—whether out of shame or denial—refused to talk about his marriage with Tallman and other friends.

After trips to Stockton and Nashville, the couple returned to Auburn and rented an apartment on Western Promenade Avenue. Soon, Lenny was back playing at the Cellar Door and various other clubs in central Maine with Steve Grover and Les Richards. Lenny also did a short-lived duo act with Jewel performing folk and pop material such as Dylan's "Gotta Serve Somebody" and James Taylor's "You've Got a Friend." Jewel's voice was a taste few acquired, however, and club owners did not rebook the team.

Lenny was now playing regularly with Brad Terry at various clubs and concerts including a stellar appearance at the Augusta Jazz Festival. Terry had continued to record his performances with Lenny, building up a stock of material that he would first release in 1988 on an LP titled *The Living Room Tapes, Volume I*. Volume II of the recordings was released on CD several years later and, in 2003, Art of Life Records reissued both albums on a two-CD set with previously unreleased material that included their first recording session from early October of 1978. Terry didn't keep an exact log of recording dates, but recalls that the performances on the albums took place between that date and January 1982. Lenny's playing on *The Living Room Tapes* does not always have the pristine, focused quality that marked his work on *The Legendary Lenny Breau . . . Now*, but it surpasses his work on that album in terms of its adventurous spirit in general and, specifically, in the depth of his harmonic ideas. One of the most dazzling tracks is his performance of "Stella by Starlight," in a sense the apotheosis of his life's work. In its opening chorus, Lenny underpins the stunning, reharmonized chord sequence that supports the melody with a gentle, Atkins-style alternating half-note bass line. It's an astonishingly successful combination of the influences of Evans and Atkins into a unique whole that brings to mind a harmonically updated stride piano style. "Emily," taken at a midtempo ballad pace, is perhaps the most flawless and exquisitely rendered piece on the disc, and ranks with Lenny's best recorded playing. At eight minutes and fourteen seconds, there is not a wasted note or uninspired bar of music as Lenny glides through the piece, prodded gently at times by Terry's laconic, imaginative phrases. Lenny's single-note playing does not quite match the level of his harmonic brilliance on this material, but there are superb solos throughout the recordings. Occasionally Lenny falls into the trap of using his stock of sequenced modal riffs to fill dead air space, but for the most part his lines are well formed and organized, and played with great lyricism and finesse. Despite the occasional rough edges and cul de sacs on *The Living Room Tapes*, it's easy to imagine that the possibility of advancing his music to this level, particularly in harmonic terms, was precisely what had kept Lenny's eye on the sparrow for two decades through some very trying times.

Not all his performances with Brad Terry during this time were quite so inspired, however. In January 1982, the quartet of Lenny, Terry, Grover, and Les Richards were booked to play at a lavishly renovated vaudeville theatre in the town of Waldoboro, Maine. "I was very pleased to do it," recalls Terry. "A lot was riding on it. But Lenny started drinking just before the show and, after the second tune, we had to physically remove him from the stage and finish the concert without him." True to form, Lenny offered no apology for his conduct, but this time there were signs that Lenny felt some real remorse over the fiasco he had created. Not only was he completely clean and sober for the next few gigs with Terry and Grover, in mid-January of 1982 he voluntarily checked himself into a six-week recovery program at The Merry Meeting House, a drug and alcohol treatment center in Bowdoinham, Maine. (Some friends suggest that Chet Atkins, who had long tried to persuade Lenny to go into a rehab program, footed the bill for the treatment.) Lenny spoke daily via phone with Terry during his treatment, and seemed optimistic and positive about its benefits. When he graduated from the program in late February of 1982, he moved in with Brad Terry and his family in Brunswick, determined not only to stay drug and alcohol free but to end his marriage as well. Jewel had stayed with Terry during part of Lenny's treatment, but he ordered her out of his home after an incident involving his son Aaron. Lenny was very close to the four-teen-year-old and had allowed Aaron to call him daily at The Merry Meeting House, a privilege that his doctor had advised Lenny not to extend to Jewel, says Brad Terry. Towards the end of Lenny's stay at the facility, Jewel became furious when Lenny did not send her a card for Valentine's Day. She pressured Aaron into calling Lenny and snatched the phone from the teenager when he answered, raging at her husband for his selfishness until he hung up. When Terry found out how she had used his son in this subterfuge, he demanded that Jewel leave and she rented a motel room in downtown Brunswick. Terry and Lenny went to the motel shortly after Lenny's return to pick up his guitars, but Jewel would not allow him to take his instruments. Terry finally summoned a police officer who watched while Lenny retrieved his guitars. Without a further word to Jewel, the men returned to Terry's house where Lenny would take refuge for the next few weeks.

Lenny's friends were pleased with his efforts to end his chemical dependency, but they were not able to savor his sobriety for long. Soon, Lenny was getting high on pills acquired from local doctors for invented aches and pains. During one of these jags, Lenny's bizarre behavior so alarmed Terry and Grover that they called an ambulance and had Lenny taken to a nearby hospital where he spent the night. The next day when Terry had finished his day job as a school bus driver, he visited the hospital to find that Lenny had checked out early that morning. Neither Grover nor Terry ever saw Lenny again.

Lenny had picked up his guitars and purchased a bus ticket to Bangor after calling Gene Hooper in Machias to tell him he was on his way north. Alerted by Hooper, Dick Curless met Lenny in Bangor and drove him to the town of Ellsworth, where Hooper connected with him later that day. Lenny, deep in a chemically induced fugue state, did not recognize his uncle and would not allow him to help him with his two guitars. "He had a deathly grip on them," says Hooper. "I had a little theme song that I used to sing that went 'my name's Gene Hooper. I'm just here to sing an old radio song.' I got right in his ear and sang it and he smiled at me and he came right out of it." In Machias, Lenny greeted and embraced his aunt Flo and after a large, home-cooked meal, he was put to bed. "He got up late the next day and we gave him a nice, big breakfast," says Flo Hooper. "Then he took all these pills he had and threw them in the toilet. He said, 'I'm done with this. This is it,' and he flushed them all right down the toilet."

Under the Hoopers' nurturing care, Lenny remained entirely straight for the next two months. His days were spent practicing for hours at a time and walking or riding a bike through the streets of Machias dressed in the western-style clothes that his aunt made for him. In the evening, after large helpings of his aunt Flo's cooking, Lenny loved to sit and talk over old times, Hooper says. "His memory was amazing. All that abuse he'd given his poor body and he could still recall all them stories from when he was just a kid."

Lenny managed to maintain his drug-free existence even when he traveled on his own to California to work with Jim Ferguson on his monthly column for *Guitar Player* magazine. Ferguson, says Hooper, was delighted to find Lenny in such good shape. "After they was done there, Jim called me and said 'Lenny's on his way back and what a treat it was to see him the way that he was.'" This victory was followed by a weeklong trip to Nashville during which Lenny continued to maintain his sobriety. When Lenny returned, the Hoopers helped him organize a concert at the nearby university. Lenny was not optimistic about pulling much of an audience for the show, but the performance was sold out, with fans turning up from as far away as Montreal and Boston. "Lenny was so surprised that all these people came out to see him," says Gene Hooper. "He played beautiful, too. He'd play 'Autumn Leaves' and you could see 'em falling."

The longest period of sobriety in Lenny's adult life came to an abrupt halt in early May. During the months that Lenny stayed with the Hoopers, Jewel had besieged the couple with phone calls, demanding to know the whereabouts of her husband. Hooper told her that Lenny was working in a remote logging camp and was unreachable but Jewel wasn't taken in. "One day," says Flo Hooper, "Lenny looked out the window and said 'Oh my God: Jewel's here!' His face turned white as snow." Lenny's stories of his physical and psychological abuse at Jewel's hands had horrified the Hoopers. When his wife turned up on their doorstep, the Hoopers' first impulse was to turn her away but at the sight of Lenny's infant daughter, they relented and reluctantly asked her in. On the second day of her visit, she and her husband took a long walk. When Lenny returned he was acting strangely, and confessed to the Hoopers that Jewel had supplied him with an unspecified hallucinogen. Jewel left the next day, but the effects of her visit on Lenny did not. He began to visit doctors in the area complaining of muscle pains in order to receive prescription drugs, and drinking cough syrup and wine when he was refused. Soon, the Hoopers, heartbroken by the condition of their out-of-control nephew, were no longer able to handle him. With great misgivings, they packed a very stoned Lenny into their Cadillac, and drove him to his mother's house in Lisbon Falls where they bid him farewell for the last time.

Lenny's stay with his mother was brief. Within a month, he was back in Nashville, living with Richard Cotten and his new wife, Darci, while collaborating with John Knowles on an instruction book of his style. The book—*Lenny Breau: Fingerstyle Jazz*—uses a unique, informal format in which textual commentary is taken from conversations between Lenny and Knowles.

> I said to Lenny, "what I'd like to do is talk to you about your music and have you play some examples. . . . I'll see if I can't guide you in a direction, and when we get through I'll write down some of the things that you've recorded. But up front, it'll be a chance to hear you talk about your music." I would say, "Now play me the first four bars of a blues and use that idea so we can see how that's gonna go." And he would start playing and you couldn't stop him. He'd keep playing and then look up and say "now what were we gonna do?" I'd think "OK, maybe I can edit that out." I'd say "Let's do it again and do all twelve bars" and he'd do it again and get into it and harmonics would be in there and everything. So it was very difficult to extract out a little thing. But we finally got there.

Still in print after more than twenty years, the book contains well-organized, succinct examples of Lenny's harmonics, melody against abbreviated chords, and polyrhythms illustrated with exercises as well as three complete transcriptions from Lenny's repertoire: "Little Blues," "Five O'clock Bells," and "Freight Train." Lenny was murdered before the book was released, but John Knowles says that he was clearly pleased with the final manuscript.

Later that summer, Richard Cotten introduced Lenny to a young bassist/vocalist named Jim Ferguson. Once a pupil of Bill Evans' bassist Chuck Israel, Ferguson had arrived in Nashville from South Carolina the previous fall with a masters degree in music and experience that included a stint as a vocalist in the New Christy Minstrels. An excellent timekeeper, Ferguson had a good ear for harmony, a rich, booming tone and the flexibility to shift tempo and feel on a dime. These qualities and his relaxed, easygoing temperament made him an excellent musical mate for Lenny.

The duo's first gig was at Faisson's, followed by dates at the Bluebird Café, Bishop's Corner Restaurant, and a number of Nashville taverns. Ferguson, who has played with many top notch jazz musicians including Stephane Grappelli, Gene Bertoncini, and Marian McPartland, says that these gigs were extremely significant ones in his musical development. "Lenny was really kind to me, really supportive," says Ferguson. "Some of my fondest memories of playing with anybody was playing with Lenny—the freewheeling nature of it. I'd just hold on for the ride because you never knew where he was going, which is how I love to play. I admired him because even as great as he was, I don't think he ever arrived at any sort of plateau where he felt like he could coast. He was always stretching the boundaries of what he could do: 'I've been working on this, doing that,' you know."

Ferguson frequently played sessions at Audio Media Studios, and one day he mentioned to a recording engineer there that he was working with Lenny Breau. "I told him that I hoped someone would get Lenny down on record before he killed himself," says Ferguson. "Well, he told [Nashville record producer] Paul Whitehead, and Paul called me up right away and said he was interested in doing an album on Lenny." Whitehead offered Lenny a contract to make an album with material and concept that would be entirely Lenny's choice.

Lenny eagerly accepted the offer, seeing it as an opportunity to realize his idea for an album of country/jazz fusion that he had mentioned to Ted O'Reilly the summer before.

Lenny recorded the album in two sessions. The first of these was an acoustic duo session with Jim Ferguson on August 12, followed by an electric session two weeks later using a group made up of Ferguson, drummer Kenny Malone, and Buddy Emmons. From the moment the musicians set up in the studio, says Whitehead, the spirit of camaraderie was high. "The sessions were very, very friendly. All the players were deeply impressed with Breau and he always challenged their musical skills. It was just a great experience." Lenny was in good spirits and brimming with playful spontaneity, says Ferguson.

> When we were playing "Bonaparte's Retreat," all of a sudden in the middle of the take Lenny just leans down and starts singing and the engineer is freaking out saying, "I didn't put a vocal mic out!" There were no charts on the sessions. He'd just start playing. The changes of tempo and feel on the duo tunes were totally spontaneous. We might have repeated some of those things, but in general I never knew what direction he was gonna turn. I was holding on for dear life most of the time.

Ferguson demonstrates his survival skills well on several tunes—the duo's recording of "You Needed Me" being an excellent case in point. The piece, which Lenny and Ferguson had played in a very different form on a local noontime TV program called *Channel 4 Magazine* a few weeks earlier, is replete with shifts in feel, tempo, and mood, and includes a tremolo section and a chorus played rubato with several short modulations. Throughout, Ferguson manages to follow these spontaneous shifts with an aplomb suggesting a worked-out, memorized arrangement.

Lenny's single-line solos on "Any Time" and "She Thinks I Still Care" are breezy and melodic, sparkling with a jaunty bop feel. His soloing on the quartet tracks is a little stiffer by comparison, particularly on "Back in Indiana," where he stumbles slightly, perhaps caught off guard by Emmons who kicks off the tune with a stunning solo.

Ferguson says that Lenny was "very pleased" with *When Lightn' Strikes*, as well he should have been. His melding of country and jazz on this album is masterful, and entirely respectful of material that he had played and loved since childhood, while still approaching it in a spirit of musical adventure. Despite its quality, Whitehead—who had recorded the album on spec—had difficulty finding a label interested in releasing the recording. "Trying to find [a label] in 1982 that was interested in a jazz guitarist who did what Lenny did," says Whitehead, "well, you may as well as have been throwing darts into the ocean to hit a fish. There was no jazz opportunity at the time." Eventually Whitehead licensed the master tapes to Tudor Records, a tiny New York-based label. No photo of Lenny was available for the cover because he had failed to show up for a scheduled photo shoot after the album was made. Instead, the company released the recording in a jacket with grotesque, poorly drawn graphics (depicting a bolt of lightning striking a guitar), no liner notes or personnel listing, and a mystifying title containing what is perhaps the most glaring typo ever to appear on a record cover. Few ears had the chance to hear the recording inside the garish cover. Tudor Records folded not long after releasing *When Lightn' Strikes*, and the album quickly lapsed into out-of-print status until Art of Life Records reissued it as *Swingin' on a Seven String* in 2005.

Lenny's Holmes seven string had been stolen or pawned the year before and, according to Darci Cotten, Lenny had returned to Nashville that spring with a Gibson RD Standard.[11] This two-pickup, extra long scale instrument was the guitar Lenny used on the electric session for *When Lightn' Strikes*. While the RD Standard was a fine instrument with a bright full tone, after a year of playing the Holmes seven string, Lenny felt constrained by six-string guitars. The electric seven string had become an integral part of his musical explorations and he wanted desperately to replace it. Fortunately, not long after the completion of *When Lightn' Strikes*, Lenny met a man who would provide him with a new seven-string guitar that he would cherish for the rest of his life. Based in Laguna Beach, California, luthier Kirk Sand was just establishing a reputation as a guitar builder when, in the summer of 1982, he met Lenny while passing through Nashville on his way to the Atlanta NAMM show. Lenny also attended the show and there the two men discussed the possibility of building a seven-string guitar that could be tuned to pitch without breaking strings. Sand told Lenny he was convinced that it could be done and promised to have the guitar ready by January 1983.

The breezy feel that permeates *When Lightn' Strikes* did not reflect the tenor of Lenny's personal life at the time. Jewel had followed Lenny to Nashville in early June and while Lenny did his best to avoid her, she turned up unannounced at the Cottens' home where she harassed and threatened him until Richard Cotten had a restraining order sworn out against her. Much to the relief of her terrified spouse, Jewel backed off for a time, but she hadn't given up. One night after a gig at Faisson's, she confronted Lenny and, when he would not speak to her, she became violent, says Darci Cotten. "She attacked him, hands to his throat and knocked him to the floor," she says. "We had to pull her off him. Richard got him out the back door and we called the police. She just left, but it didn't stop there."

Despite subsequent incidents of this sort, Lenny and his wife reunited and moved into an apartment in the Greenhill area of Nashville. Stephen Anderson says nothing was resolved between the couple and that Lenny was simply taking the path of least resistance. "Because she was such a forceful, overbearing person, Lenny just didn't have the emotional stamina to withstand her," he says. "It was easier for him to let her ruin his life than fight it. Many times he'd knock on my door at midnight and say 'she's going to kill me.' I'd put him up and then she'd come around to harass him 'til finally I got a restraining order against her. But he'd always come back to her."

That August, Chet and Melody arrived in Nashville to visit their father and were disturbed to discover that he was once again using alcohol and heroin. They were also shocked by Jewel's blatant antipathy towards their father, an animosity that was soon extended to them. This was directed towards Melody in particular and within days of her arrival, she left her father's house to stay with Stephen Anderson. "Jewel was obsessively jealous," says Chet Breau. "She would never let us go out alone with Lenny. We couldn't even talk about Melody. Jewel had to have control. The first night we were there, my dad and I were listening to Jimi Hendrix, and she grabbed the record off the turntable and threw it on the ground saying 'this is evil!'" Chet and others close to Lenny urged him to divorce Jewel, but he explained that even broaching the topic with his wife would enrage her to the point of violence and, he said resignedly, the subject was best left alone.

After another two-week gig at Bourbon Street in October of 1982, Lenny and his wife returned to Stockton. A few months later, Lenny took possession of his new Kirk Sand seven string at the January 1983 NAMM convention in Anaheim, California. "He just took off on it like crazy," say Sand. "I'd had to shorten the scale length up to 22¾ inches [in contrast to the 25-inch scale Holmes had used] to get the strings not to break, but Lenny had very little hands and he thought I made the scale so short because he had such short fingers. The fact that the neck was so short made the reach so quick. It would be the same as capoing your guitar at the second fret. So he was really impressed with how easy it was to play because of the short scale. He just flipped out and loved that guitar. Later he told me, 'I can't really play other guitars anymore. Well, I can but this is my instrument.'"

Sand equipped the guitar with tone and volume controls that he artfully embedded on their sides in the instrument's exquisite bird's eye maple top, situating them almost immediately below the guitar's high A string for easy access. "They're like what you see on a Fender Jazzmaster with potentiometers turned on their side," says Sand. "The knob is like a thumbwheel that comes up and rises slightly above the surface. He could move it back and forth and get a sort of tremolo thing [by] turning the volume up and down." The Sand seven string was powered by two Seymour Duncan pickups, which gave the guitar a very different sound than the Holmes. The Nashville-built guitar had had a very bright, penetrating tone with accentuated highs compared to the more balanced, darker and rounder sound of the Sand. In every respect the guitar suited Lenny well, and he seemed to have finally found the instrument for which he had searched so long.

Lenny had agreed to demo the guitar at Sand's NAMM show booth, but was incapacitated by midafternoon after managing to finagle several fans into buying him drinks. John Knowles, who had come out from Nashville to go over some details on Lenny's book project, recalls his irritation with his friend. "In all those years," he says, "I had never really said anything to Lenny about that stuff, but it kind of bummed me out. I thought 'these guys are expecting something from you; where's your sense of responsibility?' I guess I came on like his mom or dad. I thought he was going to jump across the table and strangle me. He said to me, 'hey man. Cut that out. Who the hell do you think you are?'"

The wasting effects of Lenny's drinking problem are evident in a video of a clinic he did a few weeks later at the University of Southern California. Kirk Sand's close friend, the late Paul La Rose, was head of the guitar department at the school and a longtime fan of Lenny's. Sand introduced the two men and La Rose put together the clinic, which was attended by twenty or so students. In the video, Lenny appears to be straight and sober but his eyes are bleary and sunken in his drawn, fleshy face, and he somehow manages to look simultaneously bloated and haggard. (His teeth, however, were in good condition due to extensive dental work paid for by Chet Atkins.) He plays well—particularly on a beautiful version of "The Nearness of You"—but his rapport with the class is far less engaged and energetic than usual in these situations. He seems distant, distracted, and nervous, answering questions perfunctorily without his usual humor and enthusiasm. One gets the impression that Lenny, although sober, was giving more thought to his next drink than the students' questions.

Upon returning to Stockton, he made another stab at abstinence. He joined AA and a few weeks into his sobriety, called Kirk Sand to belatedly praise his guitar. "He just went on and on about the details of the guitar, how beautiful the guitar was and apologizing that he had never noticed that before," Sand says. "He said, 'I was so drunk all the time I couldn't focus on these little things.' He described the binding, how it nestles up against the frets and caps off the edge of each fret and how the trim around the top was so pretty. He said 'Man, I never saw that before. I've had this guitar awhile, but I was too drunk. But now that I'm sober I can see all the work you did. Thank you!'"

Toronto audiences saw Lenny's new seven-string guitar for the first time in June of 1983 when he arrived in the city to play what would be his last appearance at Bourbon Street. Paul Grosney had booked Lenny to play with Dave Young from June 13 to 18, a stint which the duo would follow with four nights at a lounge in the upscale Chateau Laurier Hotel in Ottawa. Rehearsal time and preparation for the gig,

Dave Young says, were minimal. "Lenny had a few lead sheets, a few things that he notated and we followed those from time to time," says Young. "If You Could See Me Now" was one of those things. But there was nothing formulaic about it. We wouldn't play a tune necessarily the way it should go and that was the beauty of it. Usually I'd have to follow him. His harmonic sense had improved greatly over the years. In fact, I thought his playing was then the most creative he'd achieved."

Fortunately for Lenny's fans, a serendipitous act preserved one of these dates when Ted O'Reilly came by the club on opening night armed with a digital recorder that CJRT-FM had recently acquired. Young and Lenny allowed O'Reilly to record them, asking only that he give them cassettes of the performance. O'Reilly agreed and after recording the show, returned to CJRT to make a master reel to reel tape from the digital recording—a fortuitous move, as it turned out. The next morning, O'Reilly arrived at the station to find that another employee had erased the digital recording, leaving O'Reilly with only the reel-to-reel copy he had made. From this, O'Reilly made the musicians cassette copies of the performance and, a few months later, sold the master to Relaxed Rabbit Records. In late 1983, the label released some of this material on *Legacy*, the last of Lenny's albums to be issued during his lifetime. Two years later, Electric Muse Records acquired the master and put out most of the remainder of the material on the master on the album *Quietude*. Guitarchives acquired the original master in the mid-nineties and released the content of both albums along with previously unreleased material on an excellent double CD set called *Live at Bourbon Street*.

These recordings bear out Young's glowing assessment of Lenny's playing at Bourbon Street. The date was a straight ahead jazz set with no flamenco or country tunes. (Lenny brought his Dauphin to Toronto, but Young doesn't recall him using it on any of their gigs.) Lenny gets a luminous, burnished sound out of his Sand that well suits the slightly dark, melancholic feel with which he suffuses much of the material. His touch is exquisite, and his luscious chord voicings seem to melt into each other almost pianistically as on "If You Could See Me Now," an arrangement that he told Bob Thompson was inspired by the playing of pianist Alan Broadbent. Other highlights of the album are a beautiful performance of Bill Evans's composition

"Two Lonely People," and a fifteen-minute version of Lenny's signature tune "Vision" bristling with shadowy menace and dark energy. The dialogue between Young and Lenny on "Vision" borders on the uncanny. Young—extracting an eerie wail from his bass with some excellent bow work—doesn't merely follow Lenny; he is in absolute accord with him on every twist and turn, matching effortlessly his dynamics, mood, and feel. The piece is a highlight of the album but not unique in terms of the duo's level of interplay and flow of creative ideas. While the set may not have had the wide-eyed, breathless energy that marked Lenny's playing on his RCA albums fifteen years earlier, his technical élan, range of creative expression, and the ability to evoke and evolve a mood, were at least the equal of earlier days. Lenny played with a mature refinement and a total lack of self-consciousness on this recording, as though finally he had transcended all expectations, imagined or otherwise, of fans and mentors, and was playing only what had meaning to him.

Lenny also made an album of quite a different sort during this trip to Toronto. Bob Erlendson's brother John and his wife Pat Silver headed a group called The Sphere Clown Band and mentioned to Lenny that they were in the process of making their first children's album. "He said 'how come I'm not on it? Get me a demo and I'll play on your album,'" says Silver. "We were very flattered and blown away by the offer." Lenny added his acoustic seven-string guitar work to three cuts and was typically apprehensive about the quality of his work. "Lenny was so sweet and insecure," says Silver. "He kept asking 'is that all right?' We'd say, 'Lenny, it's brilliant.' He'd say 'well, no, maybe it's not all right. Maybe I should do it again.' He was eager to make it perfect but not confident, which shocked me." The album, *I Can do Anything* was nominated for a Juno Award the following year and remained in print until 2001.

After the week at Bourbon Street, Lenny and Dave Young drove to Ottawa for a four-night booking at the exclusive Chateau Laurier Hotel. (Jewel remained in Toronto, apparently trusting Young to keep Lenny out of temptation's way.) Lenny was in good spirits, Young says, and talked eagerly of the possibilities his future might hold. "He was saying things like 'I really want to straighten out, I really want to go to Europe,'" recalls Young. "He was talking about getting a manager, doing some recording. That was the state of mind, the kind of focus he had in 1968 when he came here [to Toronto]. Instead he wasted those years between 1968 and 1983. In a sense, his music did develop, but it was more in spite of things." During their stay in Ottawa, Young says, Lenny struggled with his demons, but kept them at bay and turned in the same level of performance he had at Bourbon Street. He gave a well-delivered workshop at an Ottawa guitar store before returning with Young to Toronto where he spent the next few days at Bob Erlendson's home. The old friends jammed for many hours and Erlendson says Lenny was "at the top of his game." In late June, Erlendson said goodbye to Lenny at the Toronto airport. It was the last time he would see his old friend.

From Toronto, Lenny and his family flew to Chicago, where he was to play for four days at Kirk Sand's booth at the summer NAMM show. Sand made the mistake of paying his friend his full fee before Lenny's first afternoon's performance and at the end of the day, he disappeared without a word to Sand or Jewel. Guitarist Pat Smith, a friend and former student of Lenny's, was at the show and had connected with the Breaus before Lenny's vanishing act. He did his best to console Jewel who, left alone to care for an infant child without money in a strange city, was understandably panic stricken. Smith spoke with her many times during her husband's forty-eight-hour absence, and says that their conversations took some surprising turns. "Once she asked, 'why is it that Lenny isn't popular like Chet?'" Smith says. "She just didn't understand. She thought 'well, if Chet says he's the greatest guitar player in the world, why are we so broke?'" Smith did his best to explain the vagaries of the music industry, but Jewel remained mystified that a talent that others held in such esteem and awe should yield up so little financial return.

Smith was on the phone with Jewel early Sunday morning when Lenny unceremoniously returned to the hotel room. "I heard Jewel say something like 'Lenny, where have you been? I've been so worried,'" recalls Smith. "Lenny just said, 'Oh yeah, man. I was worried about you too.'"

That night, Smith and his wife took the Breaus to dinner and afterwards Lenny insisted that he and Smith have a drink at the bar. Lenny rapidly downed two shots of tequila and became teary-eyed as he explained to Smith why he had blown the NAMM show. "He felt it was too much pressure always having to be the best, being what people expected of him," says Smith. "He said when he played at NAMM and looked at the people around him, he felt like they were thinking, 'come on and prove it.' Then he complained that he couldn't get gigs and I said, 'well, you actually have to show up for gigs to get booked.' He mumbled, 'yeah, yeah.' By then he was drunk and crying, and he started talking about wanting to go out like Bill Evans."

The couple returned to Stockton but Lenny spent little time in the city and often traveled to Los Angeles without Jewel to stay with various friends. On one of these forays, he took the train to Laguna Beach and arrived unannounced at Kirk Sand's home where he spent the next several weeks. He explained that he was escaping Jewel and asked Sand to tell his wife that he hadn't seen him if she should call. During this visit, Lenny contracted Sand to build him a guitar that incorporated design and construction elements from a number of the unique instruments with which he had experimented over the years: Frank Gay's nine string, his acoustic and electric 6/12 double necks, the seven strings, and even a nod to his sitar. Kirk Sand says that considering Lenny's very detailed description of the guitar he envisioned, it appeared that he had given the instrument serious thought:

> He wanted a two-neck guitar with one neck a seven string and the other a ten string with eight principal strings and doubled A and D strings like on a twelve string. He wanted the doubled strings a little further apart near the bridge so he could pick individually the little string [high unison] and not the big one. [This allowed him to] play a bass note that was an octave higher than what you would normally have there. Before, he would have to utilize his index finger in order to play a harmonic on that bass string which raised the note an octave. Then with his m, a, i fingers play a three-note chord. So he was playing a bass note that was thrown up an octave with his index and thumb and the three note chord with his remaining finger. So with the guitar he had in mind he wouldn't have to get the harmonic in the bass. It would be already an octave higher and then he could play a four-note chord on top with that bass note an octave higher. Then the bass note would be brought into the chord to get those minor seconds in there; chords you never hear on anything but piano. He wanted to tune the seven-string neck the

same as he did on the other guitar I built him but the ten string was to be tuned [from bass to treble] B E A D F# B E A. On the body between the two sets of strings he wanted ten tunable sympathetic strings that he could tune to a chord and strum. Because he had most of the details worked out when he talked to me about the guitar, I got the feeling that he'd been thinking about it for a long time and had it down exactly the way he wanted it.

Sand was fascinated and agreed to build the guitar after accepting a $750 deposit from Lenny (recent payment from *Guitar Player* for his columns). Unfortunately, the instrument was never completed; Sand got no further than making detailed templates for the instrument before Lenny was murdered that summer.

After enjoying Sand's hospitality, Lenny spent two weeks in Los Angeles with Paul La Rose. He then moved on to Nashville where he stayed with Chet Atkins for a time before traveling to New Orleans to visit Guitarp innovator Phil DeGruy,[12] a friend and former student whom he'd met in Nashville in 1976. "He said he was coming down to sell one of his guitars and hang out," says DeGruy. "He ended up staying at my house for over a week. He was messed up at the time but too loaded to care. His playing [abilities] depended on what time of day it was. By early afternoon, he was too messed up to do much." Still, one evening Lenny sat in with pianist Ellis Marsalis (father of jazz trumpeter Wynton Marsalis) and played well enough that DeGruy decided to put together a small concert for Lenny. The first set went well, he says but somehow Lenny managed to lay waste to a bottle of gin during the break between the second and third set and the concert ended on a low note.

Jewel, says DeGruy, was not happy with Lenny's protracted stay in the Crescent City. "She would call up and go freaky on the phone," he says. "The phone rang constantly, to the point where I'd have to disconnect it. And when he did talk to her, it was terrible. She would yell and scream at him and he would be half drunk and go [imitates fog horn] into the phone, pissing her off even more."

Despite his long distance defiance, Lenny rejoined his wife in Stockton in late September. Within the month, the couple once again pulled up stakes and relocated to Los Angeles, where Lenny Breau's wandering would finally come to an end.

10.

Meanwhile Back in LA
November 1983—August 1984

"You'd better change your way of living 'fore the good lord says 'that's all.'"

—Merle Travis[1]

Scott Page says that in mid-1983, the Breaus lived for a time with a friend in an upscale home off Barham Boulevard in the Hollywood Hills area of Los Angeles. However, when they returned to live in the city that fall, their lodgings were considerably more humble. The Breaus spent their first month in Los Angeles living in a small apartment at a now forgotten address before moving to the Langham Apartments at 715 South Normandy Avenue in the Wilshire district of Los Angeles. Built for Al Jolson in 1927, the 190-unit, eight-story building was bought by Clark Gable four years later as a present for his second wife, socialite Rhea Langham. Langham never lived in the building, but proudly bestowed her name on the landmark that would house many residents from the upper crust of Los Angeles society over the next few decades. But by the time the Breau family took up residence there, the apartment and the area around it had deteriorated so precipitously that Rhea Langham would likely have been horrified to have her name associated with the building. The Breaus' tiny studio apartment with its hot plate and few sticks of fourth-generation furniture was as far down the residential ladder as they had ever stepped: "a crummy, small, dumpy place," as Kirk Sand describes it. The building's one saving grace was its rooftop swimming pool—the world's first at the time the building was constructed. Lenny did not swim well and was not comfortable in deep water, but he loved to sit by the pool, high above the turbulent city life below, and play his guitar in the warm California sunshine.

This was not the Langham's selling point for the Breaus, however. The cramped room in the crumbling building was simply all they were able to afford. During their first two months in Los Angeles, the family lived largely on Jewel's earnings as a part-time teacher at a local Sunday school while Lenny scuffled to find work. Despite the resurgence of interest in jazz that had begun in the late 1970s, there were few jobs for Los Angeles musicians who were not involved in pop music or the movie/jingle session scene. Straight ahead jazz musicians were relegated to three small clubs: Carmelo's, the Baked Potato, and Donte's. In January 1984, Lenny once again managed to secure a regular Monday night gig at the latter, playing with a rhythm section that was put together by the club's owner, Carey Leverette. Leverette hired Ted Hawke, a seasoned drummer who had worked with trombonist Kai Winding, among many other jazz musicians, and asked him to choose a bassist to complete the unit. Hawke brought in a series of men for the bass chair before settling on John Patitucci. The New York-born Patitucci was only twenty-one at this time, but had already received attention for his work with Victor Feldman, George Van Eps, Joe Farrell, and Freddie Hubbard, among others. He would later spend ten years as a member of Chick Corea's Electrik and Akoustic bands and work with Wayne Shorter while recording his own albums, one of which—*Songs, Stories and Spirituals*—earned him a Grammy award in 2003. "I'd just known Lenny's name at that point," says Patitucci. "He was one of those legendary figures but at the time I didn't know his playing that well. It turned out to be a special gig for me because as a musician you play with a lot of people but then there are the ones who are the real artists—like Chick Corea and Wayne Shorter—and Lenny was one of them: a real jazz musician. His playing was killing and I loved it. I just felt really thankful to be there, you know."

Word that Lenny was back in town spread quickly in LA's jazz community and within a few weeks the club was packed with fans for his Monday night gigs. Lenny was in excellent shape for these performances, and gave his admirers everything they had come to hear and more, says guitarist Raj Rathor. Now a professional jazz guitarist living and performing in Las Vegas, Rathor had met Lenny in Nashville in 1976 and solidified his friendship with him when Lenny and Sinde Shubert came to Los Angeles in 1978. He'd heard Lenny play many times at Donte's during the following year but says, "the difference between his playing then and 1984 was remarkable. In 1984, he had completely consummated his style on the seven string, and what he was doing on the stage was astounding. Lenny had every aspect of music under his control. His melodies were keen, sharp, and very creative. His harmony was one of his biggest areas of expression, his chords were otherworldly and his rhythm was just incredible. We witnessed all of this at Donte's, and—needless to say—our jaws fell to the floor."

At this point, Lenny seldom performed his country-oriented or flamenco material and confined his playing to his electric instrument. His repertoire consisted largely of Bill Evans's originals such as "My Bells" and "Very Early" as well as many standard tunes associated with Evans. Evans's influence was also manifested in the improvisational approach the trio took to playing this material, says Patitucci.

Lenny was somebody who already had a strong identity in what he did and his own way of looking at the music. He was a virtuoso and played like an orchestra. He could cover everything but he was also very sensitive. He allowed plenty of room for me to express myself. He didn't approach it like "I'm the leader and you guys do what I tell you." He wasn't like that at all. He was a very sensitive, humble guy and very kind. He obviously had his thing and that was advanced. You had to follow him in that, to support it, and let it happen because it was unique. But within that, he was listening,

always listening. Lenny knew what I was doing and what I was trying to do: going in that direction of bass players who were trying to
stretch out a little bit in the tradition of the Bill Evans trio and [two
of Evans's bassists] Scotty LaFaro and Eddie Gomez. They were
always reaching—not just as accompanists but as soloists. I was
definitely into expansive harmony and playing more like a horn
when I played my solos. But you had to be sensitive to support
what Lenny was doing and not play too much, which is not to say
that you couldn't be free and approach it loose like the Bill Evans
trio did, but you had to be in tune with what he was doing because
he was doing a lot. It wasn't busy; it was just right—dense but correct. The guitar trio is a beautiful sound because it's very open,
especially the way he played. He had a beautiful touch in his sound
that was his identity. It allowed me to play softer, more sensitively,
and with a lot more dynamic range. We played dynamically. He
wasn't a guy who cranked up his amp, so there was a lot of nice
texture to it.

Dynamics, says Rathor, were indeed a salient aspect of the
group's sound. "Lenny would start at such a soft, gentle, beautiful,
quiet place and somewhere along the line you realized that the tune
was now just burning," he says. "Ted Hawke once said about those
tunes that they just 'levitated.' Somehow a tune would naturally
grow from a very quiet beginning to this pure, bebop thing, and
every stage along the way had been masterfully traveled through.
And then the whole thing might come all the way down again.
Another amazing thing was that in those higher moments, when the
whole thing was exploding, while he was improvising and comping
chords at the same time during the heaviest jazz tunes in the middle
of a deep serious solo, Lenny would conduct the band with body
movements to activate them to play counter rhythms!"

Before long, Lenny had a coterie of guitar students gleaned from
his adoring audiences at Donte's, whom he taught in his apartment.
He also began teaching clinics at the Guitar Institute of Technology, a
one-year guitar immersion program with a faculty that included guitarists Joe Pass, Howard Roberts, and Joe Diorio. Diorio, currently
on the faculty of the University of Southern California, has recorded
his creative bebop-based guitar work with, among others, Sonny

Stitt, Anita O'Day, and Horace Silver. He is also a highly respected jazz educator whose credits include a number of popular books on the craft of jazz guitar. Diorio had met Lenny one night at Donte's and they spent the next afternoon jamming together, becoming fast friends in the process. "He was a very sweet guy and I loved his playing," says Diorio. "It was so mature—probably the most mature guitar playing I'd ever heard at that time. This guy had so much finesse. He'd go to places that were so interesting harmonically. He was just a beautiful player that inspired all of us." It didn't take Diorio long to become aware of Lenny's tenuous financial situation and he spoke with GIT's owner Pat Hicks and Ron Benson, the school's manager, about the possibility of Lenny's joining GIT's staff as a full-time instructor.[2] "We just didn't know if Lenny could handle that kind of thing, showing up at a certain time a few days a week and all that," Diorio says. "You put him in a room with seven kids and it would be like locking a lion up; he just didn't seem to have the temperament."

Hicks and Benson arranged for Lenny to teach a series of guitar clinics at the school. These clinics, in which Lenny would play a short concert followed by a masterclass, were essentially trial runs to see if he could handle a full-time teaching position with the school. His battle with substance abuse was no secret among the LA guitar community and before committing to hiring Lenny, GIT wanted to make sure that his problem would not affect his work at the school. At this point, Lenny seemed to be over his heroin and methadone dependency and Raj Rathor says that his drug use was confined to an occasional line of coke or a shared joint. He was also being more moderate in his alcohol consumption although he still needed a few drinks to get him through tense situations, recalls Rathor. "One night, Lenny did a gig over on Sunset Strip at the Hyatt Regency with Tal Farlow,' he says. "We were out in the parking lot and Lenny had bought a little tiny flask of brandy. He was so nervous that he just wanted to have a couple of sips. He said 'Man, I'm so nervous about playing with Tal.' And then he was just spectacular and played rings around Tal." This sort of moderation was not a constant, however, and his binge drinking continued to be a problem. Hired by Sand to man his booth at the January NAMM show, Lenny downed a bottle of gin prior to the show and spent the day sleeping it off in a nearby motel without making it into the convention building. A few weeks later he was arrested for public drunkenness and locked up in a drunk tank overnight. Alcohol often plunged Lenny into a sullen, withdrawn state in which he seemed to retreat from the world around him, as Ted Greene witnessed one afternoon.

One day Jewel called me up and said "Please come over. Lenny's got to see you. He's doing really bad. He's really depressed. He needs you." I drive over and when I get there Lenny is working hard practicing some new run in harmonics. I mean really hard. He's having trouble. My suspicion was he had been drinking because when he drank enough, he'd turn from the world's finest guitarist into a sincere candidate for Mel Bay Book One [a beginners guitar method]. He looked up at me and says "phew, man this stuff is hard.' I sat down and thought "well, how can I cheer him up?" So I played "I'll Remember April" as if it were harmonized in the Wagnerian era with romantic harmony without jazz colors. He said "wow, mannnnn!" and seemed to brighten up.

But while drinking deepened Lenny's depression, it did not cause it. Even during periods of sobriety, he was often gloomy and distant. "He just seemed so sad sometimes," says John Patitucci. "Some guys are up and bouncing around but Lenny was more depressed. He seemed beaten down." This was reflected in Lenny's manner on stage. The comedy routines and tongue in cheek versions of "Back in the Saddle" had disappeared, and Lenny spoke little to his fans beyond naming tunes and introducing band members.

The catalyst for Lenny's depression and the alcoholic bingeing that was his questionable method for assuaging it, was his worsening marriage. Jewel continued her abusive treatment of Lenny and his usual response was to run to the ostensible safety of the bottle, as Scott Page witnessed during one of Lenny's gigs. "One night at Donte's," Page says, "Jewel came in and started screaming at Lenny at the top of her lungs while he was on stage playing: 'You little f—g guitar genius. You think you're so good. Blah, blah, blah.' Poor little Lenny. He was so non-confrontational. He just started shaking uncontrollably and ran over to the bar and started drinking. I thought, 'Oh my God, Jewel, what are you doing?'"

To avoid Jewel, Lenny often stayed with friends for days at a time, but his absences simply increased his wife's rage and further aggravated the already difficult situation in which he found himself. By the early spring of 1984, Lenny wanted permanent shelter from the storm of his marriage and was prepared to take drastic steps to find it. The previous October, Chet Breau had visited his father in LA and the two men discussed the possibility of Lenny's returning to Winnipeg without Jewel. They spoke of sharing an apartment and starting a jazz club where Lenny could play nightly. Chet would manage this club and keep his father out of harm's way by making sure that the venue was drug-free. Desperate to put his plan in motion, Lenny contacted Ray St. Germain with whom he had maintained a telephone relationship over the past several years. "He would phone me from Nashville or wherever in the middle of the night, kind of tanked and wanting to recover the old times," says St. Germain. "Then one night he told me that he really wanted to come back. I was hosting a TV show called *Ray St. Germain Country* on Global [television network], which ran for thirteen years. He wanted to know if there was some work and I said 'Certainly. There'll always be work for you.'"

Lenny managed to scrape together airfare for a flight to Winnipeg and, one morning in April, flew out of Los Angeles with a suitcase and his guitars. Upon his landing in Calgary, Alberta, several hundred miles west of Winnipeg, Lenny was detained for lack of proper identification, and a Canada Customs official contacted Ray St. Germain to verify Lenny's story of employment.

I've felt so sorry about this for all these years but I know there's nothing that I or anybody could have done. Customs called and said they had Lenny and asked if he had a contract with me. I said "yes he has," although he didn't. And they said, very sarcastically, that if I could get it there in twenty minutes, they'd let him in. This was before fax machines so I said "well, you know I can't do that" and they said, "we know." I spoke with Lenny and he was straight, but scared and stuttering. He kept saying, "Geez man I don't want to go back. I don't want to go back." But they put him on a plane back to LA. And that was the last I heard of him until his brother [Denny] called me and said he was dead.

Lenny returned to Los Angeles badly shaken by the experience. There seemed no way out of his dire situation and he felt hopelessly trapped by his marital circumstances. But not long after his foiled escape attempt, another opportunity to return to Canada—at least temporarily—presented itself. Bob Erlendson had moved to Calgary in 1982 and a few months later began working with bassist George Koller. Koller managed to line up a full-time job for the duo in a club that was to open later in the summer of 1984. Knowing that Erlendson was in touch with Lenny, Koller suggested that the pianist persuade his old friend to come to Calgary and make the unit a trio. Erlendson ran the plan by Lenny who was only too happy to join the trio and said he would be on his way north as soon as the club owner confirmed the gig.

In the meantime, other doors opened for Lenny. One night, he was playing a gig at the Baked Potato when Chicago-born jazz/R&B guitarist Phil Upchurch dropped by to listen. Upchurch, who often worked with George Benson, had first heard Lenny on *The Velvet Touch* fifteen years earlier. "It just blew my mind," says Upchurch. "It was the same thing as hearing Wes [Montgomery] or Jimmy Smith for the first time." Upchurch was so impressed by Lenny's playing at the Baked Potato that he decided on the spot to invite Lenny to add some parts to his new album, *Companions*, which featured a smooth pop/jazz fusion sound. "I said 'If you would honor me with your playing, I would like to go into the studio and wipe out the piano player on two tracks of the album and put you in his place,'" says Upchurch. "Lenny said 'cool, let's do it!'" Lenny asked for a tape of the tunes so he could prepare his solos for the session, which Upchurch had scheduled for August 6.

A few days later, he dropped by Upchurch's house to pick up the tape and the two men spent several hours jamming. Upchurch says he was so astonished by Lenny's playing that he called JAM records, his Washington DC-based record company, to persuade them to record Lenny. "I said 'man, if you don't make a record on Lenny Breau, you oughta get out of the business,'" Upchurch says. "The guy said, 'OK, hook him up.'" Once JAM had given him the go-ahead, Upchurch invited Lenny to his house to record a few numbers on his four-track recorder. "This was pre-production," says Upchurch. "I was going to produce the album and play on maybe three tracks, just for the honor of playing with the guy. The rest would be him with bass and drums." Upchurch recalls that the men recorded a duo version of Ramsay Lewis's hit "The In Crowd" with a heavy funk beat, and Lenny played solo versions of "Emily" and "No Greater Love."

Lenny was overjoyed with the sudden turn in his fortune, says Rathor. "He felt it was really a big thing that Phil Upchurch had asked him to play on his record," Rathor says. "He seemed happy and optimistic, that things were finally happening for him and he was more serious than ever about his music." Even some bad news from Bob Erlendson did not shake his mood. In July 1984, Erlendson called Lenny to explain that the Calgary club owner had postponed the opening of his club for at least a month. Consequently, the trio's starting date had been moved ahead until late September. Lenny, Erlendson says, seemed nonplussed and took the news in stride.

> He said "oh, that's cool because I'm doing this thing with Phil Upchurch. We've just been in the studio and we've got two songs and they're talking about a tour in the fall. As soon as we finish the album in August, they're gonna do a quick release and a tour of two guitars. So it's perfect. We'll finish the album, come up to Calgary, do the gig with you. [Then we'll] go back to LA, wait around 'til October 1 and we'll be on tour. So it'll work out just great." He was obviously feeling much better than other times I'd spoken with him over the winter. He said nothing about Jewel except that the baby was fine and he and Jewel were getting along fine. He said that the only thing that she was complaining about was that every so often he would lose a day and go out bingeing and get drunk. He said, "I don't have to do that anymore." It was my impression that he was doing really well.

Lenny may have cut back on his drinking but the circumstances of his marriage had not improved. One afternoon, Raj Rathor dropped by Phil Upchurch's house to pick Lenny up and drive him home. Lenny had just closed Upchurch's door behind him and was greeting Rathor when he was confronted with his angry spouse. "Jewel showed up at the house," says Raj Rathor. "She was literally foaming at the mouth. As we left, she grabbed Lenny's guitar and slammed an iron gate between us." Later that day, Lenny and Rathor managed to retrieve the guitar and then drove to Rathor's home in Ojai, seventy-five miles north of LA. Lenny, says Rathor, had had enough and had made up his mind never to return to his wife.

Lenny spent much of the two weeks in Ojai jamming with his host and showing him various techniques and ideas. Rathor recalls that during one of these informal lessons, Lenny explained a number of ways to improvise through 2-5-1 chord progressions, but then told Rathor that there was more to music than simply learning its rules. "He said that someone had once asked McCoy Tyner how he played the way he did. McCoy said, 'well, that kind of music only happens when you do it on faith.' Then Lenny looked right at me and he said, 'So, you have to take music as a religion. You have to say, "music, I'm your student for life." And that's where he'd always been musically."

On Sunday, August 5, Lenny celebrated his forty-third birthday with Rathor and his grandmother who gave Lenny a book on Impressionist art. "He just took right to that book," says Rathor, "and talked to us about the meaning he saw in those paintings. That's the way he played: painting pictures with his chords." Later that day, Lenny received a call from a Los Angeles guitarist whom Jewel had asked to plead her case on her behalf.[3] During his stay in Ojai, Jewel had called Lenny constantly and then made a trip to Ojai to retrieve him. Unable to find Rathor's address she went to the police who refused to intervene. She then returned to Los Angeles where she asked a friend of Lenny's to call him and persuade him to come back to LA. Rathor says that after this call, Lenny's resolve not to return to his wife weakened and he seemed remorseful about leaving his daughter.

Lenny was still mulling over his marital dilemma when Rathor drove him to Sage and Sound Studios in Los Angeles on August 6 to lay down the two tracks with Upchurch, but his gloomy reflections did not stop him from recording his parts in one take. "Lenny was straight and focused in the studio," says Upchurch. "After he'd play a solo he'd say real quietly 'I hope it's all right.' Man, he nailed it like he'd been listening to it all his life." This may be so, but Lenny's playing on the cuts is non-descript at best. He sprinkles the first cut with generic chordal harmonics before taking a lackluster solo and only begins to come alive briefly during the tune's fade-out. On the second cut, "Song For Lenny," a lugubrious funk/blues piece, Lenny does little of merit and is actually upstaged by Upchurch who plays a solo with enough grit to give the anodyne piece a well-needed kick.

Rathor says that Lenny was still unsure of his next move in regards to Jewel when the pair arrived at Donte's that night for what would be Lenny's last gig at the club. A few minutes into his first set, Jewel arrived and stood quietly in the back of the club as Lenny, unaware of her presence, began to play a soft, unaccompanied ballad. "He was really into this beautiful solo piece and his head was down and his eyes were closed," says Rathor. "Right in the middle of this, Jewel goes marching up to the stage with this lighted birthday cake and totally disrupts what he was doing. Lenny's head just kind of shot up in shock." During the set break, the couple talked and when the gig was done, Lenny told Rathor that he was going to return to Jewel. Rathor wished him well, shook his hand and said goodbye to his friend for the last time.

Despite his ups and downs during the preceding year, Lenny's clinics at GIT were unqualified successes, and Joe Diorio says that Benson and Hicks were ready to hire him as a full-time teacher when Lenny did his last clinic at GIT on Friday, August 10. A student tape made of this clinic captures Lenny in excellent form as a teacher. Chatty, relaxed, and completely engaged in the class, Lenny Breau articulately covers a number of topics including root motion of chords, reharmonization, harmonics, and care and feeding of nails. He also gives some interesting insights into the practical side of being a professional guitarist, explaining to his students one of the problems that came with playing a guitar with an unconventional design. "You could take this guitar [his Sand seven string] into a pawnshop," he complains passionately, "and you'd be lucky to get fifty bucks for it!"[4] (A few weeks earlier Raj Rathor had rescued one of Lenny's two Dauphin seven strings from a pawnshop. Lenny refused to take it back and bequeathed it to Rathor, who still owns it.)

The three-hour clinic seemed to have taken its toll on Lenny by the time he wrapped it up at 4:30 that afternoon. Joe Diorio drove him to the Langham Apartments and, on the way, tried to make small talk with his friend. Lenny, he says appeared drained and preoccupied, and gazed blankly out the window as they drove towards Wilshire.

He seemed a little nervous, I think. Not nervous from anticipating anything, but I think he was coming down a little bit and seemed a little on edge. I think he needed something, to be honest. We were talking about music and I told him how much I liked his flamenco playing. He said "oh, I don't even care about that anymore." For a second I had the feeling that he was giving up, that he just didn't give a shit. I realized he was getting real negative and seemed tired, as though his blood sugar was low, so I didn't pursue it. I just dropped him off and said "I'll see you soon, I hope."

Jewel Breau would later tell the press that over the course of the following day and evening, Lenny consumed three bottles of alcohol.[5] At about 6:30 on Sunday morning, he called his mother in Maine. He seemed sober but frightened, Betty recalls.

He said "it's getting real bad, real violent around here. I don't know what's going to happen." He said, "I'm going up on the roof to the swimming pool with my guitar. I've got music to write. I have a feeling I'm not going to live too long." He says, "they say geniuses die young, but I'd like to have enough time to write what I have in my head." And then three hours [sic] later it was her [Jewel] that was screaming on the phone: "they found Lenny. He's dead!"

Jewel later claimed that she had left the apartment with her daughter at about 9:30 a.m. to attend church. Lenny, she said, was in low spirits that morning, depressed by his inability to give up drinking. She said that he had asked her to pray for him and told her "I'm sick of this . . . it's got me. I'm drinking now just to feel normal." Lenny had had a premonition of his death that morning, she said: "He knew his life was drawing to an end . . . [he told me] 'I feel I am going to die. I feel I only have a short time.'" According to Jewel, Lenny then took his guitar and music and went up to the rooftop pool just before she and her daughter left for church.

Somewhere between 10:30 and 10:45 a.m., a resident of the Langham Apartments went to the rooftop pool. There she glimpsed a body clad in a bathing suit lying at the bottom of the pool and returned to her apartment to call for help. A team of paramedics arrived, pulled the body from the water and at 11:10 a.m. on August

12, 1984, one week after his forty-third birthday, Leonard Harold Breau was pronounced dead. The Los Angeles coroner's office later determined that Lenny had probably been in the pool for between thirty and forty-five minutes, but was unable to fix the precise moment of death due to his body's submersion in the warm water. Factoring in a margin of error of half an hour, this would mean that Lenny's death could have occurred anytime between 9:30 a.m.— about the time his wife said she had left for church—and slightly before 10:30 a.m., when his body was discovered. Jewel arrived home at about 11:30 a.m. and was told by the apartment's maintenance man that her husband had drowned. While she called Betty to tell her of her son's death, Lenny's body was taken to the Los Angeles morgue to await an autopsy.

The next day, a few newspapers noted Lenny's passing in brief articles that—although there had not yet been an official coroner's verdict—reported the cause of his death as accidental drowning. Jewel appeared satisfied with their verdict, and told one reporter, "Lenny was swimming and the Lord took him." But the drowning hypothesis puzzled family and friends who knew that Lenny was a poor swimmer and extremely uncomfortable in water above his waist and they were not surprised when a few days later the official coroner's report declared that Lenny's death had not been accidental. Water was not present in Lenny's lungs, indicating that he was dead before his body entered the pool, and marks on his neck revealed that he had been strangled.[6] (Jewel continued to tout the death by drowning theory, insisting that an ill-fitting collar of a recently purchased shirt had caused the marks.) Two days after Lenny's body was found in the rooftop pool, Bill Gold of the Los Angeles coroner's office stated that "asphyxia caused by compression of, or to, the neck consistent with those found in strangulation" had ended Lenny's life, and the LAPD officially declared his death a homicide.[7]

The coroner found no traces of drugs in Lenny's system, but the autopsy report states that his blood/alcohol level was .27, almost three times the reading defining legal inebriation in California (.10). This is not, however, an unusually high reading for a long-term heavy drinker and doesn't indicate that Lenny was not in control of his mental faculties and motor functions up to the moment of his death.

The investigating detectives Richard Aldahl and Larry Bird determined that Lenny was killed in his apartment and carried up a flight of stairs to the roof of the building where his killer dropped his body into the pool's deep end. They initially examined the possibility that Lenny had been the victim of a drug deal gone bad or revenge for an unpaid drug debt. These scenarios, however, seemed unlikely considering that there were no signs of a struggle in the apartment and the killer or killers did not take the Sand guitar—the only thing of value Lenny owned—from the scene.[8] The murderer, they posited, had probably been known to Lenny and may have murdered him in a moment of blind rage. As Bird and Aldahl pursued their investigation, they became aware of the volatile nature of the Breaus' relationship through neighbors who had overheard Jewel's abuse of Lenny. These observations were supported by the Cottens, Tallmans, and other close friends of Lenny's, all of whom described to the detectives the details of Jewel's violent behavior towards her spouse. It was at this point that the officers began to consider Jewel Breau as their prime suspect. Her well-documented history of spousal abuse and flaws in her testimony (which remain confidential in the unclosed case) convinced Bird and Aldahl of her guilt and they requested that she submit to a polygraph test. Jewel agreed initially, but balked at the last moment and refused to have further contact with the police except through her lawyer. Bird told this author that her refusal to be tested confirmed his belief that she was complicit in her husband's murder, and he and Aldahl considered bringing a formal charge of murder against Jewel Breau. However, the detectives decided that the Los Angeles District Attorney's office would not have a strong enough case to bring her to trial. Despite Larry Bird's abiding conviction that Jewel Breau was involved in the murder of her husband, she was never charged with the crime. Jewel Breau returned to Stockton to work as a critical care nurse, and in 1995 she became Jewel Flowers when she remarried. In the 1999 Canadian documentary, *The Genius of Lenny*, Detective Aldahl states bluntly that "the primary suspect on the case is Lenny Breau's wife at the time, Jewel . . ."[9] Still, without a conviction arrived at through due legal process, in the eyes of the law the identity of Lenny's killer and the precise circumstances of his murder remain as enigmatic as the restless, questing spirit that fled Leonard Harold Breau's body at the instant of his death.

Epilogue

Like his father before him, Lenny Breau died in penury and his remains lie in an unmarked grave at the Forest Lawn cemetery in Glendale, California. Richard and Darci Cotten covered his funeral costs with money raised through a memorial benefit at Nashville's Blue Bird Café. Other memorials took place in Winnipeg, Los Angeles, and Toronto and were attended by family members and hundreds of close friends, acquaintances, and fans.

For a time, it appeared that the memory of Lenny's life and music would be sustained only by this cadre of people and the relatively small group of jazz fans who had been fortunate enough to see him perform or owned his recordings, most of which were out of print by the early 1990s. The obscurity that had threatened to overtake Lenny Breau during the latter third of his life appeared to have completely enveloped him ten years after his death.

This began to change in the mid-1990s. Randy Bachman—guitarist for Bachman, Turner Overdrive and The Guess Who—had known and idolized Lenny while growing up in Winnipeg. In 1995, he formed Guitarchives Records, a label that was initially devoted entirely to the music of Lenny Breau. With the help of his associate Dan Casavant, who had been a student of Lenny's in the 1970s, Bachman tracked down and released several CDs of Lenny's previously unreleased or out-of-print material. One of these—*Live at Bourbon Street*—was nominated for a Juno award in 1997 and, at that year's ceremonies, Lenny Breau was inducted into the Canadian Music Hall of Fame. Other small labels—notably Art of Life Records—have followed suit, and Lenny's playing can now be heard on nearly three times as many recordings as were collectively in print at any point during his life. The instruction book that he put together with John Knowles is currently still in print, and in 2000, Lenny's old friend Stephen Anderson published *Visions*: a comprehensive, in-depth study of virtually every facet of Lenny's playing. Ottawa guitarist Paul Bourdeau illustrated Lenny's techniques in an instructional video format with an accompanying book, an idea that had intrigued Lenny since the late 1970s, when the instructional video industry was just getting under way.

It's difficult to say exactly what this upsurge of interest in his music says about Lenny Breau's place in the history of jazz guitar. Some of his techniques—his chordal harmonics in particular—turn up occasionally in the playing of guitarists of various stylistic stripes. Many jazz guitarists, Canadian Lorne Lofsky prime among them, have taken their own approach to assimilating the ideas of Bill Evans into their playing, as Lenny did. But unlike Django Reinhardt, Charlie Christian, and Wes Montgomery, Lenny didn't leave behind a significantly large school of jazz guitarists who have adapted and personalized his idiosyncratic style. It may be, as George Benson once suggested, that Lenny Breau was "guilty of being ahead of his time,"[1] and it's possible that more guitarists may eventually come to emulate his ideas and assimilate them into their own playing. But, breadth of influence aside, Lenny should be remembered as an adventurous, dedicated musician who brought the totality of his musical intelligence and passion to bear on mastering his instrument in order to articulate an inner life that found solace and a sense of order only in the act of creative expression. To know that he had effectively shared his musical vision with his audiences and moved them in the process was the only kind of success that had real meaning to him. That so many continue to be drawn to the humanity and beauty of his music two decades after his death suggests that he achieved this success and that it is enduring.

Quoted Interviews Conducted by Author

Interviewee	Location	Date
Allen, Chad*	Vancouver, BC	10–02–03
Anderson, Stephen	Nashville, TN.	08–17,30–00
Appleyard, Peter	Toronto, ON	08–24–02
Balis, Peter	Lewiston, ME.	08–09–00
Baron, Joey*	Berlin, Germany	02–29–03
Beckwith, Skip*	Afton, NS	10–19–03
Bickert, Ed*	Toronto, ON	01–02–03
Breau, Chet	Winnipeg, MB	04–12–00
Breau, Denny	Lisbon Falls, ME	01–26–00
Breau, Dickie	Lisbon Falls, ME	01–06–00
Breau, Dickie*	Lewiston, ME.	11–12–00
Breau-St. Germain, Valerie	Winnipeg, MB	04–23–00
Breau-St. Germain, Valerie*	Winnipeg, MB	10–25–00
Breau-St. Germain, Valerie*	Winnipeg, MB	08–06–02
Capon, John	Victoria, BC	10–20–04
Christie, Cedar	Galiano Island, BC	09–08–02
Christie, Cedar*	Galiano Island, BC	10–02,11–03
Clarke, Terry	Toronto, ON	07–31–00
Cody-Binette, Betty	Lisbon Falls, ME	01–20,25,26–00
Cody-Binette, Betty*	Lisbon Falls, ME	08–7,10–00
Coryell, Larry*	Los Angeles, CA	02–19–04
Cotten, Darci	Nashville, TN.	08–23–00
Couture, Ray*	Claresville, OH	02–17–00
Couture, Ray*	Claresville, OH	08–06–01
Davis, Danny	Nashville, TN.	08–29–00
DeGruy, Phil*	New Orleans, LA.	11–13–01
DeStefano, Lorenzo*	Pender Island, BC	02–22–04
Diorio, Joe*	Los Angeles, CA	02–18–04
Doyle, Dan*	New York City, NY.	16–01–04
Erlendson, Bob*	Toronto, ON	05–12,13–00
Erlendson, Bob	Toronto, ON	06–16,17–00
Erlendson, Bob	Toronto, ON	07–24–00
Erlendson, Bob*	Toronto, ON	09–20–03
Ferguson, Jim	Nashville, TN.	08–21–00
Ferguson, Jim*	Nashville, TN.	02–11–04
Fewell, Garrison*	Boston, MA	10–24–03
Finucan, Wayne	Vancouver, BC	08–27–02
Francks, Don.	Toronto, ON	07–17–00

Sawyer, Dan* .... Los Angeles, CA 04–02–04
Shapira, Jack* .... Winnipeg, MB 10–29–02
Silver, Pat* .... Toronto, ON 03–05–04
Singh, Judy .... Vancouver, BC 10–01–04
Smith, Eugene .... Duncan, BC 12–12–03
Smith, Hank .... Edmonton, AB 04–30–02
Smith, Pat* .... Los Angeles, CA 10–12–01
Spicher, Buddy .... Nashville, TN. 08–22–04
St. Germain, Judy .... Winnipeg, MB 04–13–00
St. Germain, Ray .... Winnipeg, MB 04–11–00
Sukornyk, George* .... Toronto, ON 11–10–00
Sukornyk, George* .... Toronto, ON 08–20–02
Terry, Brad. .... Bath, ME. 01–28–00
Testa, Bart .... Toronto, ON 07–20–00
Thompson, Bob .... Portland, ME 01–21–00
Thompson, Don .... Toronto, ON 07–26–00
Thompson, Don "DT" .... Deep Cove, BC. 08–27–02
Titcomb, Brent .... Toronto, ON 07–23–00
Udow, Len .... Winnipeg, MB 04–10–00
Udow, Len* .... Winnipeg, MB 08–07–02
Upchurch, Phil* .... Los Angeles, CA 02–07–04
Wedding, Terry* .... Nashville, TN. 12–04–03
Whitehead, Paul* .... Nashville, TN. 02–15–04
Wilkins, Rick* .... Toronto, ON 10–05–03
Williams, Doc* .... Wheeling, WV 08–06–01
Willis, Sleepy. .... Providence, RI 01–17–00
Yandell, Paul .... Nashville, TN. 08–23–00
Young, Dave .... Toronto, ON 07–17–00

*Telephone interview

Discography

This discography includes every 45, LP, and CD on which Lenny Breau is known to have played as leader, collaborator, or sideman. Entries are listed chronologically by recording date rather than release date. On albums where Lenny does not play on every track, I've listed only those tracks on which he is present. These tracks are not listed in the same numerical order as the recordings on which they appear.

In some cases, album liner notes list Lenny as being one of two or more guitarists on the recording but the tracks on which he plays are not specified. In these instances, I've relied on an educated but admittedly fallible ear to determine which tracks include his guitar work. If I haven't been able to identify his playing with certainty on particular tracks, I've listed all tracks on which he may have played. In some cases, I have listed only the session leader and Lenny, designating further musicians as "other personnel."

I have included as much detail on recording, release dates, and re-release dates as possible, leaving out specifics only when thorough research failed to turn up this information. Release dates are included only when they occurred in a different year than recording was done.

I gratefully acknowledge the assistance of Paul G. Kohler of Art of Life Records and Event Records founder Al Hawkes in compiling this discography. I also referenced writer Jack Litchfield's excellent book *The Canadian Jazz Discography 1916–1980* for information on some entries.

Note: Between 1963 and ca. 1966, Lenny Breau worked regularly for Arbuthnot Studios in Winnipeg where he played guitar on many 45s, mainly reproductions of international pop hits using local musicians. Information on these sessions is not available.

Entries 1 through 11 were recorded at Event Studios in Westbrook, Maine. The first nine entries were issued as 45s. Information on dates and personnel was taken from Event Records session logs and catalogue.

Personnel Key for all Event Recordings:

A Lenny Breau—electric guitar

B Lenny Breau—acoustic guitar

C Hal Lone Pine—vocals/rhythm guitar

D Dick Curless—vocals/rhythm guitar

E Dick Curless—rhythm guitar

F Curley Isles—steel guitar

G Sleepy Willis—electric guitar

H Sleepy Willis—electric bass

I Unknown drummer

J Jimmy Daughtry—bass

K Bob Gosselin—drums

L Dave Miller—bass

M Curtis Johnson—vocals/rhythm guitar

N Roy Aldridge—vocals

O Donnie Harrison—vocals/rhythm guitar

P Audrey Harrison—harmony vocal

Q Harold Carter—fiddle

R Ray Lemeiux—drums

1. ***Prince Edward Island Is Heaven to Me/Down by the Railroad Tracks***
   Hal Lone Pine and His Kountry Karavan (Event 4257)
   A, C, D, F, J, Q
   May 26, 1956

2. ***Streets of Laredo***
   Dick Curless (Event 4258). Re-released with other material in 1995 on
   Dick Curless: A Tombstone Every Mile. See entry 11.
   A, D, F, J, Q
   May 26, 1956

3. ***Hot Mocking Bird/German Waltz***
   Harold Carter (Event 4260)
   A, E, F, J, Q
   May 26, 1956

4. ***Blues in My Mind/China Nights***
   Dick Curless (Event 4266). Re-released with other material in 1995 on
   Dick Curless: A Tombstone Every Mile. See entry 11.
   A, D, F, G, Q
   Fall 1956

5. ***It's Not Easy to Forget***
   Roy Aldridge (Released on Emperor Records, Emp. 209). Re-released in
   2004 on *"That'll Flat Git It" Vol. 20—Rockabilly From the Vaults of
   Event Records* (Bear Family Records-BCD 16440)
   A, D, F, L, N, Q
   ca. Fall 1956

6. ***Baby, Baby/Teenage Love Affair***
   Curtis Johnson and the Windjammers (Event 4268). Re-released in 2004
   on *"That'll Flat Git It" Vol. 20—Rockabilly From the Vaults of Event
   Records* (Bear Family Records-BCD 16440)
   A, E, K, L, M
   July 15, 1957

7. ***Baby, Let's Play House/I Don't Care If the Sun Don't Shine***
   Curtis Johnson and the Windjammers (Event 4282). Re-released in 2004
   on *"That'll Flat Git It" Vol. 20—Rockabilly From the Vaults of Event
   Records* (Bear Family Records-BCD 16440)
   A, E, H, M
   July 17/18, 1957

8. ***Rock-A-Billy Boogie/Let 'em Talk***
   Donny Harrison (Event 4273). Re-released in 2004 on *"That'll Flat
   Git It" Vol. 20—Rockabilly From the Vaults of Event Records*
   (Bear Family Records-BCD 16440)
   A, F, L, O sides A and B
   P on Side A only
   Nov. 3, 1957

9. *Nine Pound Hammer*
   Dick Curless (Event 4274). Re-released with other material in 1995 on
   Dick Curless: A Tombstone Every Mile. See entry 11.
   A, D, G
   Nov. 11, 1957
   All non-rereleased Event Records material is out of print.

10. *Lenny Breau: Boy Wonder*
    Lenny Breau (Guitarchives TNSD 0172-CD)

    Tracks 1–7 B
    1. I'll See You in My Dreams
    2. Cannon Ball Rag
    3. John Henry
    4. Alice Blue Gown/It's a Sin to Tell a Lie/Unknown/I've Been
       Workin' On the Railroad
    5. Birth of the Blues
    6. Correna, Correna
    7. By the Light of the Silvery Moon/Back Home Again in
       Indiana/Barnyard Frolic/Mr. Sandman/I'm Confessin' That I Love
       You, Third Man Theme
    8. Sonny's Special (A, L, I)
    9. Side by Side (A, I)
    10. Dizzy Fingers #1 (Mislisted on CD as Rainbow) (A, L, I)
    11. The Blues Doubled (aka Multiple Blues) (A, E)
    12. Speedy Blues (aka Sonny's Speedy Blues) (A, L, I)
    13. Blue Echo (aka Blue Ocean Echo) (A)
    14. Indian Love Call (A, G)
    15. Dizzy Fingers #2 (Listed as Indian Love Call Alternate Take)
        (A, probably G)
    16. Mystery Swing (Listed as Muskrat Ramble)
    17. Knock, Knock (A, E, F, G, L, I)
    18. Caravan (A)
    19. Chinatown, My Chinatown (A)
    20. Dance of the Golden Rods (A)
    21. The Waltz You Saved for Me (A, G)
    22. Out of Nowhere (A, G)
    23. It's Wonderful (A, G)
    24. Blue Heartaches (A, G)
    25. Blues in Extension (A, G)
    26. Speedy Jazz (A, G)
    27. September Song (A, G)

Tracks	Rec. Date
1–7	July/August 1957
8–13	Alternately listed as in log as ca. January 1957 and August 1957
14–17	1956
18–20	March/April 1957
21–27	August 12, 1957

Released 1998

11. *Dick Curless: A Tombstone Every Mile*
Dick Curless (Bear Family BCD 15882 GI)

1. Cottage in the Pines (A, D, F, H)
2. Cupid's Arrow (A, D, F, H)
3. Baby Darling (A, D, F, H)
4. Naponee (A, D, F, H)
5. Rocky Mountain Queen (A, D, F, H)
6. Streets of Laredo** (A, D, F, J, Q)
7. China Nights** (A, D, F, G, L, Q on maracas)
8. Blues in My Mind** (A, D, L)
9. Lovin' Dan—60 Minute Man* (A, D, G, L, R)
10. Blue Yodel (aka Midnight Turning Day Blues/She Left Me This Morning)* (A, D, G, L, R)
11. Bright Lights and Blonde Haired Women* (A, D, G, L, R)
12. Travelin' Man (A, D, G, L, R)
13. I'm Ragged But Right (A, D, G, L, R)
14. Please Don't Pass Me By (A, D, G, F, L, R)
15. Nine Pound Hammer (A, D, G, F, L, R)
16. Nine Pound Hammer w/recitation** (A, D, G)
17. I Am a Pilgrim (B, D)
18. Tuck Me to Sleep in My Old Kentucky Home (A, D, F, G, L, R)
19. I Ain't Got Nobody* (B, D, G, L, R)
20. Rainbow in My Heart (A, D, F, L, R)
21. Something's Wrong with You* (A, D, F, G, L, R)
22. Evil Hearted Man Blues (aka Evil Hearted Me)* (A, D, F, G, L, R)

* Previously released in 1966 as *Soul of Dick Curless*. Dick Curless (Tower Records DT 5013)
** Previously released on Event 45s, see above for details.

Recording dates:

Track	Rec. Date
1, 10	Nov. 1957
2, 6, 9, 11	Nov. 4, 1957
3, 4	June/July 1956
5	Fall 1956
7, 11, 17, 18, 19, 20	Nov. 11,1957
8, 12, 13	Nov. 5, 1957
14, 15, 16	Nov. 10, 1957
21, 22	June/July, 1956

Released 1995

Instrument Abbreviation Key for Entries 12–62

7 str. el. gtr.	7 string electric guitar
7 str. nyl. gtr.	7 string nylon guitar
12 str. gtr.	12 string guitar
ac. bs.	acoustic bass
cl.	clarinet
dr.	drums

el. bs	electric bass
el. gtr.	electric guitar
fdl.	fiddle
fl.	flute
har. vcls.	harmony vocals
kybd.	keyboards
ld. gtr.	lead guitar
nyl. gtr.	nylon string guitar
p.	piano
perc.	percussion
rhy. gtr.	rhythm guitar
st. gtr.	steel guitar
vcl.	vocals
vbs.	vibes

12. *She's a Square/If You Don't Mean It*
    Ray St. Germain and the Satins (Chateau Records C107) (45)
        Rereleased on several compilations including *Shakin' Up North*
        (Bear Family CD 16289)
    Personnel: Ray St. Germain—vcl./rhy. gtr. Lenny Breau—el. gtr. Reg
        Kelln—dr. Shadow Saunders—el. bs.
    Winnipeg, June 1960
    Out of Print

13. *The Hallmark Sessions*
    Lenny Breau (Art of Life Records AL1007-2-CD)
    Personnel: Lenny Breau—el. gtr. (tr. 1–9, 14–19) nyl. gtr. (tr. 10, 11, 12, 13)
        Rick Danko—ac. bs. Levon Helm—dr.

    1. It Could Happen To You
    2. Oscar's Blues
    3. I'll Remember April
    4. Undecided
    5. My Old Flame
    6. "D" Minor Blues
    7. "R" Tune
    8. Lenny's Western Blues
    9. Cannonball Rag
    10. Solea
    11. Taranta
    12. Arabian Fantasy
    13. Brazilian Love Song (Batucada)
    14. Oscar's Blues*
    15. I'll Remember April*
    16. Undecided*
    17. My Old Flame*
    18. "D" Minor Blues*
    19. "R" Tune*

    * Bonus Tracks. Stereo Version
    Toronto, November 11, 28, 1961
    Released 2003

14. ***Lenny Breau, Don Francks, Eon Henstridge: At The Purple Onion***
Lenny Breau/Don Francks (Art of Life Records AL1009-2-CD)
Personnel: Lenny Breau—el. gtr. Don Francks—vcl. (tr. 1–7)
    Eon Henstridge—ac. bs. Joey Hollingsworth—vcl. (tr. 8)
    tap dancing (tr. 10)

    1. Introduction
    2. A New Electric Chair
    3. The Surrey with the Fringe on Top
    4. The Newspaper Song
    5. Gum Addiction
    6. Tea for Two
    7. A Gentile Sings the Blues
    8. Work Song
    9. Oscar's Blues
    10. Joey's Solo

Toronto, August 1962
Released 2004

15. ***God Bless the Child/Nobody Knows You***
Lenny Breau/Don Francks (CBC RM95)
Personnel: Lenny Breau—el.gtr. Don Francks—vcl.
CBC studios, Montreal or Toronto Fall 1962
Promotional acetate. Not commercially released

16. ***Jackie Gleason Says "No-One in This World Is Like Don Francks"***
Don Francks (Kapp Records 4501-LP)
Personnel: Don Francks—vcl. Lenny Breau—el. gtr.
    Eon Henstridge—ac. bs.

    1. Things
    2. Jazz Whot Is!
    3. My Hometown
    4. I'm Going To Love You Like Nobody's Loved You
    5. Children's Hours
    6. Loneliness Is A Lady
    7. Dear Brother
    8. The Turn of the Century

New York City, May 1963
Out of Print

17. ***Don Francks: Lost . . . and Alone***
Don Francks (Kapp KL 1417-LP)
Personnel: Don Francks—vcl. Lenny Breau—el. gtr.
    Pat Williams Orchestra (tr. 1)

    1. Nobody Knows You
    2. Sonny Boy

Out of Print

18. *Introducing Ted Rivers*
Ted Rivers (REO RLP 650-LP)
Personnel: Ted Rivers—vcl. Lenny Breau—el. gtr. Bob Erlendson—p.
(Tracks 1, 2, 6) Reg Kelln—dr. Ron Halldorson—st. gtr. (listed as Ron
Molderson on jacket) Bob Jackson—bs. The Bluebells—har. vcl.

1. Do It for Me
2. Better Luck Next Time
3. Where in the World
4. I Wish She'd Come Back
5. Angel Sittin' Home
6. Book of Memories
7. Dollar Bills
8. I Don't Believe
9. Kickin' Me Around
10. The Only Love I've Known
11. Ain't Comin' Back
12. Spring Heart Cleanin'

Winnipeg ca. 1962
Out of Print

19. *Cool Yule*
Donny Burns (ARC Records Catalogue # unknown—45). Reissued in
2002 on Norton Records: EP-111
Personnel: Lenny Breau—el. gtr. Donny Burns—vcl.
Winnipeg, 1964
Out of Print

20. *Raise Your Rockus/She Can Leave Me*
Ray St. Germain (Capitol 7237-45)
Personnel: Ray St. Germain—vcl./ rhy. gtr. Lenny Breau—el.gtr. Reg
Kelln—dr. Dave Young—bs.
Winnipeg, 1966
Out of Print

21. *Ten Golden Years of Country*
Hank Smith and the Rodgers Bros. Band (Point Records P311)
Personnel: Hank Smith—ac. gtr./vcl. Lenny Breau—el.gtr.
Ray Dussome—el.gtr. Other Personnel.

1. Singin' the Blues
2. My Special Angel
3. Oh Lonesome Me
4. He'll Have to Go
5. Alabam
6. Walk on By
7. Wolverton Mountain
8. Talk Back Tremblin' Lips
9. What's He Doing in My World
10. Almost Persuaded

Edmonton, 1967
Out of Print

22. **_Soft and Groovy_**

Jimmy Dale (CBC LM-40/Capitol Records SN 6290-L)
Personnel: Orchestra led by Jimmy Dale all cuts

1. I Should Care (Ed Bickert—ld. gtr. Lenny Breau—rhy. gtr.)
2. Norwegian Wood (Sonny Greenwich—ld. gtr. Lenny Breau—rhy.
   gtr/ld. gtr on 2nd solo)
3. Music to Watch Girls By (Lenny Breau—12 str. gtr.)
4. The Look of Love (Sonny Greenwich—ld. gtr.
   Lenny Breau—rhy. gtr.)

Toronto, Feb. 16–20/ Mar. 2, 1968
Out of Print

23. **_Catherine McKinnon: Both Sides Now_**

Catherine McKinnon (ARC Records AS 777-LP)
Personnel: Catherine McKinnon—vcl. Lenny Breau—el. gtr./nyl. gtr.
   Other personnel

1. Beautiful Morning
2. The Look of Love
3. Why Did I Choose You
4. This Girl's in Love with You
5. If You Must Leave My Life
6. Both Sides Now
7. Rising Sun
8. Hard Lovin' Loser
9. If You Were A Carpenter
10. Suzanne

Toronto, 1968
Out of Print
Rereleased on CD by ARC Records UBK-4074
Out of Print

24. **_Diane Brooks: Some Other Kind of Soul_**

Diane Brooks (Revolver RLPS-503 LP)
Diane Brooks—vcl. Lenny Breau—el.gtr. Other personnel

1. Leave My (Wo) Man Alone
2. When I'm All Alone
3. Show Him (He's Not Alone)
4. Cheat On Me
5. Season of the Witch
6. The Boys Are on the Case
7. No Turning Back
8. But I Smiled
9. He's Not the Man
10. Show Me
11. You've Got to Grow

Toronto, probably spring 1968
Out of Print

25. ***Guitar Sounds From Lenny Breau***

Lenny Breau (RCA LSP-4076 LP)

Personnel: Lenny Breau—*el. gtr. —**nyl. gtr. —***12 str. gtr.
   Reg Kelln—dr. Ron Halldorson—el. bs.

1. King of the Road*
2. Taranta**
3. Don't Think Twice, It's All Right**
4. Hard Day's Night*
5. Georgia on My Mind*
6. Monday, Monday*
7. My Funny Valentine***
8. Freight Train**
9. Cold, Cold Heart*
10. Music to Watch Girls By***

Tracks 1, 4, 5, 7, and 9 recorded Nashville, April 2, 1968
Tracks 2, 3, 6, 8, and 10 recorded Nashville, April 3, 1968
Out of Print
Released on CD in 2005, Wounded Bird

26. ***The Velvet Touch of Lenny Breau. Live!***

Lenny Breau (RCA LSP-4199/ RCA Canada KYL1-0462-LP)

Personnel: Lenny Breau—*el. gtr. —**nyl. gtr. —***12 str. gtr.—vcl. (tr.5)
   Reg Kelln—dr. Ron Halldorson—bs.

1. Tuning Tune*
2. No Greater Love*
3. The Claw**
4. Indian Reflections For Ravi***
5. That's All*
6. Blues Theme*
7. Mercy, Mercy, Mercy*
8. Spanjazz**
9. Bluesette*
10. A Taste Of Honey*
11. Blues Theme #2*

Tracks 1, 3, 5, and 10 recorded Hollywood, California, April 28, 1969
Tracks 2 and 9 recorded Hollywood, California, April 29, 1969
Tracks 4, 6, 7, 8, and 11 recorded Hollywood, California, April 30, 1969
Out of Print
Released on CD in 1994 by One Way Records (OW 29315 CD)
Out of Print

27. ***Lenny Breau: Live at Donte's***

Lenny Breau (String Jazz Records SJRCD 1008-CD)

Personnel: Lenny Breau—el. gtr/nyl. gtr.(tr. 10) Ray Neopolitan—ac. bs.
   Dick Berk—dr.John Pisano—el. gtr. (tr.10)

1. Too Close for Comfort
2. Time after Time

3. When I Fall in Love (Version 1)
4. Autumn Leaves
5. All Blues
6. Will You Still be Mine
7. Green Dolphin Street
8. 24/36 Blues
9. When I Fall in Love
10. Georgia on My Mind

Los Angeles, May 1969
Released April 2000
Out of Print

28. *Golden Guitar Magic/Guitar Magic*
Lenny Breau (RCA Custom for Reader's Digest Records RD4-75-4
   LP Box Set)
Personnel: Lenny Breau—el. gtr. and nyl. str gtr. Unknown bass and drums

1. Lullaby of Birdland (Lenny Breau—el. gtr.)
2. Seguerillas (Lenny Breau—nyl. str. gtr.)
3. Solea (Lenny Breau—nyl. str. gtr.)

October 10, 1969
Out of Print
Tracks 1 and 3 only released on CD (Reader's Digest Records RF7-112 &
   LGUI-A-36-CD)
Out of Print

29. *Curried Soul*
Moe Koffman (Kama Sutra Records KSBS 2018-LP)
Personnel: Moe Koffman—fl./sax Lenny Breau—el.gtr.* Dave Lewis—dr.
   Dave Young—bs. Doug Riley—kybd. String and horn sections arranged
   by Rick Wilkins
* Although not listed, Lenny Breau may be the guitarist on all tracks.

1. L'il Bitty Pretty One
2. Sunshine Superman
3. Country Song
4. Cantelope Island

Toronto, December 1969
Released 1970
Out of Print
Rereleased on LP as *Sorcerer's Dance* (Hopi VHS 902 CD&LP)
Out of Print

30. *Beverly Glenn-Copeland*
Beverly Glenn-Copeland (GRT Records 9233-1001-LP)
Personnel: Beverly Glenn-Copeland—vcls./rhy. gtr. Lenny Breau—el. gtr.
   (tracks 1–3, 8) Doug Bush—bs. (tracks 5,6. 2nd bs. on 8) Terry
   Clarke—dr. Doug Riley—kybds. (track 3) Jeremy Steig—fl. Don
   Thompson—el. and ac. bs, vbs. perc.

1. Color of Anyhow

2. Ghost House
3. Complainin' Blues
4. Swords of Gold
5. Song from Beads
6. Cumberland Passing
7. My Old Rag or The Hysterical Virgin
8. Erzili

Recorded Toronto, February 1970
Out of Print
Released on CD in 2002 (Songcycles Records SP02)

31. *George Hamilton IV: North Country*
George Hamilton IV (RCA Records MSP-4517-LP)
Personnel: George Hamilton IV—vcl./rhy. gtr.
    Lenny Breau—el. gtr/el. 12 str./nyl. gtr. Other personnel

1. I'm Not Sayin'
2. Countryfied
3. Love Is Still Around
4. North Country
5. Snowbird
6. It's All Over
7. My North Country Home
8. Goin' Down the Road
9. Moody Manitoba Morning
10. Put Your Hand in the Hand

Toronto, February 1–7, 1971
Out of Print

32. *Lord of the Dance*
John Allan Cameron (Columbia ELS-38-LP)
Personnel: John Allan Cameron—vcl./fdl. Lenny Breau—el. gtr./12 str. el.
    gtr. Other personnel

1. Lord of the Dance
2. Trip to Mabu Ridge
3. Elizabeth Lindsey Meets Ronald MacDonald
4. Streets of London
5. The Patriot Game
6. I Can't Tell You
7. Glasgow Police Pipers/Donald Willie and His Dog
8. Dirty Old Man
9. Mist Covered Mountains
10. Robbie's Song for Jesus

Toronto, September 1972
Out of Print

33. *Danny's Song*
Anne Murray (EMI Records SN-16211-LP)
Personnel: Anne Murray—vcl. Lenny Breau—el. gtr. Other personnel

1. What About Me
2. I Know
3. Ease Your Pain
4. One Day I Walk
5. Put Your Hand in the Hand

Ottawa, October 1972
Released 1973
Out of Print
Released on CD (EMI Records 72434-9540 CD)

34. *Dracula Is Coming to Town/So Long My Friend*
Richard (Capitol Record 72685-45)
Personnel: Lenny Breau—el.gtr. Skip Beckwith—bs. Andy Cree—dr.
   Pat Riccio Jr.—p. Don "DT" Thompson—sax.
Toronto, October 1972
Out of Print

35. *CBC Radio Canada Broadcast Recording*
Len Udow (CBC LM403)
Personnel: Len Udow—rhy. gtr./vcl. Lenny Breau—el. gtr.
   Ron Halldorson—bs.

1. Sweet Baby's Arms

Winnipeg, December 1974
Out of Print

36. *Cabin Fever*
Lenny Breau (Guitarchives TNSD 0158-CD)
Personnel: Lenny Breau—nyl. gtr.

1. Lenny's Warm-up and Improvisation on "Autumn Leaves"
2. Why Did I Choose You? (listed as "Lenny's Mood")
3. East Side
4. You Came to Me Out of Nowhere
5. What Is This Thing Called Love
6. Days of Wine and Roses
7. Lenny's Mode
8. Here's That Rainy Day
9. Celtic Dream Stream

Toronto, Summer 1975
Released 1997

37. *Chet Atkins and Friends*
Chet Atkins (RCA APL1-1985-LP)
Personnel: Lenny Breau—el.gtr. Chet Atkins—el.gtr

1. Sweet Georgia Brown

Nashville, 1976
Out of Print
Released on CD in 1995 (BMG Records 07863 61093-2 CD)

38. *Me and My Guitar*
Chet Atkins (RCA APLI-2405 LP)
Personnel: Chet Atkins—resonator gtr./nyl. gtr./el. gtr. Lenny Breau—nyl.
gtr./bs./rhy. gtr. John Baker—perc.

1. Long, Long Ago (Chet Atkins—resonator gtr. Lenny Breau—nyl. gtr.)
2. You'd Be So Nice to Come Home To (Chet Atkins—nyl. gtr./
el. gtr. Lenny Breau—bs./rhy. gtr. John Baker—perc.)

Nashville, 1977
Out of Print
Released on CD (One Way Records 35112 CD)
Out of Print

39. *Yesterday and Today*
Buddy Spicher (RCA APLI-2405-LP)
Personnel: Buddy Spicher—fdl. Lenny Breau—el. gtr. Charles Dungey—ac.
bs. Mike Leach—el. bs. Buddy Emmons—st. gtr. Kenny Malone—dr.
Bob Mater—dr.

1. Lady Be Good
2. Georgia on My Mind
3. I Remember

Nashville, May 1977
Out of Print

40. *Buddies*
Buddy Spicher/ Buddy Emmons (RCA APLI-2405-LP)
Personnel: Buddy Spicher—fdl. Buddy Emmons—st. gtr.
Lenny Breau—el. gtr. Other personnel

1. Uncle Pen
2. Magic Swing

Nashville, 1977
Out of Print

41. *Pickin' Cotten*
Lenny Breau (Guitarchives GTR 0005-CD)
Personnel: Lenny Breau—el. gtr. Richard Cotten—el. bs. Spoken homage
by Darci Cotten (track 9)

1. On Green Dolphin Street
2. I Love You
3. Emily
4. Scrapple from the Apple
5. Autumn Leaves
6. La Funkallero
7. Stella by Starlight
8. Tuning/The Two Lonely People/Nardis
9. Lenny and Richard Remembered (spoken by Darci Cotten)

Nashville, September 23/24, 1977
Released 2001

42. *Five O'clock Bells*

Lenny Breau (Adelphi Records AD 5006-LP)
Personnel: Lenny Breau—el. gtr (tracks 1, 3, 6, 8) nyl. gtr on all other tracks, vcl. track 5

1. Days of Wine and Roses
2. Toronto
3. Amy (For Cinde)
4. Other Places, Other Times
5. Five O'clock Bells
6. Little Blues
7. My Funny Valentine
8. Visions

New York City, October 1977
Released 1979
Out of Print
Released on CD in 1987 with #41 (Genes CD 5006/12)

43. *Mo' Breau*

Lenny Breau (Adelphi Records AD 5012-LP)
Personnel: Lenny Breau—el. gtr. (tr. 2, 5–8) nyl. gtr. all other tracks. Vcls. tr. 5

1. Ebony Queen/Pam's Pad
2. Autumn Leaves
3. . . . But Beautiful
4. Emily
5. New York City
6. Please Release Me/Cold, Cold Heart (listed as "I Remember Hank")
7. Beautiful Love (listed as "Marlborough Street")
8. I'll Remember April/Back in the Saddle (listed as "Lone Pine")

New York City, November 1977
Released 1981
Out of Print
Released on CD in 1987 with #41 (Genes CD 5006/12)

44. *Last Sessions*

Lenny Breau (Adelphi Records AD 5024 Direct Metal Mastered LP) (Genes CD Co. GCD 5024-CD)
Personnel: Lenny Breau—ny. gtr. (track 3) el. gtr on all other tracks

1. Ebony Queen/Pam's Pad
2. Meanwhile Back in L.A.
3. Paris
4. Ba De Da-Da
5. Feelings
6. I Love You
7. Untitled Standard
8. But Beautiful #2

9. Beautiful Love

New York City, December 1977/ January 1978
LP and CD released 1988
LP Out of Print

45. *Killin' the Wind*
Bucky Barret (Ocean Records BB 8888 LP)
Personnel: Bucky Barret—el. gtr. Lenny Breau—el. gtr. Other personnel

1. Good Lick
2. Killin' The Wind
3. Lipstick
4. Steely Dance

Nashville, 1979
Released 1981
Out of Print

46. *The Living Room Tapes Volume 1*
Lenny Breau/Brad Terry (Living Room Records LRR 1-LP1).
Personnel: Lenny Breau—7 str. nyl. gtr. (tracks 3, 4, 7),
    el. gtr (tracks 1, 2, 5, 6) Brad Terry—cl.

1. How High the Moon
2. You Needed Me
3. Blues for Carole
4. The Claw
5. Secret Love
6. Sweet Georgia Brown
7. Foolish Heart

Recorded between October 1978 and January 1982
Released 1986
Released on CD in 1988 Musical Heritage Society Records (MHS
    512294M)
Re-released on CD in 1995 DOS Records 7503
LP and CDs out of Print. See #48

47. *The Living Room Tapes Volume 2*
Lenny Breau/Brad Terry (Musical Heritage Society Records (MHS
    512627L-CD)
Personnel: Lenny Breau—7 str. nyl. gtr (tracks 1–5, 11, 12)
    el. gtr (tracks 6–10) Brad Terry—cl.

1. I Fall in Love Too Easily
2. Send in the Clowns
3. Nine Pound Hammer
4. Cannonball Rag
5. Flamenco
6. It Could Happen To You
7. Visions
8. Remembering the Rain

9. Autumn Leaves
10. Indiana
11. Stella By Starlight
12. Emily

Recorded between October 1978 and January 1982
Released 1990
Out of Print. See #48

48. *The Complete Living Room Tapes*
Lenny Breau/Brad Terry (Art of Life Records AL1004-2-2 CD Set)
Personnel: Lenny Breau—7 str. nyl. gtr. (tracks 3, 4) el. gtr. (tracks 1, 2)
  vcl. (track 3) Brad Terry—cl./whistling
CD reissue containing all material on *Living Room Tapes Volumes 1*
  and 2 plus tracks below:

1. My Funny Valentine
2. Autumn Leaves
3. Johnny Cash Sings Jazz?
4. Lenny's Radio

Same recording dates as entries 46 and 47
Released 2003

49. *The Legendary Lenny Breau . . . Now*
Lenny Breau (Soundhole Records NR10462-LP)
Personnel: Lenny Breau—nyl. gtr. (tracks 5–8) el. gtr. (tracks 1–4)
  John Baker—dr. (track 3)

1. I Can't Help It
2. Always
3. Our Delight
4. Freight Train
5. Ebony Queen
6. I Love You
7. It Could Happen To You
8. Visions

Nashville, September 1977, August/September 1978
Out of Print

50. *Musical Buffet*
Shep Spinney (EAB Records 8093N9-LP)
Personnel: Shep Spinney—el. gtr./vcls. Lenny Breau—el. gtr.
  Other personnel

1. The Blind Man's Song

Lewiston, Maine, Summer 1978
Out of Print

51. *Betty Cody: Singing Again*
Betty Cody (EAB Records 790816-LP)
Personnel: Betty Cody—vcl. Lenny Breau—el. gtr. Denny Breau—el. gtr.

1. Hopeless Woman

Lewiston, Maine, Summer 1978
Released 1979
Out of Print

52. *Hopeless Woman/The Way You Treated Me*
Betty Cody (Family Records 228-45)
Personnel: Betty Cody—vcl. Lenny Breau—el. gtr. Denny Breau—el. gtr.
Lewiston, Maine, Summer 1978
Released 1979
Out of Print

53. *Minors Aloud*
Lenny Breau/Buddy Emmons (Flying Fish Records FF 088-LP)
Personnel: Lenny Breau—el. gtr./vcl. (track 5) Buddy Emmons—st. gtr./vcl.
   (tracks 2 and 4) Charles Dungey—ac. bs. Randy Goodrum—kybd.
   Kenny Malone—dr.
   1. Minors Aloud
   2. Compared To What
   3. Killer Joe
   4. Long Way to Go
   5. Secret Love
   6. Scrapple from the Apple
   7. On a Bach Bouree

Nashville, August 1978
Out of Print
Released on CD in 2005 (Art of Life Records AL 1014-2)

54. *Lenny Breau*
Lenny Breau (Direct to Disc Records DD-112 (D to D LP))
Personnel: Lenny Breau—el. gtr. (tracks 2–5) nyl. gtr. (track 1) Chet
   Atkins—nyl. gtr. (track 1) Claude Ranger—dr. Don Thompson—ac. bs.
   1. You Needed Me
   2. Don't Think Twice (It's All Right)
   3. Mister Night
   4. Neptune
   5. Claude (Free Song)

Nashville, February 22, 1979
Out of Print
Re-released in 1985 as *Lenny Breau Trio* (Adelphi Records AD 5018-LP)
Out of Print
Released on CD in 1999 as *Lenny Breau Trio* (Adelphi/Genes Records
   GCD 5018-CD)

55. *Standard Brands*
Lenny Breau (RCA AYL1-4191-LP)
Personnel: Lenny Breau—nyl. gtr. Chet Atkins—nyl. gtr./ res. gtr.
   1. Batucada
   2. Tenderly
   3. Cattle Call

    4. Taking A Chance On Love
    5. Somebody's Knockin'
    6. This Can't Be Love
    7. This Nearly Was Mine
    8. Going Home
    9. Polka Dots And Moonbeams

Nashville, 1979–1981
Out of Print
Released on CD in 1994 (One Way Records OW 29316 CD)
Out of Print

56. *Chance Meeting*
Lenny Breau/Tal Farlow (Guitarchives Records GTR-0003-CD)
Personnel: Lenny Breau—el. gtr. Tal Farlow—el. gtr. Lyn Christie—bs.
    (Tracks 4 and 6) Nat Garratano—dr. (tracks 4 and 6)

    1. I Love You
    2. Satin Doll
    3. My Funny Valentine
    4. All The Things You Are
    5. Conversation (Tal & Lenny)
    6. Cherokee
    7. What Is This Thing Called Love?
    8. Broadway
    9. My Foolish Heart

Rumson, New Jersey, May 21, 1980
Released 1997

57. *A Touch of Bryant*
Boudleaux Bryant (CMH Records 6243 LP)
Personnel: Boudleaux Bryant—vcl. Lenny Breau—nyl. gtr.
    Chet Atkins—nyl. gtr. Other personnel

    1. When I Stop Loving You

Nashville, 1980
Out of Print

58. *When Lightn' Strikes*
Lenny Breau (Tudor Records. TR 113004 LP)
Personnel: Lenny Breau—7 str. nyl. gtr. (tracks 1–5, 7, 8, 10) el. gtr.
    (tracks 6 and 9) Jim Ferguson—bs. Buddy Emmons—st. gtr. (tracks
    6–10) Kenny Malone—dr.

    1. Anytime
    2. I Can't Help It if I'm Still in Love with You
    3. You Needed Me
    4. She Thinks I Still Care
    5. Please Release Me
    6. Blue Moon Of Kentucky
    7. I Love You Because
    8. Bonaparte's Retreat

9. Back in Indiana
10. I'm So Lonesome I Could Cry

Nashville, August 12, 22, 1982
Released 1985
Out of Print
Re-released on CD in 2005 with bonus track "Blue Eyes Cryin'
in the Rain" as *Swingin' on a Seven String* (Art of Life Records
Al1013-2(CD))

59. *I Can Do Anything*
Sphere Clown Band (One-Eyed Duck Records DL 001-LP)
Personnel: Lenny Breau—nyl. gtr. John Erlendson—vcl./gtr./bs.
Patricia Silver Erlendson—vcl./ac. gtr./kybd. Other personnel

1. Ride
2. Don't Monkey Around
3. Only A Kazoo

Toronto, June 1983
Out of Print

60. *Legacy*
Lenny Breau (Relaxed Rabbit Records RR 427-LP)
Personnel: Lenny Breau—7 str. el. gtr. David Young—ac. bs.

1. There Is No Greater Love
2. I Fall in Love Too Easily
3. Blues In My Case
4. What Is This Thing Called Love?
5. The Two Lonely People
6. Riot-Chorus (incorrectly listed as "Sparkle Dust")

Toronto, June 1983
Out of Print, see #62

61. *Quietude*
Lenny Breau (Electric Muse Records UMM 1001-LP)
Personnel: Lenny Breau—7 str. el. gtr. David Young—ac. bs.

1. On Green Dolphin Street
2. If You Could See Me Now
3. Summertime
4. Quiet And Blue
5. All Blues
6. Visions

Toronto, June 1983
Released 1985
Out of Print. See #62

62. *Live at Bourbon Street*
Lenny Breau (Guitarchives TNXD0119-Two CD Set)
Personnel: Lenny Breau—7 str. el. gtr. Dave Young—ac. bs.
CD release of *Quietude* and *Legacy* with previously unreleased material:

1. All the Things You Are
2. My Foolish Heart
3. My Funny Valentine
4. Beautiful Love
5. There Will Never Be Another You
6. Riot-Chorus

Toronto, June 1983. Released 1995

63. *Companions*
Phil Upchurch (Jam Records JAM 021-LP)
Personnel: Phil Upchurch—el. gtr. Lenny Breau—7 str. el. gtr. Others.

1. Companions
2. Song For Lenny

Los Angeles, Summer 1984. Out of Print.
Re-released in 1985 on Paladin Records (PAL4) (LP). Out of Print.
Released in Japan only on CD (PSCW-1168) (CD). Out of Print.

64. *Great Hits of the Past*
Chet Atkins (RCA AHL 1-4724)
Personnel: Chet Atkins—el. gtr/ nyl gtr. Lenny Breau—el. gtr/nyl. gtr (?).
Other personnel.

1. Chet's Medley
2. Sweet Dreams
3. Amos Moses
4. Abilene
5. That's What I Get for Loving You
6. Oh Baby Mine
7. And I Love You So
8. Java
9. Detroit City
10. The Three Bells

Nashville, 1983

65. *Mosaic*
Lenny Breau (Guitarchives BOOOIHY9RK)
Personnel: Lenny Breau—7 str. el. gtr. * el. gtr. ** 12 str. gtr. ***
nyl. str. **** 7 str. nyl. *****. Phil Upchurch—bs./gtr. (tracks 1–3)
Ron Halldorson—bs. (track 4) Reg Kelln—dr. (track 4) Land Richards
(track 1–3) Brad Terry—cl./whistling (track 7)

1. No Greater Love * (Recorded Los Angeles, Summer 1984)
2. Emily * (Recorded Los Angeles, Summer 1984)
3. The In Crowd * (Recorded Los Angeles, Summer 1984)
4. Georgia On My Mind ** (Recorded Nashville, April 1968)
5. Lenny's Ragadelic Dream *** (Recorded Winnipeg, August 1968)
6. Warm-up and Improv. of Autumn Leaves **** (Recorded Toronto, Summer 1975)
7. Blues for Carole ***** (Recorded Maine, probably 1981)
8. Answering Machine (Spoken Word)
9. Phil Upchurch Remembers (Spoken Word)

Released September 2006

Notes

(See Bibliography for details of articles cited.)

Introduction

    1. "CBC" stands for Canadian Broadcasting Corporation, Canada's national radio and television network.

    2. Lee Major, *One More Take.*

Chapter 1. On the Trail of the Lonesome Pine

    1. Hal Lone Pine's opening theme song: WLBZ radio, ca. 1936.

    2. Pine later claimed that Native Indians from a nearby reserve had given him the name. However, Betty Cody and many old friends insist that the name was suggested by Maine's designation as the "Lone Pine State."

    3. The group would change its name several times over the years, often using monikers designated by the radio stations for whom they worked. Pine did not call his group The Lone Pine Mountaineers until 1950 when he and Betty began recording for Bluebird Records with RCA Canada. Afterwards, the group continued to use a variety of other names until RCA president Steve Scholes dubbed the group name Hal "Lone" Pine and his Mountaineers in 1952. From the mid fifties onwards, Pine used "Caravan" in most of his band names.

    4. Anonymous, *Lewiston Evening Journal.*

    5. Major, *One More Take.*

    6. Lee Major, "Between Ourselves," radio interview.

    7. James Marck, "Breau's Variation on a Theme."

    8. Jim Beardon and Linda Butler, "Lenny Sings the Blues."

    9. John Knowles, "Quiet Genius of Fingerstyle Jazz."

    10. Major, *One More Take.*

    11. Walter Carter, "Lenny Breau."

    12. Knowles, "Quiet Genius."

    13. Ibid.

    14. Ruth Dutten, "Lenny Breau Was Admired, Worshiped, and Respected, by Family, Musicians and Fans."

    15. The Event Records catalogue lists the date as March 26, 1956. However, Hawkes says the label's first record was released on April 2 of that year and Pine recorded his first sides a month and a half later.

    16. Jason Perry, "Music World Loses Great Guitarist."

    17. Ibid.

2. Song of the Prairie

    1. The album was *The Poll Winners: Barney Kessel with Shelly Manne and Ray Brown*, issued by Contemporary Records.

2. Lorenzo DeStefano, *Talmage Farlow.*
3. This quotation is taken from the CBC Radio transcription of the broadcast.

3. Lullaby of Birdland

1. Joan Sadler, "Shed No Tears for Lenny."
2. Knowles, "Quiet Genius."
3. Ibid.
4. Julie London with Barney Kessel and Ray Leatherwood. *Julie Is Her Name* Liberty 3006.
5. Jimmy King, "Nightbeat."
6. Sadler, "Shed No Tears."
7. W. Carter, "Lenny Breau."
8. Martin K. Webb, "Atkins Style Jazz on a 6-string 12."
9. Carter, "Lenny Breau."
10. Major, *One More Take.*
11. Brawner Smoot, "Lenny Breau—Fingerstyle Jazz Impressionist."
12. Ibid.
13. Carter, "Lenny Breau."
14. Mona Coxson, "Lenny Breau."
15. In the liner notes of his album *Live at Donte's* (Pablo 2620 114) Joe Pass advises guitarists to use open string chords only sparingly and to avoid the keys of E, A, and D. "They tend to become syrupy sweet," he says, "and can put you to sleep. Boring."

4. Out of Nowhere

1. Carter, "Lenny Breau."
2. *Christmas with Chet Atkins*, RCA LPM/LPR-2423-1961.
3. Tom Gannaway, "Remembering Lenny Breau."
4. Quoted in Anne Henry, "With Any Range."
5. Ibid.
6. In his interview with the author, Francks said that he decreed that the trio's name would be written in lower-case letters.
7. Ralph Thomas, "They Marvel at Guitarist's Mastery."
8. Don Owen, *Toronto Jazz.*
9. Recorded by John Coltrane in 1961 on his album *My Favorite Things.*
10. Anonymous, "New Acts: Three—Songs & Comedy. 46 Minutes at L'Hibou in Ottawa."
11. Anonymous, Goings on Around Town: Cabarets, *New Yorker*, March 23/31, 1962.
12. Anonymous, Goings on Around Town: Cabarets, *New Yorker*, April 6/13, 1962.
13. Francks says that an offer to appear in the Broadway show *Kelly* led to his decision to leave the trio. However, *Kelly* did not run on Broadway until February 6, 1965—opening and closing the same night. (Internet Broadway Database http://www.ibdb.com/production.asp? ID=3225.) In the fall of 1965, Lenny came to Toronto to do a spot with Francks on a CBC show called *Other Voices.* Francks began rehearsals for *Kelly* shortly after this appearance and it's probable that his recollection of "three's" demise is informed by events in this time period.

14. Kapp Records released and promoted the recording as a Don Francks album and Ren Grevatt's liner notes contain only a brief mention of Lenny and one short reference to "three." Francks made a second album for Kapp in 1964 called *Lost . . . and Alone.* Francks is backed by an orchestra on most tracks, but Lenny—who is not listed on the album—accompanies him on two duet cuts. The origin of these tracks is unknown. Both albums are out of print.

5. Workin' Man's Blues

1. Major, "Between Ourselves."
2. Major, *One More Take.*
3. Ibid.
4. Ted Allan, "Moe Koffman Brings Out Best of Breau's Guitar."
5. Ted Allan, "Peter Appleyard at the Jazz A Go-Go."
6. David Baines, "Lenny Breau Aims for the Top . . . Again."
7. "Windy," a 1967 pop hit for the band The Association.
8. Ross Porter, "The Mystery of Lenny."
9. Marck, "Breau's Variation on a Theme."
10. Bart Testa, "Lenny Breau Found: After Five Years in Exile, a Jazz Genius Plays Again."
11. Smoot, "Lenny Breau—Fingerstyle Jazz Impressionist."
12. Anonymous, "Beat of the City," *Winnipeg Free Press,* February 6, 1968.
13. Recorded as incidental music in fall of 1967, this piece was included on "Between Ourselves," radio interview.
14. Bart Smoot, "The Immortal Lenny Breau."
15. Major, *One More Take.*

6. Days of Wine and Roses

1. Anonymous, "Beat of the City."
2. Peter Harris, "Franks: His Super-Hipster Bag Obscures Talent."
3. Lee Major, "The Kid From Canada," interview.
4. Bill Piburn, "Chet Atkins: Guitarist of the Millennium."
5. Major, *One More Take.*
6. Major, "The Kid From Canada."
7. Lee Major, "Between Ourselves," interview.
8. Major, *One More Take.*
9. Jim Robertson, "Sunday Supplement," interview.
10. Adil, "Lenny Breau-Instrumental-Riverboat, Toronto."
11. In fact, all tunes on the session were done in one take except when a first run-through was incomplete. No third take was required for any of the tracks.
12. John Burke, "Guitar Sounds From Lenny Breau."
13. Testa, "Lenny Breau Found."
14. Leonard Feather, "Blindfold Test with Barney Kessel."
15. Jim Ferguson, "Lenny Breau Remembered."
16. Carter, "Lenny Breau."
17. Lee Edwards, "Heard and Seen: Lenny Breau, February 10, 1974."
18. Susan Janz, "Jazz Guitar Praised in Doctor Music."
19. Alastair Lawrie, "Breau: The Great Guitar Returns."
20. Peter Goddard, "Lack of Imagination Sometimes Hinders Guitarist's Skills."

21. Alastair Lawrie, "Breau Jazz Pleases, But It's All Too Brief."

22. Although Beckwith, Thompson, and especially Titcomb were not heavy drug users, Murray described the entire group as a "band of junkies and drunks" in a November 2002 *Reader's Digest* interview.

23. Jamie Craig, "Anne Free of Heavy Burden."

24. Ian MacDougall, "Audience on Its Feet."

25. Susan Janz, "Breau Treats Jazz Fans."

7. Turn Out the Stars

1. David Baines, "Lenny Breau Aims for the Top."

2. Jack Batten, "Two Other Virtuoso Musicians Doing Fine Work in Town."

3. Jeani Read, "Reviews."

4. Anonymous, "Court Frees Guitarist," *Winnipeg Tribune.*

5. Jack Batten, "Breau Teases and Listeners Love It."

6. Kevin Prokosh, "Breau's Name Will Live On, says Atkins."

7. Hazrat Inayat Khan, *The Mysticism of Sound and Music* (Boston: Shambhala Publications Inc., 1991).

8. Webb, "Atkins Style Jazz on a 6-string 12."

9. Wyman Collins, "Lenny Breau in Great Spirits."

10. Mark Miller, "Caught: Lenny Breau—The River Boat, Toronto."

11. Ross Porter, "The Mystery of Lenny," radio documentary.

12. Brawner Smoot, "Lenny Breau—Fingerstyle Jazz Impressionist."

8. Back in the Saddle

1. Testa, "Lenny Breau Found."

2. Natalie Dunning, "Jazz Picker Lenny Breau Back in the Saddle Again."

3. Chet Atkins and Russ Cochrane, "Me and My Guitar."

4. Sadler, "Shed No Tears."

5. In the fifties, Gibson offered buyers of their J200 model the option of a customized truss rod cover. Hal took advantage of this offer and had a pine tree engraved on the cover. This served to identify the guitar.

6. Lenny joined the Nashville Musician's union on May 5, 1977, to gain the union card required to do session work in Nashville.

7. John Martin and Emily Hughes, *The Genius of Lenny Breau.*

8. Burton met Atkins when he was seventeen years old and working with Nashville country/jazz guitarist Hank Garland. The three men performed together at the 1961 Newport Jazz festival. Atkins may well have recommended Lenny to Burton in late 1967 but could not have given him Lenny's first album which was not recorded until late spring of 1968.

9. Smoot, "Lenny Breau—Fingerstyle Jazz Impressionist."

10. Testa, "Lenny Breau Found."

11. Peter Welding, "Reviews: Lenny Breau, Buddy Emmons/Lenny Breau—Minors Aloud."

12. Lee Underwood, "Lenny Breau, Sound Room, Studio City California."

13. Ibid.

14. Walter Carter, "New Breau Not Just Old Jazzer."

15. Welding, "Reviews: Lenny Breau."

16. Peter A. Dammann, "A Legendary Guitar."

17. Sadler, "Shed No Tears."
18. Dave Kyle, "Chet Atkins 1996: A Work in Progress."
19. Andrew Periale and Mike Hughes personal recording, Orono, Maine, ca. April 1976.
20. Dammann, "A Legendary Guitar."
21. Roger Siminoff, "Atkins."
22. Sadler, "Shed No Tears."
23. This birthdate is taken from Lenny and Jewel Breau's marriage certificate. Glasscock's marriage certificate from a second marriage in 1998 lists the date as January 12, 1962, but she was indisputably long out of her teens when she met Lenny in 1979.
24. Atkins, "Fingerstyle Guitar: The Genius of Lenny Breau."

9. Cold, Cold Heart

1. Martin and Hughes, *The Genius of Lenny Breau*.
2. DeStefano, *Talmage Farlow*.
3. Jean Bannerman, "Musician with Soul of a Poet."
4. Sadler, "Shed No Tears."
5. Dan Rooke, "Guitarist Lenny Breau: Colored Notes Tell His Story."
6. Mark Miller, "Breau's Guitar Work Evokes Reverence."
7. Personal recording Toronto, April 1981, supplied by Ron Casey.
8. Porter, "The Mystery of Lenny," radio documentary.
9. Mark Miller, "Lenny Breau Needs No Introduction."
10. CJRT-FM Radio interview by Ted O'Reilly.
11. This guitar is pictured on the back cover of the Guitarchives CD, *Pickin' Cotten*, although it was not used on the session from which the CD was derived. Lenny used this guitar until the late fall of 1982, when he gave it to Richard Cotten to cover outstanding loans. Darci Cotten currently owns this guitar.
12. Designed by DeGruy, the Guitarp is an electric guitar with a seven-string neck and a ten-string frame of sympathetic strings on the body. Larry Coryell would later dub DeGruy "the most unique solo guitarist of the '90s."

10. Meanwhile Back in LA

1. Merle Travis, *That's All*, American Music Inc. 1949.
2. Lenny was already known to Hicks and Benson through clinics he had done at the school in 1979.
3. Rathor has asked that the name of this well-known guitarist be withheld.
4. Tape supplied by Ron Casey.
5. Jewel Breau's description of that morning's events and the quotations she attributes to Lenny are taken from Andy Blicq and Kevin Prokosh, "Breau Found Dead in Swimming Pool," *Winnipeg Free Press*, August 14, 1984, and Associated Press, "Guitarist Lenny Breau Found Dead on Coast," *Portland Herald*, August 15, 1984, and Kevin Prokosh, "LA Police say Breau Murdered," *Winnipeg Free Press*, August 18, 1984.
6. The coroner—for reasons of confidentiality—will not divulge whether the marks were left by a pair of hands or a medium such as rope or cord.
7. Nicole Yorkin, "Guitarist's Death Not an Accident."

8. Lenny's Kirk Sand guitar was stolen from Jewel Breau while she was in the process of trying to sell it in the months following Lenny's death. Its current owner is unknown. The whereabouts of Lenny's stolen Holmes seven string and Baldwin Vibraslim are also unknown. Two Toronto residents own his Holmes six string and second Ramirez and Raj Rathor still has his second Dauphin seven string. Lenny's other seven-string Dauphin is unaccounted for but it's rumored that Lenny pawned it on the day before his death.

9. Martin and Hughes, *The Genius of Lenny Breau*.

Bibliography

Books:

Brault, Gerard J. *The French-Canadian Heritage in New England.* Hanover: University Press of New England; Kingston: McGill-Queens University Press, 1986.

Khan, Hazrat Inayat. *The Mysticism of Sound and Music.* Boston: Shambhala Publications Inc., 1991

Litchfield, Jack. *The Canadian Jazz Discography 1916–1980.* Toronto: University of Toronto Press, 1982.

Miller, Mark. *Jazz in Canada: Fourteen Lives.* Toronto: Nightwood Editions, 1988.

Articles:

Adil. "Lenny Breau-Instrumental-Riverboat, Toronto." *Variety,* April 10, 1968.

Allan, Ted. "Moe Koffman Brings Out Best of Breau's Guitar." *Winnipeg Tribune,* December 18, 1965.

Allan, Ted. "Peter Appleyard at the Jazz A Go-Go." *Winnipeg Tribune,* February 15, 1966.

Anonymous. *Winnipeg Free Press,* October 12, 1967.

———. "Beat of the City." *Winnipeg Free Press,* February 6, 1968.

———. "Court Frees Guitarist." *Winnipeg Tribune,* May 10, 1973.

———. "New Acts: Three—Songs & Comedy. 46 Minutes at L'Hibou in Ottawa." *Variety Magazine,* October 31, 1962.

———. "Around Town." *Lewiston Evening Journal,* October 2, 1948.

———. "Goings on Around Town: Cabarets." *New Yorker,* March 23/31, 1962.

———. "Goings on Around Town: Cabarets." *New Yorker,* April 6/13 1962.

Associated Press. "Guitarist Lenny Breau Found Dead on Coast." *Portland Herald,* August 15, 1984.

Atkins, Chet. "Fingerstyle Guitar: The Genius of Lenny Breau." *Frets Magazine,* July 1986.

Atkins, Chet, and Russ Cochrane. *Me and My Guitar.* Hal Leonard Publishing, 2001–2003.

Baines, David. "Lenny Breau Aims for the Top . . . Again." Focus/Youth. *Winnipeg Tribune,* May 19, 1973.

Bannerman, Jean. "Musician with Soul of a Poet." *Ottawa Citizen,* October 18, 1969.

Batten, Jack. "Two Other Virtuoso Musicians Doing Fine Work in Town." *Globe and Mail,* January 25, 1973.

Batten, Jack. "Breau Teases and Listeners Love It." *Globe and Mail,* June 20, 1973.

Beardon, Jim, and Linda Butler. "Lenny Sings the Blues." *Saturday Night,* September 1981.

Blicq, Andy, and Kevin Prokosh. "Breau Found Dead in Swimming Pool." *Winnipeg Free Press*, August 14, 1984.

Burke, John. "Guitar Sounds from Lenny Breau." *Rolling Stone Magazine*, RS30, April 5, 1969.

Carter, Walter. "New Breau Not Just Old Jazzer." *The Tennessean*, February 22, 1979.

Carter, Walter. "Lenny Breau." *Down Beat*, September 6, 1978.

Collins, Wyman. "Lenny Breau in Great Spirits." *Edmonton Journal*, November 15, 1974.

Coxson, Mona. "Lenny Breau." *Canadian Musician*, Spring 1981.

Craig, Jamie. "Anne Free of Heavy Burden." *The Vancouver Sun*, June 17, 1972.

Dammann, Peter A. "A Legendary Guitar." *Maine Times*, January 4, 1980.

Dunning, Natalie. "Jazz Picker Lenny Breau Back in the Saddle Again." *The Tennessean*, July 18, 1976.

Dutten, Ruth. "Lenny Breau was Admired, Worshiped, and Respected by Family, Musicians and Fans." *My Country Magazine*. September 1984.

Edwards, Lee. "Heard and Seen: Lenny Breau, February 10, 1971." *Coda*, April 1971.

Feather, Leonard. "Blindfold Test with Barney Kessel." *Down Beat*, July 1970.

Ferguson, Jim. "Lenny Breau Remembered." *Guitar Player*, November 1984.

Gannaway, Tom. "Remembering Lenny Breau" *Fingerstyle Guitar Magazine*, September/October, 1997.

Goddard, Peter. "Lack of Imagination Sometimes Hinders Guitarist's Skills." *Toronto Star*, April 1972.

Harris, Peter. "Franks: His Super-Hipster Bag Obscures Talent." *Toronto Star*, February 1, 1968.

Henry, Anne. "With Any Range." *Winnipeg Tribune*, May 11, 1962.

Janz, Susan. "Breau Treats Jazz Fans." *Winnipeg Tribune*, September 19, 1972.

Janz, Susan. "Jazz Guitar Praised in Doctor Music." *Winnipeg Tribune*, July 24, 1971.

King, Jimmy. "Nightbeat," *Winnipeg Tribune*, date unknown, 1960.

Knowles, John. "Quiet Genius of Fingerstyle Jazz." *Frets Magazine*, March 1982.

Kyle, Dave. "Chet Atkins 1996: A Work in Progress." *Vintage Guitar: Online Friday*, July 27, 2001.

Lawrie, Alastair. "Breau's Hands Fly Like a Butterfly's Wings." *Globe and Mail*, February 14, 1969.

Lawrie, Alastair. "Breau: The Great Guitar Returns." *Globe and Mail*, April 1972.

Lawrie, Alastair. "Breau Jazz Pleases, But It's All Too Brief." *Globe and Mail*, May 4, 1972.

Marck, James. "Breau's Variation on a Theme." *Now Magazine*, Sept 30–October 7, 1983.

MacDougall, Ian. "Audience on Its Feet." *Toronto Star*, August 25, 1972.

Miller, Mark. "Caught: Lenny Breau—The River Boat, Toronto." *Down Beat*, July 17, 1975.

Miller, Mark. "Breau's Guitar Work Evokes Reverence." *Globe and Mail*, April 1, 1981.

Miller, Mark. "Lenny Breau Needs No Introduction." *Globe and Mail*, August 13, 1981.

Perry, Jason. "Music World Loses Great Guitarist." *Lewiston Sun Journal*, August 15, 1984.

Piburn, Bill. "Chet Atkins: Guitarist of the Millennium." *Fingerstyle Guitar*, January/February 2000.

Prokosh, Kevin. "Breau's Name Will Live On, Says Atkins." Winnipeg Free Press, August 15, 1984.

Prokosh, Kevin. "LA Police Say Breau Murdered." *Winnipeg Free Press*, August 18, 1984.

Prokosh, Kevin. "Breau Case Stumps Police a Year Later: Death of a Guitar Great—Part 2." *Winnipeg Free Press*, August 4, 1985.

Read, Jeani. "Reviews." *Vancouver Province*, April 5, 1973.

Rooke, Dan. "Guitarist Lenny Breau: Colored Notes Tell His Story." *Performing Arts*, Summer 1981.

Sadler, Joan. "Shed No Tears for Lenny." *Trib Magazine*, January 12, 1980.

Siminoff, Roger. "Atkins." *Frets Magazine*, October 1979.

Smoot, Brawner. "The Immortal Lenny Breau." *Guitar World*, September 1986.

Smoot, Brawner. "Lenny Breau—Fingerstyle Jazz Impressionist." *Guitar Player*, October 1981.

Testa, Bart. "Lenny Breau Found: After Five Years in Exile, a Jazz Genius plays Again." *Globe and Mail*, January 10, 1979.

Thomas, Ralph. "They Marvel at Guitarist's Mastery." *The Daily Star*, September 4, 1962.

Underwood, Lee. "Caught: Lenny Breau, Sound Room, Studio City California." *Down Beat*, March 8, 1979.

Webb, Martin K. "Atkins Style Jazz on a 6-string 12." *Guitar Player*, September 1974.

Welding, Peter. "Reviews: Lenny Breau, Buddy Emmons/Lenny Breau—Minors Aloud." *Down Beat*, December 1979.

Yorkin, Nicole. "Guitarist's Death Not an Accident." *Portland Herald*, August 15, 1984.

Radio Interviews with Lenny Breau:

Major, Lee. "The Kid From Canada." CBC Radio, August 8, 1968.

Major, Lee. "Between Ourselves." CBC Radio, May 4, 1968.

O'Reilly, Ted. "Jazz Scene." CJRT-FM Radio, August 18, 1981.

Robertson, Jim. "Sunday Supplement." CBC Toronto, January 26 1969.

Film and Radio Documentaries:

DeStefano, Lorenzo. *Talmage Farlow*. Rhapsody Films, 1981.

Martin, Jim, and Emily Hughes, *The Genius of Lenny Breau*. Sleeping Giant/ Buffalo Gal Productions, 1999.

Major, Lee. *One More Take*. CBC Documentary. June 25, 1968.

Owen, Don. (dir), Kroitor, Roman (producer). *Toronto Jazz* 62. National Film Board Documentary 1963.

Porter, Ross. *The Mystery of Lenny*. CBC Radio Documentary, 1991.

Selected Filmography:

Only a handful of the hundreds of CBC and other network television programs on which Lenny Breau played are extant. The author consulted the following during his research:

The Lenny Breau Show. CBC TV, August 12, 1966.

Music Hop. CBC TV, February 15, 1967.

A Song For You. CBC TV, May 23, 1964.

A Touch of Jazz. CBC TV, March 2, 1965.

Music To See. CBC TV, October 11, 1971.

In Person. CBC TV, December 31, 1966.

Channel Four Magazine. Channel 4, Nashville, TN, exact date unknown, summer 1982.

Index